C000242540

Far to Go
and
Many to Love

ALSO BY LESLEY BLANCH

BIOGRAPHY

The Wilder Shores of Love

The Sabres of Paradise: Conquest and Vengeance in the Caucasus

Pierre Loti: Portrait of an Escapist

Pavilions of the Heart: The Four Walls of Love

Round the World in 80 Dishes:
The World through the Kitchen Window

From Wilder Shores: The Tables of My Travels

The Game of Hearts: Harriette Wilson and her Memoirs
(edited & with an introduction by Lesley Blanch)

Farah, Shahbanou of Iran: Queen of Persia

MEMOIR

Journey into the Mind's Eye: Fragments of an Autobiography

On the Wilder Shores of Love: A Bohemian Life

FICTION

The Nine Tiger Man: A Tale of Low Behaviour in High Places

LESLEY BLANCH

Edited by Georgia de Chamberet

Far to Go
and
Many to Love

People and Places

QUARTET BOOKS

First published in 2017 by Quartet Books Limited
A member of the Namara Group
27 Goodge Street, London, W1T 2LD

A catalogue record for this book is available from the British Library.

ISBN 9780704374348

Text design and typesetting by Tetragon, London
Printed and bound in Great Britain by TJ International Ltd, Padstow, Cornwall

For Pickles, genius of the blue pencil,
admired by godmother and god-daughter alike

CONTENTS

The eyes of the artist see life in its entirety whereas the man in the street is never able to see the forest for the trees. The artist has visions of what is hidden beyond the foggy horizon of material reality, whereas the average man is conscious of little beyond his nose. The greater the work of an artist, the less likely it is to be accepted by the crowd, who can appreciate what is new in art only after they have become accustomed to it, and that requires time.

THEODORE KOMISARJEVSKY

LESLEY BLANCH: LAST OF A KIND

Georgia de Chamberet

'WITH THE DEATH OF LESLEY BLANCH, AGE 103, ENGLAND AND FRANCE have lost one of their last links connecting them to White-Russian Paris, Free-French London, and many other lost worlds. Her friends would leave her Ottoman eyrie in Menton invigorated and inspired. The subjects of her conversation were well beyond the conventional boundaries of time, space, nationality and fashion. I often went to see her, attracted by her warm personality and colourful, cosmopolitan past. With a unique turn of phrase, she would talk equally passionately about film stars, racism, Arab culture, or the Mitford sisters.' So wrote the historian, Philip Mansel, in *Le Figaro Littéraire* in May 2007. When she died, Lesley Blanch may have been a century old, but her mind remained young, alert and inquiring. She had made her way out of the suburbs and up in life through her creative talents, her ability to learn, and her passionate curiosity.

A Londoner by birth, Lesley Blanch spent the greater part of her life travelling about those remote areas her books record so vividly. She did her own thing against the odds, choosing to fulfil the potential of her own nature and escape from strait-laced Edwardian suburbia to become a working woman at a time when few women had careers. She had a soft spot for Russian men, was very open-minded and a true internationalist.

The author of twelve books, her writing brings to life something of Russia and the Middle East as they once were, before war and terrorism became the norm. She was ahead of her time, and prescient in the way she attempted to bridge the West and East. Most people today associate her with *The Wilder Shores of Love*, her best-known book about four nineteenth-century women who travelled east, *escaping the boredom of convention* as she liked to put it. The book pioneered a new approach to history writing. But her greatest work is *The Sabres of Paradise: Conquest and Vengeance in the Caucasus*. The way she writes about the struggle of the people of the Caucasus to remain independent of Russia is dramatic and disturbingly relevant to our world today. As Philip Marsden wrote in his introduction: 'Like Tolstoy's, her sense of history is ultimately convincing not because of any sweeping theses, but because of its particularities, the quirks of individuals and their personal narratives, their deluded ambitions, their vanities and passions.'

In the 1920s she studied painting at the Slade School of Art where Oliver Messel and Rex Whistler were among her contemporaries. Her subsequent work as a book illustrator, caricaturist, and scenic and costume designer for her mentor and lover, the Russian émigré director Theodore Komisarjevsky, culminated in a selection of her designs being included in MoMA's Theatre Art International Exhibition in 1934. His impact on her was galvanic. He was the subject of *Journey into the Mind's Eye*, in which he is only ever referred to as 'The Traveller'. Lesley's romantic obsession never lessened, even once he had gone.

In the early 1930s, she was among the few who adventured across the USSR, tracing history and literature, rather than politics. As features editor of British *Vogue* from 1937–44 she was on the front line of women journalists covering universal topics alongside writing about women, collaborating with Anne Scott James and Lee Miller.

She went on to travel through post-war Europe with her Polish-Russian-French diplomat-novelist husband, Romain Gary. By the time they reached Hollywood in 1956, they were at the peak of their writing careers. Films were made of their books and friends who came for dinner included many of the major cultural figures of the time. In the words of the historian Philip Mansel, Lesley was 'not a school, a trend, or a fashion, but a true original'.

As far as godmothers go, Lesley Blanch was as good as it gets. Everything about her was unconventional and romantic: her writing; her tumultuous love life;

her sartorial style and seductive glamour; her mischievous humour. She was erudite without being stuffy or pompous. Fearless and headstrong, she was passionate about all things Russian and Oriental. She opened windows on to the world. An understanding and generous friend, she was a good listener. A free spirit, she never apologised for who she was; she took risks and relished writing about her adventures. Some of Lesley's favourite Arabic sayings are a comfort on dull days, one being: *Enjoy this world, for it may be the only Paradise you will ever know.*

As the Hollywood actress Dana Wynter put it: 'She was the greatest influence in my life and I'll be forever thankful and grateful... for her mad sense of humour... speaking French and Russian with that tooth-rattling Brit accent was endearing.'

A tunnel of green leaves, jasmine and datura wound up to the front door of a small pink villa on the hill overlooking the blue bay of Garavan and its tiny Victorian railway station. It was the last stop before the French border with Italy. To visit Lesley was to enter many different worlds.

She could turn the most ordinary of objects and places into a story. Her sitting room was filled with treasures and memorabilia found on her travels: an eighteenth-century Staffordshire rabbit, the first possession she ever bought; a portrait of Empress Elizabeth of Russia; a collection of Russian silver snuff boxes; antique rugs of all kinds from Bessarabian to kilims; a court painting of Fath Ali Shah's Persian ministers; a teak rocking elephant from India, once a child's toy; her Oriental book collection left to New College Oxford – all destroyed by a fire in 1994 which gutted her house (she had it rebuilt).

A *takht*, or raised dais, and *mensofas*, or narrow divans, were strewn with cushions and bolsters for lolling, Turkish style. She recreated *a land of memory stretching from Cairo to Constantinople* as gros point cushions which were coveted by friends: 'Nile-side idyll'; 'Samarcand'; 'Beyond Kandahar'; 'In Arabian waters'; 'Egyptian night-piece'; 'Roquebrune village'; and 'Afghan teahouse', which shows crouching tribesmen on a local rug, shelves of teapots, a giant samovar and blue mountains in the distance. She wrote: *I turned to gros point as a distraction, during some emotional entanglement. Through many successive uproars of emotion and daily life, gros point has proved wonderfully calming. Then, it helps me to concentrate, thinking out a sticky chapter, or listening to music.* Some were done as gifts, with a motif designed around the friend in question: *For Nancy Mitford*

The *moucharabiyeh* and *takht* in Lesley Blanch's main room, Garavan

I worked a large pink-pawed mole, part of her family crest, with a huge sunflower indicating her book, The Sun King, *and for Violet Trefusis, an evocation of Russia, to recall our shared love of all things Slav.* A gros point cushion which I have shows her enjoying tea with her lover under a spray of roses on the banks of the Nile; another, the Dome of the Rock. Things mattered a great deal to her. She'd say: *Surround yourself with the things you love and your house will make you happy.*

During one visit to Garavan in the 1970s, my late mother, Gael Elton Mayo, and I went junking with Lesley in Nice. When we returned home out came little pots of paint and rags, and she set to, embellishing the stool she had bought using the artisanal technique of painting on wood. Much of the furniture which she had decorated was destroyed later by the fire. I particularly loved the mottled azure-blue cupboard in Lesley's kitchen. On the four door panels, she had painted the golden domes of Novgorod, Moscow, St Petersburg, and the Tartar domes of Kazan which she said: *Spanned the vast surface of the Orthodox religion.*

Domestic uproar was a feature of home life. Lesley was mischievous and entertaining when describing *Darling Self* turning away unwanted visitors; her cats and their moods (at times, really her own); or the housekeeper's inability to create some of her favourite recipes (kidney pilaf, Balkan pastry tart with

4

Gros point cushion made for Violet Trefusis

spinach filling, *pirozhki*, goulash, Syrian lentil soup). She was a great storyteller, and conjured Bukhara, Samarcand and Khiva on the ancient Silk Road at the dinner table.

Lesley could be infuriating, stubborn and proud. When in grandiose *Grande Dame*-diva mode she put on a very good show as she went out and about to dine with *Vogue* photographer Henry Clarke and chic Parisian antique dealer, Raymond Poteau; architectural historian and diarist James Lees-Milne; or Lord Iliffe, part owner of the *Daily Telegraph*, and Renée, his Mauritian wife of French descent.

Lesley and my mother had met in New York in 1951 through their Russian husbands. With their nomadic tendencies, tumultuous relationships, and a curious ambivalence about confronting profound and difficult personal feelings, they were women of their time. Both were pulled between marriage and career. Neither was particularly maternal (although my mother had three children). My late mother's bohemian life – recounted in her memoir *The Mad Mosaic* – was no less eventful than Lesley's.

In June 2007, as I gathered together papers and manuscripts, fragments of reminiscences written at different times over a long and adventurous life floated up at me in the sultry Mediterranean air. One read: *Perhaps it was due to those exceptional travellers whom, as a child, I had followed from the armchair, that when at last I began to travel for real, I discovered no flesh-and-blood companion could compare with the company I had kept between the covers of a book. Going alone seemed best. Thus, when I went to Russia in the early thirties, I sought the background of Tolstoy's novels, the Moscow of the young Herzen, or many other fascinating characters of Slav literature who had become my friends.*

Lesley's father, Walter, was cultivated and idle, and spent his time in museums and galleries, while her elegant and artistic mother, Martha, longed to travel, but never did. She wanted her daughter to fulfil her potential and be independent at a time when few women had careers. She was a supporter of the suffragettes who fought for women to win the right to vote. In 1913, their leader, Emmeline Pankhurst, declared: 'Never underestimate the power we women have to define our own destiny... I'd rather be a rebel than a slave.' Encouraged and supported by her avant-garde mother, Lesley rejected conventional conformity and turned her back on Edwardian Chiswick, then a London suburb.

In her posthumous memoirs, *On the Wilder Shores of Love: A Bohemian Life*, Lesley describes how a Gypsy woman once came to the door selling clothes pegs and stolen honeycomb and predicted that the sixteen-year-old had 'far to go and many to love'. She lived her life by that prophecy.

I must have been about four years old when Russia took hold of me with giant hands: the opening line of Lesley's autobiography, *Journey into the Mind's Eye*, immortalises not only the 'giant hands' of Russia, but also the firm, lifelong hold on her heart and imagination of her mentor, lover and lost companion, the theatre director Theodore Komisarjevsky, whom she only ever referred to as 'The Traveller'.

A portfolio containing some of her work as a scenic and costume designer came to light in January 2014. 'The owner wishes to remain anonymous,' said the fine-art dealer's voice at the other end of the telephone line. 'The portfolio was found after her mother died. There are original sketches and photographs of Lesley Blanch's designs. The best ones were framed and hung up, but were stolen by the housekeeper when she was sacked.' I went to Pall Mall, and arranged for seventy theatre designs, book illustrations, caricature-portraits, sketches for wall panels and whimsical animal drawings to be photographed.

A reading of theatre programmes in the archives of the Bibliothèque historique de la Ville de Paris, the Bibliothèque-musée de l'Opéra, and the Bibliothèque nationale de France, alongside the designs in Lesley's portfolio, enabled me to pinpoint and verify certain pivotal events she describes in *Journey into the Mind's Eye*. Komisarjevsky's imprint on her was such that he would influence her later travels, and choice of husband.

Russian London

A mesmeric character full of the legends and fairy tales of Russia, bearing gifts of Fabergé eggs and ikons, Komisarjevsky was always a welcome visitor to the Blanch household in Chiswick. To a starry-eyed, pretty and precocious young girl living with ageing parents, his flow of ideas and international way of life must have been mesmeric. He offered passion, escape and adventure.*

Alleged to have had a passionate affair with Martha before her marriage to Walter Blanch, I never heard Lesley speak of it, other than an oblique reference: *I asked her once why she had not gone to Russia – long ago, when she first knew The Traveller, and was grown up and free to go anywhere she liked. 'One is never really free,' was her enigmatic reply.*

Komisarjevsky had left Moscow for Paris in July 1919, having produced and directed at the Bolshoi Theatre during the Russian Revolution where he had fought for his avant-garde theories. At the suggestion of his friend the ballet impresario Sergei Diaghilev, he headed for London – an artistic and political safe haven. In *Myself and the Theatre*, he describes what he left behind: 'At night both streets and houses with smashed windows and empty shops were in complete darkness, as there was no longer electricity or gas... On special days after hours of queuing at the rare government shops a salted herring, some dried peas or perhaps a black biscuit, tasting like sawdust and stale beetroot, were supplied as food for a whole family. Very often instead of tea people drank a liquid made of grilled carrots... It may well seem strange that in such circumstances

---

* Lesley writes in detail about The Traveller's comings and goings at the Blanch household in Part One of her posthumous memoirs, *On the Wilder Shores of Love: A Bohemian Life*.

7

the theatres were still open… Frequently during performances, the breath of the singers on the stage was visible in such clouds of vapour that they called themselves samovars.'

Young Stanislavsky, Stravinsky, Turgenev and Mussorgsky had been regular visitors to his operatic-tenor father's house in St Petersburg. His first experience as a director was in 1906 with Meyerhold in Petrograd. In 1909 he moved to Moscow where he was director of the Imperial Theatres and, after 1917, of the State Theatre. In 1919 he came to London to stage Borodin's *Prince Igor* for Sir Thomas Beecham and became known chiefly for his staging of Chekhov and Pirandello. His sister, Vera, created the role of Nina in the ill-fated premiere of Anton Chekhov's *The Seagull*, at the Alexandrinsky Theatre, St Petersburg, in 1896.

Komisarjevsky promoted realistic acting and produced a 'synthetic' universal theatre, 'Where all forms of art could be harmoniously united in one single show. I introduced music into the plays, rewrote the librettos of the operas to suit the character and the rhythm of the music, and inserted dialogues and speaking parts in the operas. Hence the singers took part in the plays as well as the operas and, similarly, the dramatic actors took part in the operas.' John Gielgud, one of Komisarjevsky's students, said of him, 'His influence has been considerable and his contribution to the English theatre and its artists leaves us greatly in his debt.'

Komisarjevsky set up Lahda in 1920, a society for the promotion of Russian culture in London, with Laurent Novikov and Vladimir Rosing. They organised 'Opera Intime' concerts, ballet performances and 'at home' events at which they performed in the homes of prominent figures in London society. When he taught at the Royal Academy of Dramatic Art during the 1926–7 season, he inspired intense devotion in his students. He loved young people and knew how to encourage them and bring them out. He produced sixteen operas in Europe in 1919–28, with an interlude at the Theatre Guild in New York in 1922–3 – a likely explanation for his djinn-like manifestations at the Blanch household in Chiswick.

Larger-than-life, brilliant and headstrong, his education was encyclopaedic and he spoke and wrote seven European languages fluently. Disdainful of business practices, he was dedicated to art and non-commercial ideals and was invariably beset by financial problems. Softly spoken and short, he was self-contained and a superb storyteller, instilling a lifelong love of all things Russian and exotic in Lesley. According to her, *he possessed that curious magnetic power found in the street.* By the 1930s, Komisarjevsky was recognised as being one of the most flamboyant and influential figures in European theatre.

The City of Dreams

The newly opened art deco Théâtre des Champs-Élysées was on the front line of the European avant-garde. The premiere of Diaghilev-Nijinsky-Stravinsky's *The Rite of Spring* in 1913 had provoked a riot. In 1925, the opening night of *La revue nègre* headlining Josephine Baker caused a sensation. Komisarjevsky worked there from 1923–24, again in 1929, and in 1931.

After leaving the Slade, Lesley had to support her parents. Martha's money, inherited from her grandfather, John Stewart, was running out. The family was sliding into a state of distressed gentility.

Komisarjevsky's production of a comedy by Henri Duvernois and Pascal Fortuny, *Le Club des Deux Canards Mandarins*, was performed in November 1923, inaugurating a smaller sister theatre of the Théâtre des Champs-Élysées, Le Studio, founded with reference to Meyerhold's Studio and Stanislavsky's Moscow Art Theatre. A black-and-white photograph of Lesley's sketch for the character Orchidée is very likely her first costume design.

She describes their visit to the City of Dreams: *Diaghilev and Rachmaninov were among The Traveller's circle, and once or twice, Diaghilev or Sergei Pavlovitch as he was to The Traveller, allowed us, O rapture! O rare privilege! to attend a rehearsal flattened in the wings. The Sakharovs, Alexandre and Clotilde too, sketched out their stylised dances for The Traveller's opinion dancing to Faure and Bach. Komisarjevsky presently joined this eclectic band, with projects for the production of an Ostrovsky play; and*

Costume design by Lesley Blanch for Orchidée in *Le Club des Deux Canards Mandarins when Chaliapin appeared, and none of these lofty personalities seemed to object to the presence of a gaping schoolgirl in their midst, I was able to savour, first-hand, some of the greatest aspects of Russian theatrical genius. It was transplanted in its full bloom and, for a while, it did not wither.*

The Théâtre des Champs-Élysées's programme for the 1922–23 season features a roll call of modernist talent, including recitals by Vladimir Rosing; a series of dance performances by the Gurdjieff Institute; the Shakespeare Association and Pitoeff's versions of *Hamlet* and *Macbeth*; and Komisarjevsky's production of Pirandello's *Six Characters in Search of an Author*. In May, June and July 1924, a series of *Soirées de Gala des Ballets Russes de M. Serge de Diaghilew* were held there. The *Comité d'honneur* featured a glittering international array of crowned heads, ministers and patrons of the arts from across Europe, South America and the Far East. Komisarjevsky's productions of *Siegfried* and *Tristan and Iseult* headlined the theatre's Wagner Festival in October and November of 1924.

The pair attended a private concert for friends given by Rachmaninov in his house in Rambouillet and, wrote Lesley: *In a more frivolous vein, there was Nikita Balieff, whose family life was quite as stylised as his Chauve-Souris theatre, and Vertinsky, who was then enthralling the nightclubs of Berlin and Paris with his cracking voice and air of a disillusioned Pierrot... Russian artists and musicians with smoky voices were also in his circle from early exile in Turkey.*

Her description of Komisarjevsky's rooms in Paris is reminiscent of how she decorated her home: *With waves of colourful rugs flowing from floor to divan, a medley of Russian and Turkish objects and gros point Victorian cushions.*

Parisian nightclubs in the 1920s were renowned for the romanticism and burning excitement of Russian Gypsy music, made famous later by Django Reinhardt. She wrote: *Now I understood the spell they cast over Pushkin and Dostoyevsky, the young Tolstoy and so many more.* An advertisement in one of Théâtre Pigalle's programmes from 1926 is evocative: 'Cercle artistique Russe Paris 2 et 4 Rue des Batignolles – five o'clock tea, diner, soupers dansants – attractions – cuisine excellente Russe et Français – American bar – surprises – cabaret.'

Komisarjevsky seduced Lesley on the Train Bleu, after taking her to hear Gypsy music in a nightclub. She describes it in *Journey into the Mind's Eye*, and writes: *How I loved him! How I loved his Traveller's Tales and the way he brought the Trans-Siberian thundering through the house.* The connection between sex, travel and fantasy was irrevocably established.

From 1925–26, Komisarjevsky transformed English theatre with his productions of Chekhov's *Ivanov, Uncle Vanya, The Three Sisters* and *The Cherry Orchard*; Andreyev's *Katerina*; and Gogol's *The Government Inspector* at Barnes Theatre. Lesley witnessed his techniques first-hand, known as the Komisarjevsky Method of Acting. (See Appendix: The Komisarjevsky Method of Acting, p. 345.) Lesley's small, battered copy of Chekhov's *Three Sisters and Other Plays* translated by Constance Garnett, published in 1923, has crossings-out and annotations in pencil in the margins of *The Three Sisters*. Two A4 pages of roughly drawn circles and lines are folded inside.

Brian Howard, who scandalised the older generation as a leader of the 'Bright Young Things' and was immortalised by Evelyn Waugh in two novels – Ambrose Silk in *Put Out More Flags* and Anthony Blanche in *Brideshead Revisited* – was an admirer of Komisarjevsky's work. 'The best play I've seen was *The Three Sisters* by Tchekov, produced by Komisarjevsky, with John Gielgud in it. It was really great. The best stage management I've ever seen. The lighting and decorations were productions of genius.'

Most of the originals in Lesley's recently-discovered portfolio are for thirteen characters in Cimarosa's *Giannina e Bernardone*, one of a trio of Théâtre Pigalle's 'Opera-ballet de Michel Benois' 1931 summer season. On the reverse of her drawing for 'Bernardone, Maestro di Musica, 1er acte,' is a very rough pencil sketch of a disconsolate woman sitting on a stool, her back to the bar, and the words: *Sample – tart May-June 1931, Paris*. Prokofiev's *Symphonie Classique,* was choreographed by Thadée Slavinsky who later joined de Basil and Blum's *Ballets Russes de Monte Carlo*. His name features on one of Lesley's costume sketches.

An art deco temple to modernism, the Théâtre Pigalle's new scientific and technical innovations – including four stages with lifts and stylish electric lamps – were eulogised by Jean Cocteau. It was the home of the Chauve-Souris theatre company, and Jean Giraudoux's *Amphitryon 38* played there. Lesley's design for the stage setting of Ashley Dukes' 1933 production at the Mercury Theatre has the words 'Amphitryon, Giraudoux' scribbled on the lower right-hand corner.

Costume designs by Lesley Blanch for Cimarosa's *Giannina e Bernardone*

Scenic design by Lesley Blanch for *The Merchant of Venice*

Costume design by Lesley Blanch for
Portia in *The Merchant of Venice*

Costume design by Lesley Blanch for
'Macbeth and household servant' in *Macbeth*

Her portfolio also contains scenic and costume designs for two of Komisarjevsky's productions at Stratford-upon-Avon: *The Merchant of Venice* with Randle Ayrton as Shylock and Portia played by Fabia Drake, July 1932; and *Macbeth*, performed in spring 1933, using modern dress with howitzers and World War I field uniforms against a backdrop of aluminium scenery. Eight of Lesley's costume and scenic designs for various productions were included in the Theatre Art International Exhibition, MoMA, New York, 16 January to 26 February 1934.

He introduced Lesley to many different exiles in London, including aristocratic émigrés whom he railed against, and *the intelligentsia, a shabby brilliant lot who still believed in liberalism, still quoted Herzen.*

Books from Lesley's library hold riddles. Inside Komisarjevsky's memoirs, *Myself and the Theatre* is the handwritten *dédicace*: 'I am never sad but when I hear sweet music… / I am never merry when I hear sweet music,' and on the next page the dedication reads, 'To my dearest Lesley from

T. K.' Inscribed in Russian in the top right-hand corner is an indecipherable term of endearment. *Das Buhnenfortum in ultertum mittelalter und reuzeit* by Mar von Boehn is inscribed 'Lesley Blanch' followed by the initials 'ThK—, Paris 1931.' *The Costume of the Theatre* by Theodore Komisarjevsky is inscribed 'To P—, Ж—— a / P, / w —, l—, h. /— XII — 1931.'

In *Journey into the Mind's Eye*, Lesley writes of The Traveller using various terms of endearment, *rocokoshka*, my little rococo pussycat, or *pussinka moiya* among them. The Russians to whom I have shown the indecipherable inscription in *Myself and the Theatre* tell me it is a hybrid, and not a specific Russian word per se.

Lesley Blanch's copy of Theodore Komisarjevsky's memoirs, *Myself and the Theatre*, with dedication

A Balletic Mystery

When Diaghilev died in 1929, the *Ballets Russes* evaporated after twenty years of activity. Some of his dancers continued with other organisations, while others started their own. Léonide Massine had joined the company in 1914. A well-respected choreographer, dancer and mime artist, he wanted to start up a ballet company in New York performing Diaghilev classics with American dancers, but the Wall Street Crash made it impossible. So in 1933 he joined the *Ballets Russes de Monte Carlo*, replacing George Balanchine.

During the period 1932–35 the company was under the direction of Colonel Vassili de Basil – a White Russian émigré Cossack officer turned impresario – and financier René Blum – brother of Léon Blum, the first socialist and the first Jew to serve as prime minister of France, in 1936. It had reunited thirty dancers from Diaghilev's former company, and veteran stage manager, Sergei Grigoriev. Massine devised new ballets reflecting his version of the concept of 'the transmutation of music into pure dancing,' as well as producing ballets from the old Diaghilev repertoire. A roster of artists was called upon to design sets and costumes for the incessantly touring company – including Joan Miro, Raoul Dufy, André Masson and André Derain.

Three 'baby ballerinas' formed the core of the company, giving it a fresh, youthful zing. Their glamour concealed a difficult daily life and a background of deprivation since losing status, money and a way of life because of the Russian Revolution. The *Ballets Russes de Monte Carlo* gave them a home and a means of supporting their parents.

Lesley describes the dancers as constituting: *A world of their own, turbulent, and magnetic, glittering Harlequin figures for whose public and private lives the British public were soon avid. There was much shouting, melodrama, intrigue, rivalry and obsessive dedication to their art. During their first unpampered seasons they lived in small dingy hotels round the British Museum, their narrow bedrooms stacked with steamer trunks. Massine was at the Savoy, but the rest were more modest. Their mothers, (for they moved in family units), darned tights and fought amongst themselves for the supremacy of their children: some spoke nothing but hissing encouragement, over-boiling like kettles at some fancied slight to their progeny.*

The *Ballets Russes de Monte Carlo* had reached the Alhambra Theatre in London from Europe in 1933. Three weeks became four months, due to its success. Tamara Toumanova and David Lichine were the principal dancers in *Choreartium* which provoked an uproar. By 1935 the Russian ballet had become a cult, with devotees from all classes of society.

Her portfolio contains unsolved mysteries. There are two costume designs for Chloé's father and Chloé (Act 3 'the Winter Scene') from the Balanchine-Ravel ballet, *Daphnis et Chloé*, on which the name 'Lydia Lopokova' appears. Three sketches titled *Baroque*, coloured greenish white, or reddish brown, with a terpsichorean theme are, possibly, Lesley's way of achieving a transmutation of music into costume for Massine. On one, in the Russian (Cyrillic) alphabet, is written the name 'Toumanova' – one of the child star 'baby ballerinas' – and on another it reads 'Delaroria: dance with Shabelevsky'. There are also two costume sketches for the ballet *Rouge et Noir* – her design for 'The King' was included in MoMA's 1934 Theatre Art International Exhibition in New York. Matisse did the costume and set designs for Massine's 1939 production of *Rouge et Noir* which was an abstract piece with a vivid colour theme.

David Lichine's two-act ballet, *Les Imaginaires*, with geometry its theme and a score by Georges Auric, premiered at the Théâtre des Champs-Élysées in Paris and came on to the Royal Opera House, Covent Garden, in August 1934. Lesley designed the costumes with her friend Frieda Harris, who went on to design Aleister Crowley's Thoth Tarot deck. Lichine had studied dance in Paris with Lubov Egorova and Bronislava Nijinska, created star roles as principal dancer for de Basil's company and started choreographing in 1933.

When Massine fell out with Colonel de Basil, he launched his own company in 1938. Lesley wrote about its premiere in British *Vogue*: *All London, Paris, New York focused on Monte Carlo, where, in the tiny gilded baroque theatre, United Art Incorporated made their massed debut at Easter. The little principality was jammed with celebrities, élégantes, critics, musicians, painters and balletomanes. The Casino sulked, its thunder stolen. The Sporting Club was a pandemonium of ballerinas essaying the Big Apple. Prince and Princess Jean-Louis de Faucigny-Lucinge, the Grand Duke Dimitri, Chanel, Kreisler, Bruno Walter, and David Herbert were thick as thieves or autumn leaves in Vallombrosa.*

The End of a Dream

Lesley wrote, in *Journey into the Mind's Eye: The Traveller's companion – mistress – wife – my status is never quite clear.* Komisarjevsky was a master at creating

Costume designs by Lesley Blanch for the *Ballets Russes de Monte Carlo*

anticipation and mystery, and held his women in the tension of love, leaving an indelible impression. His father had married his second wife before divorcing the first. Like father, like son: both ignored conventions when it suited them.

Komisarjevsky visited Lesley in Italy with his sons, Kamran and Sergei, proposed marriage, and then disappeared for a year. They wrote to each other, but Lesley was fretful: *I felt myself abandoned – marooned on an island of conventional living – and sulked accordingly.* He returned to London and side-stepped questions with his usual skill: *'When I am here with you, you know all about me – why do you want to know all about me when I am elsewhere?'... he would launch into tangled theories of time and place, and the non-existence of persons, or objects, except when in direct contact with other persons or objects. It was all very confusing, but his meaning was clear: don't pry.*

She describes a train journey to Corsica from the Gare du Nord with The Traveller's two sons and his *mad Montenegrin aunt*, Countess Eudoxia, screeching, *'Scandalist! He was always a scandalist!'* after a row with the ticket inspector about their dog. The hilarity masks a dark undertow. During their holiday, marriage was planned, and Lesley's parents informed via telegram. But the lovers' slow end-of-summer drive along the French Riviera to Garavan, Menton, marked the end of their relationship.

Theodore Komisarjevsky
aka The Traveller

Peggy Ashcroft took him off me were Lesley's words to me the last time I saw her in 2007. Known as 'the Russian Don Juan', Komisarjevsky had nine officially registered marriages by the time he left London for the United States. As in a French farce, his women invariably overlapped as one made her entrance and the other her exit. A son, Vadim, with Elena Alkopian, was born in England in 1921, though they are not mentioned in *Myself and the Theatre*. Because of Lesley's portfolio, we know he was with her in Paris in 1923–4, and again in 1931. Peggy Ashcroft parted from her husband, the actor-turned-publisher

Rupert Hart-Davis, in 1931, and moved into Berkeley Gardens, Camden Hill with Komisarjevsky in 1932. Lesley's scenic and costume designs may have been used for his productions at Stratford in 1932–33, but she was no longer his favourite. (This pattern was repeated years later when she was left by her husband Romain Gary for Jean Seberg: Lesley still worked with George Cukor in Hollywood on the film production of his novel, *Lady L.*)

Ashcroft divorced Hart-Davis in 1933. According to Komisarjevsky's biographer Victor Borovsky, the pair married in 1934, even though he had already met the young dancer Ernestine Stodelle whom he married in 1937 – after divorcing Ashcroft. Komisarjevsky and his new young wife left for the United States at the outbreak of war in 1939.

Komisarjevsky's younger brother and his wife were charged with spying for British intelligence and arrested by the KGB in 1937. Nikolai was shot and Anna was sent to a concentration camp in Karaganda, Kazakhstan. (She returned to Moscow after Stalin's death and died there in terrible poverty in 1970.) When Lesley asked The Traveller why he had chosen Corsica for their summer holiday, he answered that it was because he was a spy. His idealism, work in the theatre, linguistic skills, and love of adventure were appropriate attributes for the job. Was he collaborating with his brother? Komisarjevsky died in 1954, the year *The Wilder Shores of Love* was published.

Paradise Lost

A man of extremes, Komisarjevsky would suddenly break off relations for no apparent reason like his friend Diaghilev. Once he had gone, there was no turning back. Lesley writes, *he left me, as casually as ever, on one of those sudden departures which had become an accepted pattern.* In his farewell letter, he says: 'Now it is time for The Traveller and his tales to go out of your life, and for you to begin your own journeys. The Turkish people say farewell beautifully, '*Güle,*' they say – Go with a smile.'

In an interview with Philip Mansel, Lesley said of her faithful friend and fickle lover: *I loved him unreservedly... it seemed that I had always known and loved him and in his world I would at last come home.*

She attended Prince Mirsky's lectures on Russian literature when London University was at Somerset House and learned a little Russian. Her first journey travelling alone was to Russia, in 1932, the year Komisarjevsky moved in with Peggy Ashcroft. She describes her despair: *as time passed, and the certitude of my loneliness became apparent to me, I noticed that all which had seemed real in myself was lost, with him. With his disappearance part of myself had vanished too. What was left did not belong to the setting in which it remained. I had been formed in a mould of his creation, and all my longings and instincts were now fixed on some remote and seemingly unobtainable world – his – which I was determined to reach... The Traveller's spirit seemed as ardent as ever, always beside me, luring me deeper into the horizons of my desire.*

She visited Prague, Poland, Czechoslovakia, Salzburg, Munich and Berlin. Her books offer clues: *The Robber Brothers (Bratya razboyniki), Gypsies, Poltava* by Pushkin published in Leningrad in 1930 is a very battered paperback, in Russian, inscribed *Lesley Blanch Moscow*; her 1929 edition of Gogol's *Dead Souls* reads *Lesley Blanch Moscow – Leningrad 1932*, and the title in Russian is written under the English title along with Lesley's notes in the back; *Two Hundred Years of Russian Ballet 1738–1938* published by Leningrad School of Choreography in Russian, in 1938, records *Lesley Blanch, Leningrad*; *Russian Architecture (Russische Baukunst)* published in German in 1922 is inscribed *Lesley Blanch Munich 1935*; *Pushkin 1799–1837 in Portraits and Illustrations*, published in Moscow in 1937 in Russian, reads *Lesley Blanch, 3 The Paragon Richmond Surrey* and also *Lesley Blanch Moscow/Berlin 1934-'36-'37*; *Konstantin Paustovsky on Orest Kiprensky* published Leningrad 1938, in Russian, is inscribed *Lesley Blanch, Paris, August, 1938.*

Lesley came across Komisarjevsky's son, Kamran, by chance at the Russian Orthodox cathedral in Rue Daru, Paris, and they had a tempestuous on-off liaison. She was searching for echoes of his father while he relished the thrill of making love to his father's former mistress. They had no money and their relationship was condemned by friends as unsuitable. The idea of a conventional marriage was rejected.

Pavilions of the Heart

The most intense and formative period of Lesley's life was the decade she spent with The Traveller. The power of place on the imagination and on the heart is a recurring motif in her writing: *A tattered blue volume carries me to Bakhchysarai, where the celebrated 'Fountain of Tears' recalls a Tartar khan's unrequited love for his beautiful Christian captive and inspired Pushkin's romantic poem of that name – that's travelling.*

Komisarjevsky was a talismanic figure Lesley returned to again and again throughout her long life: *Although he was international in his way of life and Tartar in his remote ancestry, he was, in essence, the most supremely Slav being imaginable. I use the word Slav rather than Russian, for how to define or pin down the prototype of this race which is the blend of a hundred different peoples from the Arctic to the Black Sea, from Poland to China?... He was impossible to classify.* The last time they made love was in the cemetery for Russian émigrés above Menton on the French-Italian border where she lived, and was to die, over eighty years later.

The cemetery for Russian
émigrés above Menton

Her book, *Pavilions of the Heart*, combining love and place, is Lesley at her most romantic: *commemorative plaques often mark houses where distinguished persons have lived. But they do not necessarily indicate where they have loved... Yet the settings for high passions or profound love are surely worth recording and, as surely, should reflect something of the emotions they once framed.* She had her favourites: Bibi Hanum's *medressa* in Samarcand, built by Tamerlane in memory of his best-loved wife; Aurélie Picard and her Saharan idyll with Prince Si Ahmed Tedjani; Balzac and Madame de Hanska in the Rue Fortunée; a cave beside the Black Sea which sheltered, briefly, the meetings of Pushkin and Countess Woronzov.

The Ballet Club

Marie, or 'Mim', Rambert had collaborated with Diaghilev's *Ballets Russes* and danced in the corps de ballet from 1912–3, but moved to London where she studied under Enrico Cecchetti. She married the playwright and drama critic

Ashley Dukes in 1918. Lesley's interest in Rambert dated from 1926. She wrote: *It was she who trained and developed the talents of Fred Ashton, Harold Turner, Pearl Argyle, Walter Gore, William Chappell and many more. Her pupils were the nucleus of English ballet, and it was her sorrow, but never her bitterness, that as they matured they left the Ballet Club for wider scopes and greater glories.*

Dukes bought the freehold of a simple stone hall in Ladbroke Road, behind Notting Hill Gate. He walled off two sections for the ballet company at the back and the theatre at the front. The proscenium opening was tiny, and a flight of steps up the back of the stage led to the dressing room. The Ballet Club opened on 15 February 1931. The Mercury Theatre opened in 1933 with the play *Jupiter Translated* by W. J. Turner, after Molière's *Amphitryon*. Lesley designed the scenery and costumes, some of which were included in New York's MoMA exhibition. Also in her portfolio are costumes for Ashley Dukes' play, *A Woman of this World* – a new version of Henry Becque's comedy *La Parisienne*. The first London productions of T. S. Eliot's *Murder in the Cathedral* were performed at the theatre in 1935 – Lesley had designed book jackets for T. S. Eliot at Faber. The dramatists and artists working together at the Mercury Theatre in Notting Hill were like a European alternative to the Bloomsbury group.

Lesley and Mim remained lifelong friends. A letter dated 20 February 1968, conveys her affectionate appreciation:

Darling Mim,

    This is just to wish you a very, very happy birthday and <u>many</u> happy returns of the day. Dear Mim: what a wonderful woman you are — + how many marvellous things you have achieved in your life! Whenever I think of you, I feel such admiration for your integrity as an artist, your courage as a woman: + then I remember your warmth, + wit, + I know there is no one in the least like you, anywhere in the world. You are unique, + it is a privilege to be counted among your friends.

    Today I was in bed with la grippe, + listening to Woman's Hour, in a fit of homesickness for London — + then, your voice, your views, to keep me company. How great and good, what you said about an artist's work — to do your best — + then reconsider, do again, scrap, rework, on + on, till you have done all you can. I try to do that in my books: one is never satisfied, except in snatches.

Costume design by Lesley Blanch
for Jupiter in *Jupiter Translated*

Costume design by Lesley Blanch
for Alcmena in *Jupiter Translated*

Homage to Marie Rambert by Lesley Blanch

The trouble is, as you said – it never gets easier, for one expands, + we hope, progresses. That is – you cannot go back, to the first formulae of success, or you are stone dead, static, a pastiche of your old self...

Every book I write has to have its own pattern + rhythm + I am conscious that many readers would prefer me to rewrite *The Wilder Shores* for them... I can't. My new book, only just finished is rather peculiar, + chiefly on Siberia... I will send you a copy when it comes out, which won't be for a while.

My darling mother died last January. I feel amputated... Nothing to be said, or done – except work. As Gogol said: 'Life is a sad business Gentlemen...' But that is not the right tone for this letter which set out to embrace you + congratulate you on 80 years of a life well lived, a life crowned, I think, in so many senses, crowned + fulfilled.

Darling Mim, a loving hug from Lesley

Romantic Moderns

Lesley readily admitted to marrying advertising agent Robert Bicknell, in 1930, for love of his Georgian house, The Paragon, by the River Thames in Richmond.

Caricature-portrait for Philip
Gosse by Lesley Blanch

It was not a happy union and two years later he returned to his previous wife. Lesley's parents had also moved in to The Paragon. Walter died in 1933 and Martha took in lodgers.

In 1934, Lesley acquired a room in G1, and at some point later in G4, Albany, Piccadilly. Friends had apartments there: theatre critic James Agate; man of letters Clifford Bax, whose book *Ideas & People* is dedicated to her; Dr Philip Gosse, author of *The History of Piracy*, whose father Sir Edmund Gosse introduced Henrik Ibsen and other continental European writers to English readers; crime writer and poet Dorothy L. Sayers who *had an attractive voice and was usually alone, drinking wine.*

Caricature-portrait for Clifford Bax by Lesley Blanch

Many of Lesley's friends were *those people in the set who always discover every-thing first* – the composer, novelist and aesthete Gerald Lord Berners; incipient novelist Nancy Mitford; conductor and composer Constant Lambert; Harold Acton, co-founder of the avant-garde literary magazine *The Oxford Broom*, and author of *Memoirs of an Aesthete*; Peter Quennell who commissioned Lesley to write for him after he became editor of the *Cornhill Magazine* in 1943; travel writer Robert Byron; art and drama critic John Steegman who liked to 'throw her on wet leaves'; the photographer and interior designer Cecil Beaton, and brothers Osbert and Sacheverell Sitwell who formed a literary and artistic clique around themselves as rebels against 'philistine' values and 'accepted' artistic conventions.

The English village and rural life were a source of inspiration for many art-ists and writers. Arnold Bax moved into the White Horse Inn at Storrington. Mim Rambert and Ashley Dukes had a cottage in Dymchurch, Kent where the Shakespearean actress Sybil Thorndyke was a neighbour. Cecil Beaton was at Ashcombe. Gerald Lord Berners at Faringdon. Lesley developed *a new kind of caricature-portrait* based on her interview with the sitter. Those of Ralph Layton and Carol Mary Layton, the first husband and daughter of one of her oldest and dearest friends, the artist Eden Box, were done at Elmtree Cottage, West Wittering.

The Shell Guides overseen by John Betjeman and *The Weekend Book* appealed to a new kind of motor car weekender. Country inns attracted a fashionable crowd. Fragments from Lesley's unfinished memoirs offer glimpses of her life at that time. She and her friends enjoyed outings to John Fothergill's Spread Eagle in Thame with its *gate-leg tables, excellent food and port wines... despite the awful climate we tasted the joys of a village cricket match.* They weathered outdoor productions at the new Open Air Theatre in Regent's Park: *Clifford Bax loved it: the damp grass, the deck chairs and rain-sprinkled bushes; setting up in a chill corner round some laurels. It was the precursor to Glyndebourne, which would add the penalty of evening dress: trailing audacious finery, women hugged their décolletés in wraps along wet platforms on a biting June afternoon while their escorts struggled with picnic baskets along the platform at 2.30 p.m., in black tie!*

British *Vogue*

Lesley worked briefly as a copywriter in an advertising office and designed a poster for London Transport in 1933, but turned to journalism. Her article 'Anti-beige' published in *Harper's Bazaar* in June 1935 was spotted by Alison Settle, editor of British *Vogue*. Lesley joined the features department and became features editor in 1937.

Opinions expressed in the press dominated all classes in a time before TV, radio or the internet. British *Vogue* was the ultimate fashion-and-society bible which also presented a potpourri of the best artistic and literary talents of the contemporary avant-garde: Aldous Huxley, Nancy Cunard, Clive Bell and Virginia Woolf; Noël Coward, Vita Sackville-West and the Sitwells. Cecil Beaton, Hoyningen-Huene and Horst turned fashion photography into an art – all three would become lifelong friends of Lesley's.

By the end of the 1930s, British *Vogue* began to cater for a mass readership, showing women how to dress stylishly on a budget and weighing up working girls' wardrobes. In the magazine's May 1938 issue, Lesley wrote: *Chanel demonstrated the fact that grey flannel trousers and a hairy wool sweater are nothing if not allied to swags of pearls, wrists clogged with barbaric bracelets, and a netted coiffure top-knotted with masses of geraniums and chenille plumes. And why not?*

Couturiana by Lesley Blanch

What an object lesson to those ladies who think country clothes spell beige tweeds and ghillie shoes, and who sit back on their shooting sticks, preferring boredom to bravado, sartorially speaking.

After Britain declared war on Germany in September 1939, Londoners settled into chaos, living day-to-day in an atmosphere of danger, but they pulled together. Air raids enforced night-long blackouts, but it was business as usual at theatres and restaurants – although they closed early so after-hours clubs sprang up in the reinforced, shored-up basements of hotels and restaurants. Society was much more fluid than people realise today. Men and women married frequently and love affairs were not unusual. Sirens and blackouts gave an immediacy and frisson to life, absent in peacetime.

A fragment from Lesley's unfinished memoirs describes life under fire: *During the Blitz, I would leave home with a small piece of carpet under my arm, as one never knew where one might have to sleep the night. London was full of foreign men in those days; there were Czechs and Poles, you could take your pick! Every day was possibly your last. When you went to sleep in a friend's cellar, if you brought a handsome stranger with you, nothing was ever said. It was a free-for-all.*

Lesley's letter to her friend Diana Gould, the striking beauty who danced *Leda* with Freddie Ashton and later married Yehudi Menuhin, gives anecdotal insights into working life, wartime deprivations and irritations. Written on *Vogue* notepaper, it is dated 4 December 1941, and is addressed to her c/o The Russian Opera and Ballet Company, Grand Theatre, Leeds:

Dear Diana,

Your saga of misery was highly entertaining except that my heart really bled for you. I know something of those northern provinces, which, unless you do, are quite as unimaginable as Tahiti. I spent some weeks in Leeds many years ago, working on a production of *The Cherry Orchard* with Komisarjevsky + I remember he used to become quite hysterical with horror, on Sundays at, I think, the Queens Hotel. He used to say, lowering round, take any moujik, any serf, of the dark ages + they will not stand such living conditions. They will rebel. I will rebel, we will rebel. Waiter bring me another half bottle... + so on. All very Slav.

But of course, you cannot send for half bottles now, or even half pints. Nor can you live riotously in restaurant cars (on flannel fish + gravy soup). I speak with feeling, for I too have been ploughing the northern furrow, on a Calvary of my own, in Anglesey, doing a reportage on the Mixed Gun Teams, Men v. Women, or, and – I really forget – who are practising their lethal arts on remote mountain slopes, where the cold is legendary. Not uninteresting though; the journey down, also, like yours, undertaken on a Sunday, began at 8.30 a.m. dragged on, nine to a compartment + the heat jammed on – so that we were tearing at our collars by early blackout + shut window time – no restaurant car, of course, + none of us were prepared for the siege – + every buffet a troop concentration, most of the halts spent outside the station anyhow + four hours delay, in all. Paddington reached at 12.20 a.m. Pitch black, no taxis, I was marooned in Bayswater.

Vogue has been particularly bloody lately. So many really insane, unnecessary fusses, I really think the atmosphere rivals a rehearsal, sometimes. Anyhow, one trial was that after all the trouble I gave you all taking pictures, getting the story, etc. etc. I was given so much to do in the rest of the issue (signed stuff) that the

Spotlight page, of course, had to go in as a picture page, unsigned, + only the most mignon captions − + no sort of chance to be critical, informative or have a viewpoint about anything. I wish they would realise you cannot say anything worthwhile if there are 15 pictures (mixed subjects) on one page. And 11 words is not space to discuss a flea. Of course, hats, boots, brassières, all get <u>columns</u> − even with the paper shortage as acute as it is. But not ballet, books, music − oh no. Oh dear me no.

Lesley Blanch at home in Chelsea, 1944

However, I did get in Firtolani's picture, + one of the rehearsal, + a note about the Christmas season + *Tzar Sultan*. That comes out 17 Dec. Also, in the present issue, I've forced them to print a small notice, on a page called Notice Board, to the effect that you were all coming back for Christmas, so that's about all I can do, at present.

Who will do your décor for *Tzar Sultan* − let me know quick. I may be able to put in yet another line, somewhere. It's good to keep reminding the apathetic audiences. And who will make the clothes?

Do you belong to a library? If so, read Maurice Collis' *The Great Within*. All about Pekin (history of) quite absorbingly entertaining + wonderfully escapist, for railway journeys.

The London theatre is full of refined gutless whimsies, I sat in a torpor of boredom at *Ducks and Drakes* <u>such</u> clean fun: such really nice people, so jolly. I walked out of *The Nutmeg Tree*. I'm looking forward to Clark Gable in *Honky Tonk*. That's my cup: or Ibsen. Either or both. But not Dodie Smith, please.

I have never written such a long letter before. I think my pen has got the bit in its teeth. I hope the screed will serve to while away an odd half hour on some blasted platform.

Love + sympathy − + to Devillier,

Lesley Blanch

Romain Gary

London, 1944. A divorced, older woman meets a handsome young man in airman's uniform at a party. So begins a love story with echoes of Flaubert's *Sentimental Education* and Stendhal's *The Red and the Black*. She was 41, and he 31. A Polish-Russian-Jewish navigator, his deep, gravelly voice was irresistible. She had *found The Traveller again in him*.

Born in Vilnius in Lithuania, Romain Gary's actress mother, Nina Owczyńska, was from Koursk in Russia, and his father's identity uncertain, though probably also Ashkenazi Jewish. (His original patronymic, Kacew, was from his mother's first or second husband, Lebja Kacew, who abandoned her.) When he was fourteen, his mother moved with him to Nice. Alone and impoverished, she fought fiercely to give her adored son the very best. A naturalised Frenchman, he served with General de Gaulle's Free French Squadrons flying with the RAF, and took part in numerous successful sorties and was greatly decorated for his bravery, receiving medals and honours after the war ended.

His first novel, *Forest of Anger*, was reviewed by Lesley in British *Vogue* in January 1945. She arranged to have him photographed for the press by Germaine Kanova and Haupt in the state-of-the-art *Vogue* studio, newly opened to cater to the magazine's roster of photographers. The novel was first published in English – translated by Viola Garvin – because of paper shortages.

Nostalgia in exile is potent. Lesley, with her love of all things Slav, was a link to the man Gary liked to say was his father, *the arch seducer of his moment, Mosjoukine of the silent screen*. She describes the actor and Komisarjevsky during a trip to Paris in *Journey into the Mind's Eye*, *flung back on the low Turkish divans which ran round the room; beside them, the samovar, humming comfortably; above them, one of the many glittering, silver-cased ikons which studded the walls*.

Romain Gary (or Kacew, as he was then called) and Lesley Blanch married on 4 April 1945 and celebrated at Prunier's in St James's. They went to Budapest for their honeymoon. Anne-Scott James, beauty editor at *Vogue* and Lesley's flatmate in Chelsea (they had both been to St Paul's Girls' School) describes the couple in her thinly disguised autobiographical novel, *In the Mink*. She uses fictitious names: 'Jean-Pierre Lasalle was at least as tough as Amy. He was a pilot of the French resistance with a fine war record, French by nationality,

Romain Gary, 1944   Lesley Blanch and Romain Gary, 1944

but Russian by ancestry, and as Slav as they come. He was brilliant, witty and good-looking, and I adored him at sight, but he lived in a state of *Cherry Orchard* gloom. He never saw a gleam of hope in any quarter.' Of his wife, she writes: 'Amy had a fund of stories concerning racy adventures that had befallen herself – a smuggling episode in Turkestan, a misunderstanding with a procurer in Lisbon, acting with a touring company in Mexico, dancing with a bandit in Macedonia – and she did not spare herself in the telling. She pictured herself always as the innocent victim of misfortune, a cork buffeted on stormy seas, an ill-starred heroine of a new *Arabian Nights*. Indeed, there was something about her of Morgiana or Scheherazade.'

Lesley's words about Isabel Burton, one of the four women profiled in *The Wilder Shores of Love*, capture the lure that glowing far horizons held for her: *From the start she had known what she wanted, and proceeded single-minded, with the force of a steam engine towards her goal. There was never a moment's doubt or regret. She wanted the East.*

31

An unsent postcard addressed to her husband at the Ministère des Affaires Etrangères, Quai d'Orsay, Paris, is evocative:

London

In my little, lonely room, darling, my thoughts turn constantly to you + your gay life in the glittering city. How silly! Here are both of us, figuratively, fretting away our summer in attics which are either too hot or too cold. I hear Paris is blazing warm. Here, it's like wild December. Peter Ustinov passes through Paris for filming in Italy, + will try + reach you for a cosy crone. He is killing and wears a red waistcoat + side whiskers now. Witty as ever + as nice. Keep this card for my collection please.

A big kiss, Pussuna

In 1946 Lesley left England, never to return except as a visitor, to travel across war-torn Europe and join her husband. There was food rationing, most borders were closed, and trains were the main form of transport. Bulgaria had collaborated with Hitler. With the unconditional surrender of the Axis powers it was now occupied by Allied military forces – the American Army alongside the Russian and British armies, while the French were represented by a diplomatic mission. Gary was posted to Sofia as part of the French diplomacy delegation.

On the ship from Marseilles to Istanbul Lesley befriended a Turkish passenger who showed her around the city of light and shadow in return for her smuggling a package of precious gems. She was stunned and seduced by Istanbul – it was love at first sight.

It turned out that her husband had also been seduced, having acquired a mistress in her absence. Nedi Trianova was beautiful and gifted, and came from a distinguished family. The two women became close friends and helped each other in different ways. Lesley asserted emphatically that she did not mind and was not jealous.

The consulate was empty of furnishings, yet Lesley was supposed to entertain visiting

Nedi Trianova

dignitaries and ambassadors. So she bought Nedi's family silver, which also meant that Nedi had some money. Since everyone knew that Trianova spied for the Americans, at the diplomatic dinners to which she was invited, the guests chit-chatted about trivia and never discussed politics.

The Russians made it difficult to travel around, but thanks to Nedi, Lesley had no trouble. She jumped on a train when she could, and visited the Black Sea and mountains and Thracian plains on her own. She'd say: *I like to reach different horizons, to break away from the present and look at the past in far distances.* Her husband was left to his diplomatic duties and he spent every available hour working on his novel. In her posthumous memoirs, she writes: *Sometimes it seemed as if he regarded his life as a sacred trust, something quite above mere egomania, rather, something which at all costs must be preserved until it had fulfilled its purpose. Which was to write, to write all that inner döppleganger master had decreed and achieve all that his mother had decreed for him too, social status – money – glory; but first the writing. Nothing must threaten that. People, or events, or the intrusion of daily life were all enemies blocking the way to the ultimate goal of fame.*

After eighteen months, much to Lesley's despair, Gary was summoned back to the Quai d'Orsay. They left in December 1948. Nedi left with the American consul.

On the Road

Life in the French diplomatic service took Lesley and Romain to Berne, New York and Los Angeles. From these postings they extended their travels further – to Turkey, North Africa, Mexico, Central America. Unorthodox and passionate in their search for adventure, they were an odd couple in a diplomatic world riddled with protocol. Lesley fulfilled her wanderlust by travelling to, and writing about, those places she craved: *Whenever I could not stand the formality of the Corps Diplomatique I would take a train as far away as possible, usually the Sahara, to wander in wild places.* A postcard dated 15 March 1951, sent to her husband at the Ambassade de France in Berne, reads:

> Darling, it is all quite beyond everything – I am bored with the oasis, bored with palms – but O! The faces, the people, the incredible life in this lost, lost boundary town full of camel trains from the Sahara. I get up at 5, + out before

light... exhausted, very dirty, + living on eggs + cous-cous. Never better. Love from a Happy Traveller.

Post-war Britain still had rationing (butter, meat, tea and coal) and all manner of state regulations and high taxation to endure. Cities were scarred by bomb sites, half-ruined houses, temporary prefabs and gardens turned into allotments. The countryside was littered with wartime military bases, some abandoned and others reactivated because of the Cold War.

A fragment found on Lesley's desk, overlooking the green shade of her terrace, describes her happy release at a difficult time: *At a moment overcast by all kinds of travel restrictions that had been applied during World War II and lingered on to frustrate the would-be voyager. Many people had come to share my childish longings for 'Abroad' – for other scenes and skies, and I was even told that what I had written acquired a forbidden, or hallucinatory, flavour for the frustrated stay-at-homes. 'Abroad' was not for most British citizens just then. They had only lately emerged from the stress and trauma of those four grim war years, when England was a beleaguered fortress, its inhabitants severely rationed and under constant attack. Then, when at last peace was declared in 1945, they found themselves almost as cribbed and confined, still rationed, still yearning for the inaccessible 'Abroad'.*

Turkey, which in time grew to be my most loved 'Abroad', was then beyond my limited means, although travel was cheap enough at that time for those who accepted the rough and tumble of the now-vanished Third Class. Even so, Turkey seemed out of reach and I returned to reading and re-reading Pierre Loti's haunting and beautiful descriptions of the Sublime Porte, biding my time, consoled by less exotic expeditions within easier European horizons.

America was a never-never land, attained by expensive and lengthy crossings on one of the big liners refurbished after years of disuse or war service. Atlantic flights were just getting under way again, long costly flights that had to come down to refuel en route. Jet flights were unheard of then; jumbo jets quite unimaginable. Yet presently the word 'jet' passed into the language, synonymous for luxury and chic, and the privileged few who 'jetted' were referred to by the media as 'the jet set', soon to have their very own ailment: jet-lag.

While those post-war years of restriction were frustrating so many would-be travellers, and I had escaped, a whole new and revolutionary concept of travel was taking place. A vast international network of big business became aware of the financial benefits to be obtained from an interlocking system of tourism on a mammoth scale. Suddenly, everywhere was accessible to everyone and a rush of nations began sweeping across the globe: the West going East and the East coming West – a ceaseless, seasonless tide, here, there, anywhere, (the further the better, was how a large section of an untravelled public saw it). The age of charter flights and package holidays had begun. Giant hotels rose where coral atolls had been and mileage became the new status symbol. But it was not travel in the sense of my writing.

Lesley's books and articles took readers whose senses had been starved by wartime austerity to places they had never been to, which is easily forgotten in our age of easy travel. She knew what they wanted and gave it to them: 'local colour', adventure and high romance. Both the travel writer and the translator shape the perspective one culture has of another, like a nomad bringing news from faraway places. She opened up the landscapes, cultures and cuisines about which she was passionate. Researching in depth, she rewrote and romanticised the cultures which obsessed her, then considered exotic. Her words carried worlds in their wake. She was at home in, not just conversant with, the cultures of many different countries.

Roquebrune

Lesley's artist friend, Evelyn, lived with a Russian who had known Romain before the war in the south of France. Their villa was on the Moyenne Corniche below

Roquebrune's mediaeval *vieux village*, on the coast between Nice and Monte Carlo.

The Garys arrived in Roquebrune on foot in 1948, wearing heavy woollen army coats. Her Bulgarian embroidered leather boots were striking; a military cap was pressed down flat on his shoulder. To the local community it was as though aliens had landed from Mars.

Le Vieux Village, Roquebrune-Cap-Martin in the 1950s

The villagers grew vegetables and had rabbits. Every old stone house had a fire to keep warm. It was a spartan way of life. The couple acquired three rooms arranged vertically like a tiny pile of sugar cubes, known as 'the Tower'. The room at the top was his. Later she bought two small cellars below to create a kitchen; and then the adjacent donkey-stable which was larger, known as 'the Turkish room'. It became their base.

Gary often sank into depression and lay marooned in darkness. In 1955 he had a mental breakdown in London and was hospitalised. He convalesced in Roquebrune, and wrote. Lesley neither pandered to him, as advised by his doctors, nor got sucked into his emotional undertow. She bought him a piece of land: three terraces behind an ancient olive tree. There was a stone trough full of spring water for the vegetables, an orange tree, and an earthenware Grecian-style urn by the wall in which to store odds and ends. But he did not like it. So their housekeeper's husband cultivated it.

The Garys were the only foreigners to live in the *vieux village* until the 1960s when artists and writers began to come from outside. An outlandish and theatrical pair, the villagers thought they were odd, but accepted their eccentricities. He would walk down the narrow, car-free streets in a cowboy hat and American blue-green snakeskin boots with wooden heels. She dressed like a Persian houri,

Lady Frieda Harris

in Oriental trousers, a shawl or a scarf, and gold bracelets that jingled. As she passed the children playing games on the cobblestones, her white caftan or pleated burqa worn like a cape billowing behind her, they'd shout, 'There's a ghost! There's a ghost!'

Mireille Dagostin, the daughter of the Garys' housekeeper, Ida, never forgot Lesley's friend Frieda Harris who stayed for a while in what came to be known as the 'Lovers' House' at the top of the village in Rue du Château. Eccentric and elderly, she had handkerchiefs with little bells on them. If she dropped one she'd hear, and pick it up. Since it was too damp for her, she returned to India – her homeland – to die. Harris had been a suffragette; was half-Indian, half-English and wore *churidars*. She had a boat on the Ganges and sailed with the crew to the Himalayas. When the two women went down to Menton dressed in an assortment of Indian and Moroccan clothes, everyone called them old hippies.

The Non-Conformists

Gael Elton Mayo's description of the Blanch-Gary couple in 1950s New York offers a rare snapshot:

> Then Romain Gary arrived in New York, followed by Alastair Forbes, and all was changed. *'Comme ce pays est razoir,'* said Romain, continually amazed that the girls wore girdles – the most unsexy arrangement he had ever encountered.
>
> I met him with Vsevolod [Gael's husband]. He appeared one day with a Russian friend called Sasha Kardo-Sasayev, but he knew my sister and Alastair and it felt that he came from 'home'. His wife, Lesley Blanch, was due to arrive soon, after closing their house in the Balkans, where he had been a diplomat. She was writing her book, *The Wilder Shores of Love*, dedicated to 'Romain Gary, my husband'. He must have been the wildest and most difficult, if also the most amusing husband any woman could have had. Sasha was his 'samovar', a Russian expression for a loyal and ever-present friend. He had a fine Slav face with high cheekbones.
>
> *'J'ai besoin de Sasha parcequ'il est con,'* said Romain, and Sasha did not seem to mind. He probably did not grasp the subtleties, and Romain was in many ways obscure. He was established as an author but not yet great; it was not for another five years that Zanuck filmed *The Roots of Heaven*. He was obsessed with women but declared that he believed in love. 'It is a duty to be happy,' he said. 'If you love someone, send everyone else to hell; stay with your person.' He was an idealist, he was a mixture, for he was also unscrupulous; he was honest enough to dislike puritans for their confusion of other duties with love – certainly much of his preoccupation was about love and sex. At times it seemed that he was playing a role, looking at himself from the outside – or perhaps looking for the idea of love more than the object of love. He himself was two people; one really watched the other. He would ask with sudden anxiety: 'Do you think I am handsome?' Indeed he was, with blue eyes and nearly black hair, but the diffidence in the question was not in keeping. In the war he had been a navigator in the Free

French Lorraine Squadron (attached to the RAF), and had been given the Croix de la Libération, a rather special decoration. He spoke English with a Russian undertone, but his true language (not his character) was French.

When Lesley arrived Romain's sense of proportion changed. She was very funny, and teased him for the way he fussed about his diet (which had not been apparent before). As a couple their irritations with each other were constant but entertaining. They were having a lawsuit concerning their furniture, Romain having 'lost the papers on purpose'. She gave dinner with Balkan dishes: meat with green peppers and yoghourt sauce. The Romain who made passes at women was not the same as the Romain lying on the bed in their darkened room, 'not understood', asking to be left alone. He had indigestion, during which time Lesley was in the next room (their flat in New York was small) at the head of her dinner table talking to Arabs, who never got indigestion. She was very keen on Arabs. One of her guests was the son of the Pasha of Port Lyautey, his great uncle was 105 years old and had been Ambassador of Morocco in Madrid in 1875 – he remembered Victoria's jubilee. Romain would appear looking tragic like an El Greco saint. He worried about his weight and his appearance, yet when he went out, or when he forgot about them, no one would have guessed from his jokes. His conversation was brilliant, and like Lesley, he was exceedingly funny. She called him the Japanese Overlord.

They lived in the Hungarian quarter, where their fishmonger played the violin. Lesley found a stray dog and adopted him. He was chocolate-brown and she named him Moony. One day she dressed him in long lace robes and asked some elegant ladies to a christening tea. They didn't know if she was serious or mocking, but she really did dote on the dog.

In some ways Romain was mad. He would suggest to a near-stranger that they go off and live together far away – in Teheran for instance. (Later he was there as Conseiller.) His eyes would look beyond her into the novel he was perhaps imagining and acting out, not with his pen but with his person... he could see himself fleeing the staid world with his imagined love. The great future Goncourt had to *live* his creation, not just write it.

The seeds of his suicide thirty years later were possibly already sown then. It is tragic to remember that he lost his laughter and that they were such an original couple. How unnecessary the subsequent events now seem. By 1980 he thought that all the world's ideals were lost, which cannot have helped.

Christmas card by Lesley Blanch sent to friends in 1951

Writers' Rooms

Gary wrote his novels in the tower above Lesley's snug terrace which was festooned with bougainvillea, honeysuckle and jasmine. Writing was a visceral
necessity, he was consumed by it. His room had a chair, an ironwork bed, a
bench, a shelf for books and a kind of pulpit painted black which served as a
desk, although he generally sat on the floor to write since it was a small space.
Like Lesley, he wrote longhand – preferably with a fountain pen – and used
wicker baskets for his drafts. They each had someone to type up their writing.
(Since Mireille was eight or ten years old at the time, she did not type up Gary's
manuscripts as has been claimed.) The little girl was allowed to look at his
books about Africa, which had pictures of animals, so long as she did not lose
the page-markers. She preferred his books to the ones downstairs; they were
exotic, or about the East. He'd send her off to buy his Gauloises or Gitanes. Gary
liked to work in a kimono-style dressing gown which was made by Madame
Maingoucie, the local seamstress, whom Lesley supplied with special fabrics:
cool, light cotton for the summer and *laine des Pyrenées* in the winter to keep
her husband warm.

Mireille was scared of Gary, although he could be kind. Once at school, during a lesson, the Catholic nun ordered the girls to obey her because she was the wife of Christ. A girl laughed, 'Ouah, he had lots of women!' Mireille added, 'Just like Mohammed who had several!' The nun thrashed her in front of the statue of St Joseph. When she got home, her mother and Gary were chatting in the kitchen. He noticed the flushed, silent little girl slinking past the door, and asked why she was crying. When she told him, he laughed out loud, but then went to complain to the nun. He said it was very wrong to beat a child.

Lesley's historical biographies and travel articles were written at a rectangular bistro table on her terrace with a blue view of sea and sky. Dr Chan said of her, '*Ecrire c'est son moteur*; writing is the engine that drives her.' She worked in a warm caftan, or a *jellabiya*, acquired on her travels; a rug on her knees and maybe a pashmina in winter; a parasol and refreshing drink in the summer. She often had a bottle of wine to hand – preferably a good vintage offered by wealthy friends – and took a sip from time to time, but did not always finish what was in her glass; she just liked having it there. There was also the caviar she had loved since childhood when she had been initiated by The Traveller, saying, *it tastes so much better from a spoon.* In the late afternoon whiskey made its appearance – a ritual she never missed. She was not a smoker although she would occasionally light up a Turkish cigarette from a special box which she offered to guests.

Mireille often ran small errands for her after school, or carried her paint pots. Lesley liked to make marbleised endpapers for books, or to embellish a picture-mirror frame. The wooden trunk which she decorated with Russian artisanal floral designs was used to transport the Garys' manuscripts around the world, from one posting to the next. When Mireille was older she learned how to sew. Lesley would sketch what she wanted – a caftan, Turkish or Egyptian style trousers, or a straight skirt to be worn with a belt in the day – so the clothes could be made up for her. She sometimes added buttons or decorative trim brought back from her travels. A great improviser, nothing was wasted.

Lesley was tolerant when it came to the complexities of human relationships and desire, and accepted her husband's need for women and sex. She rented the 'Lovers' House' at the top of Roquebrune's *vieux village* in Rue du Château, where he could meet his French or American mistresses. He, in turn, accepted his wife's disappearances, letting her go off alone to travel across the Sahara and other faraway places. He said nothing, and respected her privacy. No one ever stayed in Lesley's place when she was away.

Mireille remembered them laughing a great deal and enjoying each other's company. Although they talked to one another in English, a French observer could sense their intellectual affinity which she described as being *'fusionelle'* ('it was as though they had fused into one'). But as relations deteriorated there were screaming scenes. Husband and wife crossed paths, but were rarely in Roquebrune at the same time. *He was so absorbed in his writing when he wasn't being a fascinating ladykiller. So I was very free,* was how Lesley described it.

He gave her status and the means to travel. She gave him domestic stability and opened doors into many different worlds. Their tempestuous relationship was punctuated by repeated separations and reunions; it was not an easy or particularly happy one. It was, however, a creative marriage of minds, and they fuelled each other's imaginations and ambitions. Contradictory, complex personalities, they were romantic idealists and fantasists, each in their own way. Over the years, they got used to each other's idiosyncrasies: *We had quite a different social metabolism: at a dinner, if one of us was bored witless and the other was the centre of attention, one would just get up and go.*

Although Lesley went away on trips to research new projects, she increasingly succumbed to the demands of domestic life that are as fatal to feminine creative talent as the demands of marriage. Her writing was constantly interrupted by moving not only house, but continent, and by her duties as a diplomat's wife. She was becoming tired of her husband's endless affairs, and he was fed up with her literary success. They nearly divorced, but decided to give it another go.

Tinseltown

By the time the Garys reached Hollywood their writing careers had taken off. Her success with *The Wilder Shores of Love* in 1954 was followed by his winning the Prix Goncourt in 1956 with his novel *The Roots of Heaven* in which he championed animal rights, ecology and land conservation. It was filmed – directed by John Huston with Errol Flynn, Juliette Gréco, Trevor Howard and

Christmas cards by Lesley Blanch sent to friends in the 1950s

Orson Welles. As was his satirical novel *Lady L*, published in 1959 – directed by Peter Ustinov with Sophia Loren, Paul Newman, David Niven, Daniel Emilfork. Lesley illustrated the cover for Michael Joseph's edition, and collaborated on the film production in 1961. Her 'agent to the stars', Robbie Lantz, whom she met when writing for *The Leader*, took on Gary as a client.

Film rights were sold to MGM for *Aimée Dubucq Rivery: Message from a Ghost* from *The Wilder Shores of Love* – with Elizabeth Taylor cast in the lead role. Lesley's only novel *The Nine Tiger Man, A Tale of Low Behaviour in High Places* was to be directed by George Cukor and shot partly at Belvoir Castle Grantham in Rutland, with a screenplay by Terence Rattigan, who wrote: 'Romantic, outrageous, savage and comic... *Nine Tiger Man* is the purest ironic comedy, almost, let's face it, black.' But neither film was made.

Lesley read her husband's work and made editorial suggestions, though it wasn't her kind of writing. However, she acknowledged his exceptional ability. Gary was irritated by her success, and said: 'My wife may be talented, but it's always women's stories.' Yet when her biography of Imam Shamyl was published, Gary sent her a note, 'This book will remain a classic – admiringly yours...' His view was shared by President de Gaulle who sent her a congratulatory letter.

I sought, wherever I was and with whoever I might be, to recapture something of that particular climate I had known, beside The Traveller, Lesley wrote. Her London friends Peter Ustinov, Laurence Olivier, Nancy Mitford and Cecil Beaton (who designed the costumes for the 1956 Broadway production of Lerner and Loewe's *My Fair Lady*), arrived in tinseltown so they all picked up where they had left off. Lesley read and revised film scripts for the director, George Cukor. As Consul General (minister's rank), Gary's role was, in part, to be France's ambassador to the film industry, and he learned about making movies. Hollywood in the 1950s was a glorious melting pot of European avant-garde, expatriate talent.

The Garys' art deco villa in Outpost Drive was spacious. Living quarters were on the ground floor where a large sitting room gave on to a terrace and garden. Six consulate staff worked on the first floor with the Consul General. The

The French Consul in Los Angeles, 1959

couple enjoyed their diplomatic status and the fact that they had some money at last, which they had never had before.

Katia de Peyer, then married to Daniel Aubry, said that Lesley made their young lives 'glitter with fun and excitement' and remembers her as being, 'One of the most generous and witty hostesses in Hollywood. For four years when my then very young husband and I lived in Los Angeles, she warmly embraced our presence and with her ongoing hospitality made our lives a unique experience. We met an amazing array of stars, political and literary figures.'

French artists, intellectuals and politicians loved to visit, and they often returned. Lesley was fun yet erudite, and a good conversationalist. When André Malraux, the author and French minister of cultural affairs at the time, and his wife, said they were sick of always being so serious, Lesley took them to Disneyland and they all had mad fun. She said to Shusha Guppy: *I loved Malraux – he was a really romantic figure. I knew Camus, but not very well. I spoke French rather badly. I am not an intellectual in their way.* Gary also greatly benefited from his diplomatic status, and his literary fame. It amused him to lead a star-studded Hollywood life arranged by his wife when she was not away in wild Berber hill country, or the mountains of Dagestan.

Lesley created her own sartorial elegance, wearing clothes from the countries where she had travelled, the epitome of hostess chic: *I wore them long before they became the fashion and I will be wearing them long after they've gone out. My friends used to say, 'Oh, there goes Lesley in another of her funny outfits.' Now nobody thinks anything of it.*

Bestselling authors, the Garys were invited everywhere. She wrote: *We both loved it. And we knew everybody: Aldous and Maria Huxley, Christopher Isherwood,*

Igor Stravinsky and his wife Vera, George Cukor, who became a great friend, Gary Cooper, Charles Boyer — everyone interesting. James Mason, Sophia Loren, Gregory Peck, David Selznick... Grand Hollywood parties? Oh no, there was never enough money for us to do that. But we had a Russian cook, and it was sometimes very amusing to give a dinner for, oh, Cecil Beaton and Laurence Olivier and Peter Ustinov and Leslie Caron, who was one of the few intriguing women there at that time.

The actress Dana Wynter, who ran from the Pod People in the 1956 sci-fi classic *Invasion of the Body Snatchers*, described their first meeting in an email:

David Selznick gave one of his informal dinners, five tables of eight people. I arrived when people were seated as I came from the studio. When the meal was over, everyone dispersed to play either gin-rummy or strip poker. Since I have no interest in cards I headed for David's library where I had just settled down with a book when the door opened and an English voice said, 'Hello, what are you doing here?' Lesley was in the same quandary re-cards and I rather think it was a first visit to that house. Anyway right then we took an instant liking to each other. The friendship even survived my telling about one of my dinner partners whom I discovered later on to be Romain Gary, French Consul General in LA. I then launched into saying how tiresomely the man whom I didn't find a bit attractive had 'come on' and by the time the main course appeared I had to say to him 'M. Gary, I'm a happily married woman, a bit fatigued after a long day's work, and I'd appreciate it if you'd stop feeling you have to be so "French" with

Lesley Blanch flanked by Aldous and Julian Huxley, 1961

45

me.' (Remember, Georgia, how L. used to say that sometimes R. looked like 'an ikon dipped in vinegar'?) L. took it all with a straight face – no stranger to those circumstances I later learned – saying: 'Romain Gary – my husband actually'.

In the 1950s, a façade of sexual conservatism was kept firmly in place, although sexual shenanigans often went on behind the scenes. Away from the glamorous and seductive façade, husband and wife led different lives and slept in separate rooms. Their ten-year age gap now mattered. Having been so accommodating about his affairs, Lesley was blind to the possibility of his trading her in for a younger model. She wrote: *We had become very great friends and understood each other perfectly about work – and we had the same sense of humour. We both loved animals, all kinds. He used to say, 'Lesley doesn't mind my infidelities, she is very eighteenth century'.*

When the twenty-one-year-old actress Jean Seberg and her director-husband François Moreuil went to one of the Garys' suppers in December 1959, it marked the beginning of the end of two marriages. She had just finished filming Jean-Luc Godard's *Breathless* with Jean-Paul Belmondo.

Lesley had just finished *The Sabres of Paradise*, about Imam Shamyl, the 'Lion of Daghestan and Chechnya,' and his fight against Tzarist imperialism from 1834 to 1859. Despite thirteen years of work on this book, she felt there was something missing, and decided to return to Istanbul to do one final piece of research. Years later, Lesley still regretted that fatal decision. She ignored

her friends' warnings that there was more substance than usual to her husband's infatuation with this particular starlet. Leaving the cats – Norman and Titimi – to keep her husband company, she left town.

The Garys' open marriage had survived his previous affairs, but the gamine muse of the French New Wave was not mistress material. Lesley remarked icily, *like all Americans she can't make love without having to get married.* She was surprised and angry

Monsieur & Madame Gary, circa 1959

46

that her husband wanted a divorce, and held out for a year. He moved in with Seberg. Lesley travelled to Turkey, Siberia and Outer Mongolia in 1962, returning with a superb shaman's staff topped by a horned creature which looks like a sculpture by Picasso.

Divorce was particularly unpleasant and nasty. It ended a marriage of eighteen years. In her last ever interview, Lesley said: *He saw a very pretty, randy, young woman, a little bit vulgar. I was disappointed that he let it take hold of him, and made another base. He made a great mistake getting involved with someone who could not talk about books.*

Sylvia Plath and Ted Hughes, Zelda and F. Scott Fitzgerald, Anaïs Nin and Henry Miller. To this pantheon of ill-fated literary couples can be added Lesley Blanch and Romain Gary.

A Singular Friendship

After divorcing Seberg in 1970, Gary often visited his old friends Sylvia and René Agid in Nice. He spent most of his time in Roquebrune and Mireille remembered him dropping in on her mother with the novelist Joseph Kessel, author of *Belle de Jour* which had been filmed by Luis Buñuel in 1967. Ida was instrumental in reuniting Lesley and Romain, acting like a go-between. Mireille described in detail their reconciliation in 1972.

During one of his visits, Gary was waiting in Ida's house while his friend René went off to run some errands. Ida asked if he wanted to see Lesley. Gary looked at himself in the mirror, 'Oh no, no...' Fiddling with his hair and clothes, he said, 'If Lesley is willing to see me we could meet here, but I don't know if she'll agree. I won't go down, she can come up.'

So Mireille went to fetch Lesley who had been warned of his visit. She was wreathed in the scent of jasmine; primping and preening; changing her outfit; trying on scarves and bracelets. There was fuss and anxiety on both sides because of so many years of arguing over money, and Arctic emotions. Yet each wanted to see the other. Lesley went up the narrow cobbled street to Ida's house, and the couple talked for hours before decamping to her terrace down below. Ida prepared some food and Mireille served it. She was struck by how they talked non-stop: as one. He spoke English and a little French, and she did not talk in her usual way. Each spoke like the other – her intonation was like his, and his was like hers. Mireille had never heard anything like it. Watching them, she understood now that she was a little older: it was a love-hate relationship.

Lesley bought her villa in Garavan in December 1971, on Ida's recommendation. She moved in gradually, and renamed it Kuçuk Tepe – Turkish for 'little hill'. Mireille was adamant that Gary and Lesley were getting back together: an ageing odd couple, each in their house (he asked Lesley to find one for him). He craved her intellectual richness, and Lesley knew it. She could not give him a child, but she could give him knowledge and culture. He loved the way she told him stories about Russian history and its characters like Pugachev who led the great Cossack rebellion during the reign of Catherine II, or Stenka Razin, the brigand, seated in his ivory-and-silver chair high on the cliffs above the Volga. She gave him stability and support. He had a good entourage in the south: Ida, Lesley, René Agid. He was terrified of getting old, and felt frail.

Lesley was surprised by Gary's suicide in December 1980, as were his friends. Though when asked about it, she answered: *He was depressed all of his life; why should he not choose when to go?* Gary was given a state funeral at the Invalides, the home of Napoleon Bonaparte's tomb. Lesley stayed with her friend, Susan Train, former Paris bureau chief of Condé Nast magazines, who lent her a fur hat. A year later, she helped scatter his ashes in the Mediterranean.

Un monstre sacré

Romain Gary left behind him thirty-two books. A dizzying array of characters populate his novels – more often than not idealists, misfits and prostitutes. He wrote in both French and English, and enjoyed making mischief. He reinvented himself as Émile Ajar whose second novel, *The Life Before Us*, about an Arab boy growing up in a Parisian suburb, won the Prix Goncourt in 1975. Under the statutes of the prize, an author is not allowed to win it twice, but he had won it already, in 1956 for *The Roots of Heaven*.

I went to see Roger Grenier in April 2013, Gary's neighbour in Rue du Bac. He studied under Gaston Bachelard at the Sorbonne during World War II; was hired by Camus to write for the newspaper *Combat* (Fight) which was originally an underground newspaper of the Resistance; and is a prolific writer as well as a member of Éditions Gallimard's reading committee.

Most writers are forgotten twenty or thirty years after their death, but it's not the case with Romain Gary: he has become more important. His work is very varied and original. An adventurer and a force of nature, he loved to live inside the 'drama' – both imagined and real. His voice was slightly husky and he spoke French without an accent. A war hero, he was very brave. He cared a great deal about what Général de Gaulle's Compagnons de la Libération thought of him. Camus and Malraux were close friends.

He loved to play games, and to tease. I was a guinea pig in the Émile Ajar case. Only Robert Gallimard really knew what was going on, along with Jean Seberg, Gary's son, Diego, and his typist. Gary had introduced me to his nephew Paul Pavlowitch five years before, and I got him work as a ghost writer. When Pavlowitch was outed as Ajar, it was easily believable since he could write. It was only after Gary's death in 1980 that we found out the truth.

For Romain Gary to play with genres and styles was a fantastic adventure. Now, when you read *Pseudo*, written after *Gros-Câlin* and *The Life Before Us*, they are obviously Gary, but at the time everyone was blind to it. His series *Frère Ocean* was a flop with booksellers and people were indifferent to his new novels: 'Ah, another Romain Gary, we know what to expect...' Ajar revived his fortunes.

Olivier Agid, the youngest son of Gary's old friends Sylvia and René Agid, is emphatic: 'Romain Gary left behind him a body of literary work, and a rapport with "image", that makes of him a more modern writer than Sartre. He was ahead of his time.'

The Years of the Minarets

Until the 1960s, to be a traveller you had to have money and time: the arrival of the jet plane made it easier and cheaper. Lesley made Paris her base after the divorce was finalised in 1963. She told a journalist that it was *a good place to work – and that is what is important to me when I come back from my travels. Besides there are no quarantine regulations here to prevent my cats coming and going freely. The climate is just as bad as London, but I live in a very ivory tower manner in my rooftop apartment.*

From 1964 well into the 1970s – which she referred to as *The Years of the Minarets* – she took off, driven by her lodestar longing. Alone, or for work, she journeyed to Istanbul, Fez, Algeria and the Holy Cities of the M'zab, Tunis, Cairo, Oman, Isfahan, Damascus, Aleppo, Afghanistan, Bukhara and Delhi.

The books from Lesley's library tell a story. Fellow travellers and writers Freya Stark, Rebecca West and Wilfred Thesiger were admired and letters were exchanged. A note on the first page of her copy of *Desert Marsh and Mountain* reads: *First meeting in Persia – Iran, chez General Arfa, his fabled library... amusing at dinner, not generous about Freya Stark. I suggested Mme H de Hell (Mme Hommaire de Hell) – he laughed a lot, but agreed over endurance.*

She adored Gerald de Gaury – the British military officer, explorer, historian and diplomat – and treasured his letters to her. She wrote: *He spoke beautiful Arabic, and could talk Arabic lore. Living among, and as one of, the royal household in Arabia, he knew a great deal and could tell you marvellous legends. His books are a brilliant reading of the Middle East that is vanishing as we watch – he was an historian manqué.*

Camels at Dawn

In 2010, I interviewed Susan Train, my co-literary executor. She reminisced about American *Vogue*'s charismatic editor-in-chief, Diana Vreeland, whose view of the magazine's readers was that 'they don't know they want it, or are missing it, until you give it to them.' Pre-World War I Orientalist high fashion was revived by Vreeland, with a 1960s twist.

Sue described a three-week shoot in Syria and Jordan. In 1965, *Vogue* photographer, Henry Clarke, Lesley and Sue were dispatched, along with the models and stylists and the clothes. They flew from Paris to Lebanon, drove to Damascus, *the fountain city breathing apricots and roses,* and on to caravan city, Palmyra, where the last pillar of Zenobia's crumbled empire stood sentinel over the Syrian desert. It was an unsettling journey: suddenly in the middle of nowhere there would be two soldiers with guns. The expedition took over a small hotel and settled into communal living. Lesley tended to scatter things around her as she went – fans, hats, veils – so Sue ended up keeping an eye on her as well as the models. Henry Clarke needed a camel for the following morning's shoot at the ancient ruins. He and the hotelier, accompanied by Lesley and Sue, headed into the desert. They stopped at some tents. Carpets and cushions came out for the women while the men negotiated for a camel at dawn. A little boy with hennaed hair stroked Sue's hands, mesmerised by her red nail polish. Despite not speaking Arabic, Lesley communicated with the grandmother.

Team *Vogue* moved on to Aleppo, its souks held to be the best in the world, and settled in to a small hotel where Lawrence of Arabia had stayed. At the beehive village of Tareb, Lesley sat smoking a *narghilyé* in the large communal room with the elders, all the villagers watching through the window. At a shoot in Jordan, Lesley parodied herself in a photograph which she used as that year's Christmas card to friends. She is half-reclining on rugs with a parasol, beaked teapot and small glasses on a tray, reading an Arabic newspaper; the ancient ruins of Petra rearing up behind her.

A tiny fort in the desolate landscape of Wadi Rum was the setting for an unfortunate case of love at first sight. The men of the Bedouin desert patrol were exceedingly handsome: tall and swarthy in khaki caftans, with daggers and big leather belts slung around slim hips. 'They were something else!' exclaimed Sue. While Henry negotiated for a camel charge similar to the one in the film *Lawrence of Arabia*, Lesley painted swirling turquoise-and-green henna shapes, with a touch of gold, up a model's exceedingly long legs, shown off to perfection by a long blue, side-slit Madame Grès gown. One of the young soldiers was smitten. Keen to arrange his marriage to the young gazelle, he offered a number of camels in exchange for her. He had a hard time accepting she was not available.

'Match Me Such Marvel! A Rhapsody on Middle Eastern Themes' was published in American *Vogue* in December 1965. Models pose dramatically across twenty-two pages in front of Roman-era columns in the ancient Syrian city of Palmyra, the Nymphaeum at Jerash and Khirbet al-Mafjar Palace outside Jericho. Lesley's accompanying text is just as theatrical.

Lost Worlds

Lesley's first encounter with Istanbul in 1946 had left her wanting more. She returned often. Fragments of notes found after her death are seductive: *To know Istanbul truly would demand several lives, each lived on different levels, in different centuries; but it would be a mistake for any visitor to concentrate on the grandiose. Les petits décors de la vie are eloquent, too; those cobbled steep old streets of the Phanar, at Paile Pasha, or any village along the Bosphorus where, behind summer embassies or abandoned palaces, the tumbledown bleached wooden houses, with their windows sealed by* moucharabiyeh, *always wear a secretive air, and where there is always a shadowy figure within, observing us silently; or where a woman's hand emerges stealthily to pull up a basket of figs proffered by a street vendor below, his brass scales and fruit panniers carried by a donkey who wears blue beads to avert the evil eye. That is Istanbul as much as any legend of the Bosphorus, or the sweep of the Marmara, where the dolphins frisk joyously round the beaches of the Princes Islands, and the Bithynian Mount Olympus rises, majestic on the horizon.*

Lesley spent time in Iran, researching and writing a commissioned biography of the Shahbanou Farah Pahlavi whom she admired. The book was published on the eve of the 1979 Revolution which sent the royal family into exile. The piece, included here on page 309, 'Iran: Where Ancient and Modern Collide' is a mosaic of extracts from the biography, giving an inside view into the royal couple's life and the imperial coronation in 1967. Other pieces in this book are from the 1970s when she travelled extensively.

Drawn to Islamic civilisation, Lesley never intended to settle permanently in Garavan-Menton. Her traveller's tales can make for disturbing reading given the cumulative impact of a century of war on the Middle East, and the horrors of Syria's civil war, and Daesh. Aleppo was once the cultural jewel of the Ottoman Empire.

In *From Wilder Shores: The Tables of My Travels* she wrote: *Once upon a happy time, I journeyed about Syria, going from desert to oasis, from Damascus to Ma'loula, a rock village where an ancient language, Aramaic, rather than Arabic, is still spoken and is said to be the language spoken by Jesus. There, climbing dizzily to the fortress-like monastery I ate falafel, a rissole made from dried broad beans, the white kind, spiced with garlic and parsley, and deep-fried. This is enjoyed throughout the Middle East, from Egypt to Jordan, sometimes dipped in taheena, or a mixture of slivered onions steeped in vinegar. On my climb I ate in nature. Syrian food remains to me so memorable that sometimes it overcomes any geographic, geopolitic, historic or cultural recollections of my travels.*

At Homs, a small, smiling town, the rushing waters of the Orontes river have turned the huge creaking water wheels for centuries, and there are balconied houses and little cafés hanging over streams. There I ate apples stuffed with small pieces of cooked chicken, rice, sultanas, chopped blanched almonds, honey and cloves; which is a good way to make the remains of a chicken go a long way without seeming apologetic.

Another Syrian chicken dish is chicken mish-mishiya (mish-mish being the name for apricots). It is a delicious sweet-and-sour way to vary the ubiquitous fowl. Other dishes I have eaten among my Arab friends such as Kebash-el-Attarin (spit-roast leg of lamb with pistachios, honey and apricots) led to struggles for as much culinary instruction as I could disentangle. If you are going to be lily-livered about experimentation, do not embark on the Arab cuisine. Oddly enough, in all the welter of aromas, garlic is not very much in evidence and none at all is found in salads, where European gastronomes consider a trace or more essential.

The 1950s Woman

The writings of Alexander Herzen, the Russian writer and passionate political exile who lived in Britain from 1852–64, were among the books on Lesley's bedside table. After the death of his wife in Nice, he wandered with his children from home to home in London and its suburbs, and ended up living in a fractious *ménage à trois* with his closest friend, Nicholas Ogarev, and his wife Natalie.

There was a time when for a woman to live unconventionally and totally on the outside was the only way to escape from suburban gentility and the pressure to conform and be 'a good girl'. Lesley had an affinity with those women who were free when opportunities to gain independence were limited, and to do so was condemned.

As British *Vogue*'s features editor during World War II, she was on the front line of women journalists writing about a wide range of topics. Lesley documented the lives of women in the forces with the photographer Lee Miller, who was later given permission to follow the Allied advance through Europe. The war had a liberating effect: women in Britain got through it without their husbands, brothers or fathers. Some joined the ATS, or WAAF, or WRNS and drove ambulances, or worked in a government ministry.

Codes of conduct were different to now. Women had to marry and settle down, yet having had a taste of freedom many wanted independence from the restrictions of family. The old and the new pulled against each other. Trailblazers who lived purposeful, intense, liberated lives, inspired others to get out from under and do their own thing too. But to forge ahead required toughness; a thick skin to handle criticism and setbacks; a resolute self-belief in the face of ostracism and social expectation. They often had a rackety, messy, muddled time of it.

Lesley respected traditions and the rulings of domestic protocol, yet broke away. She often said that she had a strong appetite for life, and for loving. Submissive yet strong, she was a paradox. Her husband was referred to as the Japanese Overlord and herself as *poor little faded paper fan*. Although Lesley believed in equal pay for equal work, she disagreed with other feminist beliefs. Romantic disappointment could not be soothed by career satisfaction. For all her bohemianism, she could be surprisingly old-fashioned.

In the 1950s, the boundary between work and personal life was blurred, and a husband was instrumental in helping his wife get her career off the ground. Lesley took to addressing Gary as 'Chance' in reference to the poet William Henry Davies' beautiful lines, 'Sweet chance that led my steps abroad...' Thanks to his postings in the French diplomatic service, she could travel. They had an unorthodox understanding: while he was free to have affairs, she was free to roam in wild places.

When asked what inspired her to write *The Wilder Shores of Love*, Lesley answered, *Seeing young Englishwomen spoiling their lives tapping away at typewriters, and then watching them trudge home over Waterloo Bridge. I wondered how different their lives would have been if they'd managed to get away.*

One of the first generation of career women, Lesley was a mistress of reinvention. The artist became a journalist, and then a bestselling writer. She understood her audience and its aspirations. In books like *Round the World in 80 Dishes: The World Through the Kitchen Window*, she blended entertaining traveller's tales with exotic recipes. *The Sabres of Paradise: Conquest and Vengeance in the Caucasus* is history through a vibrant Technicolor Hollywood lens. As she was finishing the book, one of Imam Shamyl's grandsons proposed marriage. But Lesley turned him down, as she still hoped to salvage her failing marriage. Letters from his sister, Zubeydette El-Amroussy née Shaply-Shamyl, are illuminating.

Throughout her writing life, Lesley explored the different roles of women: *mother, wife, mistress, muse, or slave*. A subjective essayist, she is no less a part of the story than the characters the story depicts. The four women in *The Wilder Shores of Love* were each in their way escaping from the constraints of conventional European society to live the life of their choice, free and unfettered. Lesley was the fifth one who got away. Her words to Lorna Sage about them apply equally to her: *The East attracted them romantically and adventurously, they willed things into a pattern they liked. It's rare... you need imagination and will combined for this sort of transformation of your life – not into fiction exactly, but into something which becomes fact in the living of it.*

Isabel Burton, the devoted wife, is a monster of adoring, mothering control. She follows her wild explorer husband wherever he goes. In certain passages it feels as though Lesley is describing married life with Romain Gary.

Highly-romantic, highly-sexed Jane Digby – Lesley's favourite – becomes a liberated woman through having myriad affairs as she adventures across Europe, ending up in Syria where she marries Bedouin chieftain, Sheik Abdul Medjuel el Mezrab. In the 1970s, Lesley fell in love with Sheikh Zaïd bin Sultan Al Nahyan – he was instrumental in the creation of the United Arab Emirates. Their affair lasted for several years. She said she lived for a time in his harem, and often showed me a photo of them together.

Aimée Dubucq Rivery, cousin of Empress Josephine, was kidnapped by pirates and became the Sultane Validé. She was the mother of Mahmud II. Lesley first heard about her – a veiled Oriental femme fatale – from a Turkish gem smuggler on the ship from Marseilles to Istanbul when travelling to join

Lesley Blanch with Sheikh Zaïd bin Sultan Al Nahyan in the 1970s

her husband in Bulgaria. She described the veil as being a whole way of life in Muslim countries, and despaired of how it was misunderstood in the West. As Philip Mansel put it, 'For Lesley Blanch, the veil, especially the all-covering burqa of the Afghans, is a means of female self-protection, equalisation, independence, even seduction and coquetry, the garb of convenience, privacy and honour – rather than part of the mechanics of male domination.'

Isabelle Eberhardt changes her identity to become who she wants to be. She wears men's clothes, dresses as an Arab cavalier, and calls herself 'Si Mahmoud'. Lesley sees the ambiguity in the erotic: *Even in her own mind she does not seem decided as to which sex she is – or wishes to be. This indecision or ambiguity is emphasised in her* Journal, *where, for the first part, she always refers to herself in the masculine gender, and only later adopts the feminine.* Lesley too had a paradoxical quality: on the one hand very masculine, and on the other very feminine.

London's post-war publishing world was stuffy, masculine and elitist. Lesley was an unclassifiable one-off who lived abroad – an exotic outsider. She seemed to know everyone but belonged to no group, and was not a fixture of the London literary scene. She generally did as she pleased and got away with it, and was admired for her independent spirit and wit. Dramatic in action and in word, flamboyant and entertaining, she was a reminder that artists invariably go against the grain, take up unfashionable causes, and see the world differently.

Marianne Faithfull, Shirley Conran and the late Jackie Kennedy were inspired by her. In a 1957 diary entry, Anaïs Nin wrote: 'I read *The Wilder Shores of Love* and became completely devoted to her writing. It is a book of great vitality, superb storytelling. She is herself Scheherazade telling about four remarkable women. I was fascinated by the charm and wit with which she tells biographical facts. The four women became my heroines. I read the book several times. My admiration for her was total.'

A New Kind of Autobiography

Lesley claimed that she could not invent so chose biography rather than fiction. When she wrote that *Journey into the Mind's Eye is not altogether autobiography, nor altogether travel or history either. You will just have to invent a new category*, the label narrative (or creative) non-fiction did not yet exist. Today most memoirs are written in this way, as opposed to the straightforward cradle-to-the-grave approach. The narrative is based on facts about people and events, but the author uses the literary and cinematic techniques of novelists, playwrights and poets to make the story vivid and dramatic. The boundary between dreams and waking worlds is often blurred.

She writes about her time with The Traveller, aka Komisarjevsky, and their fabulous romantic and sexual passion through a series of dramatised scenes. Their liaison may have been scandalous, but to keep him anonymous had another point: it created a romantic mystery. The abrupt ending of their affair and her subsequent journey to Russia became all the more poignant. Telescoping time is a feature of narrative non-fiction. Episodic fragments create an impression, as opposed to revealing every detail as each occurs in space and time, so the reader gradually pieces together the story like a jigsaw puzzle.

Although she turned her back on the theatre when Komisarjevsky left her for Peggy Ashcroft, the lessons learned stayed for life. Reinventing herself as a writer, Lesley never lost her sense of theatre. Her dramatic control of image and narrative, whatever the context, was exuberant, intimate and finely tuned. She wrote: *Komisarjevsky understood how my taste for dramatic effects, for the theatre of stylisation such as he knew so marvellously how to create, was gratified by the settings and rituals of the Orthodox Church.*

By means of impressionistic prose and with the self-confidence of a great actress, Lesley gets under the skin of those she writes about and is able to convince her reader of the palpable existence of the most exotic characters and events.

Komisarjevsky's view that, 'There is only one theatre – *the theatre of life on stage,*' was transformed by her into the theatre of life on the page. His biographer, Victor Borovsky, wrote: 'The art of theatre is born out of a metamorphosis, out of a double life; behind it lies both inspiration and control.' While Lesley used dramatic elements in her prose writing, her actual life also featured a high degree of drama.

From 2001, I worked intermittently with Lesley, transcribing her handwritten anecdotes on to an old laptop kept on the top shelf of her cupboard during my visits. I became fascinated by the many lives she had led and the different worlds she had known. Her memoirs, *On the Wilder Shores of Love: A Bohemian Life*, were published posthumously by Virago in 2015.

We had also discussed putting together a selection of Lesley's writing. After her death, Dana Wynter and Mireille Dagostin spoke to me candidly about the Blanch-Gary marriage. Hence this book, *Far To Go and Many To Love: People and Places*, which incorporates their insights, along with a selection of early journalism, biographical essays, travellers' tales; and a selection of sketches from her recently-discovered artist's portfolio.

Lesley's first article, 'Anti-beige', landed her a job at British *Vogue* where she worked until 1945. She then freelanced for a year before joining her husband in Bulgaria, and was a regular contributor to Edward Hulton's *The Leader* (sister publication to *Picture Post*). She covered film and photography – still relatively new media – and profiled rising stars: Vivien Leigh, Peter Ustinov and Billy Wilder among them. War correspondent Germaine Kanova, the 'French Lee Miller', was in Paris for the Liberation and with General Leclerc's divisions in Germany – which won her the Croix de Guerre. Lesley inferred that she had met Romain Gary at one of her parties. Students of film studies still reference her article *Red Tape and Blue Pencil: the Autocracy of Film Censorship*. In her books, Lesley wrote about historical figures, generally women, who were misfits and eccentrics. She first heard of Pierre Loti at her mother's knee and would talk about him, or Laurence Hope, or Isabelle Eberhardt, during supper, bringing them to life as though they had only just left the room.

Specific places held a particular significance: the Sahara, Iran, Turkey, Syria, Afghanistan, Central Asia. In *Fragments of a Balkan Journal* (revised by her in 1995) she describes life in Bulgaria with Romain Gary. *Much Holy Day in Chichicastenango* is a traveller's tale from the couple's stay in Mexico where he began to write *Promise at Dawn*.

Lesley was the last in a long line of romantic English woman travellers who fell in love with the East, and went off, enduring all kinds of living conditions and experiences. The world was less accessible; less traumatised by bombs and technological inventions. A time of insouciant openness, religious fundamentalism had not yet taken hold.

As I cleared her desk, the smell of datura coming through the window, a piece of lined paper covered with her graceful handwriting emerged from under a small pile of letters from the Arabist, Gerald de Gaury; Mohammed Marmaduke Pickthall's translation of the Koran; and Alice Keppel's *Book of Common Prayer* given to Lesley by Violet Trefusis. It reads: *Dr Johnson, the Great Lexicographer, though not much given to travel himself, made one of his most majestic pronouncements on the subject. 'The Object of Travel,' he said, 'Is to Regulate the Imagination by Reality.' (The capitalisation is mine.) Today, it might be better if Imagination could Regulate Reality – the realities of mass tourism which now overrun the globe, overwhelming its multifarious flavours and traditions, and destroying forever those romantic images or illusions of remote lands which we once sought and which could, often, still be found.*

I

People

ANTI-BEIGE

ADMITTEDLY OURS IS A BEIGE CLIMATE, BUT LET THAT BE THE END OF IT. Let us no longer plead guilty to the accusation of the Distinguished Foreigner who said, 'Englishwomen's minds are becoming as beige as their clothing.' Beige, or to be exact drab, odiously indefinite, devitalised, and smugly self-satisfied, pursues almost a right-of-way through the bewildering maze of its ingenious alibis, such as Fawn, Biscuit, Cracknel, Café au Lait, Tussore, Oatmeal, Sable Foncé, Thatch, Pinky Beige, Birchbark Beige and even 'New Beige'.

Is it perhaps these misleading alibis which are responsible for the fatal preponderance of beige in our national colour scheme? Is it, alas, possible that the Englishwoman purchases a fawn coat, a *café au lait* tea-gown, and a beige two-piece in the happy conviction that she has been both selective and adventurous? Nor does the matter end here, for the beige blight has even penetrated to the realms of interior decoration. Who has not sat, chilled and repelled, in the anaemic desolation of contemporary pickling and stripping, upholstered in the perniciously anaemic off-whites, near-whites and broken-whites (I dare not say dirty-whites) so dear to the heart of every modern decorator? Moreover, food follows suit and, with the cult of various slimming Nordic biscuits, we are confronted by further excursions into *beigerie*.

I appeal to women for immediate action against this 'Up beige and at 'em' attitude of the dyers and buyers. We must resist this insidious flood which sweeps like a tidal wave, and certainly like a great bore, over sartorial Britain. Let us return to the splendours of the past. Let us, attired in hunting pink and seated upon crimson plush, demolish round upon round of underdone beef, strawberry jam, and cherry brandy. Let us, in short, see red.

If such descriptive invention is lavished upon beige, then why not upon scarlet, which is seldom classified and usually left as 'pillar-box'? Let the designers, dyers and buyers lavish their rhapsodic ingenuity upon its subtle shades. Let us have not only Pillar-box and Sealing-wax, but Chelsea Pensioner, Jam, Lobster, Fire Engine and Dining Room, or even Under-done; and if 'grey-lite' is an accepted hue, why not 'rear-lite'? Nor must we overlook the rarer 'off' reds, best described, perhaps, as Telegram or Orphan's Drawers (or Flannelette).

Even the garnet, cardinal and lacquer of the more emphatic nail varnishes do not, I feel, gauge the full possibilities of scarlet. Scarlet — I repeat the word — with what ineffable strength and richness it falls upon the ear! Surely the Scarlet Woman is preferable to the Blue Boy, whether in the guise of a social menace, public house, or national art treasure. I would even go so far as to place a purely personal preference on scarlatina, rather than, say, jaundice, which borders on the realms of beige.

The hour has struck. But where is the scarlet woman? Once roused from apathy, all sartorial Britain will impatiently await its new leader, who shall deliver them from their beige bondage, whose war cry must be 'In the pink' and whose slogan 'See more Red'.

The Legendary Miss Leigh

SHE TORE OFF HER EYELASHES – THE FALSE ONES – AND THOSE BENEATH were almost as long. She wiped off her face – the exquisite pink and white mask – and the one beneath was even more beautiful. Layer after layer. I was reminded of the onion-peeling scene in *Peer Gynt*. But coming down to the basic beauty of her face, it was still, I thought, a mask: which is as near to the true face of this actress as any casual acquaintance can come, perhaps. Impossible to say where the actress and the woman merge; where public performance leaves off and private life begins.

It is rarely otherwise, in the theatre, for it is a medium that fosters every kind of artifice, until the playing of one or many parts has superimposed another character altogether, built up by calculation, biddable emotion – technique, in fact, overlaying the original structure. Just how much this original character is overlaid depends not so much on the strength of that character as upon the weakness of the basic dramatic talents.

The Progress

By all accounts, Duse, who was born with dramatic genius, remained compartmented. As she did not have to build up the actress (but only to perfect her art) nothing encroached upon her personality. Now Vivien Leigh will, I hope, forgive me if I say that I think she began with very few dramatic abilities; but she has so progressed, so muscled into all the technical aspects of her work, that the actress now appears to dominate. To what precise extent it is impossible to gauge. One thing is certain. As an actress, she has become very polished, very able, very good.

Her progress has a spectacular, legendary quality about it. I remember the first time I saw her. It was just ten years ago. It was at her first London first-night, and there was a party afterwards. She was appearing rather than acting in *The Mask of Virtue*, an indifferent play. But she made it her triumph.

Her beauty was dazzling, it brought her fame overnight, headlines, front-page photographs, a contract with Korda, offers on all sides, bouquets, bowing and scraping. But she did not find that enough. Behind the inscrutable façade of loveliness, the crystal-clear, single-minded ambition of this most determined woman was already at work.

The Ambition

She was not content to be just a beauty, as she had not been content with the conventional role of happy wife and mother in the easy, elegant pattern of life which she once shared with a small number of other fortunate women. A home in Mayfair; seeing Cook about dinner; seeing Nanny about Baby; shopping; doing the flowers; a fitting at Stiebel's; entertaining her husband's friends; being entertained – the sort of round that used to be called a busy life.

All the while, ever since her childhood, in fact, she had eyed the stage with furious longing. She was born in India and expensively educated all over Europe – her languages are admirable. Before the war, she dubbed some of her pictures herself, speaking her lines again, in French and German, for the Continental market, which is a test few English accents could survive.

She married very young; her first husband was a lawyer. Their daughter was about four when her chance break, in *The Mask of Virtue*, rocketed her to the top. She got there by good looks and good luck. But she stayed there by stamina, sheer determination and hard work, more hard work, and still more hard work. All through the early days of her marriage she had studied, with an eye on the theatre. At the RADA; voice production at Elsie Fogerty's; singing with Baradi. Now she redoubled her attack. Inch by inch she was raising her professional abilities to the level of her looks. It was a high standard, but she's made it. The actress has won.

Her latest stage performance in *The Skin of Our Teeth*, Thornton Wilder's Pulitzer Prize winner, is a tour de force. She has the plum part, or parts; she invests the puckish, quicksilver qualities of Sabina, the eternal skivvy, with a touching, infantile charm, a special, skippish grace. Next, she is metamorphosed into Miss Atlantic City, or, in essence, the Whore of Babylon, the scarlet woman – the eternal pin-up. Here her sense of satire and perfect, stopwatch timing is displayed – as well as the most flawless underpinnings this side of

Ziegfeld's Follies. Apropos these legs – why the seductive black stockings? (Bomber-fresh from Broadway, I should imagine, for it is six years since we saw such sheer delights here.) Why not the scarlet stockings which are the symbol of adultery? The author obviously had such a pair in mind when writing the scene where Adam, or Mr Antrobus, having fallen for Lilith, or Miss Atlantic City, and recoiling before the sight of his bobby-sock-aged daughter, tricked out in a pair of scarlet ones, rounds on the Eternal Pin-up for having put the child up to such tricks. It is a small point, perhaps – or is it? It confuses a scene which should not have been confused by issues of vanity. For once Miss Leigh has let looks supersede drama; woman has come before actress.

Which is odd, for this is a play about which she feels strongly. She tells me, reverentially, that she finds new depths, new meanings, each time she plays. When I ventured a criticism as to what seemed a lack of structural development – theme, but no true variations; act I, the type; act II, the prototype; act III, the archetype, for all characters save hers, a crystallisation rather than the progression which is the essence of all comic strip characters, as these are designed to be – she suggested that perhaps I had not understood it fully; that I might appreciate it better were I to see it again; that so profound a theme needed several visits.

In the Dressing Room

Very likely: I was concentrating chiefly on her performances; I had not clarified my mind about other aspects – the production as a whole; whether the *décor* was contributive, or merely an execution of stage directions (how was the American version I wonder?). Whether the *Commedia del Arte* effects were too deliberately rammed home. Whether it was all too much of a romp, or not enough? Should it be comic, or sacrosanct? Whether it was a good play, or just a very good part – for her. Yes, I must go again, decidedly. Such a play, however you criticise, is worth serious consideration; it is very welcome after all the *blah* which most managements serve up.

Backstage, I usually find the dressing room atmosphere revealing. Among all the classic setting of cold cups of tea along with the mascara, wilting flowers, wigs, safety pins, telegrams, lonely Pekinese-and-dragon dressers, there are usually some indicative, significant touches. And always the superlatives gush round one's ears. 'Darling, you were divine…' the *leitmotif* is eternal, cloying.

'My sweet, bless you… you were heaven…' But Miss Leigh conducts even her dressing room life in a more rarefied manner. Hardly any litter, nice hot cups of tea, braced-up blooms, not too many superlatives and a much-loved, snuffly little Siamese cat, New Boy. They shared the sofa, eating bread and honey together. Both gave the impressions of purring over their tea. Both gazed at me with those pellucid, fathomless, turquoise blue eyes.

I am passionately devoted to cats, so I hope Miss Leigh will not think I am making any crude analogies or meaning any disrespect when I say she has the same delicate, exotic feline beauty as New Boy. But she doesn't snuffle, though she does insist – and here her wit flashes out, sharp and gay – that she can match his adenoids with her bronchial patch, acquired by the excessive Egyptian *décolletages* of *Caesar and Cleopatra* and all the weeks of overstrain which finishing off the film entailed.

She collects pictures, usually likes to make her dressing room an art gallery, but doesn't do so just now, since in less than two months she must start work on her new film, *Lottie Dundass*. In the meantime, a note of rarity is set by one exquisite little Renaissance drawing given her by Sir Kenneth Clark of the National Gallery.

'Have you seen the new pictures at the Wildenstein?' she asks; her eyes look far away, visionary, conjuring a distant prospect of Picasso. 'Nice?' I ask, economically. 'Out of this world,' she sighs, 'Out of this world…'

The dulcet, velvet tones which can range so flexibly are a tribute to her voice training, as the whole woman is a tribute to her own achievement. But her beauty and grace are, indeed, out of this world, from no pot of face cream (though her mother did control a beauty salon at one time) and no elaborate system of exercise, no ritual of beauty. She loathes exercise, never takes any; eats heartily and with relish; remaining porcelain fine and clear in both colour and silhouette. Legendary is the right word.

Realised Ambitions

Here is a woman who has realised several of life's ambitions and legendary ones at that; and, more wonderful still, not found them turned to dust and ashes in the realisation. She wanted to be an actress and she swept everything else to one side and became one – a good one. She wanted to play Scarlett O'Hara; this was an *idée fixe* which obsessed her from the first moment she read the book, long before there was any talk of a film, much less of a comparatively unknown English film star snatching such a much-coveted role from all Hollywood. But she did so, in the teeth of every obstacle and opposition, transferring to America to sustain this test role, armed, as everyone thought, only with a natural likeness to the southern charmer. But her perfect performance proved her abilities, and proved too, that her faith in her own limitless potential was justified. She established herself as world box office; the goods.

Her marriage to Laurence Olivier continued, or strengthened, the legendary, dramatic pattern. Together, they are a powerful force in the theatre and cinema. A self-contained unit, planning and capable of big things and deeply conscious of their potential, too.

The production of *The Skin of Our Teeth*, and the playing of Sabina were other ambitions which she had realised successfully. (Her husband produced the play.) Now she plans to alternate between screen and stage. Britain and America – that is, if it is only for brief visits, perhaps to play in something opposite Olivier; teamwork wherever possible.

To do *Caesar and Cleopatra* on the stage with him is another ambition. The stage is her true preference and she has never been sidetracked by films. Speaking of her contract with Selznick – the seven-year contract which expires at the end of this year and which she fought in the High Courts recently, to free herself for *The Skin of Our Teeth* – she maintains such long-term affairs are unhealthy, stultifying. She won't be so bound again. She only accepted this one since it was that or nothing; that or not playing Scarlett; and as such she considered it a price worth paying at the time, though she warned Selznick that she would always be restive, always troublesome, always unwilling to be so restricted. Time has proved her right and triumphant once again, since she won her case and was upheld in her claim that some clauses regarding her work in the theatre were unjustifiable. She now divides her time between screen and stage, eyeing her next picture, *Lottie Dundass*, with as much enthusiasm as she can ever muster for film work. She is loath to exchange her role of Sabina for Lottie, but likes working with Korda. And is thankful that the more inelastic terms of her still valid contract do not yet demand her return to America for an MGM picture to which she is committed. Her home and husband, and their mutual interests, are here, and here she intends to remain.

And What Now?

I do not know, but I suspect that she is moving towards new, possibly still almost unformed ambitions which, once clarified, she will undoubtedly realise once again. I think that she and her husband, 'Larry and Viv' as they are known to a small, doting coterie which surrounds them, are becoming the embodiment of a legend; embedded in an aura of brilliant mutual achievements, good looks and a serious reconstructive programme in the theatre to match the earnest times. They are, in short, rapidly qualifying to be our Royal Family of Theatreland. The way is clear and they never put a foot wrong. Given time, they may emerge as the English equivalent of the Lunt legend. The perfect team domestically, dramatically. But with this difference. The Lunt legend is, perhaps, based even more on their personality than their artistry; in the case of Olivier, his playing of Richard III places him at once among the giants – it has a Kean-like majesty, a quality of genius which overrides all else. Here is artistry, long before personality.

Still, taken as a potential team, the Oliviers are all set for a similar legendary life of domestic-dramatic triumph. Not that, since the Lunts are still happily among us, 'Larry and Viv' see themselves as pretenders to that particular throne. They are streaking towards one of *their* own.

A New Personality: Peter Ustinov

In the world of theatre and cinema, where more acts are put over offstage than on, and people fall into clearly-defined categories – dream lover, chorus girl, earnest repertory novice, commercial manager and those fading but still gilded young men who are the too precious bane of our theatre – from these and many more, Peter Ustinov stands aloof. He defies classification and is an outstanding new personality.

Already, at twenty-four, he's famous for his side-splitting turns at the Players Club and in Farjeon's Revues; he's known both here and abroad for his quality as a playwright; he's recognised as a first-class cinema actor – cinemagoers may recall his performance as the café proprietor in *The Way Ahead*; he's a much sought-after script writer and, in general, he's considered to be the most promising creative force in the world of English entertainment today.

It is said that we owe him to Mr Agate, whose eulogies, after reading his first play, *The House of Regrets*, put him among the rare and the few and made him known and respected by a public who might not, left to themselves, have discovered him so quickly nor appreciated him so greatly.

I count myself pre-Agatian; that is, I'm probably one of the first to have taken the very young Ustinov seriously. Having enjoyed his earliest comic flights when, straight from school, he was to be seen as the fat German opera singer, or the drooling bishop, at the Players Club, then in Covent Garden, I had the privilege of being one-man audience to his one-man rendering of his play, called *Uneasy Lies the Head*.

I reminded him of it the other day; he says he wouldn't own such a title now – thinks play titles shouldn't be lifted piecemeal from Shakespeare. Says the appropriations made by Noël Coward and other playwrights begin to impinge on the finest Shakespearean productions. Like the old lady who said *Hamlet* was too full of quotations, today, all Shakespeare seems too full of smash-hit play titles.

Private Performance

But to return to the one-man performance. I remember, he arrived for dinner armed with the script, swung into the first act with the soup, and while the succeeding dishes congealed, he played out two whole acts before being persuaded to take so much as a mouthful. I went on eating. We rang down the curtain about midnight. Too much of a good thing, maybe, but a good thing all the same: a strange gallimaufry of oddities and disembodied characters; the odd, displaced persons who filled all his first plays. He's choosing more positive types nowadays.

All that's eight years ago. He's gone a long way since. Now, at twenty-four, he's a man of achievement and, happily, still of promise. He's proved himself no flash in the pan and he is developing with each new piece of work. His potentialities are enormous. If he doesn't allow himself to be too easily distracted from one project to the next, from one medium to another – he's now finishing another play, writing his first book, co-directing and co-producing his first picture, having written the script – then we may expect him to fulfil, in time, all his magnificent promise.

Peter Ustinov is English-born, of Russian parentage. His mother is the distinguished painter, Nadia Benois, niece of Alexander Benois, the designer of Diaghilev Ballet fame. He is married to Isolde Denham, one of our best young actresses. She has a rare, classic sense of style. You may recall her exquisite playing of a young girl in Emlyn Williams' adaptation of *A Month in the Country*, a couple of years back.

The Sergeant-Major's Despair

Peter is a strange figure, emerging out of a semi-conventional background of school at Westminster, where he wrote plays instead of prep; the army where, as he says, he tried, but was happily switched to script-writing with the Army Film Unit.

He's a shambling, baggy figure; he must have been the despair of his sergeant-major; his tailor, too, will suffer, I expect. He's not natty. His large, pale face is set with little, intelligent eyes. When he ambles about the room, I'm reminded of a performing hippo walking on its hind-legs. But as a conversationalist, he's as mercurial as any Harlequin. He'll turn from a discussion of Chinese traditional drama or the contemporary French theatre, to one of his unhurried, malicious, brilliantly entertaining bits of mimicry.

Speaking as a ration-harassed hostess, I'd describe him as a guest who is positively worth his weight in Spam. He's a sort of dinner table chameleon, who, if he's in the mood (and happily he very often is) assumes in turn the didactic manner of James Agate holding forth at the Café Royal; the wan charm of John Gielgud holding court at the Savoy Grill; the Poet Laureate reading his own verses aloud; a Chinese diplomat being received by royalty and, of course, royalty receiving the diplomat. He's so convincing that I find myself heaping his plate for four.

The Favourite

My favourite turn is a well-known actor buying himself yet another identity-disc bracelet. Unless, perhaps, it's an imitation of his own new baby, Tatiana, arrested in full yell by the broadcast of *Peter Grimes*. He does a nice imitation of the score too, and has the glorious gift of being able to talk mock languages; to launch into a flood of near Norwegian; to describe an argument, for example, between a Polish officer, an Italian prisoner and a Doughboy. Not a word of sense, nor a word of any known language, but it's all there – Polyglopolis.

It has been suggested to me that although America, France, Russia, Sweden and Italy are all either performing his plays, or bidding for them, the general public here don't know much about Ustinov, and that his character acting in films hasn't fixed him in the fans' minds, as a classic profile would do. That his name is tricky to say, hard to remember.

Public Performances

Let's simplify.

Ustinov; it's pronounced *oo-stee-noff*. He played the bewildered, mulish North African café proprietor in *The Way Ahead* and was part-author of the script too. He was Van der Lubbe in *Mein Kampf*; the priest in *One of Our Aircraft Is Missing*. He began, theatrically, with Michel St Denis; did turns and panto at the Players Club and appeared in several Farjeon Revues. With Edith Evans, he co-produced *The Rivals*, when it was done in Bath. He produced Kataiev's *Squaring the Circle*, at the Vaudeville, in 1941. He was not, however, as American *Vogue* stated recently, either the author, or an Old Etonian. A wonderful mix up, this – Old Etonian writes Soviet smash-hit comedy – a confusion of thought irritating to all concerned, Old Etonians, Soviet playwrights and Peter Ustinov; proving once again how very far away from Europe America still remains.

But it is as a playwright, first, and film script-writer, second, that Ustinov is best known and this is the work he loves best. *The House of Regrets* was his first play, all about seedy White Russian refugees washed up in South Kensington. It was very properly hailed as outstanding. I liked *Blow Your Own Trumpet*, but most people didn't. I enjoyed its oddly assorted, tag-line characters, all hodge-podged together in the stuffy little café, with Grandmother Bossi, a perfectly inarticulate, immobile character, who only made sounds and was interpreted by the other characters; the lonely misfits, the passionate turtle doves, the atmosphere of teeming streets outside, seeming to press in, to encroach and dwarf the characters within. Whether this was Usintov's deliberate intention, or owed more to the wonderful permanent setting devised by Feliks Topolski (his first, and quite outstanding, venture in stage designing), I don't know. The play was shipped off after only a week's run and was generally dismissed as being undisciplined, lacking in architecture. It must be admitted these are faults often apparent in his work; but still, there is always so much else that is poetic, fresh and intriguing. So much that breaks away from the old, stale formula of theatre as we mostly see it today, that I don't wish to carp.

New Work

His range is wide and widening all the time. *The Banbury Nose* was all about an English militaristic family. This is likely to be seen in Russia soon and is now being played in Sweden. His latest, *The Man Behind the Statue*, is his individual interpretation of Bolívar, the great nineteenth-century liberator of South America. This is likely to be seen here shortly, with Robert Donat in the title role. Bolívar is an intriguing subject. The flashy, swarthy dandy of the cigar-box lids, all side-whiskers and epaulettes, set against a highly-spiced landscape of palms and snows, balconies and little carriages. Yet he was a great revolutionary genius in an era which bred many. Garibaldi and Kossuth were his peers.

This method of interpreting historical characters or episodes in a personal way, and also in a contemporary light, seems to be Ustinov's strongest line of new development. The play he is just completing, *Paris Not So Gay*, is on the Trojan Wars, with Homer and other great bards seen as war correspondents, whose reportage established certain heroic myths. This might be described as a Claridges play; full of kings and princes, it's quite a breakaway from his earlier displaced persons. *The Tragedy of Good Intentions*, which he finished last year, was tried out by the Old Vic Company, who hold the option, at Liverpool recently; now it waits its London presentation.

This is a subtle, curiously haunting interpretation of the Crusades; the tragic misuse of religious fervour, telling how the political, militaristic barons used Peter the Hermit, a mystically exalted dolt, for their own piratic ends, while the seeking, longing crowds followed blindly, led to their doom. I think it a beautiful and nearly great play. It fails for want of architecture, but even in its failure, it is splendid. I hope his many new cinema projects won't deflect him from the theatre, for, being at heart an utterly single-minded actor himself, he understands the theatre and writes plays as such – actors' plays, vehicles for actors; an approach more suited to stage than screen. He is now one of the small, select band, the Independent Producers, with whom much of the future quality of British pictures rests. His present picture is on the subject of radar.

Art – and Commerce

Later he hopes to go to Italy, where he'll make *The Tragedy of Good Intentions*. And, and… and… His future is full of plans; schedules and projects jostle one another. Most of them seem realisable too. He is not Johnny Head-in-the-Air, indulging in wild imaginative capers, grandiose schemes. He loves and believes in the theatre; he takes it seriously. Sees it as something besides show business, or big business. He is an artist who has succeeded both artistically and commercially.

That's why I think him such a very rare and significant person in our theatre today.

An American Director: Billy Wilder

THE FAÇADE IS AUSTRIAN BAROQUE, BUT THE STRUCTURE IS, I FANCY, Pittsburg steel. He reminds one of those ornate cherubs that swarm all over the architecture, paintings and furniture of seventeenth-century Austria. Actually, he's a solid, rather flash-looking little figure, fortyish, with thinning brown hair and round brown eyes set in a round, cherubic, pug-mug. But he's tough, all right. As tough as one of the characters in his latest picture, *Double Indemnity*, only much better fun to know. He might easily be one of the more successful gangsters: he's got their sort of tough charm; their flow of wisecracks; and their sort of cat-foot grace and precision of movement, too.

At least, that's how he struck me, watching him eat strawberry tart, at Eric Ambler's dinner table, while the two of them talked film-shop and picked over their own and other people's scripts. They were talking against the *Itma* programme, which was issuing from the radio *fortissimo*, in all its ritualistic insanity, 'on account of because', to use tough-guy idiom, Wilder wanted to get acquainted with the English sense of humour. (He's become a Sid Field fan, right away.) After listening fitfully to Mrs Mopp and the Colonel, Sam and I'll-have-to-ask-me-Dad, he gave it up. 'Too fast for me,' said the director of *Double Indemnity*, a picture which left most of us positively bruised by its brilliant hard pace.

The Happiest Couple

The name of Billy Wilder is usually coupled with that of Charles Brackett and has become synonymous with most of America's top-line pictures. They are known as Hollywood's happiest couple. As a team, they were responsible for *Ninotchka, Bluebeard's Eighth Wife, Ball of Fire, Hold Back the Dawn, Arise My Love* and *The Major and the Minor*. *Double Indemnity*, which was based on a James Cain novel, was also directed by Wilder, as were *Five Graves to Cairo* and *The Lost Weekend*, which has not yet been seen here.

Double Indemnity is generally conceded to be a piece of outstanding technical virtuosity. It is a sordid, mean, compelling story, charged with a curious quality of inferred, rather than even suggested, sex, in its most implacable, basic form; this, coupled with suspense spun out to nervewracking lengths and a polished – almost varnished – finish, makes the picture so remarkable and so highly individual.

But Wilder's talents are not to be taped. They are of somersaulting versatility: he can switch from tough, sadistic stuff, to the romantic dramatics of *Hold Back the Dawn* (one of my favourite films and his too, he says, for it was written in blood and tears, being based on his own struggles as an alien, to cross the border, from Mexico into the States) or the adult cynicism of *Ninotchka*, or the gay inconsequence of *The Major and the Minor*. Whatever they have, in the way of witty dialogue or psychological finesse, they all share the same sense of the cinema. They are, before all else, movies – not static scenes. He says America has taught him this.

Twenty years back, in Berlin, at the old Ufa Studios, when, as an indigent young Austrian, he made his first break into pictures, it was considered good cinema to go slow, to photograph one lovely scene after the next, just for the look of it. European audiences were quite content to sit there absorbing the atmosphere, but without much movement. American audiences are not given to such reveries. 'The moment you show them a skyscape they begin looking for the plane,' says Wilder, but he doesn't repine. He loves all things American; even Hollywood's sometimes inexplicable habit of distorting or adapting novels out of all recognition. 'In the book it's a submarine, but in the picture, of course, it's a bunch of roses,' is one of his favourite cracks.

He laughs delightedly and we join in. It's very funny, especially now, after some years of war pictures, when, by an inevitable process, in the book it's roses and the film gets it round to being a nicely topical submarine.

Like his mother before him, Wilder is passionately pro-American. It is the country of his adoption and his choice. His mother was an Austrian who had visited and loved the States, and thought that the best start in life her boys could have was to give them good Yankee names. The Wilder brothers were christened Willy and Billy. After a brief period studying law in Vienna, Billy turned crime reporter for a Berlin newspaper, hired himself out as a dancing partner, starved and wrote a pornographic book – Berlin in the twenties was a particularly pornographic place, he reminds you – before becoming film-struck to the point of mania. After a while, he broke into the Ufa Studios, at that time the training ground for so many great names of the cinema.

The usual bleak period followed, but his film stories, *People on Sunday* and *Emil and the Detectives*, won much praise though little cash. With the advent of Hitler, Wilder transferred himself to France, where he directed Danielle Darrieux in *Mauvaise Graine*, which I don't remember seeing here. By now he felt sufficiently established to make for Hollywood.

Snubbing and Starving

But there followed another long, disheartening spell of snubbing and starving. Hollywood was overflowing with European talents; it was rotten with self-acclaimed, over-ripe genius. 'I don't care if you are a Hungarian genius, you must have talent too,' one harassed studio executive wrote outside the doors of his office. All the while, Billy Wilder was growing more alarmed and despondent over his chances to convince Hollywood – particularly since he had, literally, not one single word of English with which to blow his trumpet. He earned his first fifty dollars by jumping into a swimming pool, fully dressed, to make a party go.

At that time, he was living at cut-price rates in the disused and roomy ladies' lavatory at an apartment house. The management made only one stipulation. He must keep the door locked. He decorated the walls with the collection of modern French paintings he had acquired in Paris. In this well-appointed room, then, he spent his time tapping out scripts and stories which were always bounced back at him. Since his rise to fame, however, they have been sold for large sums of money.

After two and a half years the tide began to turn. He made enough to return to Europe, but only just enough to return quickly to America again which, by now, he realised was his true love. Paramount put him under contract and one day, the collaboration which was to change everything occurred in the most chancey manner imaginable. 'Brackett meet Wilder,' said one of Paramount's executives, 'From now on, you're a team.' So saying, he set them to work on *Bluebeard's Eighth Wife*, which established them in the eyes of themselves, their friends and others, as a sound working proposition.

Since then, they have been responsible for many of the most memorable pictures of recent years. They work together in a two-roomed suite at Paramount: the inner room is called the bedroom and here they retreat, to nap, frankly and unrepentantly, after lunch. When working, Brackett lolls on the sofa, shoes off, taking notes and Wilder paces up and down, twisting a stick, rattling out impromptu dialogue and devising situations. They reckon a script takes them about four months to produce. It is impossible to tell where one leaves off and the other begins in this team. They are linked together, as Brackett and Wilder, in the eyes of the industry, even though credit titles and more recently, separate ventures, have proved them individual entities.

They are an incongruous pair. Brackett is an aloof easterner from Rhode Island, one-time lawyer, novelist and dramatic critic. He is academic in his literary approach. Wilder is more cinematic; more articulate, less executive, in the manner of writing. He does most of the talking.

Brackett makes a corner in the stylistic graces which distinguish their scripts. Both are witty; both know how to turn out scripts which are emotional, without being cloying. Speaking of scripts, Wilder says a good script should have everything: that the rest should just be a matter of execution; that if audiences are aware of directorial effects, or tricks, this shot, or that, then the script has sagged.

His tip is to find a new angle on a stock character. Once you've found that, he says, you can lean the whole picture up against it and take a nap yourself. What made *The Maltese Falcon* so successful, in his view, was the character of the detective: he was not just another detective, but a flesh-and-blood man, who had affairs with his clients, if it suited him to do so; that is, if it helped him as a detective, and, or, pleased him as a man. Similarly, in *The Pied Piper*, the outstanding character was really not so much Monty Woolley as the Nazi officer who bargained to get his niece away to safety – and succeeded. In *Ninotchka*, it was the conventionally high-minded Soviet girl who fell for luxury living, who could cope with life and death and revolutions and sex – but not emotion, or new hats... He sighs, 'Yes, I enjoyed doing that picture... only...' he paused. 'Only?' we asked, hanging on his words. 'Only I'm afraid I may have offended the Russians. I wouldn't want to do that.' He seems to have a lively awareness, regarding politics, or rather, to be democracy-conscious. It is evidently deep in his mind – an *idée fixe*, which recurs at the oddest moments: 'So-and-so is a swell actress, always knows her lines, is dead punctual and what legs! But her politics stink.'

His next picture, awaited with panting eagerness here, is *The Lost Weekend*, based on Charles Jackson's horrible study of a dipsomaniac. Ray Milland plays the part with all the case history horror we expect from such a story. The script is Brackett and Wilder. Movies are the great passion of Wilder's life; when he's not making them, he likes to see other people's; to mix with the other picture people and to talk shop. Hemingway, Ingrid Bergman, Lubitsch, John Ford and Claude Rains – 'that glorious ham' – are his prime favourites in their various aspects.

Hold Back the Dawn was one of his special favourites among his own pictures. He admired the way Boyer played the *maquereau* (pimp); he wrote it with this actor playing the pimp in mind. It was an intelligent, unsympathetic part in which Boyer triumphed. He thinks Ingrid Bergman has all the rest of the actresses beat at the start, not only by her dramatic abilities, but by the depth of her personality.

Wilder is married to a Californian girl and has one little daughter, Toto, or Victoria, who was so named since she was born at the outbreak of the war. They live out on the Beverly Hills, in rustic calm, far from the clubs and the people and odd joints that he enjoys. The house is filled with early American furniture and the old needlework *toile de Jouy* nineteenth-century patchwork and such, which Wilder collects fervently. He also collects Toulouse Lautrec posters and some of these, such as the famous *Divan Japonais*, will set the mood for his forthcoming film, *The Count of Luxembourg*. This is to be in Technicolor, with the splashes of orange and black and greenish-yellow which Toulouse Lautrec favoured. Long, long black gloves, frizzy-bang orange coiffures, swirling skirts and froths of madly embroidered and frilled *sous-dessous*.

This lovely, bubbly musical will have Monty Woolley and probably Bob Hope, or Danny Kaye. And women? Wilder looks truculent, then cynical. He shrugs. The cherubic pug-mug lights with malice.

'Well, I guess So-and-so could have sung the part – twenty years ago; and Such-and-such could have looked the part – thirty years back – but right now, the casting's a bit of a problem.'

Right now, however, he's up against more important problems. Which films to show the German people? He's here, passing through London on his way to Germany, accredited to SHAEF, working in their Overseas Service, in the department of Allied Film Control. The part which the cinema can play in the remoulding of Germany and the reconstruction of Europe is generally acknowledged and is being studied with scientific, almost clinical, zeal by some of the administration. Wilder argues that the German people must be re-educated subtly. Not by sledgehammer propaganda blows, for they are an obstinate lot. But by inference; by entertainment; by pointing the moral while adorning the tale. He's a good man for the job. None better. He knows the country and the people as well as he knows the cinema, which is more than somewhat.

WOMAN AT WAR

Germaine Kanova Returns to Britain Bringing with Her a Picture-Record of the Violence and Suffering

THIS WEEK I AM WRITING ABOUT A PHOTOGRAPHER, BUT NO ORDINARY one. I used to think Germaine Kanova's work, on portrait, travel or fashion photography, was sometimes very good, sometimes not so good – but always arresting. I was always interested in her sense of theatre, and by a tantalising, unfulfilled quantity of promise. Now that has been fulfilled.

Last year she was attached to the French War Office working with the Office Français Information Cinématographique. Technically, she is a war correspondent. Actually, she is the only woman to have been in the spearhead columns that fought their way into, *ahead* of, the front lines.

Not only was she the only woman on such a job, she was sometimes the only reporter, news camera, or news reel, within miles. Her battle experience, her forays with the Maquis, her adventures (smuggled into German-occupied French towns to obtain secret photographic information needed by the military) and above all her front-line coverage in open battle, in foxholes, in street fighting and in the first tanks of the first tank divisions storming Germany – such achievements dim down even the most daring exploits of other women war correspondents or, indeed, many men. Her work seems to make theirs like so many armchair excursions, sorties from base: day-return trips to the front. Now I don't mean any disparagement by this: it just happens that a combination of circumstances and events, the unique opportunities granted her by the French authorities – and her own temperament – have put her in a class by herself.

She came back here last week for a few days only, to settle some business affairs, and returned to France where she will finish up all her war reportages, posters and military-archive material before returning to civilian life, to her home here and her work. She left a portrait studio in full boom. 'In a war, portraits pay well. All those partings,' she says, her firm French logic uppermost.

She's a shrewd businesswoman and an artist; a rare mixture. As a child, in Boulogne (she's French by birth, married to a Czech, British by naturalisation) she was a 'child wonder' pianist; a pupil of Debussy, who foretold a dazzling future for her. But a long illness broke her training which she never resumed. She married straight from the schoolroom: her first husband was Scottish and concert-pitch-piano playing faded out. She still plays beautifully; switching from any comic song to French chansons, Stravinsky and Bach. Her childhood background, one of a large, typically solid, happy French bourgeois family, taught her that command of the kitchen, that sense of food and of home, which distinguishes most French women and which makes her little London flat so much of a centre to all the many people, of many nations (she herself speaks six languages) who crowd round her there, enjoying her gaiety and warm sympathy, her endearing self.

She's small, delicately boned, neat, very blonde, with a pink and white and blue prettiness. She looks frail, but she's not. She's as tough as a tank and has the vitality of a racehorse, raring to go. She couldn't have faced up to such assignments, otherwise. She became something of a legend, up beyond the front. I'm told that sometimes news came of her being seen in some inaccessible hot spot. Kanova? She's 'gonflée à bloc,' they said, which can be broadly translated as being full of guts.

She had had some experience of war already: the sort all Londoners had, during the Blitz; and as a child in the last war, she spent much of her time in the cellars, during German bombardments, or helping her mother look after the tragic trails of Belgian refugees who clogged the road, bewailing their dead and lost, from door to door. Her family have suffered much in this war. Seven were killed. Her mother died in the British bombardment. Between them, the family harboured, re-equipped and saved seventeen escaped Allied airmen.

Her war reporter's job began around D-Day. She was in Paris for the Liberation. From there she joined the Maquis. She wanted to make a complete record of these patriot bands. She went into hiding with them, first near Pointe de Grave, living in wild open country. Her adventures are too long to tell here, but included ticklish jobs like all-night forays, crawling cross-country, under the nose of enemy gun emplacements; or worming across the oyster beds, near Royau, raked by searchlights and gunfire (75mm guns: not an occasional sniper); or being smuggled through the barriers, into Royau, later pulped by American heavy artillery. Here, having exchanged the battledress, tough boots and heavy equipment she usually lugged around for women's clothes, she mingled with the French citizens, watching for her moment to get pictures of fortifications needed by the Maquis. She'd hide her tiny Leica camera under her jersey, have it hanging from her neck; her topcoat would be open, carelessly; she'd have to photograph blind, without sighting, like shooting from the hip; and, to continue the metaphor, she had to be quick on the draw; she was surrounded by Germans. She'd raise her jersey an inch or two, face the fortifications or whatever – click – she'd have the shot and go strolling on under the Nazi noses, on to the next objective. It was work with General Leclerc's divisions in Germany that won her the Croix de Guerre and the Bronze Star. Now, another citation for bravery and another award awaits her in Paris: chiefly for her work for the Maquis, at Royau, and elsewhere.

For some time, last winter, she fought with them in the mountains, in bitter snows, in the rock hideouts that were their headquarters. She'd swoop with them rounding up a German outpost, the tattered, ill-armed Maquis boys against the organised German military machine. She lost many friends that way, but she has succeeded in recording these unnamed battles, and the way the Maquis lived and died.

With the French Army Pictorial Service she was attached to General Leclerc's troops. Her place in one of the first tanks in the column was no picnic. Mostly under fire – firing mostly, as they went; she gives a terrifyingly tense picture of street fighting – just as the tank ahead blew up. Often the impact of own tank's gunfire made her nose and ears bleed for hours at a time. But she escaped miraculously from bombardment, shrapnel, snipers, street fighting with the infantry from door to door, crossing the Rhine under intensive shelling – of the the men in her boat, she alone survived, struggling to a foxhole, to wait there till nightfall. Listening to her talk, I recalled the words – I don't know whose, I wish I did, for they are very haunting – 'Man is immortal till his work is done.'

Her descriptions are as graphic as her camera. She tells terrible things, but remembers lovely little things, too. The cherry blossom over the hills beyond Dachau. The baby who'd been in a cellar two months and whose mother was killed and who tasted chocolate for the first time and laughed. The stillness and emptiness of Oradour, the French Lidice, where there are ashes and ruins everywhere, no town, no people left; and simple notices, now, saying 'Silence,' as if you were – as indeed you are – walking through a graveyard.

She tells how she, the most luxurious of women, used to fussing over down pillows and bedside lamps and sleeping tablets – slept in the straw, or the rubble, dossing down anywhere, sleeping on her feet, marching with a column of Goumiers, the native troops who fought so magnificently. She tells, graphically, how an armoured column halt as they crash through a village; a ten-minute halt, and how the tanks open up and the grimed, bloodshot, hungry, angry men are out, kicking in the doors, raiding the larders, taking what they want, anything – the spoils of victory – and out again, into the tanks, already plucking the chickens they've seized, leaving screaming confusion behind them, and as they move on, the guns nose forward through slow-falling snow-flurries of chicken's feathers... I wish I could reproduce one of her pictures of this strange, violently contrasted scene, but most of her material is still in France.

Her material on the prison camps doesn't bear speaking of; one camp after another – Dachau, Buchenwald, Vaihingen, near Stuttgart. That's not a name we hear about, it was just one of many, dotted about, where she recorded the unnameable horrors of German domination. These pictures could not be published. They are worse than anything I have seen – published or otherwise. Some of her work in the prisons is more telling by reason of its restraint; her sense of detail, her selectivity, make them more haunting than even those where the bulldozers are shovelling the massed bodies into the pits, with all the nightmare horror of a Breughel canvas.

She says she's done with hating the Germans. She's no time for that, they're not worth it. She thinks the best way to avenge the suffering she's seen would be by building up a world where Nazi and Fascist doctrines cannot rise again – ever. And if, after the six years of misery Germany imposed on the rest of Europe, Germans have a tough time, or perish this winter – well, what about it? She shrugs. She thinks they understand only one thing – force. She loathed their cringing civility, the way they fawned on the Allies. Every time they came out with their honey-talk about not being Nazis at heart, crying *Vive la France!* she made the Nazi salute; but irony is lost on such a race.

Today, she flies back to Paris, to a settle up all her war records. By mid-winter she hopes to return here for good. American newspaper offers are pressing, but she wants to stay here, for a while anyway. This is the first of her war-reportage to appear in the British press, since she was not working as war reporter for us. But readers remember her portrait of Shaw, which appeared on the cover of this magazine, a while back.

Later, I hope we may find her working not as a war-reporter, but as a world-reporter, going anywhere she thinks there is a big story to be found. She plans to bring out a collection of war pictures, for she says she doesn't want the world to forget, too quickly, those things they can hardly bear to remember. And already, she says, she finds those who saw least of war are the first to elbow it aside. For such, this profile will seem altogether out of date: too much about the war; too little about the woman.

I'm unrepentant.

A Traveller's Tales

Perpetuam Mobile: Lise Cristiani

Only an astronaut's voyage could have satisfied that fervent band of women travellers who were a peculiar manifestation of the nineteenth century. Neither before nor since have any voyagers approached travel with quite the same enthusiasm for mileage. Although the ladies recorded their journeys in detail, we do not sense so much their interest in the goal, as the distances covered. In some cases their lives became a *perpetuam mobile*. The habit of movement, of ever-changing horizons, had infected them. There was no cure. They could not come to a standstill anywhere, either in the homes they had left or in the regions they obtained, and they were forever off again, whirling round the globe like tops (or astronauts), their skirts and petticoats billowing round them as they spun onwards; a fabulous giddy-go-round. In their journals they record their mileage with the exactitude and total absorption which hypochondriacs reserve for their pulse or temperature, and we see that it becomes a positive point of honour with them to add another two or three thousand miles to any itinerary.

Mostly they went alone; sometimes they dragged a husband along; seldom, if ever, a lover, for nothing is so destructive to a love-affair as constant gaddings, packing and unpacking and the distraction of the scenery; to say nothing of admirers encountered *en route*. Occasionally the ladies seemed to believe they were following, or accompanying, a husband, as in the case of Madame Hommaire de Hell, who recorded her husband's geological findings; or Sir Richard Burton's wife, who lived by his celebrated dictum: *pay, pack and follow* – all over the world. But no man was ever so intoxicated with distance for its own sake as this band of women.

Perhaps it was the cumulative effect of so many centuries of domesticity which fired them. In the nineteenth century, keeping house had reached crushing proportions morally, socially and physically. True, for the average household there was no shortage of servants; but never had there been so many children, relatives, rooms or guests either. Never were women so chained. Every moral and legal code obliged them to live narrowly restricted lives. European or Western women, that is; in the Orient it was at once better and worse. Perhaps that too influenced the lady travellers. Perhaps those few, who escaped, enjoyed not so much the darkling glances of foreign men, as the sight of their even more restricted Eastern sisters. After an invitation to visit the harem or a glimpse of purdah, it is probable that the massive mahogany confines of the Western nineteenth-century home appeared less irksome. Though perhaps not: for while the divans of the harem hinted unimaginable delights, the double bed upstairs seemed consecrated to breeding. In any case, for the travelling ladies, home was the last place where the heart was.

A young Frenchwoman, Lise Cristiani, is the perfect example of this type: a curious girl who came to sublimate both her brilliant career as a cellist and her personal life as a woman to the chimera of distance. Let us follow the comic overtones of her essentially tragic, and brief, life. She first appears in Paris, in the 1840s, as a fragile-looking girl with large, soft, dark eyes and a pale face framed in ringlets. She had been a child prodigy and her technical mastery was matched by her interpretative quality. When first she set out to conquer other worlds she had no doubt been led abroad by dreams of purely professional ambition. No thoughts then of distance for distance's sake. She had won Copenhagen overnight. The snug little city, with its splendid formal palace, its precise parks and ships' masts piercing the chill skies between the chimney pots clustered along the canals and harbours, was very different from the sprawling, careless grandeur of Paris; but its audiences were all she could ask. In recognition of her talents she was appointed *violoncelliste du Roi*. Next, the Swedes welcomed her, and in Stockholm she was known as the *Sainte Cécile Française*. She began to eye further horizons.

Soon after her twentieth birthday she was engaged for a concert tour in the principal cities of Russia. Russia! Snowy steppes – wolves – grand dukes; Count Razoumovski, Beethoven's patron, had been Russian. Russian audiences were celebrated for their musical enthusiasm. The prospect enchanted her. All the leading musicians of Europe returned from Russia with glowing accounts of their reception. Indeed, when Liszt had disapproved of the Tzar Nicholas I talking loudly through his recital, he had firmly shut the piano, saying: 'Music itself is silent when Nicholas speaks.' And the audience's reaction, though understandably uneasy at such audacity, had been most gratifyingly on the artist's side. Mademoiselle Cristiani set out with perfect confidence, an old German pianist as accompanist beside her. But on reaching St Petersburg, she met the first check in her career. A member of the Tzar's family had died suddenly; the court was plunged into mourning and her most powerful patrons compelled to languish beside their own hearths. Her recitals were cancelled. The impresarios and concert hall managers shrugged off their losses. It was God's will, they said, displaying that Slav acceptance of fate which so closely approximates to Arab fatalism. *Mektoub!* or *Nietchievo!* are both expressions of fatalist passivity.

For Mademoiselle Cristiani there seemed no other course than to accept fate and return to France. But she had already taken the first step which led her to that passion for far distances. She had already travelled five thousand miles – why not another five thousand? Already the strange germ of mileage had taken hold. She would go on. If the Russian capital was closed to her, she would take herself further afield – east, to those Asiatic Siberian territories of which she had heard so much while in St Petersburg. They were the latest, largest developments of the great thrusting country. There, she believed, she would find appreciative audiences, unshadowed by any considerations of imperial grief. Siberia was then beginning to be envisaged in terms of colonial expansion, a rich field for agriculture and trade, besides the fabulous resources of the mines, which exploited convict labour. Irkutsk, the capital, was a prosperous place, building its university and opera house, and it was here that the Governor-General lived in state. The dread convict settlements were further afield. As the small towns sprang up, some of their most respected new citizens were first and second generation descendants of the earlier political exiles who had, when faced with appalling difficulties, retained a cultivated milieu. Everything Mademoiselle Cristiani heard of Siberia convinced her that her musicianship would be properly appreciated there. And, *en route*, there would be eager audiences in Tobolsk, Omsk and Tomsk… Three thousand miles of unknown distances to conquer! The first stirrings of her strange craving had now crystallised.

She started east, in a bone-shaking *telega*, a wooden vehicle generally used for long journeys. With her went a Russian maid and the old German accompanist. 'I practise assiduously, *en route*, for I know how much will be expected of me,' wrote the musician; while the woman wrote: 'Natasha is a real necessity on such a journey. I rely on her to look after my clothes: everything is covered in dust, or sadly crumpled, I arrive looking like a scarecrow.' But the traveller, as yet unacknowledged, remained silent before the intoxicating realities of this three-thousand-mile journey. While the old German was charged with the care of her cello, cradling it in his arms, to protect it from the jarring, pitching motion of the *telega*, Lise Cristiani sat staring around her avidly.

They drove east – ever further into the nomad steppes and each day the Asiatic landscape grew more sinister, even more sparsely inhabited, more foreboding. Gradually the difficulties of obtaining a night's lodging came to occupy all their thoughts. They followed the posting road, but even so the wayside inns grew fewer. They drove on, often sleeping where they changed horses, at primitive *stancais*, vermin-infested wayside shacks, or the *étapes*, military-controlled halts designed for the trudging lines of convicts: men, women and children, political exiles and felons, dragging their chains on the cruel stages of a forced march which often took them years to accomplish. Each night, stiff with fatigue, Lise Cristiani's little party would climb down from their *telega* and, half-frozen, stagger into whatever shelter they had reached.

Beside the stove and surrounded by wondering peasants, a handful of Cossack guards, or even some wretched convoy of prisoners, the cellist stubbornly continued to practise her roulades and cadenzas. There being no pianos in such surroundings, the old accompanist dozed and snored, waking fitfully to beat time and snore again, while Natasha, hunched over her sewing, repairing the torn hems, broken stay-laces, or bedraggled bonnet strings of her young mistress – a daily toll exacted by such a journey, but no longer strictly necessary, since appearances were becoming of less and less importance.

At last, arrived in Irkutsk, they found the city at once more primitive and even more appreciative, than they had imagined. It had none of the architectural beauties of mediaeval Tobolsk; no golden-domed cathedrals or splendid kremlins. The unpaved streets sprawled across empty acres of mud. The rough wooden houses that lined them stood back behind high fences; puddles stretched across the streets and were often knee-deep pools into which household refuse was flung. There was no street lighting, few shops, only one weekly newspaper, a handful of fly-blown restaurants or frowzy commercial hotels and a doubtful-looking pharmacy. But many of the well-to-do merchants were latecomers who treasured a certain cultural heritage from their life in Moscow and St Petersburg. Some of the settlers were those political exiles known as Dekabrists – the flower of Russia's aristocratic and cultured élite. And the Russians, from moujiks to the military garrison, were a passionately musical people.

So unusual a visitor as the celebrated young French musician intrigued the people of Irkutsk and all walks of life welcomed her. General Mouraviev, the Governor-General, was particularly hospitable, removing her from the short-comings of the Grand Hotel du Commerce, inviting her to his official residence: a large, classical white building overlooking the wide waters of the Angara, where he lived in princely state. Today it is the library of the city of Irkutsk and when I was there, the chief librarian showed me some of its treasures. But I found myself eyeing the chandeliers and the elaborate white porcelain stoves with more interest, wondering if they were the same as in Lise Cristiani's day. She speaks of a certain absence of the more accepted Western comforts, but there was such an overlay of splendours (solid silver chamber pots screened by hangings of gigantic white bearskins) that the young Frenchwoman was enthralled by the exotic turn her life had taken. Here she was, in a palace in Siberia, supping on caviar, tuning up her cello to play to dashing Cossack officers who could discuss the niceties of a Mozart quartet as knowledgeably as the latest type of rifle. Her host was an outstanding figure of his day. He had lately realised his dreams of Russia's colonial expansion along the Chinese borders of the Amur River. Moreover, he had accomplished this coup without bloodshed and was the hero of the hour, both in Irkutsk and St Petersburg. His monument, unlike many Tzarist heroes, has never been removed from its place of honour and still dominates the public gardens; and here, once again, I found Lise Cristiani dominating my thoughts, so that I saw the kind, moustachioed face on the monument as her host rather than the great administrator.

Mouraviev immediately arranged that his visitor should give a series of recitals, first in Irkutsk and then in some of the less remote provincial towns, such as Yeniseisk – centre of the convict settlements, where we may imagine the tones of her cello floating out across the twenty-foot-high wooden stockades of the prisons brought a melancholy joy to the forgotten beings who dragged their fetters round the prison yard, as they took their brief daily airing.

When the Governor-General left Irkutsk on an official mission to Kiakhta, on the Chinese frontier, Mademoiselle Cristiani accompanied him. From there she had made up her mind to push on – further east. 'I shall play everywhere – in Pekin, even,' she wrote to her anxious family in Paris. Kiakhta was only about a thousand miles from Pekin. True, the dreaded Gobi Desert lay between, but she felt no qualms. By now her passion for movement – for distance – had taken form. The further and wilder her destination, the better she was pleased. It is doubtful, had Pekin been only a day's posting from Irkutsk, if she would have felt such a surge of enthusiasm. But the doubly alluring prospect of playing to Chinese audiences and journeying yet another thousand miles to do so was positively intoxicating. She saw herself travelling in a box-litter of Chinese fashion, scarlet lacquer and carried by coolies. Under burning suns, they were following camel trains crossing the Gobi wastes; but neither thirst, nor the serpents that abound there, nor yet the bleached bones of less fortunate travellers, could turn them back.

Already she saw herself installed in some jade pavilion of the Summer Palace, executing a Paganini étude with such brilliance that the impassive yellow faces of her Manchu audiences broke at last into smiles of rapturous enthusiasm. Alas, while still at Kiakhta, and still under Mouraviev's protection, she discovered the drawbacks of being a European woman on the edge of Outer Mongolia.

Kiakhta was divided in two by a broad esplanade. Russians lived on one side, Chinese on the other. The two sections of the community seldom met. It was a merchant population, the centre of the tea trade, with yak caravans, camels and men converging there with tin-lined boxes of merchandise. After a good deal of manoeuvring, she managed to obtain an invitation to dinner from the Chinese; but it was a formal, all-masculine affair, a gesture of Asiatic *politesse*, no more. With the last bows and ceremonial leave-takings, she was once again back among the provincial Russians and she had not been invited to play, either after dinner or in Pekin. The Chinese had found a way to snub Mouraviev and the Russians, through their French protégée.

However, all the rest of Asia lay ahead. Mademoiselle Cristiani was not to be discouraged. Leaving the sheltering Mouraviev wing, she set out to visit the Buriat-Mongolian camps, playing Bach and Bellini to them in return for a night's lodging in their round felt-covered yurts. Buriat tribes had been under Cossack domination for a century or more and now knew better than to question any personage arriving from Russia. Their inscrutable flat faces showed neither surprise nor pleasure when she appeared among them. She was travelling with an escort of Cossacks, supplied by Mouraviev, so they bowed her into their yurts and listened attentively.

Although to Asiatic ears the music she played must have sounded incomprehensible, she appears to have possessed some potent magic, for, wherever she went, both civilised audiences and intractable locals fell under the spell of her playing. There is no means, today, of measuring her standing, musically; it would seem that by nature of her many engagements in the capitals of Europe she was of the front rank. That, at last, her musical career was sacrificed to far distances was eloquent of the strength of her passion. Health, professional prestige, personal life, all were sacrificed to this exacting god of mileage. She who had once known the applause of Europe's *cognoscenti* was now lured on by the thought that she would be travelling into a further horizon for her next recital.

In an overcrowded yurt, the Buriats cannot have been an altogether agreeable audience. They were a nomadic people who passed for the dirtiest race in all Asia, their sheepskin coats swarmed with lice and their tallowy skins reeked of sweat. But Lise Cristiani makes no mention of their shortcomings. She was seven thousand miles from the Salle Pleyel and found this rewarding enough. By now the maid Natasha and the old accompanist had dropped by the way, or been cast aside like the excess baggage they had become. No Buriat-Mongolian yurt possessed a piano, nor was there any more need to keep up concert hall appearances – even though there were occasional visits to the larger lamaseries, which counted as social events.

At Guisinoi Ozera, three hundred miles out of Irkutsk, the great whitewashed monastery with its red-and-gold-roofed temples flung open its doors to her and the orange-robed monks led her in state to play before the Grand Lama. He received her ceremoniously, seated on a scarlet throne piled with saffron cushions, and, offering ritualistic little cups of tea, conversed through a merchant interpreter in a most worldly fashion. He spoke of Paris – which he believed to be an ungodly city; of the Tzar Nicholas I, 'A most mighty neighbour,' he said enigmatically. When she offered to play for him, he graciously declined. 'After such a journey you must not exert yourself on my behalf,' he told her, '*My* musicians shall play for you instead.' Rising, he closed the interview by summoning a lesser lama to conduct her to the temple, where massed cymbals, drums, giant bronze trumpets and conch shells burst into a welcoming cacophony as she took her place.

From the Lamasery the obsessed girl proceeded to explore the eastern shores of Lake Baikal, 'the Holy Sea', the world's deepest freshwater lake, where brilliant green sponges and monstrous-looking fish lurk and the dark quartz cliffs overshadow waters which rise suddenly and lash the lake into twenty-foot waves. Wandering along the lake's dramatic strand, crossing it in one of the frail bark canoes of the Buriats or camping among the fisher folk, Lise Cristiani still clasped her cello, still believed she was returning, however circuitously, to France. But the pattern of her destiny was formed. She had reached the point of no return; and back in Irkutsk it was, in fact, no stopping-place on her journey homewards, but once more a starting-point.

When General Mouraviev lightly invited her, 'This crazy Frenchwoman', to accompany him on an official journey to Russia's northernmost port, Kamchatka, on the Bering Sea, he had not imagined she would accept. He had not gauged the degree of her mania. She accepted rapturously. 'I shall add yet another four thousand miles to my travels and thus complete my artist's life,' she wrote to her sadly anxious family in Paris.

In the romantic early years of the nineteenth century to speak of a woman 'completing her life' generally inferred she had taken a lover. (Later, entrenched in domesticity, the mid-Victorian woman's life was said to be 'ruined' by a lover and 'completed' by a numerous family.) But Lise Cristiani had made her own choice. For her completion was in terms of computation – miles, versts, leagues…

The Governor-General's party set out in great state with Cossack outriders, couriers, and wolfhounds. At night they still sped northwards, now bedded down in sable-lined, fur-covered sledges, the stars racing overhead, their way lit by the flaming torches of the outriders, great plumes of snow marking their progress as they cut through the deep white drifts. Heading for the Sea of

Okhotsk, they travelled by way of the Amur provinces 'drawn by wild horses which had never known a harness', writes Mademoiselle Cristiani on a note of gratification, choosing, like most ardent travellers, local colour above comfort. At Okhotsk they embarked on a steamer bound for the Kamchatka Peninsula. The young cellist's siren songs (she was playing Scarlatti on deck) so captivated a whale that it sidled round and round the boat in a most alarming manner, and the captain was obliged to put an end to the concert.

Kamchatka is the last outpost of Russian commerce, set down beside the frozen seas: it suffers fearful winters of fog and ice. But nothing discouraged the frustrated cellist. Although the late autumn was closing in, and the snows were already deep, her mania would not be stilled. Forward! Never mind where! The Governor-General became uneasy. He did not wish to be held responsible for such an obstinate guest. Finding all his warnings went unheeded, he at last withdrew his Cossack escort and turned back to Irkutsk, leaving Mademoiselle Cristiani alone. She had unfortunately learned that a government courier would shortly be leaving for Yakoutsk, in the interior, and was determined to accompany him. No matter that the snows had become exceptionally heavy, that the journey must be undertaken on horseback, under conditions of inconceivable hardship – she must go too. The route lay across the Stanovoi Mountains, crossing many frozen rivers: new territories – more mileage!

We can imagine this solitary figure, at once ridiculous and pathetic, still clasping her cumbersome cello case, her agile fingers muffled in fur-lined gloves, her ringlets crammed beneath a hood of sea-otter fur as, trembling with cold and excitement, she met the courier's refusals by every argument and persuasion at her command.

The courier appears to have been an enigmatic and sullen young man, cold as his setting, impervious to the hardships of his *métier*, and unmoved by the French girl's blandishments. No doubt he had an orderly nature, liking everything in its rightful place and knowing that wayside huts of the frozen north were not the setting for dalliance, either musical or romantic. At last, exasperated by Mademoiselle Cristiani's insistence, he shrugged a bored acquiescence. So be it! They would start at daybreak, come what might.

In a dawn darkened by a gathering tempest, the dreaded *pourga*, this ill-assorted pair set out, mounted on the small, shaggy Mongolian ponies that alone can survive such conditions. In winter, when a calm spell has left the track between Okhotsk and Yakutsk fit for fast dog sledges, the journey can be done in little over two weeks' hard going: in such a period of snowstorms and blizzards as they now encountered, the journey might take well over a month, or it might end in a wayside death by freezing, as the courier pointed out with relish. But Lise Cristiani's mind was made up.

They left the low-lying frozen marshes of the coast for the taïga, scrub regions which stretched northwards to nothingness. Here, where only the bears and wild dog-packs lived, there were no villages, no settlements, only, sometimes, hunters' shelters, dilapidated wooden shacks already almost buried in snow, which the Siberian people contrived to keep furnished with a few strips of frozen meat, flint and fuel. This was a long tradition – as long as the prison settlements, as long as convicts had been escaping from them… Few survived their wanderings, few were not hunted and shot down by the guards. 'A bullet always finds its runaway,' says a Siberian proverb. Those who reached the taïga often lay hidden there for many months, snowed-up, as did the trappers who lost their way on hunting expeditions.

The frozen expanses they traversed revealed neither vegetation nor any trace of human life and the *pourga* still howled round them. Sometimes they paused, more for the sake of the ponies than themselves, it seems; for there was no rest without warmth and the courier seldom stopped long enough for a fire to be lit. They did not speak to each other. She was too proud to admit the pass to which her obstinacy had brought her and no doubt far too exhausted to offer to play for him. She was now threatened with frostbite, while snow-blindness with its agonising pains went unalleviated. The courier did not bother to tell her of the local remedies – chewed tobacco poultices and such. He seems to have taken a sadistic pleasure in observing her increasing weakness and despair. After another week of black skies, under which the ponies inched their way, deep in snowdrifts, Lise Cristiani could stand no more. She begged for mercy – for one night's sleep in a hut, beside a fire. This was the courier's hour of triumph. He had not wished for her company. He was not interested in her as a woman, or as a musician. He had warned her of the dangers of such a journey and he was unmoved, now, by her misery.

'I stop for no one. The Tzar's orders. *En avant!*' He cracked his whip and rode forward. He did not even look back at the wretched girl huddled in her inadequate pelisse. Now she was quite alone with those far distances she had craved so passionately. They were closing on her, freezing her with their icy breath, crushing her with the terrible intensity of their embrace. Now, suddenly, she knew herself betrayed. All the miles and versts and leagues had only led her towards death...

Their promises had been empty; they had demanded everything of her and given nothing but a reckoning in return. The blizzard shrieked round her, seeming to taunt her soul, as it tormented her body. Her half-blinded eyes strained open to follow the courier's vanishing form. Another moment and he would vanish into that dread white limboland. She must either follow him, or lie down and die. But her choice had been made long ago – she would remain true to her love, however cruel. She went on, winding the bridle round her numbed fingers and, crouching down over the pony's neck, passed into a coma, 'another dimension', as she described it, later, 'where only cold remained. It seemed as if my soul floated icebound before me, seeing that body which it could no longer inhabit or warm...'

She survived this fearful journey, but her health was shattered. There were no more thoughts of cello recitals. As a concert artist, she had, not surprisingly, lost her touch. But as a traveller, she seemed content. 'I have just completed a journey of 18,000 miles,' she wrote home proudly. 'Fifteen Siberian towns living among the Ostiks, Kirghiz and Kalmucks... I have played where no artist has ever played before. I gave 140 concerts without counting private ones.' (Was the whale rated as a private or public audience, one wonders?) But later, she wrote bitterly: 'I know now that a rolling stone gathers no moss... I have death in my soul.' The moss of security she had never craved, but she could not face immobility.

There seemed nowhere else to go, or at any rate, she had no more strength; she managed to crawl south to the Caucasus, where she hoped to regain her health but, quite soon after, she died at Novocherkassk, among the Don Cossacks. Cholera was raging there and she succumbed almost overnight.

The population was touched by her youth and sad fate and erected a handsome monument to her in the public gardens. Below the large stone cross lies a cello. 'The Artist's Other Soul', reads the inscription. But they should have inscribed her mileage: I think she would have chosen it as her epitaph.

LOTI IN LOTI-LAND

JUST AS EVERY CITY HAS ITS MOMENT IN TIME, SO IT HAS ITS PAINTER OR poet who best interprets it to the rest of the world: impossible to imagine the endless birch forests of Russia without peopling them with Turgenev's characters. Even the least classical tourist sunbathing in the Aegean recalls a Byronic distillation. Any walk through the English countryside of ploughed fields and misty hills recalls Cobbett, or Marvell; the scene seems awaiting the landed gentry of Gainsborough's family groups, debonair squires leaning on stiles beside button-eyed wives, wispy little girls and frolicking gun-dogs. This is their setting: they are stamped on it for posterity, despite the pylons and the bungalows.

So with Istanbul today. When present progress has been admired and all the historic panorama unwound, it is not the grandeurs of Byzantium and the 'Greens and the Blues' that come first to mind, nor Lady Mary Wortley Montagu's pawky accounts of the Ottoman court, but rather Pierre Loti's now unfashionable writings – *Aziyadé* of course and *Fantôme d'Orient*, his finest piece of evocation. Loti found his perfect subject in this city; his melancholy genius, or rather his genius for poetic melancholy, is the city's eternal core, whether its whole goes by the name of Constantinople, Stamboul, or Istanbul.

'Loti?' a deprecating half-smile: 'I'm afraid I haven't read him since I was at school.' This is the reaction today: although both Anatole France and Courteline stoutly proclaimed him, without question, the greatest living French writer of their day, Anatole France also describing him as *'le sublime illettré'*. And Louis Barthou: 'Posterity has begun for Pierre Loti. He has been assessed... As long as there are lands and seas, forests, deserts, rivers, mountains and seasons, the name of Pierre Loti will live... As long as men suffer and love, and dread death, too. His genius springs from a double source: nature and the heart. It is because he has written of them with such incomparable art that he remains eternal.' And Gide declared, *'Grâce détendue, retombée, qui se trouve chez Loti.'* All the unfashionable adjectives, sublime, noble, incomparable, poignant, belong to Loti. His cumulative artistry, his particular charm, overcome whole chunks of bathos. It doesn't matter: we skip and then, coming to a passage of subtle evocation, we are held entranced.

When I returned to Istanbul after a gap of seven years, I found myself drawn once again into the web of nostalgia which is this city's secret. However much the surface changes, in spite of grinding trams and roaring American taxis, blaring radios and crops of new buildings mushrooming up across those empty wastes which are perpetual reminders of the Asiatic hinterland, the spirit of the city, its skyline of mosque and minaret and cypresses soaring up from Marmora, or Bosphorus, or Corne d'Or – while the chailak, a bird of prey, wheels overhead – this remains forever Loti-land.

Pierre Loti's nature responded to and found a response in its romantic decay. He loved its crumbling splendours, savoured its spectral beauty, listened for its ghostly echoes – ghostly, even in his day. He liked to think he regretted its past glories, but what he really enjoyed was the regret. In Loti's writings there is always this voluptuous abandonment to nostalgia. He found his perfect subject when the ship on which he was serving as an ensign sailed up the Dardanelles to anchor off Seraglio Point. This was in 1877: for the last ten years the young Louis-Marie-Julien Viaud to give him his real name, had been in the French navy; his voyages had already taken him to Brazil, the Pacific, Tahiti and Senegal, from which he later derived several of his best-known novels; but it was Turkey which inspired his finest work. From this first impact came *Aziyadé*, which is, in substance, autobiographical; it tells of his liaison with the little Circassian kadine who escaped from a harem to live a brief idyll in the arms of the *giaour* and then to pine and die, abandoned. A return to Constantinople, many years later, inspired its sequel, *Fantôme d'Orient;* and his last visit, the coda, *Suprêmes Visions d'Orient*, written thirty years after the fabulous city first rose up out of the Marmora before his dazzled eyes.

It was more than a city he sensed then: it was a whole way of life and a people, which cast a spell over him for the rest of his days.

Loti was at his best as a subjective traveller, turning his foregrounds into backgrounds for his tragic loves. *Le Mariage de Loti, Le Roman d'un Spahi, Aziyadé, Fleurs d'Ennui*, all these are Loti seeing himself in the various landscapes. He moves through the enchanted scenes, Loti in Loti-land, always seeking the plaintive undertones, as minor in key as the Oriental *mélopées* he loved, always draining an embittered cup to the dregs, but savouring it in delicious sips, choosing his sorrows with the deliberation others reserve for their pleasures. In Turkey, the tragicomedy reached its apogee and we see Loti going with self-conscious melancholy through the deserted streets of the Phanar, to hear the fifth, or evening, prayer at the Mehmet Fatih Mosque; choosing the *mise-en-scène* with a theatrical sense; lingering in the shadowy cypress-planted courtyard; luxuriating in the muezzin's chant, that *'gémissement religieux, lugubre à faire frémir,'* as it floated out from the spear-like minarets, to hang, vibrating, on the vapours of the chill night air; going, in positive ecstasies of grief, to search out the stele of his lost love, somewhere among the forests of graves and cypresses beyond the Byzantine walls, graves which he describes as 'sunk in solitude, drunk with silence'.

Loti longed to be part of the great stream of Eastern life: the crowds which surged through the narrow, vine-swagged street markets of Tophane, or Kum Kapou were, to him, a life-giving stream into which he plunged. The boatmen, *hamils,* beggars, Turcomen, Persians or Albanians who lay sprawled along the harbour, then, as now, brawling, sleeping, jesting – these people had, for him, an irresistible allure. In the beginning he deliberately chose a humble milieu in preference to the more Westernised élite, learning the language of the people, their ways and legends. By every means he sought to identify himself with this land of his predilection, and he found a warm response; there were no reserves on either side – although it must be admitted that Loti's role was a favoured one. He was always the pasha of, yet not quite of, the circle; not bound by local horizons, however much he might appear, even to himself, to crave them. Perhaps this detachment gave him sharper appreciations; perhaps, too, it gave the Turks an equally lively realisation of Loti's value among them, not only as an ardent Turcophile, but as a world-famous man of letters and, even in the beginning, an officer of the puissant Allied fleet then patrolling Turkish waters. In any case, his peccadilloes and games were observed with indulgence by both small fry and government officials.

Of all the many aspects of Moslem life which Loti sought to penetrate, it was those hours of retreat, of contemplation and withdrawal which he most treasured. Such stretches of deliberate, voluptuous nothingness – *kef,* to the Arabs – are known to all Eastern peoples: the Turks call it *rahat*; it is the quintessential Oriental retreat from a too-pressing reality. Again and again in his writings Loti returns to the enchantment of those timeless hours becalmed in stillness, in drifts of dreams, forming and reforming, nebulous as the smoke rising from his *narghilyé*. In today's jargon it would be called escapism: but to Loti, who fled reality down the years, it was Elysium.

In Turkey, he found it easily enough. In the haze of the hammam; beside some cypress-shaded graveyard; or in some small café with a terrace overlooking a sunset, such as one he loved beside the Green Mosque at Broussa; or equally, in the splendours such as those he describes, when, as guest of Izeddin-Ali-effendi, he is offered a traditional Turkish night's entertainment in the *selamlik*, or men's quarters, of a princely establishment. Here, with a refinement of luxury, there is no feasting, no riotous living, but a gathering of men, centred round the glowing copper mangal, stretched on divans, in their fur-lined caftans, each with their long jasmine-stemmed *tchibouk*, or *narghilyé*, to pass the long winter's night together, in stillness, in *rahat*, 'this reverie which is not thought, which is more than feeling and which no word expresses'. Timeless hours, neither haunted by the past, nor shadowed by the future, but filled with an animal sense of wellbeing. For Loti, with all his curiously pagan horror of death, these hours gave him the longed-for illusion that time stood still. They were perhaps the real secret of his hunger for the East. Later, he tried to introduce such evenings among his Western friends, but they only found it a picturesque novelty and soon began to fidget.

Even in the house for lovers' meeting at Eyüp, living what was the supreme adventure of his life, he was savouring *rahat* with the same abandon as his amorous transports. 'Only the Oriental knows how to live inwardly, within himself, his home,' he writes longingly. And in a letter describing the life at Eyüp he goes on, 'It was so good to be there, far away from everyone, everything, so still, so peaceful, so alone… (*le bien-être egoïste du chez soi*). I would lock our door and sit cross-legged, while Achmet my servant prepared two *narghilyés*, one for me, the other for himself. Aziyadé's voice sounded a sombre note as she sang the song of the djinns, striking her little drum, which was hung with twinkling coins. As the smoke began to rise slowly in bluish spirals I would find myself, little by little, forgetting all the tragic realities of human life.'

Yes, Aziyadé's lover was, first of all, an escapist.

The curiously obsessive force of Loti's writing is such that he still seems to pervade Stamboul. He is that quiet form sitting by the dervishes' cells, at the Sokullu Mehmet Pacha Mosque; he is that figure posing dramatically before an itinerant photographer's canvas backcloth painted with the crescent of Islam. He is the loiterer in the glittering souks: his is the face that stares down on the crowd from the birdcage-like yoghourt kiosk in the Great Bazaar. I see him in the dappled shade of any street café, at Beyazit, or the Atmeidan. He sits there, the eternal revenant, a faintly self-conscious figure, at once actor and audience, and greatly enjoying his own performance. He wears a fez, of course, and toys with an amber chaplet. He is handsome: *un bel homme*, in that rather pronounced-featured manner of his age. He has the sumptuous moustaches and fine dark eyes of the postcard hero; eyes which were, in the words of a friend, 'the tragic, questioning eyes of a suffering animal, haunting in their pathos'. Fascinating, too.

He was an irresistible figure in the 1890s, not only to inexperienced, untravelled girls who might be expected to revel in armchair excursions and tantalising mixtures of spirit and flesh ('It was reserved for Pierre Loti to make us savour – to the point of drunkenness, of delirium, of stupor even, the bitter flavour of exotic loves,' wrote Anatole France, quite beside himself and voicing his contemporaries), but *mondaine* hostesses in palmy salons were spellbound too. Great generals, statesmen, personalities such as Sarah Bernhardt and various royals were also under his sway, though one of his most devoted admirers, Carmen Sylva, Queen of Romania, was herself a very accomplished poseur.

Loti was not only lionised by the public; he was adored by his friends to whom he became a cult and to whom he showed a simpler side; a childish sense of fun. As to the extravagant manner in which he was lionised, it speaks for the place writers once held, that photographs of Loti sold in tens of thousands among all kinds of people. In Loti's day, to be a poet, a poetic writer, was '*la gloire*'. It was the romantic nineteenth-century conception of 'Literature', of literary demigods; the attitude which had fostered Byron, Pushkin, Victor Hugo and Lamartine.

Loti transposed exoticism from aristocratic flamboyance to a more bourgeois intimacy. It was in key with his age. The assassin's dagger had become bric-à-brac – the furnishings of a drawing room. For Byron exoticism was a medium, a way to exalt and dramatise the tragedies of his characters. But with Loti, for the first time, exoticism became a quality on its own, and from a literary point of view, a whole subject. Victor Hugo, too, made use of exoticism, but in the Byronic-romantic manner: it was reserved for Loti to tame, or present, exoticism for itself, the transposition being made by way of Gautier.

In the last decade of the nineteenth century, travel was still something remote from the general public, reserved for the rich, for commercial travellers, or the adventurers. Voyages were long and costly with unimaginable diseases lurking in every port of call. Even luggage told of the difficulties involved – gigantic iron-bound leather or tin trunks with domed lids, almost immovable even when empty and requiring storage space which by today's standards would represent an extra room. No airlines or cars brought exotic horizons within reach for the annual holiday. It was still an age when most Europeans went, in July or August, to the nearest sea and sat there, facing it, or dipping in it, until time to turn round and go home again. Their curiosity as to foreign parts remained ungratified. They attended lantern-slide lectures, or collected crudely coloured postcards. All travel, all far horizons, were invested with mystery and romance. How strong, then, the spell that Loti's writings cast. He shared with his readers his own poetic sense of wonder confronted by these horizons and his fervour was that of a lover discovering, and possessing in them, many different aspects of the beloved.

In spite of the fame and fortune Loti's writings brought him and in spite of that other dimension of dreams – that poet's limboland in which he had his true being – nothing, no philosophy, no detachment could compensate for the gnawing knowledge that he was far too short-legged for the classic perfection he craved. In vain he was photographed in tights, in athletic poses with rippling, hard-won muscles; in uniforms blistered with equally well-won decorations, or in dashing Balkan costumes, staring out with his proud wounded stare. The fact remained – he was stumpy. Even as a child he disliked his appearance, 'was not "my type",' he said. But perhaps his favourite device, *Mon mal j'enchante*, with which he decorated his blue and gold dinner service, and inscribed in many of his books, explains the various costumes and disguises which were his weakness and which, says Edmond de Goncourt, all claws out, made his life a perpetual carnival.

Loti tried to escape his limitations in other ways too: by means of high heels and not always discreet touches of make-up; above all, muscular prowess, keeping himself at circus pitch with gymnastic feats. He was inordinately proud of having appeared in a circus act, genuinely admired by the professionals and once alarmed Frank Harris by executing some dangerous backward somersaults in the course of a stroll through the garden of his friend, Princess Alice of Monaco. For many years the only means of entry to his study was by a swinging rope ladder up which he swarmed squirrel-like, enjoying, with that childish sense of fun, so oddly at variance with his morbidity, the frantic efforts of his less agile visitors who had hoped to see the master in his cadre.

Loti always worshipped physical strength: it was an expression of the eternal youth he craved, not so much for itself as for its denial of the final annihilation which was his horror. This note of dread sounds through all he wrote. He is obsessed by the ultimate darkness. Neither the Roman Catholic religion of his youth, nor the Moslem faith for which he longed, could dispel this profound despair. Like love and youth, life could not endure. Irrevocably, all led towards a tragic finale. Every joy was overshadowed. Every kiss ended on a sigh; even in Aziyadé's arms he was quoting Oriental poetry: 'Each season draws me towards the night... O! Seigneur, to where do I go? And who will be beside me when I must drink that bitter cup?'

We still find this mood echoed in Istanbul, where Loti's *hélas!*, his *other times!*, and *other places!*, take positive form, overcoming the present. Graveyards abound: that other, still grey world of the Turkish cemetery is omnipresent, even now, among markets, beside cafés and taxi-ranks, replacing the little parks and gardens of other cities. Slender-stemmed tombstones, each flowering into a turban, fez or garland, each turban carved with the fantastic windings and invention of its epoch, seems a stone bloom, a top-heavy tulip, flowering on, through the centuries, behind the grilled wall-windows that enclose these street graveyards. Peering through, we see rank grasses, knee high, where stray cats slink, stalking a bird, savaging a rag of greasy paper in which someone has thrown them a handful of scraps. Loti loved cats especially and wrote of them as no one else but Colette has done. He suffered for all animals, as *Le Livre de la Pieté et de la Mort* bears anguished testimony.

Enmeshed in what was always, to him, the tragedy of life, Loti's principal distractions, after those meditative withdrawals which I have already mentioned, were found in music and dressing up – romantic disguises. In his cabin on board the various ships he came to command in his maturity, he would surround himself with a most unnautical décor, Chinese porcelains, Persian brocades and rare prayer carpets. Here, beside cupboards filled with caftans and gandouras and burnouses, he would sit at his piano for hours at a time playing Chopin – only Chopin. The pellucid phrases floated out across the water and along the shores of the Bosphorus to the *yalis*, or summer palaces, where, behind the *moucharabiyeh*, many pairs of melting eyes were turned towards the ship. Loti was the *coqueluche* of drawing room and harem alike.

Shutting the piano with a sigh (*Hélas!* everything passed; even the afternoon was sliding irrevocably from his grasp) the Commandant would order the cutter to be brought alongside in half an hour; and opening the wardrobe he would select some fancy-dress outfit, by which he hoped to escape from reality into that exotic ambience he craved.

Wherever he went, Loti flung himself into the masquerade with an enthusiasm which was touchingly childish and quite at variance with his world-weariness. He plays his heroes with bravura, or pathos, as the role requires. He poses before the photographer's backdrop: Moroccan Loti in a burnous, in a gandoura, among the Senegalese, in Zouaves costume, living every page of *Le Roman d'un Spahi*; Loti with a fan beside Madame Chrysantème, though here he retains Western dress and a certain air of superior detachment; or, garlanded by caramel-skinned charmers, celebrating *Le Mariage de Loti*, a book which he illustrated himself with the same elegant facility with which he played the piano. *Le Roman d'un Spahi* first appeared with his haunting evocations of Senegal, where the story is set. We see the shores of huge rivers, sands, broken only by a group of monstrous baobab trees or a solitary, crouching negress, beside the conical huts of a village stifled under a pall of leaden heat, and where the great birds of prey circle ceaselessly.

Loti's habit of adding an element of fiction, or ambiguity to his experiences, of placing a *moi* in every landscape, was summed up by one critic who, in writing '*mais les mariages de Loti se font partout*', could not avoid sounding a faint note of envy, perhaps. But if Loti displayed a Don Juanistic attitude towards many countries and their women, Turkey (and Aziyadé) was his real love to which he remained faithful.

Thus, above all the rest of the fancy dress, we see Loti the Turcophile; he wears baggy trousers, a gold-embroidered jacket and a fez. In the novel, Aziyadé's lover is a young English naval officer. The *Deerhound* is anchored up the Bosphorus and at night, assuming Turkish dress, in which he has the grace to admit he feels uncomfortably like an operatic tenor, the English Lieutenant, who, rather bewilderingly, is still called Loti, keeps a series of reckless rendez-vous with his mistress, first in a gilded *caïque* massed with cushions, 'a floating bed' and later, hidden away in the small house up the Golden Horn, at Eyüp. But after a great deal of unnecessary suffering it all ends badly. Fate separates them. Loti is ordered to sea. Aziyadé's imprudence is discovered by her old master and she is left to pine and die. When Loti returns, it is, of course, too late. *Hélas* and *Jadis*...! He quits the navy, joins the Turkish forces and dies in the flower of his youth, fighting for Turkish independence.

When, twenty-five years later, Loti returned to Constantinople as a world-famous writer, he was captain of his ship, still a dashing figure, but the sun was sinking. He loved his life on board and was adored by his crew, among whom was the youthful Claude Farrère, whose life followed superficially something of the same pattern – naval officer, exotic novelist and Turcophile. Again the ship was anchored in the Bosphorus; again a cutter brought Loti ashore. But now the cutter took him less often towards adventure and the cut-throat alleys of Tophane than towards the world of Pera and the embassies, where, an adulated figure, he presently entangled himself in the snares of three mischief-making women (one of them a French journalist) posing as stifled victims of the harem. Loti, the romantic revenant, going back on the elusive tracks of his youth, became their gullible victim. With touching eagerness he would tiptoe off to those clandestine meetings in the mysterious house behind Ahmedieh. When in *Les Désenchantées* he described it all, he placed it elsewhere; but there is no mistaking that he saw himself as the hero, André Lhéry. The ladies led him on without scruple and when the whole ignoble affair was exposed, Loti's reputation suffered. The book is indifferent and, save for some beautiful descriptions of Stamboul, not worthy of the man who could write *Vers Ispahan*.

But this was only one episode of so many, acted out against the city which remains forever his. Truth and fiction, autobiography and posturing, all are interwoven. Haunting Loti! His power is such that there is no street, no aspect that does not conjure him.

Such is Loti's obsessive quality that however much we know he was, in his protracted Turkish farewells, really only taking an egoist's leave of his youthful heyday, we still search out the scenes of his joys and sorrows, as if they were some historic site. We still go through the streets of Khassim Pacha recalling his description of a sunrise seen from the house where he first lodged, waiting for Aziyadé to rejoin him. 'Sketched in rose-coloured tints, a dome and its minarets emerged... little by little, the silhouette of the Turkish city appeared, as if suspended in the air...' And then, firmly placing himself in the landscape, 'And then I remembered that I was at Stamboul and that she had sworn to come there.' That was the rose-coloured morning. There are many other, more sombre evocations. Loti's lyricism could give place, at times, to dramatic effects as startling as a clap of thunder over the minarets; as in the terrible description of Fatou-Gaye finding the body of the Spahi: or the opening page of *Aziyadé*, where the hanged men kick and dangle along the waterfront of Salonika; or that dark note of passion sounding in a scene where Loti is telling his mistress of his love and she seems not to be following:

'Aziyadé,' I said, 'Are you listening?'

'No,' she replied. And then, in a low voice, at once gentle and feral: 'I would like to eat the sound of your voice.'

Such words must have quite taken the sting out of any suspected inattention, and been balm to any man, let alone such an egoist as Loti. 'Ah! Who will give me back my Eastern life?' he asks, again and again.

In Istanbul, as in Loti's writing, there is the same thread of violence lying behind the beauty, something sensed rather than seen. This city is not facile. It does not offer itself at once. Its essence is uncomfortably uncompromising and remains hidden from those who do not search for it. Above all, it is dramatic, and as such, it was irresistible to Pierre Loti. The quarter behind the Sülimanyé, or those vertical streets which go down towards the Seven Towers and the sea wall, are, before all else, sinister. The bleached, greyish wooden houses, with the windows of their top-heavy upper storeys sealed by close-grilled *mouchar-abiyeh* seem to conceal dark secrets: we walk there and are suddenly aware of a presence, observing us, a watcher, a shadow with eyes. This is the stealthy, forbidding city of which Gérard de Nerval wrote that it was like scenery, to be viewed from the front, without going behind. (Loti took us behind the scenes, but it was still theatre.) Nerval goes on: 'These painted houses, zinc domes and minarets are always charming to the poet, but 20,000 wooden houses so often visited by fire, the cemeteries where doves coo in the yew trees, yes, but where jackals dig up the dead when the great storms have loosened the soil... these are the reverse of the Byzantine medal.' Today, if the more picturesque aspects have faded behind the city's advancement, this Oriental mixture of the sinister, the beautiful and the sordid, remains the true Loti-land.

To the Turkish people themselves, Loti is still a legend. They will talk to you of Sinan's architecture, point out the delicate perfection of some street fountain, show you a radiance of blue tiles in some forgotten mosque; and with equal pride indicate a plaque on a particularly uninteresting-looking house in the Divanoglu where Loti lived. 'Have you been to Eyüp?' they ask, earnestly, as much on account of its association with him, as the fact that it is the holiest place in all Turkey, with sanctuaries no Christian may penetrate, the burial place of Eyüp Ansari, the Prophet's comrade and standard bearer.

We climbed the hills above its valley where the thousand pigeons strut and flutter in their chosen mosque and where, half-hidden in foliage, fragments of Turkish rococo gazebos and fountain courts lie beside the ornate *turbehs*, or sepulchres. They are remnants of an imperial palace; today, even the fez factory which was later established among its decaying splendours seems as remote as those sultanate glories, vanished, along with the fez, along with the little house where Loti and his love dallied. But Loti's legend still lingers there. 'Loti... Loti café,' said the vendor of the blue bead amulets and crude Koranic prints. He pointed to the scrubby hilltop. 'Loti... To Loti?' asked the peasants we met on our way. They waved us on, up, pointing to the shack where, under straggling vines, some weatherbeaten benches overlooked the windings of the

Golden Horn, a panorama to silence all the guidebook rhapsodies. An old Turk sat there, smoking his *tchibouk*, contemplating the distant city, as Loti loved to do. The café proprietor lit a samovar and brought us the ritual glasses of tea. With the exquisite politeness of his race, he switched the radio from roaring Oriental moans to a Western station, equally insistent. The visitors, he inferred, would no doubt prefer European strains. He fiddled the knobs, and the machine screeched across a political agitator in Cairo, and a snatch of crooning, to settle into Chopin's Funeral March.

It could scarcely have been more appropriate, for most walks about Istanbul could be described as funeral processions: outings have a curious way of centring round graveyards, or ending beside the sumptuous catafalques of some imperial *turbeh*, which, however drawing room in conception with crystal chandeliers, pearl-embroidered velvet hangings and carpets, is still a tomb. So many tombs, all echoing Loti's 'Never more!' By boat, or tram, or taxi, all roads lead to the grave: foxy old Barbarossa's tomb in the little park at Beşiktaş, where the children and nursemaids play among the lilacs: the Giant's Grave, Joshua's, they say, overlooking the inky expanses of the Black Sea: the tomb of Mahmoud II's favourite charger at Usküdar, or Scutari, where everyone makes a pious pilgrimage to the Crimean War cemetery and the scene of Florence Nightingale's heroic labours. Tombs everywhere; on Fridays, the Moslem holy day, there are picnic outings to the cemeteries where, quietly, but cheerfully, the Turks sit beside their dead in confident communion, often bringing the departed's favourite food, for in the midst of life we are in death and to the Turks, the dividing line is slight. In Loti's day, quick and dead were linked in even more aspects of pleasure. It was customary for prostitutes, at night, to flit about the cemeteries, where, having acquired a client, they would gratify him, there and then, on stony couches shadowed by the cypress and the yew.

Even now, on jolly bathing expeditions to the Princes Isles, someone is sure to point out the rock on which the Turks cast many thousands of stray dogs, bane of the streets, to die lingeringly, in Allah's own time – a more humanely organised end being contrary to Moslem tenets. A shadow falls on the picnic outing and the dog-loving infidels try to think of other things... but once again, they have looked on death.

At Usküdar, where efficient car ferries now chug ceaselessly between Europe and Asia, the dominating impression still has this sombre quality. The cypress thickets rise steeply behind the town, to the most celebrated cemetery of all. 'Mighty death field, PANORAMA,' says Murray's *Handbook* for 1892, which is the vintage I like my guidebooks to be. Besides, it is Loti's heyday, and essentially, still applicable. Murray may remind us that Osküdar derives from the Persian word for courier, or runner: that Osküdar was the first station of the Asiatic couriers heading eastwards: that it was the assembly point of the great camel caravans heading towards Asia, to Bukhara, the Turcoman steppes – all Central Asia. We, less adventurous, may set out to follow the Bulbul Derisi, or Nightingales' path, but are, first of all, conscious of that dominating cemetery. Wherever we go in Istanbul, if we ask the way, we are certain to be told to keep the cemetery on our left, or our right, or to go past some 'little field of the Dead'. Everywhere, in the uproar, or in the stillness, the shades close in. We may go to the Sublime Porte in a tram, but it is the tram which seems unreal. Everywhere we are more aware of the dead than the quick; and Loti is always there, brooding among the steles with a dread of death, a repugnance, and yet a morbid fascination for graveyards, wholly at variance with the fatalistic Eastern beliefs he admired.

If melancholy inspired Loti's finest work, it seems that in Istanbul, too, sorrow and remorse have produced some of the loveliest expressions of Turkish architecture. The Shahzadeh Mosque, for example, commemorates the unhappy princes Mohammed and Jehangir, sons of Süleyman the Magnificent, who met their end through the machinations of their stepmother, Roxelane, determined on the advancement of her own son. The Mosque of Mihrimah at Scutari tells of that day when, at its consecration, the populace rebuked the sultan for his little son's arrogance towards them. On the instant the sultan stabbed the child in public amendment for his omissions as a parent. The fatal dagger was walled up in the prince's tomb and its outline can still be seen along the marble side.

Tragedy, drama, decay, all three elements of the Turkish scene stimulated Loti. Could he have borne seeing the old thrust aside to make way for the progress so necessary to this race he loved? A welfare state would not have inspired him, I think, however much his sense of humanity might be in theoretic agreement. Sunset was better than sunrise; endings appealed more than beginnings. Eyes were more fascinating seen through a grille, over a yashmak. Aziyadé's tomb held him as perhaps her bed would not have done.

Except for the simplicity with which he writes of animals, Loti often sounds a thoroughly theatrical note; but then that is all part of his magic. It has something of the intoxicating unreality of grand opera. Although he liked to use his landscapes, his local colour, as backgrounds for his own pinings, to us, the readers, they always become foregrounds. Loti saw them as a framework in which he played out the perfect role – perfect from the masculine viewpoint, that is. He loves, and sails away before the problem of satiety arises. There are tears, and Loti's wonderful evocations gleam through them, sharpened by finality. These Circassian kadines, these Serbian shepherd girls, these dusky beauties waving farewell from the Bosphorus, from a rooftop of the kasbah or a tropic beach, it is always the same pattern of voluptuous partings, elegiac sorrows. Death or malign fate always overtakes them. Loti always sails away. 'Adieu' or 'Come back!' they cry. But he does not: cannot. And if he does, it is too late. 'Eûlû! Dead!' the old negress Kadidja hurls at him, when he returns to search the quarter where Aziyadé lived, those grey, silent streets beside the Fatih which have not, I think, changed much since he wrote of them so beautifully. The wrenching farewells reach a last orgy of grief in *Suprêmes Visions d'Orient*, where, in spite of Loti now being accompanied by his grown-up son Samuel, the melancholy is quite overpowering.

All sorts of spiteful things have been written about Pierre Loti. He had his enemies, or rather his detractors, for someone of his largeness and essential goodness had few enemies. Aziyadé was said to have been no odalisque, escaped from the harem of a rich old Turk, but a prostitute, astutely presented to Loti in this more romantic guise... She was said to have been a boy... she was said to have been a figment of Loti's imagination; but Loti himself was categorical in his denials. It had all happened as he wrote it: her name was Hakidjé: he would remember her until his last breath. In Farrère's description of Loti's end, it seems that he did. Even then, his sense of theatre prevailed. A dying man, he received his guests in the chill candle-lit dusk of the private mosque he had installed in his house at Rochefort, where Aziyadé's stele reigned supreme.

However much Loti dramatised, he had, too, a camera eye for verity. Some of his straight reporting, such as that on the Boxer Rebellion, has a steely impact.

Even when romanticising, he never writes of places or ways of life he does not know well. Thus, he tells us little of the one place, above all others, of which he should have written – the Seraglio, or Vieux Sérail, fabulous palace of the Ottoman dynasty, at once fortress and prison which dominates the straits between Europe and Asia. Today, most of it (excepting the inner labyrinths of the *sérail*) is open to the public as a museum, filled with treasures beyond description. Its towers, domes, kiosks and outer bastions rise from the wooded slope of the lower gardens, now given over to an amusement park where, amid swings and roundabouts, sober Turkish families sit drinking tea and taking their pleasures rather austerely.

Another link, this, between Loti and the Turks. He too could be austere.

For all his exoticism he came from a severe northern French province: his family background was also strict. This northern quality is apparent to all who know the Turks beyond their superficially glowing Levantine legend. Turkey, it must be remembered, is not Mediterranean; it is a northern, Asiatic land where, sometimes, a southern sun blazes down; but, more often, the wind from the steppes howls wolfishly round. Loti loved best this chill aspect of Constantinople and although his descriptions seem to glow with colour and light, they are, in fact, more often concerned with winter scenes: rain lashing across the landing stages; the livid skies of snowstorms; winter nights, winds moaning down the conical, hooded chimneys; rain beating down to foam through the refuse-piled gutters; damp mists closing in, muffling sight and sound. All these aspects of the city we find reflected in Loti's writing.

There are contradictions in both Loti and in the land. Opulence beside austerity. Take the Turkish passion for richness, seen in their palaces, their cuisine, jewellery and arts: Loti shared this love of the extravagant. But in his house at Rochefort, the home of his childhood (and it was part of his cult for the past that he kept the house, the old servants, his mother's room, all unchanged; a sort of hallowed temple of yesterday), he also allowed his flamboyance full rein. Here he amassed a varied collection of Eastern splendours, even to the acquisition of an entire mosque, transported stone by stone, from Damascus. It was of the Sunnite cult – red marble pillars and a gold-encrusted mihrab, very splendid. Loti admitted he thought it the most beautiful mosque he had ever seen. Besides this, he had gratified his sense of theatre with vast Renaissance halls, a mediaeval salon, Chinese and Japanese rooms, Turkish divans and Algerian alcoves, all

Pierre Loti's house, the Mosque, Rochefort

placed behind the discreet façade of the original house and the neighbouring ones into which he had gradually spread, to accommodate his treasures.

It is eloquent of his tact, his respect for the old forms, that outwardly the little street remained untouched, sober Rochefortaise architecture.

Some aspects of the Seraglio, particularly its hugger-mugger of glories and ruin, would have been very much to his taste and beneath the gilding lay trage-dies which would have nourished him for years. Yet, it seems that he was never familiar with it. In his day, it was still imperial property, though the sultans had withdrawn, one by one, to other, less haunted palaces along the Bosphorus. While the Seraglio lay abandoned, the Sultan Abdul Hamid II lived among his menagerie, his concubines and his fears, at Yildiz, or in the zebra-striped marbles of Tcheregan.

When, as often happened, Loti was shown some special marks of imperial esteem and received by the sultan, it was, unfortunately, always at some other, less historic palace, or at the Friday *selamlik*, or *levée*, usually held in the sugar-cake décor of Dolmabagtche, 'not quite in the best of taste', according to the censorious Murray.

To the Turks whom he always championed, particularly in the dark hours of the Balkan wars, Loti had become a national figure. On his last visit, it was decided to bestow some exceptional favour upon him and they found a graceful way to do it. A house near the Sultan Selim Mosque, high above the Golden Horn, was furnished in the old Turkish manner with treasures from the imperial palaces: rugs beyond price, embroideries, divans, jewelled *tchibouks*, all the settings of Loti's dreams. Here he was installed as the sultan's guest. Servants from the palace dressed in their traditional costumes waited on the master, serving him and his friends with the rarest dishes. Nothing could have given him greater pleasure. No one could have been worthier of the compliment. Later it was regretted that he had not been offered a suite of rooms in the Seraglio. Its *revenants?* He, of all people, would have welcomed them, feeling himself one among them. Among its splendours and miseries he would have heard the pulse of the old Turkey he loved and to which, today, we can still return, through his eyes.

Whatever else I have missed by the accident of having been born in the twentieth century, a hundred years too late for a person of my backward inclinations, I have, nevertheless, been able to know something of that old city which is the core of Loti-land. There is a Turkish saying, a farewell benediction, *Güle* – go with a smile. They always say it to me, when I leave. But I always go with a sigh.

Undulators and Adulators

The café looked like any other; it was small and dirty and dark and getting darker, for it was dusk, and the electricity had broken down. A ha'penny dip guttered in the corner, where a decrepit Arab fanned a little brazier for the clients' tea and coffee. Gradually the place filled up. Some elegantly dressed elderly men – rich merchants, I afterward learned – came in followed by what appeared to be young pages, beautiful, very dark-skinned boys. Some wore elaborate white turbans, most of them were veiled like houris, or Touaregs. Over the thick folds, they cast limpid glances at our table. One group was followed by a tame sheep. A few pompous-looking old men sat stiffly in the corner and were obviously standing treat for several shy-looking creatures from the desert, I guessed, and new to the city. Presently the flower vendors came round and did a brisk trade with the little jasmine bouquets which are typical of Tunis. The starry flowers are mounted on pine needles, like tightly furled umbrellas: gradually they unfold, the spokes open, umbrella-like, and the little bouquets spread out, perfumed toys. Tunisians love this plaything, and in the cool of the evening you will see soldiers, policemen, taxi-drivers and beggars all savouring them voluptuously. In the café, the boys were sniffing them in ecstasy, or pinning them into their turbans, where they spread out over their dusky cheeks in a most enticing way. There was a lot of coming and going, and a strongly familial or tribal atmosphere.

This was the favourite meeting-place of the Ouarglis and their friends, I learned. In Tunis the best servants are Ouarglis. They come up from their country on the edge of the Sahara, in eastern Algeria, to work in the cities, but keep very much to themselves, a lone community. They are markedly effeminate in both appearance and bearing; but it is the delicate, romantic effeminacy often found among Arab men. It has nothing of the degeneracy associated with over-femininity in the West and watching them, you are reminded how small a place women have ever played in Arab civilisation. If they bred sons they were ensured a respected old age. Otherwise, after a few brief seasons of delight – the rest was silence.

The Ouarglis appeared to be a world of their own, enclosed and self-sufficient. They have their own caïd, who ruled over them with considerable indulgence, I fancy. Their own cafés and caravanserais, or hostels, were hidden away in the labyrinthine souks. Their Bureau de Placement, or Registry Office, was always crowded with these graceful, coquettish creatures, looking for situations as cooks or house-boys. I reflected how welcome they would be in Europe or America.

The night we chanced on their café, somebody was celebrating something – I never knew what – and there were to be dancers and musicians. The Ouarglis are famous for their dancing, which it is claimed, can rival that of the Ouled Naïls. But whereas the Ouled Naïl women are traditional prostitutes, their costumes, beauty and sensual delights celebrated all over North Africa, the Ouarglis are strictly amateurs, only dancing among themselves, with no calculated tourist effects. Straying into their café, being allowed to stay, all this was because my companion, a Turk, was known to the establishment. We lurked in the darkest corner and watched. There were the endless, monotonous, yet strangely stimulating songs of Arab tradition: the plaintive flute, the hot, wild drumbeats of the *derboulka*, all Africa in its rhythm, a sort of lute and a toy violin daubed with gold paint and played across the knee. Sometimes the musicians sang, hurling a long thread of melody above the café's din.

The Ouarglis began to dance: undulating, vibrating rather than moving. Their rich elderly adorers looked on entranced. These persons are prosperous – mostly merchants from the same part of the world. They trade in ostrich plumes, dates and particularly, ostrich marrow fat, considered an infallible cure for rheumatism. Lately they have been much disturbed by bootlegging competition, a black-market substitute made from donkey's marrow. Not at *all* the same thing, I was told, heads shaken in condemnation.

The merchants lapsed in silence again, their eyes following the dancers' undulations. But soon, these languorous delights were broken up by the arrival of their celebrated teacher, Amarr Ould Djella, famous all across North Africa. From the Tiznit dancers of Morocco to those of the Kerkennah Isles, Amarr was respected. The Ouled Naïls used to send their star performers to him for coaching (so did Egyptian impresarios perfecting their best belly dancers, before Cairene nightlife was cleaned up). He came across to us, and accepted an English cigarette. He was about fifty – small, pale, finicky, with cat-like gestures, and was wrapped in a large European overcoat under which some gaudy rags draggled round his white tennis shoes. He looked like one of those seedy tumblers who entertain provincial theatre queues.

When he stood up to dance and removed his overcoat, I was reminded of the Widow Twankey. He wore an electric-blue, long-sleeved under-vest, his turban had worked askew, and low round his hips a dazzling sequin belt was safety-pinned to a flaming salmon-pink satin skirt. But when he began to dance, there was no more of the grotesque pantomime droll. The shoddy costume, the tennis shoes, the safety-pins… all faded. It was the fabled Orient, Haroun Al Raschid's dancer, Salomé and her seven veils; all seduction, all provocation, the lure of the flesh incarnate. He danced the traditional slow, almost static dances, where only head and neck sway; the curious fluttering finger and wrist dance of the Ouled Naïls and the immemorial love-dances of the East, where writhing muscles and erotic belly swayings leave nothing unsaid, but which were, in this instance, rather hampered by the under-vest.

The circle of Ouarglis closed in, watching, enthralled. The ha'penny dip gleamed feebly on the rapt faces. The coffee pots boiled over unchecked; only the sheep seemed unmoved by the frenzies and dozed in a corner.

Next day, we were invited to the Ouarglis caravanserai, a big covered courtyard, where many of them lived and received their friends in little cells opening off the square. Amarr was to be there giving a lesson to some particularly promising young dancer. It was a Thursday, generally the Ouarglis' servants' afternoon off. Most of them repair to the caravanserai, where a convent, rather than monastery, atmosphere prevailed (the sort of Venetian convent of which Casanova wrote: a worldly scene); much chatter and comings and goings of visitors and inmates; tiffs and reconciliations. Newcomers up from their home town were sitting round, regaling the boys with family news. There were the usual refreshments – tea, the intoxicating green Arab tea and slender pipes for opium, or *kef*, which though strictly speaking, proscribed, is still sometimes enjoyed. Its sickly, unmistakable smell hung on the air. Their caïd arrived, and the traditional pot of basil was placed before him. This is a refinement of taste, of living, found in many Arab countries, where it is quite customary to enter a café and order a glass of water and a bouquet, or a pot of basil. The Arab is often content to sit contemplating a plant, nourished on beauty, in place of buns.

The orchestra filed in, but now, primed for the photographs we wished to take, they were a colourless band, transformed by what they proudly considered a more photogenic get-up – gents' natty suitings. Amarr arrived, his blue vest and sequin skirt glittering in the sunlight which filtered through the trellised vines. The new pupil had the same feline grace of all his tribe; his eye-lids curved like scimitars above the muffling white veils. He was Valentino and Salomé in one, and everyone suddenly looked faint with longing...

The lesson began. Amarr led, the pupil followed, turning and twisting, shuffling and posturing. The musicians changed their beat, and Amarr slashed his way through a fiery sabre dance. The new pupil panted after him, watching every step. Do it this way – try it again! One! Two! One! Two! I seemed to hear all the echoes of the many great teachers I have watched. Kesschinskayas' class in Paris. *Ras! Dva! Tri!* Simienova rehearsing in a classroom of the Bolshoi Theatre of Moscow. Marie Rambert at the Ballet Club... The echoes merged with the one, two, three, hop, of my first dancing-class polkas.

The lesson lasted a full two hours. Amarr is a perfectionist, giving value for money. Times were hard he said, and pupils were fewer, poorer. He was compelled to eke out his living by taking in washing (shades of the Widow Twankey once more). After the lesson he obliged with a solo dance – one of his star turns. Balanced on glass tumblers, a pitcher poised on his head, he executed a particularly erotic number. The rich merchants applauded frenziedly and money rained round. Bowing right and left, like a *prima ballerina assoluta*, waving and smiling his thanks, Amarr backed gracefully out of the ring taking his pupil with him. The audience repaired to their cells with their admirers. Doors slammed shut. It was time to go. We left Amarr and his pupil resting in one of the more elaborate cells, a sort of star's dressing-room, adorned with pictures, mirrors, flowers, and dominated by a large velvet covered sofa, style Louis-Philippe. There they would repose after their efforts, sip tea, gossip and discuss what sort of future lay in store for an Ouargli dancing boy today. But in North Africa, that today is already yesterday. How much traditionalism will survive, tomorrow, I wonder?

OULED NAÏLS

THE PERFECT FEMALE IMAGE? THAT DEPENDS ON HOW YOU DEFINE
female: mother, wife, mistress, muse, or slave? It is a shifting image. Woman the
refuge, the dispenser of comfort (expressed variously in terms of sympathy,
good cooking or the bed) would, I fancy, still be most men's ideal. This is the
subjective approach. Taking an objective view, I suggest the most successful
female image is that of Oriental woman, who in general does not yet struggle
greatly to be other than what untold generations of ancestors have been before
her – pleasing to man. In the West, this basic attitude has become subservient to
careers and Women's Lib. Thus the image of my choice might be regarded as
remote, retrograde; for the mysterious hieratic figure shown here is an Ouled
Naïls, from the tribe of that name, living in the Djebel Amour mountains

of Algeria. There, women are celebrated for their wild, dark beauty, their
hereditary seduction, and the furious
allure of their dancing. In short, they
are prostitutes – but with a difference.
These legendary charmers come early
to their calling leaving their villages in
all honour and when they have earned
their dowry, around age twenty-six or
so, return to their homes to marry
well, breed and become matriarchal
figures. No raddled, lonely old age
in a concierge's lodge, or as lavatory
attendants, for them. Some used to be
found lending contrived local colour to
the tourist circuit.

The remaining real stuff, a declining band, have haunted me, ever since

Ouled Naïl

I spent spellbound evenings in an Arab café frequented by the Foreign Legion and the Chaamba – an Algerian camel corps patrol who gathered there to slake their various thirsts with green tea, raw red wine or the Ouled Naïls, who offered themselves with such panache. There were no striptease, Bunny Club tricks there. Their supple, tawny flesh was always hinted, never revealed, by bunchy gauze skirts and sequin-strewn pantaloons. As they danced, the circle of men crouched round would offer coins or banknotes which the dancers placed on their brow, pasted by their sweat as the dance became more and more furiously expressive. Not all Ouled Naïls danced: most were content to hold court and conduct their commerce with a wonderful mixture of abandon and dignity. When one had been chosen, she would lure him into the shadowy alleyway where each woman had her small cell: candle-lit and piled cushions, perhaps a *narghilyé* to puff on, when the transports were done. It was always a festival of the senses...

Peace and Plenty: A Plea for Polygamy

In our monogamous society the institution of polygamy is surrounded by a miasma of misconceptions. It has highly-coloured and vaguely pornographic connotations – even in today's permissive mood. It spells unbridled licence, if not licentiousness. A certain smacking of the lips is still observed among men, and in general, a pursing of them among women. Few see beyond the clichéd cushions of the harem to the social, economic and physiological benefits it represents. Polygamy still conjures some sultry harem interior recalling Delacroix's *Femmes d'Alger*, where ladies of assorted pigmentation, lily-white and gold, or with the dusky sheen of a black pearl, loll in perfumed alcoves, satiated, or in anticipation...

Somehow, the bracing setting, the high endeavours and the mahogany and mutton interiors of Brigham Young's Salt Lake City do not leap to mind. Yet this too was polygamy. But it did not last. Alexis de Tocqueville, returning from a visit to America, wrote 'pulpits flame with righteousness,' and of the uplifting moral tone of the country. Presently the overall consensus of opinion went against Mormon plenitude; although as yet I have not discovered any passage in the Bible where polygamy is condemned.

St Paul's grudging 'Better to marry than burn' becomes Holy Matrimony, or rather, Holy Monogamy. But the exponents of this creed seem to ignore the fact that, at the present rate of divorce, monogamy is nothing more or less than polygamy with a time lag. American women are generally acquisitive – never more so than in the matter of husbands. The rapid succession of wives experienced by many American men, often acquired by the woman's volition rather than theirs, make these ladies, in essence, concubines. Holy Matrimony it may be, for as long as it lasts, but usually it does not last long, couples whisking in and out of the courts almost before you can say alimony; this makes for odd man or woman out, disturbed children and general disorder.

To the races who practise polygamy it is just as holy an institution, and surrounded by considerable formality. The rulings of domestic protocol impart great style to daily life in the harem, or *zenana*. As all over the Far and Middle East, age is greatly respected; thus the first wife, past child-bearing age, and no longer offering the stimulus her husband seeks, seldom finds herself abandoned and forced to start life all over again, or to fight to provide well for her children, if she obtains custody. Moreover, if she has retained her husband's confidence and friendship, it is she who will probably choose a younger wife for him, and mould the newcomer to his liking. And she will probably remain powerfully installed in the domestic hierarchy, if, later, other debutantes appear. It is a sensible arrangement. But then, like eighteenth-century Europe, the East has always taken a practical, rather than romantic view of marriage. I am reminded of the wise Egyptian lady of quality, cited, I think, by Lady Duff Gordon, in her *Letters From Egypt*, written well over a hundred years ago. This wise lady married her fourteen-year-old son to one of her favourite slaves, a woman verging on thirty. 'She will teach him what he must know about love,' she said, 'and when it is time for him to marry well, she will choose the right wife for him; and when I die she will look after the household properly.'

Why should we imagine we can be, throughout our lives, all things to one person? Or that person, to us? It can happen: it does – remember the unity of Aragon and Elsa Triolet, only broken by her death; or the unity, without marriage, of Sartre and Simone de Beauvoir, and a whole gallery of great romantics in the past, who never looked away from their beloved. But it is rare. In my life I have known exactly two truly happy monogamous marriages; but many happy polygamous ones. In polygamy, the man enjoys the spice of variety (in the comfort of his own home, too), and the woman, that of competition. Healthy competition, for the most part, for no wife will let herself go if there are other wives around. Jealousy? This is the burning question: of course it exists, but far less than we or the West imagine, for when the husband springboards out of one bed into another, if so vigorously inclined, the wife he leaves does not see this as infidelity, but the normal pattern of domesticity. Nor does she lose face, or suffer invidious comparisons from the outside world. Jealousy, here, is less a matter of love for a person, than desire for some particular gain – property, for example.

Polygamy solves many problems that harass Western society, such as broken homes, surplus women, the shortage of domestic help, loneliness, old age and babysitting. In case of absence or illness, there is always another mother to hand, for so the ladies are regarded and addressed by the assorted brood, who generally love and are loved without discrimination. Particularly in the more modest households, where affection is not clouded by those questions of inheritance and fortune, which according to *The Arabian Nights*, are responsible for much cupidity, and many a cup of cold poison, behind the latticed windows of the more sumptuous harems.

Polygamy is not promiscuity and if we view the practice impartially, without prejudice, or those ingrained, or rather instilled, tenets of possession – the total possession which is monogamy and which, in other circumstances, would be condemned as most unchristian greed – we must admit that domestic plurality works as well for women as men. Or so I have come to believe, from my many travels about lands where establishments of plenty still flourish. Contentment and peace, rather than fretful strain, is apparent everywhere. It seems both sad and ironic that the East, with its infatuation for the superficial aspects of the West (blue jeans, dark glasses, Coca-Cola and such) which are, oddly, interpreted as expressions of progress and civilisation, should also begin to adopt Western strictures on one of their fundamental principles of living.

Alas, polygamy is on the decline. Among the more sophisticated, it now seems old-fashioned; not in line with the West. I accept that it may have become economically difficult to maintain more than one wife in those conditions of scrupulous equality, material and physical, enjoined by the Prophet (which is why he set the limit at four – more being, we suppose, too much of a strain for any man, both materially and physically). But when the East begins to dwell on the superior virtues of monogamy, it does not ring true. To me, at any rate, it smacks more of fashion than conviction – of a wish to conform to Western ways without weighing their value when transplanted.

Yet, in reverse, were the West to adopt, or try out polygamy – which I repeat, is not promiscuity; we have that in plenty, but without structure or form – the transplant might take root and flourish. The industrialised, materialistic West has overstrained itself, and brought its human relationships, judging by many marriages we see around us, to a point of no return. In the New York area, which is a giddy, international zone by comparison with the rest of the country, six out of ten men commit adultery, four out of ten women, and seven out of every ten marriages break up. England is going the same way, and in France, once the bulwark of family life, the rot sets in too, however much the Church thunders. Those young, free-living, free-loving exponents of group-living, such as some settlements in California, are regarded as eccentric exceptions to the general rule; but I think they are instinctively moving towards the more basic, simplistic approach to human relationships which the East still knows, and which, in principle, polygamy expresses.

I do not suggest it as an imposed, or general solution. (Imagine the headlines: *President Vacationing with Second Lady*, or, *First and Fourth Lady Honour Dodgers' Wives' Brunch...*) No... it wouldn't do for everyone, there will always be some single-minded souls around. But in order to give it a chance, woman's whole attitude to man must change fundamentally. This is the crux of the matter. She must see him, and accept him, as master. Those embattled ladies who make a noise about equal rights and careers seem to be searching for happiness through justice, an odd route, for justice is not to be found on earth, and happiness is.

I have come to believe that woman's acceptance of her more passive role, is the secret of those still harmonious relationships which exist between men and women, in the less developed, or industrialised, lands – notably those where polygamy continues to be practised. Whether single, or married, or embedded in marital plenty, rich or poor, the issue is simple: women know instinctively, and do not resent, their role. They may stand or crouch behind the man, to serve his meal, as do the Turcoman women in the Afghan steppe country, or walk behind the mule or camel he rides, but they do not see this as a cause for strife or unhappiness, like realities such as hunger, or pain... Now were those mules or camels along Madison Avenue, I fancy the sort of American woman I have in mind would be riding ahead, her husband trotting after. And here is the rub: not so much because she wanted to ride, but because she had trained him to trot behind, and he could no longer keep up the pace, let alone call the tune.

Turning away from this painful scene, where every other door proclaims a doctor's or analyst's office, and calming pills, or the pep kind, proliferate, my mind turns to simpler lands... lands of peace and plenty, at any rate, in the polygamous sense. Whether the mud and palm frond huts of a *fellah* on the Upper Nile, or one of those refulgent palaces favoured by the great Arab nobles, or the goat-hair tents of the nomads, the same note of serenity is apparent. This is not a purely domestic calm; nor is it the outward stillness of a setting far removed from the roar of urban life. It is something much deeper, something stemming from a vibration of intense animal magnetism – by that I do not infer that man and woman represent only the positive and negative; but here, senses are certainly gratified to the full, and there are no nervous tensions. The atmosphere, which is sensuous, rather than sensual, also proclaims a marked stability, or balance, as if each individual were sure of their place and purpose in an established order.

Such is the peace I have observed among polygamous peoples. At the price of considerable effacement and restriction (by Western standards) woman reaps great returns here: she is loved and protected. In old forms of Arabic address she was referred to as 'the hidden jewel and the guarded treasure'. Perhaps this is what Stendhal – most worldly of European men – had in mind when he wrote: 'It is in the black tents of the Bedouin that we must seek the model and the land of true love.'

The West has tried monogamy and successive polygamy. Why not now try the classic, concurrent kind?

Sultan Murad's Room

The plurality implicit in a harem, seraglio, *zenana* or *anderoun* means that, in general, it is not a pavilion of the heart but a pavilion of the senses, while its furnishings reflect its Oriental nature, and are generally little more than bedding. The Khan of Kokand, in his turquoise palace in the Ferghana, beyond Bukhara, cannot have had much time for the pursuit of true love, for it is said there were three thousand or more concubines chattering, parakeet-shrill about the rooftop terraces which overlooked the wastes of Central Asia. Here man's life was composed of hunting sorties or battle. Like many other Oriental overlords, the khan probably regarded his harem in the light of an oasis – somewhere he found refreshment (though scarcely rest) after the violent tempo of these territories.

Yet, on occasions, polygamy gave place to some overwhelming single love such as that of the Tartar Khan Sahin Ghirei, one of that exotic band, the Krim (or Crimean) khans, who descended from the Mongol hordes. His love is said to have been a Polish noblewoman, Marie Potocka, captured in a raid; though she is also said to have been a Georgian slave in his harem, one Deliareh Bekhé, before becoming his adored and only wife. She was in any case a Christian, who displayed the most inflexible religious scruples which quite blighted the bliss she might have shared with her Moslem adorer. When she died, pining away as if in condemnation of her apostasy – or marrying outside her faith – he was inconsolable, building a noble octagonal marble mausoleum to commemorate his love. And here, beside her tomb, unmoved by the blandishments of any other woman, he mourned the years away, monogamous in grief as in joy.

But his love is better remembered by a fountain – that celebrated Fountain of Tears which he also erected in her memory. It is still to be seen, set among the overgrown cypress trees and now rather neglected rose gardens where once they wandered together. The melancholy of this romantic scene inspired one of Pushkin's loveliest poems, *The Fountain of Baktchiserai*.

Deathless loves have a way of producing splendid memorials.

After such elegiac sorrows it is positively tonic turning to the recusant sensuality which prevailed, generally, in the Vieux Sérail or Seraglio, Top Kapou Serai to the Turks, fortress and domain of the Ottoman sultans from the sixteenth century until the fall of their dynasty in 1918. The Seraglio (an Italianate derivation of the Eastern *sérail*, or palace) has always been surrounded by legends of terror and debauch.

Among all the beautiful, sinister or dramatic settings within the complex of the Seraglio, the divans, kiosks, places for strange doings, inner courts and corridors such as that one where 'the Djinns hold Consultation', or that 'Golden Road' down which each new odalisque was ceremonially led to the imperial couch, it is Sultan Murad's room which remains the heart of the honeycomb. It has been said to be the loveliest room in all the world, and is the perfect setting for lovers' meetings, romantic beyond measure. Even in its present deserted state it retains some overwhelming quality of emotion, as if the shades of Sultan Murad and his Italian kadine still lingered there, 'emparadised in one another's arms'.

But first something about the Seraglio as a whole, since through many centuries, to the world outside, its name alone epitomised some fabulous enclave, all love and all desire. Desire, yes, but love less often. With rare exceptions the lives of its inhabitants were conducted in a cynically businesslike manner, while that of the concubines might, except for the initial circumstances of their being there at all, have been compared to the inmates of a rigidly run boarding school.

The Palace of Top Kapou was finally abandoned as an imperial residence in 1853 when Sultan Abdul Medjed transferred his harem and court to other less historic and rather less haunted retreats along the Bosphorus. Since then no sultan has lived within the Seraglio, but it has remained inviolate, still steeped in mystery, and there, until the rise of the Turkish Republic, a few raddled old eunuchs and some elderly ladies, last remnants of former imperial harems elsewhere, lingered on among the decaying splendours. Nothing was repaired, rats scuttled, and broken window panes were stuffed with tattered silk against the icy winds which lashed round in winter. There these forgotten derelicts continued, living in the past, in the manner of inmates in some poorly-endowed almshouse, until at last they were removed – 'liberated', in official parlance – and found themselves thrust out into a world they had never known and could not now comprehend. With their departure most of the Seraglio was set in order as a museum, its treasures classified, its principal buildings restored and its history recounted in guidebooks designed for the visitors who now invaded it in strength.

Only the harem remained apart, unseen by the majority, a palace within a palace, core of the complex, and object of the liveliest curiosity to every frustrated tourist. But as I have had the rare privilege of wandering about it freely over a number of years, I came to know something of its secrets. This intricate and awesome interior has, as might be expected, an obsessive quality. There a strange hush falls – not only the silence of an abandoned building, but some brooding apprehensive stillness reigns. The revenants are at home here, in these halls of yesterday.

Harem – or, more correctly, *haremlik* – signifies the women's quarters, from the Arabic *haram* – forbidden, or sanctuary – the men's quarters being known as the *selamlik* – a place of meeting, from *salam*, a greeting. Thus the harem of the Seraglio was sacrosanct, inviolate and, in a sense, remained so until lately, though no curators or directors of the museum should be blamed for having withheld this section from the general public for so long. How could they do otherwise? How hasten the laborious, and delicate process of restoration when all was dangerously dilapidated, and every door, cupboard, or attic was a significant part of the whole?

You cannot put a whole rambling warren behind glass. A single careless cigarette stub could kindle the bleached wooden kiosks and frescoed passages of Osman III. One spark could destroy the gilded splendours of the Sultane Validé's apartments, where gilded rococo intricacies (decoration, if you admire them, trimming if you do not) are imposed on the flower of mediaeval Ottoman *faience*. Thus the authorities had no other choice but to set this most marvellous of national treasures apart for so long. And lingering there, within this last bastion of mystery, I used to rejoice selfishly.

When almost all the historic mansions of England, like the châteaux of France, are thrown open, when the great palaces of Vienna or Venice are often turned consulates or government offices, when we can enter the last Tzarina's rather suburban, but ikon-studded bedroom at Tzarskoe Selo, left intact as an awful warning against superstition and autocracy, it was particularly enthralling to know that one fastness remained round which to build every romantic flight of fancy. Although no imaginings could exceed the mysterious atmosphere which is the *haremlik*'s own.

The Seraglio has always been surrounded by misconceptions as well as mystery. But besides its sultry reputation there were other aspects of intellectual and mystic austerity which would confound those whose notions were based on whispered Levantine gossip, or on a performance of the ballet *Scheherazade*, where eunuchs, slaves and sultan alike conduct themselves with an impetuosity quite alien to the rigid canons of etiquette which, in fact, prevailed. Moreover, it is often overlooked that within the Seraglio there existed, and still does, one of the most sacred shrines of all Islam. This is the Pavilion of the Mantle, Khirqa i Sherif (curiously placed between the Baghdad Kiosk, representing the flesh, and the Kefés, or prison cage, representing the devil). The Khirqa i Sherif contains the Prophet's mantle, three hairs from his beard, his footprint on a stone, and one tooth, lost in the battle of Bedr. Each sultan was by tradition their guardian, and venerated accordingly throughout the entire Moslem world, and his guardianship was believed to be proof of his divine mission on earth.

The Ottoman court was celebrated not only for its extravagance, but for its culture, the sultans having a long tradition as patrons of the arts, both within and without their palaces. They endowed mosques, hospitals and public buildings, employing the finest talents of their age. Gentile Bellini was among the painters at one time resident at the court of Mohammed II. It was this enlightened sultan who founded the celebrated Seraglio School, designed to educate, with extremely high standards, those boys levied by tribute, seized in wars, or, as some young princes, taken as hostages, but invariably Christian children. They were educated to become royal pages, or to hold high office. The chief white eunuch was in charge of all educational questions here, while his sable counterpart, the chief black eunuch, in charge of the women of the harem, was responsible for such education as they received; though this was generally rather superficial, concentrating more on the finer shades of pleasing.

Besides the institution of the state school, the Seraglio housed numbers of master-craftsmen. By custom every sultan acquired a trade. Some were carpenters, some goldsmiths, some calligraphers, the Turks being acknowledged masters of this art, who perfected their skill on the parchment firmans or imperial decrees, on those sweeping arabesques which form themselves into the name of Allah, or on the *tughra*: imperial seal or sign of each ruler.

Everything within the Seraglio bears evidence of those standards of perfection which successive rulers enjoined. Here, when a coffee cup is chunked from a single emerald, it is not vulgar, for the quality of its setting, the delicate gold workmanship of the *finjan*, or casing which holds the cup, whether this is of porcelain or a precious metal, makes the whole a work of art. A solid silver cradle, buttoned in rubies, is not ostentatious here: harmony prevails over everything, design, colour, form... Door locks and bolts – so vital a part of the *haremlik* – are superb examples of the metalsmith's craft, bronze, damascened with gold or silver; bolsters are tasselled with strings of pearls, hangings marvellously worked in gold thread; velvets are blistered with precious stones, while the sumptuous silks from Broussa, like the Iznik tiles and the carpets of Ghiordes, Melés or Bergamo, are the perfect flowering of Turkish artistry.

Every extravagance was controlled, not only by strict canons of taste, but by etiquette and protocol. This applied to the manner in which a person lived, dressed, or was killed. Erring women were sewn into weighted sacks and drowned off Seraglio Point, this operation being ritually performed by the *bostanji* – gardener-boatmen – in the presence of the black eunuchs who supervised the women in death as in life. Those dignitaries whom the padishah had decided to liquidate were also removed in style, their doom being announced to them by the arrival of the deaf-mutes, presenting the ritualistic bowstring for strangulation. In the case of princes, a silken one was decreed. Deaf-mutes were always employed about the Seraglio, carrying messages, running errands; they were a particularly useful lot, for in theory they could neither overhear, nor repeat what went on around them. Though in fact it was otherwise, for they had, over the generations, perfected a sign language which, combined with some mysterious technique of lip-reading, kept them well informed.

Were a foreign ambassador to be received in audience by the padishah, Allah's Shadow on Earth, Brother of the Sun, to give him only a few of his titles, etiquette reached its peak. Stumbling on carpets gravelled over with pearls, the visitor was required to don an enveloping garment of gold tissue (much as, today, visitors to maternity clinics are put into sterilised overalls).

Colours, perfumes, fabrics, jewels and furs, too, all had their hieratic significance. The sultan's turban — and his alone — could be tufted with herons' plumes. Ermine was for one dignitary, fox for another. Certain members of the imperial family might wear sable, others not. By yellow or red leather boots, a soldier's rank was marked.

Life within the House of Felicity was seldom that luscious world of nineteenth-century romanticism pictured in Miss Pardoe's *Beauties of the Bosphorus*, all sweetmeats and roses. To most inmates of the Seraglio, the House of Felicity was also known as the Palace of Tears. Here, in this formalised world, everything revolved round one man — the sultan, Padishah of the Faithful. From here, he dispensed justice and injustice, gratified his senses and enlarged his domains, which at one time stretched from the Sahara to Vienna. Beyond the Gate of Felicity, Bab-i-Saadet, where everyone who entered must first prostrate himself to kiss the threshold, successive rulers lived lives of despotism and indulgence; yet, as has been remarked, sometimes tinctured by extreme cultivation, scholarship and piety too.

The Seraglio reflects this counterpoint at every turn.

In its form, or plan, the sultan's palace follows those of the Sassanian Persian kings, which must have inspired the first princely Turkish dwellings. The particular model seems to have been the palace of Haouch-Kouri, where, archaeologists tell us, three courts succeeded each other in a direct line. The first, or outer court, for guards and commerce; the second, for administrative buildings and personnel; the third, forbidden to all but a chosen few, containing the monarch's palace and household. And behind that, inviolate territory — the inner sanctuary of his harem.

So it is at Top Kapou Serai. After passing through the first, or outer court, where Janissaries gathered round their legendary tree, sharpening their scimitars and rattling their kettle drums in displeasure, a menace which even the sultans dared not ignore, one arrives at the Ortakapi, gateway to the second court. But before reaching its ordered green peace, with the alleys of cypress and delicate colonnades leading to the Divan and the inner Gate of Felicity, a wall fountain 'of the Executioners' recalls that here they cleansed their swords after spiking their victims' heads above the gatehouse, or piling the niches beside the fountain with the ears, hands or noses of others, an inducement to obedience which few could ignore. On reaching the *haremlik* gardens, beyond the third court, the lovely terraces, pools and parterres of the tulip gardens which extend towards Seraglio Point, a promontory lying between the waters of the Corne d'Or, the Bosphorus and the Marmora, are strewn with fanciful little kiosks and gazebos, each an exquisite toy set in groves of myrtle and box. Yet how haunted, still, those ornate empty shells; how evocative their names…

The House of Desire, the Kiosk of the Sofa, the House of Joy, the House of Security (a foreboding note, here), the Pearl Kiosk, the Kiosk of the Turban, or, most celebrated of all, the Baghdad Kiosk. Some were for informal audience, a meeting between sultan and vizier, perhaps, some contrived solely for the pleasure of contemplating a sunset over the minarets of the distant city, or for the ecstasy of breathing the fragrance of roses. One sultan devised a domed roof cooled by a constant flow of water, where he liked to take his siesta. Most were for amorous play. The Baghdad Kiosk, named after a sultan's Eastern conquests, embodied every voluptuous dream – *le repos du guerrier*. Each of its four cushioned alcoves are framed in a shimmer of pearl and ivory inlay and the intense blues of intricate tiling. Each alcove seems to invite another houri, each divan a new embrace…

Amid all these delights of the flesh, of the perpetually replenished ranks of seductive slaves (the Sultan Ibrahim of abhorred memory at one time requiring twenty-four virgins in as many hours, until, overcome by nervous exhaustion, he fell back on powdered ambergris with coffee as a restorative), both sultan and concubine must sometimes have been uncomfortably aware of shadows menacing the alcove where they sported, for throughout the Seraglio death always lurked. The concubine, her eye falling on a little ornamental boathouse amid the bosky shade of Seraglio Point, far below, was no doubt reminded that it was from here that those of her kind who had failed to please were drowned. This thought must have chilled her blood while no doubt encouraging her ardours.

'Let her disappear!' was the fatal phrase which the sultan had only to pronounce for the slave's doom to be sealed. It is recorded that one padishah, in a fit of ennui, ordered his entire harem of tried favourites to be liquidated overnight, in order to make a fresh start in the morning. We imagine him, Bluebeard in person, idly fingering his amber *tespeyh*, or prayer beads, and issuing the command, 'Let her,' or, in this case, 'Let *them* disappear!' Small wonder then, that terror took root, and love, in romantic terms, scarcely at all.

Even maternal affections were corrupted by the lust for power. By custom, the sultan was always born of a slave, one of foreign blood, never from a Turkish woman, for they were never recruited for his bed. Every inmate of the *haremlik* could possibly become mother of a sultan, and herself acclaimed Sultane Validé, Queen Mother, Crown of the Veiled Heads, that is, of all women throughout the realms. The Sultane Validé ranked only second to the sultan himself, and wielded absolute power within the *haremlik*. During the century and a half known as the Kadinlar Sultanate, they so influenced their imperial sons or husbands that they came to dictate most of the Sublime Porte's affairs of state, and foreign policies too. Every woman dreamed of achieving supremacy, rising through all the hierarchies of pleasing, first as a novice, attached to the court or room, *oda*, of a highly placed inmate (thus odalisque, but having originally no erotic connotations, as assumed by the West). Then, proving successful and perhaps lucky, nominated *güzdeh*, 'one who has caught the royal eye'. At which she was set apart, groomed and schooled in all the intricacies of pleasing, provided with her own *oda* and slaves. From there, were she to continue pleasing, and now promoted as *ikbal*, an established favourite, she might become one of the four kadines, equivalent of the four wives sanctioned by the Prophet.

Before that fortunate state was reached, were she to become pregnant, and the sultan to favour her state, she would be known as Kassachi Sultane, of princess's rank. But if the sultan were to fall under the sway of a rival *ikbal* and lose interest or command the pregnancy to be terminated, the court abortionist would be summoned and all her hopes dashed. If the unfortunate creature continued to conceal her condition, and escape his attentions, and a child be born, a girl risked being drowned or stifled forthwith. But even if it were a boy, and the sultan smile upon it, her troubles were far from over. On the contrary: from now on her own life, and that of her child would be forever more threatened by the jealousy of every other mother, each jockeying for power, not only for their child's possible accession to the throne, but their own consequent aggrandisement. As I remarked earlier, love, the tender passions, had little place here, but ambitions raged, bringing with them intrigue, violence and terror.

This uneasy climate prevailed everywhere: in the grandiose state apartments, or the sinister quarters of the black eunuchs, as in those dormitory-like galleries where the novices languished, awaiting their summons to the sultan's bed. The contents of these rooms or the more splendid apartments of the favoured ladies were much alike, only varying in their degree of luxury. Eastern living does not require furniture on Western terms. Carpets are of first consequence: then quantities of padded quilts and mattresses, coverlets and cushions. These comprise the typical bedroom, which, by day, when the bedding is stacked or hidden in cupboards, changes its character and use, to become the living room, plenty of space being now free for the *tchibouks*, or water pipes, the mangals, or braziers, and those relays of coffee which punctuate the day.

Painted chests or coffers contained clothes, and smaller caskets, inlaid with silver and tortoiseshell, held the jewels, paints and unguents with which the women enhanced their beauty. Food was served by the African women servants, brought on huge round platters; these *tabla* were sometimes five feet across, and of solid silver. The mangals were of brass, beautifully worked, or silver, too; both warmed well enough, save in winter, that dread damp chill of winter in Constantinople, when the more pampered ladies were installed in rooms possessing fine chimney pieces. Bronze lanterns and candles lit the rooms – the wax candles being brought from Wallachia – while incense, an indispensable adjunct to every Eastern house, like ambergris to perfume the coffee, came from the Yemen. Specially scented soaps and essences were manufactured in the Seraglio, like the *surmah*, or kohl, with which the women darkened their eyes. Mastic, precursor of chewing gum, was used constantly, being said to sweeten the breath and whiten the teeth, though through several centuries teeth were blackened artificially, like kohl-rimmed eyes, and as much admired, while feet and hands were tinted with henna. Looking glasses were imported from Venice, often ornamented with pearls and enamels. The women passed the long, empty hours of their cloistered existence studying how best to enhance their appearance. Their extravagances were indulged, and their bills for finery seldom questioned. Hair was plaited with pearls or threaded with fine gold chains to which diamonds were attached, like dew drops. Even the lowliest novice was accorded lavish trimmings.

Such hours of embellishment were almost their only occupation. Books were not encouraged, unless a study of the Koran, and many could not read. Embroidery was admitted, musical accomplishments and dancing were favoured. Among themselves they would assume those sidling, writhing poses, undulating their bellies and striking on little tambourines, to perfect themselves against the day when such seductions might help to win the sultan's love. An occasional promenade into the tulip gardens, or to the menagerie — captives contemplating other captives — or surreptitious consultations with fortune tellers, smuggled in as purveyors of silks or gewgaws, or the languorous pleasures of the hammam were, apart from involvements of a lesbian nature, all the distractions upon which the sultan's women could count. Not all of them reached the imperial alcove, or, once there, were required to linger, let along exercise their charms, for the sultans were capricious. Were the rebuffed girl to be returned to the ranks untried, empty years stretched ahead, years of humiliation and taunting.

Every aspect of the Seraglio, its courts and gardens and such of its furnishings and the objects, clothes and possessions of its inmates as are still to be seen, *in situ* or housed in the sections now arranged as museums, reflect not only its history, but the character of its inmates and their daily life. While the Seraglio as a whole housed several thousand persons, the *haremlik*, which the West loosely supposed to be its sole purpose and content, was only one small part — but it was its core. Here the padishah and his family lived, their quarters, *haremlik* and *selamlik*, were contained within the jumble of dark courts and corridors, pavilions, hammams and guardhouses which had come, over the centuries, to form the whole. Only their immediate suites, and, of course, the sultans' women, lived here, behind that great doorway comprising four doors, two wooden and two of iron.

The quarters of the women were ruled by the black eunuchs under their chief, His Highness the Kizlar Agha, a personage of the greatest consequence, entitled, among other privileges, to three hundred horses for his sole use. The white eunuchs, a legacy of the Byzantine court, had been the original guardians of the *haremlik*, but were ousted from this internal — could one say domestic? — charge after long years of struggle, and henceforth were about the *selamlik* or Seraglio in general, but no longer in the holy of holies.

After the Kizlar Agha, the first post of importance in the *haremlik* was that of the Lady Stewardess, comptroller of the household, then the treasurer, the mistress of the robes, and the mistress of the jewels; the reader of the Koran, the head nurse, the keeper of the baths, and the court abortionist, an overworked person, by all accounts.

In the *selamlik*, the sultan's immediate suite included pages, scribes, treasurers, grooms, the keeper of the royal turbans, the chief turban winder – Dulbendtar-agha, *dulbend* being Turkish for muslin (as used for turbans) and hence the English 'turban'. Then there was the keeper of the jewels, reader of the Koran, and the imperial barber, whose position was an onerous one, since the sultan's beard had an almost sacred significance, every hair being meticulously preserved, as well as his dressers, grooms, bath attendants, apothecaries and many more who revolved around the imperial presence at close quarters. A host of others, still within the *selamlik*, did not approach closely, innumerable dwarfs and buffoons, the keeper of parrot cages, musicians, astrologers, and the royal taster, who must always sample each dish in the presence of the sultan; and since to err is only human, the royal toxologist, who was ever at the ready should dangerous symptoms be manifest. Here organisation had been brought to perfection.

Were any men from the outer periphery of the first and second courts of the Seraglio to be admitted – those who stoked the copper boilers for the hammam, gardeners, carpenters or plasterers perhaps, convened on some special task – their approach was signalled well in advance and the black eunuchs saw to it that their charges were invisible, under lock and key. Were the sultan and his kadines walking in the gardens, the warning cry, '*Helvet! Helvet!*' would ensure that no one lingered there. If by some error, the warning had not been heard, or was neglected, and the petrified intruder be detected by the black eunuchs, death was likely to follow such an imprudence. The Tressed Halberdiers, a corps of manual workers, woodcutters and bodyguards, were most often about the place, but even so, subject to the strictest rules. Their name derived from the two long locks of artificial hair that fell each side of their face. These were originally worn, it is said, to prevent their casting any sidelong glances where they should not. Secrecy was everywhere, an inherent instinct of succeeding generations to preserve the sacred mystery surrounding Allah's Shadow on Earth. And when he issued forth from his fastness, to go in state about his cap-ital, he was scarcely visible to its citizens; riding his charger at the heart of the vast cortège hedged by a special guard whose headdresses of towering fan-like plumes screened him from mortal view.

In spite of the padishah's seclusion, and the rigid sequestration of his women, the *haremlik* and *selamlik* quarters of his palace were oddly adjacent, hugger-mugger even, separated in some cases only by a door – though all were massively barred. There was no architectural plan or symmetry about the *haremlik* – only a congeries of rooms and courts. Succeeding sultans had added to the jumble, destroying and rebuilding haphazardly. State apartments adjoined windowless inner bedrooms, libraries abutted on hammams, the black eunuchs' quarters were close by the Sultane Validé's splendid suite. But however casual, there was an evident insistence on plumbing. Small marble-walled lavatories, each with their fountains of running water, were attached to every suite, for a most fastidious attention to cleanliness has ever been next to godliness, in Islam. Not far from the grandiose Hall of Audience Within – within the *selamlik*, that is – lay the Kefés or Cage, the prison-dwelling of those wretched princes whose existence might threaten the sultan or his direct heir. Succession passed to the eldest male relative; thus uncles and brothers were immured there for life, awaiting either a summons to the throne, or the silken bowstring which announced their end.

The Kefés is a small, rather squat stone pavilion with closely barred windows giving on to an inner courtyard. All around, the windows of other suites are also barred or screened by close-carved *moucharabiyeh*, while inside, lesser windows, or spyholes, are apertures through which dishes or messages were passed, connecting room to room. This was a feature of most Turkish domestic architecture, which catered for the total sequestration of harem life. But in the Seraglio, especially the Kefés, it implied a sinister system of observation too. A dim twilight pervades these ill-lit rooms. Even the charming tilework of the princes' schoolroom, with its map of Mecca and its lovely pointed, chequered chimney piece, cannot overcome the sinistry. In its abandonment, it still envelopes the stranger with a powerful sense of dread, of shadows lurking everywhere... the watcher and the watched...

Now a soft scuttle is heard... a rat? No, rather, the stealthy approach of the deaf-mutes bringing that message of doom for which some princes listened a whole lifetime. Down the Corridor Where The Djinns Hold Consultation another procession pads past... some of the black eunuchs are escorting a suitably barren odalisque to distract the imprisoned princes. In the Kefés, while appetites were gratified, the question of progeny must not arise, and the selected concubines, if not already proven sterile, were usually made so. Thus, in an atmosphere of cunningly fostered debauch, the princes were kept apart from all knowledge of the outside world or affairs of state. Their *khodjas*, or tutors, permitted very few books: not for them the educational opportunities of the Seraglio school. Apart from learning a craft, as did every man in Turkey, including those of highest estate, they were left to rot. Small wonder, then, that when, as occasionally happened, one was fetched out of obscurity to rule, he was seldom fit to do so. Some, having been incarcerated for fifty years or so, emerged as vengeful lunatics.

Phantoms everywhere. Brooding shadows, the women, the princes, and the abused and humiliated ranks of eunuchs too, for whom no advancements or honours could altogether compensate.

Now, standing in that marvellous alleyway of turquoise and sapphire-blue *faience* known as the Golden Road, I hear the muffled tread of a ceremonial procession, one headed by the Kizlar Agha no less, for it was down this Golden Road that he, by tradition, must conduct each new untried favourite-elect, or *güzdeh*, to the sultan's bed. Yet it is not a joyous procession, for too much apprehension and envy surrounds it... More steps, the capering antics of the dwarfs and buffoons, desperate in their determination to amuse. Now the dragging step of a prisoner led off between guards, but quiet, even in terror. All these phantoms tread softly, on bare jewelled feet, or feet slippered in yellow leather, high pattens or furred overboots, but always quietly, stealthily, in hushed silence, as they did in life.

This hush was always remarked by any outsider invited to enter the Seraglio; ambassadors, clockmakers, or physicians, perhaps. 'Horses as well as men know how to tread soft here,' records one amazed visitor. It was a stillness — as before a storm — an awesome quiet, and it must have hung over the most festive occasions. Even now the state apartments retain this sense of oppression. We read that a fountain played in the Arz Odasi, or Hall of Audience, just inside the Gate of Felicity: this was not so much to please the assembly as to ensure any whispered exchanges from the throne were lost to those around. Stealth everywhere. The ceremonies and galas held in the Throne Room Within, where the sultan fêted religious or family occasions, circumcision festivals and such, and where the women were ceremonially paraded before him, must still have breathed tension and dread. All the refulgence of Turkish rococo and the splendours of the Ottoman court were once centred round this salon, and still much of its magnificence remains. Yet the velvet hangings worked in gold, like the jewelled *tchibouks*, or those solid gold ewers, their handles of crystal or amethyst, like the vessels for amber-scented coffee, in which sherbets made of sugar and violets were served, all remained traps, where dangers lurked. Jewelled daggers, however ornamental, could strike home as ably as scimitars; poison – slow but sure – could lurk in a sip of coffee. Danger was everywhere in this abode of intrigue. Not an *ikbal*, nor even a kadine, could relax. The sweep of a peacock feather fan, or the flutter of a rival's gauze kerchief could conceal the death-dealing phial; and the excitement of such occasions was a perfect screen for mischief. The elaborate canopied throne, or *lit à baldaquin* (for their form and use was indistinguishable) represented to every lovely creature gathered round her sole chance of advancement, if not survival. Not even the glitter of the countless Bohemian glass chandeliers, shimmering and brilliant, could really lighten the scene. These chandeliers and candelabra (which had to contain a certain mystic number of candles) were imported from Europe during the eighteenth century, replacing the earlier bronze and horn lamps. Such bonbon colours, ruby, rose, pea-green and sky-blue, had a succulent, almost edible quality which appealed especially to sensual Turkish taste, and they continued to be imported in large quantities, not only for the Seraglio, but for every rich house and many mosques about the city too, where they still strike a singularly *mondain* note. But in the *selamlik*, even their sparkle could not produce a truly festive air. And when the sultan 'cast the handkerchief' to the charmer of his choice, an envenomed hiss must always have sounded behind the applause, the music of an orchestra (strictly blindfolded) or the tinkling merriment of the professional laughter-makers. This body, the reverse of those professional mourners or wailers found throughout the East, were employed much as, today, some hostesses use discreet mechanical music as a relaxing social background.

Yet many women accepted their lot willingly, for the luxury it offered and the possibilities of dazzling advancement it held. And not only the women, for strange as it may seem, the ranks of eunuchs were also largely recruited from willing victims. Oddly enough, those women who were selected for the Seraglio (which always had first pick of the slave market) were, in a sense, far less well placed than those taken into less august households, for they seldom obtained their freedom, as the others often did, unless, retired from the *haremlik*, they were presented to some indulged eunuch who retained a morbid interest in women, or were married off to a notable who had earned a mark of imperial esteem. Still, not every girl recoiled from her fate. Many saw it as an easier way of life then they had known in Europe, or in the rigours of a Caucasian *aôul*. Freedom is, after all, comparative, and the prospect of luxury universally seductive.

Safieh Baffo, the beautiful Italian concubine who was for many years Sultan Murad's only, and adored, kadine, she who shared with him the loveliest of all rooms for loving, had no need to better herself. Luxury and rank were her birthright. She came of a noble Venetian family, rich and proud in their splendid palazzo. To her, the opulence of the Seraglio must have seemed almost barbaric; and we can imagine the despair of her family when they learned she had been abducted by corsairs and sold into the Seraglio of the Grand Turk. It is not known how she came to be seized, for young girls of her kind were strictly kept, though abduction by corsairs was one of the hazards of earlier centuries. The Barbary pirates operated from Algiers and the ports of North Africa, doing a thriving trade with fair-skinned Europeans, both men and women, whom they sold to the slave merchants. Perhaps those who made off with Safieh Baffo were lying-to beyond the lagoons, and swept down audaciously, within sight of the Doge's Palace, to snatch their prize as she was sailing to Chioggia or some family estates on the Brenta.

I know of no existing portrait, such as that of the Russian kadine Roxelane, by which we could gauge something of her beauty. But it is certain she enslaved the sultan to the exclusion of every other woman. It was for love of her, I like to think and maintain, that he built that perfect room known as Sultan Murad's Bedchamber. Admittedly this sultan ended up with an enormous harem and left 103 children, though that was at the end of his days, and owing to the machinations of his mother, jealous of Safieh's ascendancy over her son. But for many years Safieh reigned supreme, and it was her son, Mohammed III, who succeeded as sultan, and, in turn, her machinations which disposed so ruthlessly of any possible rivals. It was, no doubt, also through her influence that the Italian Domenico Hierosolimitano was appointed a court physician — an unimaginable innovation in this closed world.

I imagine the young Safieh in her Venetian girlhood as one of those smooth-faced blonde beauties such as Carpaccio painted, sunning themselves on a roof-top terrace, bleaching their long crimped golden hair in the summer sunshine. Carpaccio's models were the courtesans of Venice, but most noble women also repaired to the rooftops for the same purpose. Golden hair — that particular reddish gold which Venetian painters and notably Tintoretto immortalised — was especially prized, and said to be maintained not only by regular exposure to sunlight but by assiduous applications of urine.

Daughters of the princely families and courtesans alike shared much the same setting; over several centuries the scene changed little. The frieze of tall, funnel-like chimneys, so characteristic of Venice, was always there. The terraces were embellished with pots of tall carnations, laurel and bay. There were pets to tease: skinny Italian greyhounds or those small, fluffy, muff-like dogs that are everywhere in paintings of the period; and peacocks, strutting and shrieking, or apes, chained by jewelled belts. The women wear stiff brocaded gowns, their sleeves puffed and slashed. Their hair is unbound, or plaited with pearls, or sometimes confined by a little meshed cap. They read poetry to each other, embroider silks, whisper of smuggled loveletters and wonder what the future holds for them... girls' talk everywhere. It is a serene and softly flowing life, quiet as the still green canals below. How overwhelming that destiny must have seemed, which flung the young Safieh into the Seraglio.

Her beauty and that warm nectarine and gold colouring of the Venetian woman would have attracted immediate attention there, and very soon she was singled out for the sultan's attention — probably by no less a personage than the Sultane Validé Nur Banu, mother of Sultan Murad, who was herself of Venetian origin. The convenience of placing a fellow countrywoman beside the sultan, and through her, acquiring even more influence, must have struck Nur Banu Sultane, for she was a woman of implacable ambitions, prototype of those who made the Reign of the Women notorious.

By tradition, it was the Sultane Validé who, on the Night of Power, at Bairam, personally selected the virgin whom she conducted in state to her son's bed, in the expectation that his ardours, agreeably renewed after long abstinence, would ensure a lusty heir. The trembling aspirant was always well coached: she knew that she must approach Allah's Shadow on Earth with proper humility; it is said, by entering the imperial bed symbolically, from the foot only, inching up by degrees. Etiquette even here, between the sheets. No doubt Safieh Baffo followed this formalised beginning to her days of love and power.

Let us look now at the setting of her life. This room, an expression of romantic genius, was conceived by Sinan Agha, supreme architect of Ottoman glories, of the greatest mosques and secular buildings of the sixteenth century. He was of Greek origin, but brought up in Turkey. He considered himself wholly Turkish, and his work, breaking from Seldjuk traditions, came to embody the purest Ottoman style. He worked for three successive sultans: first for Sulieman the Magnificent, then his son, Selim I, and last, his grandson, Murad III. During those reigns he built a large number of mosques, among the loveliest being the Sokölumehmet Paçha, the Rustem Pasha, and, greatest of all, those at Edirne. His particular genius was to unite the noblest proportions with a sense of intimacy. This is particularly apparent in the Mosque of Rustem Pasha, where colour, the glowing, almost carpet-like intricacies of tilework and decoration imparts a special richness.

A mosque, it should be remembered, is not a consecrated building in the sense of a Christian church. There is a subtle difference. It is the house of Allah — as sacred, but more personal, more approachable, open by day and night, not only for prayer but for shelter, repose and contemplation; study too, for students are often to be seen there, quite apart from the *medressa*, or theological college, usually attached to the mosque. In the house of Allah, the poorest outcast finds hospitality — a place of refuge — of beauty and luxury too. Here, cool fountains, exquisite *faience*, fine lamps and carpets, often beyond price, surround him, as they do the sultan in his palace. Such is Allah's hospitality.

When Sinan Agha designed Sultan Murad's room he seems to have been inspired by some special grace, as if he were aware that he was building for love rather than majesty. For all its stateliness, this room retains, to an extraordinary degree, a sense of emotion, as opposed to the sensuality of the kiosks. It is a secret enclosure 'in palace chambers far apart'. Sinan Agha probably built this room when he was rebuilding much of the Seraglio after the fire which ravaged the earlier palace in 1574. It lies at the heart of the *haremlik*, as it were, embedded in successive layers of mystery, secrecy and silence; and is reached either through the Corridor Where The Djinns Hold Consultation, or by the majestic Vestibule of the Fountain, also by Sinan's hand.

But nothing prepares one for the impact of Sultan Murad's room. Crossing the threshold, it is as if the curtain has risen on some marvellous dramatic scene. 'An Eastern Tale of Enchantment' such as the young Disraeli evoked in his letters from Turkey, yet having nothing of such tinselled pantomime. This is drama, all romance, with some bold, almost barbaric flavour, which gives it force and passion.

> Act 1. *Scene 1*: The Corridor of Consultation with the Djinns
>   *Scene 2*: The Vestibule of the Fountain
>   *Scene 3*: The Bedroom of Sultan Murad

And the cast? Grand Turk, Venetian kadine, viziers, courtiers, black eunuchs, dwarfs, djinns, attendant slaves and guards... How well it lends itself to the idiom of the theatre. And since, as has been told, clothing was regulated according to the rank and occupation of the wearer, scarlet for an admiral, sable for a vizier, and so on, it has been rightly remarked that the history of Constantinople was in fact a costume drama.

The Corridor Where The Djinns Hold Consultation is as ominous as its name, narrow and stone-flagged; on one side its thickly barred windows give on to an inner court beside the Kefés, and from where, no doubt, a wan face was sometimes to be seen – one of the incarcerated princes peering out for a sight of that world he must never know. On the inside wall of the corridor, a door, heavily barred and bolted but beautifully worked with inlays of pearl and ivory and a great damascened lock, led to the *haremlik*, the kadine's quarters and outer cells of the honeycomb. In the sombre beauty of the Vestibule of the Fountain, those few privileged persons summoned to the sultan's presence in his private apartments were set to wait his pleasure. Although Sultan Murad's bedroom was always known as such, it also served as a living room, in the turnabout Eastern system already discussed.

Two vast *lits à baldaquin*, the canopied beds which served as such, or as thrones, are the dominant feature, and have given the room its name. They are placed symmetrically flanking a huge chimney piece, hooded in bronze, one of those tall, pointed, helmet-shaped structures, the *achmak*, found in old Turkish houses and recalling the headgear of Asiatic conquerors. Reminding us, too, that behind all the outward Ottoman luxuries lies a Mongol past, harsh as the wind that howls down from the Asiatic hinterland beyond the Black Sea. The size of this hearth would reduce tree trunks to firewood proportions. In such a gaping maw logs were habitually placed upright, so that the upward draught kept smoke from belching out into the room. The canopied beds are carved and gilded, and must once have been spread with innumerable cushions. Their hangings, or some similar ones used elsewhere in the Seraglio are described as being particularly magnificent, 'of black Velvet, with an Embroydery of great Pearls, whereof some are long and others round, and in the form of Buttons… There is another of white Velvet set out with Rubies and Emeralds… a third of a Violet coloured Velvet, embroyder'd with Turquoises and Pearls'.

The posts supporting the *baldaquins* were gilded and painted, and also worked with precious stones, the curtains roped back with swags of pearls, while coverlets of tufted velvet or cloth-of-gold lined with lynx or sable were flung about among the cushions. Even without these furnishings, or the wonderful carpets, Ouchaks, Karabaghs or Konias to make the mouth water, this room is never bleak in its present abandonment. The textures of its lost glories are still sensed, for with all its spacious splendour there is warmth and harmony too. The soaring ceiling is domed, yet it does not seem remote, for the walls rise to meet it without straining, their lofty proportions, which might chill, are rendered intimate, or brought to living level by a deep gilded dado of Koranic inscriptions which circle the entire room and are set above panels of superb *faience*. Almond blossom, carnations or tulips bloom here on a background of burning blue, edged with that thread of coral red which is the signature of *faience* made at Iznik, the old Nicaea. There are double rows of windows: those placed high – very high, above the dado and almost merging with the dome – do not shed that chilling top-light found in studios, for they have panes of jewel-coloured glass and cast pools of colour on the stone floor, though since this was certainly once criss-crossed with carpets overlaid one on another in that prodigal fashion peculiar to the East, the shafts of light streaming down from the windows must have overlaid colour on colour most sumptuously. The lower lines of windows are deeply embrasured and typify those low-set, door-like apertures, almost at ground level, which are so significant a feature of Eastern architecture, whether domestic or religious.

Such low placed windows, precursors of the modern picture window, always remind me of the raised tent flap in encampments, where the desert's rim is ever visible to those inside. It was from such nomads, roaming the steppes, that the pattern of living and so many tenets of Eastern taste developed. Thus in the Seraglio, as in so many other Oriental palaces, notably those of Moghul splendour, for all its luxury and apparent sophistication, some lavish disorder or wildness lurks. This is the careless, open freedom of a desert or steppe encampment, extravagance beside harshness. The tents of Genghis Khan were of leopard skins lined with ermine.

Throughout the arid East, water is regarded as the ultimate luxury, venerated for its scarcity and man's thirst. The finest gesture of hospitality is to offer a glass of pure water, while fountains and pools obtain almost mystical qualities. Thus, in placing a wide, three-tiered marble fountain stretching the length of one wall in Sultan Murad's room, Sinan Agha set the seal of splendour and pleasure on this room. Curiously, although Constantinople is not a city of great heat and is surrounded by water and green forests where springs abound, the element is apotheosised in the number and beauty of its street fountains. Some are set exquisitely under gilded eaves, some behind lace-like marble grilles; some gush from porphyry basins in the courtyards of mosques, or beside the entrance to a hammam. Everywhere such hammams, known loosely as Turkish baths, have an element of the temple about them, where the rituals and worship of water prevails. The image of water is found translated into many terms: in the Anatolian cemetery rugs of tradition, which were taken to the cemetery upon which to pray beside the tomb, and to picnic, too, for graveside feasts with the departed's favourite foods were *de rigueur*. Such rugs are all woven with a blue ribbon of water, a stream, traced round the flowers and cypress trees representing the Gardens of Paradise. Nor do the mourners forget the birds, for Turkish graves often have a little scooped-out hollow where dew collects, and where the birds may drink their fill... Water everywhere, life-giving water, treasured and symbolised in many ways, in mosques or palaces, sacred or profane... Those fabulous diamond sprays that tremble on fine gold wires, a typically Turkish type of jewellery — surely these too were inspired by showers of raindrops, dewdrops, or the jet of a fountain?

Thus in Sultan Murad's room it is the fountain – the marvellous wall fountain – which is the supreme symbol of luxury. Two tiers of white marble stretch almost the entire length of the wall facing the throne beds, and each tier is set with a row of nine bronze taps, so that cascades of water fall in a shimmering curtain. Moreover, each tap is contrived to sound a different note, thus making a sort of liquid symphony to lull the sultan's slumbers. Here moonlight, starlight or firelight glittered across the water as it fell, or shafts of sunlight from the jewel-coloured windows above played over it in rainbow arcs. Here is a setting worthy of true love. Here the silences and sighs of passion must have lost themselves in the shadowy dome, or sunk, muffled by the murmuring splash of the fountain. Here the sultan and his Italian kadine lived becalmed, shut away from the terrors and tragedies of the Seraglio, indifferent to the extravagance of their setting, perhaps, but figures of unparalleled magnificence themselves. Veronese should have painted them in all their splendour.

I like to imagine the scene and the figures for whom this pleasance was made. They are couched among the tufted velvets and lynx skins. Sultan Murad is a bearded, beetle-browed, long-nosed man, his gigantic turban, heron-plumed, is laid aside, like his jewelled dagger, as he puffs at his turquoise-studded *tchibouk* and fondles the woman at his side. He wears the traditional caftan or surcoat, which changed little through thirty successive sultanships, only in the nineteenth century giving place to the Western frock-coat, or Stambouline, as its local variation was known. Caftans were always monstrously stiff and heavy, in cut velvet and brocades, often lined with sable and fastened by a line of jewelled clasps.

It was the custom to preserve all the garments and state robes of the Ottoman sultans. They were parcelled, listed, and preserved in the treasury of the Seraglio, from the fifteenth century onwards. This marvellous record contains bloodstained caftans, telling of violence, as well as the whole art and development of Turkish silk weaving. Upon each sultan's death, their clothes were packed in numbers of wax cloth wrappers and labelled with both precision and veneration. For example: 'The garments of His Majesty the Deceased Sultan Osman the Ghazi Victorious, unto whom all sins are forgiven. In three wrappers.' Many of these sultans' robes are to be seen in the Seraglio museum – tremendous garments which, topped by towering turbans, gave the impression of having clothed a race of giants. Their stiff, cut velvets and brocades, weighted further by jewelled embroideries, were of Seljuk weaving, and later came from Bursa looms. Against the chill, some were fur-lined, some wadded with raw silk, for the cold of winter in Constantinople was penetrating. To the Greeks, Turkey was 'the land beyond the north wind', and no doubt, compared to Hellenic azures, they saw its pearly skies and vaporous clouds as an overcast grey. Odalisques and kadines were perhaps sometimes compelled to appear naked beneath their gauzy *chalvari*, those bouffant trousers known as Turkish, but sultans, viziers and such are always portrayed in comfortably padded garments.

Thus I see Sultan Murad resplendent in his blue shot-silk under-caftan (now preserved in the treasury) printed with gold and silver circles, the lining embroidered with crescents. Over this he wears a violet-coloured caftan of *kemha*, velvet brocade, woven with gold thread. Its lining is of sable, and the sleeves of his undershirt emerald-green taffeta. His feet are thrust into yellow leather slippers; his hands are heavily ringed, and while the buttons of his outer caftan are diamonds, the size of gooseberries, those of his undercaftan are gigantic sapphires.

Beside him, Safieh Sultane, as splendidly arrayed. She sits cross-legged, so that her crimson taffeta *chalvari* emerge from beneath a flowing lemon-coloured damask robe, or *entari*, the basic garment of every Turkish woman of quality, worn loose over undershifts and tunics, its sleeves trailing almost to the floor. It is buttoned with topazes, and belted by a wide, heavy girdle, a mosaic of precious stones, the stomacher clasp fashioned of enormous diamonds. Her gauze chemise is left open to the waist, revealing her breasts; between them dangle chains of pearls and rubies. The loose sleeves of the *entari* fall back from the gauze sleeves of her chemise, and on each wrist there are bracelets without number. Her feet are bare, and tinted with henna. On her head she wears the traditional *talpock*, a little flat round tasselled cap, studded with pearls and worn rakishly to one side. On the other side, pinned to her hair, a large aigrette of diamonds springs from a brooch which is marvellously contrived to represent a bouquet, a typical Turkish style, with ruby roses, pearl buds, emerald leaves, diamond dewdrops and other such opulent conceits. Her long blonde hair is left unbound, and falls over her shoulders in a molten shower where diamonds glitter, for they are attached to fine gold chains threaded through her locks. She is painted in the bold manner of the Seraglio, her lips crimsoned, her eyes darkened by kohl, and her eyebrows marked emphatically, being joined in one ebony sweep, for this is the fashion from Samarcand to Cairo. We must hope, in the interests of romance, that her teeth were not also blackened in that manner admired and followed for some centuries by ladies of the *haremlik*.

She holds a lute of Venetian workmanship, tulipwood inlaid with ivory, but now she puts it aside and turns towards her lord and master. On a signal from the sultan, a eunuch steps forward and draws the silk curtains round the throne which, on the instant, becomes their bed. Eunuch, pages and buffoons steal away; it is quite silent in that great room: only the shift of smouldering logs and the faint music of the fountain sounds. Moonlight streams down from the high windows above, and outside, silvers the dark spears of the cypress groves where there are nightingales. Firelight, moonlight, birdsong and the sound of a fountain… Such was the pavilion Sinan had devised for these lovers.

Conjuring them in their paradise, it does not do to remember the sour finish to such a love, yet it came to pass. After many years, Safieh Sultane's influence became such that Murad would make no decisions of any kind without her approval, and his mother, the redoubtable Sultane Validé Nur Banu, determined to end the idyll. She succeeded, at last, by acquiring numbers of the most lovely slaves imaginable, virgins of such voluptuous promise and variety that even Murad's single-minded devotion wavered and, at last, vanished. He spent his remaining years in ceaseless debauch, a puppet at his mother's command.

Safieh Sultane, whose character remains obscure, but who, we suspect, was first of all ambitious, accepted her banishment philosophically (which is not the sign of true love) and turned to politics – particularly fostering good relations between Venice and the Sublime Porte. She was in correspondence with the Doges and ambassadors, and also with Catherine de Medici. She does not appear to have made any effort to obtain her release from the Seraglio or return to Venice, so we must assume the power game was, at heart, her chosen way of life. Perhaps she had never really loved Murad, or loved better the power she obtained through him. And then, there was her son, the future Mohammed III, whose position, and accession, was forever shadowed by rival brothers and half-brothers: there must be no weakness. Murad's frenetic sensuality had produced over a hundred children, many of them male. Were any one of these to obtain power, she, Safieh Sultane, would never obtain the long-desired position of Sultane Validé. It was evident that she must allow no supine sentiment on Mohammed's part to undermine her plans. When Sultan Murad died and his son was proclaimed successor, there is little doubt that it was Safieh Sultane who steeled him to the frightful holocaust which followed. Nineteen of his brothers were strangled by the ceremonial bowstring, and seven of his father's pregnant concubines (big with possible claimants) were drowned off Seraglio Point, again with due ceremony. Thus the way was clear for Mohammed as Sultan, and for his mother, Safieh Sultane, to become Sultane Validé, Crown of the Veiled Heads, ruler within the *haremlik*, and soon, beyond. Following in the footsteps of her predecessor Nur Banu Sultane, she continued the supply of lovely slaves, thus keeping her son besotted and befuddled, the better to rule as she pleased.

Yet that game of love and power Safieh Baffo knew how to play with such ruthlessness could also be played by others. One day she was found strangled in her bed, that sumptuous bed in the Sultane Validé's quarters which, for many years, she had occupied in triumph, as once she had triumphed in Sultan Murad's bed. I prefer to think of her as she had been then: the Venetian kadine, forever 'emparadised' in Murad's arms... the Grand Signor and his golden favourite, the perfect lovers in the perfect setting, Sinan's own.

Aurélie Picard: A Saharan Idyll

Stendhal was snugly installed in a northern Italian consulate when he wrote his celebrated dicta on love; but he was emphatic. 'It is in the half-light of the Bedouin Arab tent that one must seek the model of true love.' Although he never budged from the straitjacket of polite European living himself, he seems to have been aware of that curious climate of fervent sensuality and extreme discretion, spiced with a wildness to match the surrounding deserts, which has proved so irresistible to generations of Western persons of romantic inclination, particularly the English, both men and women. Like the pine tree of Heine's poem, they dream, on their northern shore, of some faraway palm — until, one day, sweet chance leads their steps abroad, and they are enthralled for evermore. There must have been, over the centuries, uncounted numbers of crusaders, travellers and traders, besides the raiding corsairs and even their captives, who, finding themselves in the half-light of the black tents, took root there and never returned to the West.

Such was the case of Aurélie Picard, a little provincial French girl who was to become known as Lallah Yamina, la Princesse des Sables, a power in the Sahara and all across Algeria, a woman upon whom the French authorities, both civil and military, came to rely in their endeavours to achieve their 'pacific penetration' of the Sahara and to be accepted, in particular, by the Tedjanis, one of the most fanatic religious confraternities of North Africa. It was the Sahara which became the passion of Aurélie Picard's life, so that Kourdane, the fabled domain which, under her hands, sprang from the desert, became the pavilion which held her heart to the exclusion of every other thing, or person.

Her life of love and adventure begins in a small, glum provincial town, Montigny-le-Roi, in northern France, where she was born in 1849. Her father served under General Bugeaud in the French conquest of Algeria. At the end of his service he joined the local gendarmerie at Montigny, while eking out his meagre means giving riding lessons. On his retirement, the family moved to another grey little town, Arc-en-Barrois, where, with so many younger brothers and sisters to be fed, Aurélie went out to work at fifteen. She was neat-fingered and quick, and soon made herself indispensable to the milliner to whom she was apprenticed. At night she returned home to more work, washing and mending for the family; a pinched existence. Aurélie dreamed of escape to glowing horizons; where, she could not define. The only colour in her life was when her father recounted his adventures in North Africa. She listened, rapt, to stories of the desert slashed by a line of charging Arab warriors; of Moorish palaces, of blazing stars and mysterious deserts — a world very far from her own.

To study the pattern of Aurélie Picard's life is to believe in destiny. Over and over again we find this recurring intervention of fate, bringing her undreamed-of chances. It has been said that character plus chance brings fortune. Aurélie's character was both audacious and tenacious, and she never missed a chance. Fate's first appearance was in the classic guise of the fairy godmother. Aurélie had quit the milliner's establishment to better herself as housekeeper in the château of Arc-en-Barrois, property of the Prince de Joinville, but leased to a *député* of the Haute Marne, a Monsieur Steenackers. His wife took a fancy to the girl, and soon Aurélie found herself installed as her *dame de compagnie*.

It was the open door she had craved. In these easy circumstances she set about improving herself. She read studiously and was able to ride the fine horses in the stables, for she was already a good horsewoman, having profited by her father's tuition. Above all, while learning to set off her natural good looks by an acquired polish, she was observing the general style of those around her, so that, one chance leading to another, when the decisive turning-point of her life came, she was ready.

It came in 1871 heralded by gunfire — the cannons of the Franco-Prussian war.

And now the scene changes from northern France to Bordeaux, glowing among vineyarded hills, its mellow elegance set beside the wide waters of the Garonne. Here the provisional government settled, having removed from beleaguered Paris. Monsieur Steenackers, now *directeur général des postes*, followed the provisional government, and he and his family were lodged in a hotel reserved for persons of consequence. Aurélie accompanied them, leaving behind her forever the pinched existence of her family at Arc-en-Barrois. And if her new life did not, as yet, compass the glowing horizons of her dreams, it was no longer drab.

At this moment, almost the only means of communication with Paris was by carrier-pigeon, messages being sent regularly to and from the besieged capital by this means. In his official capacity as *directeur général des postes*, Monsieur Steenackers received all such messages, but at whatever hour they arrived, the pigeons were first brought to Aurélie, who detached the tiny cylinders and took them to him. She was also allotted care of the birds, and so it happened that one day, as she stood among the swooping, muttering, pecking multitude, an impressive figure in Arab dress approached, staring intently. He was a romantic-looking fellow, very dark-skinned, his face framed in a short black beard, his costume magnificent. A dark burnous was flung over another white one, and that over a white robe belted with a silk scarf, through which was thrust a jewel-handled dagger. His boots were of soft crimson leather spurred with gold, and pinned to his robe were a number of orders and decorations, some of which Aurélie recognised as French. As he approached her, wafts of some heady perfume accompanied him, so that he seemed to move in a special aura of exoticism.

This remarkable personage was surrounded by an entourage of guards, black slaves, courtiers and interpreters who waited obsequiously at his heels. Next day, and for several days following, he reappeared, always silent, always fixing Aurélie with a gaze at once romantic and incredulous, as if contemplating some celestial vision. And perhaps this *Roumia* (or European), so fair-skinned and surrounded by the pigeons which are venerated by Moslems as sacred, did indeed seem such.

By now Aurélie had recognised her admirer as the Prince Si Ahmed Tedjani, a young Arab ruler from southern Algeria who, with his half-brother, Si Bachir, had been for some time of absorbing interest to all Bordeaux, object of the most flattering attentions in governmental circles, even being given a standing ovation when attending the opera from the préfet's box. Public enthusiasm knew no bounds, for the brothers were representatives of such of the feudal Arab chiefs who now offered their allegiance and material support to the hard-pressed French. Not so long ago, the French had been their invaders, overcoming, at last, the great Arab leader, Abd-el-Kader, but that was the past. Abd-el-Kader was in honourable exile in Damascus, and the French were accepted by most of the Algerian leaders as a chivalrous ex-army worthy to guide (if not wholly subdue) them. Curiously, most Algerians, while still straining at the leash, found French domination − if domination was Allah's will, as it then seemed − infinitely preferable to the abhorred Turkish yoke, even though the Turks were their co-religionists. But the Kabyle revolts were still causing much bloodshed, and Algeria was far from calm.

Si Ahmed's background was as exotic as his appearance. He was the child of a Sudanese slave girl and the shareef of the Tedjanis − the mighty Prince Si Mohammed-Seghir, the marabout and absolute ruler of the Tedjanis, a religious sect, one of many, throughout northern Africa. The slave girl, though *enceinte* by the prince, had left his harem to follow another master, a not unusual procedure in that age of slave traffic and quickly satiated masters. She vanished and nothing more would ever have been heard of her, or her child, had not Si Mohammed-Seghir died suddenly, leaving from among all his wives and concubines only one sickly baby son. (His fourteen daughters were of no account: 'I have three children − and two daughters,' a Moslem father of five will tell you.) The Tedjani nobles were uneasy that their dynasty rested with one frail boy, and when it was remembered that the slave girl was said to have borne a son, they dispatched messengers in search of her. When at last she and her child were found, it was a robust little boy of seven who was brought back in triumph to the *zaouïa*, to be installed in state beside his half-brother, the weakling Si Bachir.

Between them the two princes were co-heirs to the absolute power and glory accorded shareefs. Such hereditary princes were of a special religious nobility, invested with spiritual as well as temporal power. They were marabouts, seen as saints who, in however secular a manner they lived, were still holy, venerated figures, their *bordj*, or *ksar* dwelling being not only a fortress, but also the *zaouïa*, monastery and sanctuary, with mosques, theological college and almshouses within the complex. The great doors were always open to pilgrims and the needy who, by tradition, must be lodged and fed for three days: often, the blind or dying came there, and were never turned away. These confraternities might be likened to powerful Masonic lodges − but fanatic too. Since the shareefs wielded enormous influence among the Arabs throughout

North Africa, their goodwill was of paramount importance to the French or any rare person venturing into the unmapped interior.

This, then, was the puissant figure whom Aurélie Picard had captivated and was to subjugate entirely, first by her blonde charms, and, later, by her force of character. To begin with, the courtship hung fire, for they had no common language, and no doubt the presence of an interpreter was stultifying to one so passionately enamoured as the prince. Aurélie met his advances with the downcast eyes and missish deportment then *de rigueur*. But her modest calm concealed a turmoil of hopes and fears. Here before her stood the means of realising her wildest dreams. Demure and unattainable, she launched an occasional death-dealing glance from beneath her long lashes, and the prince could think of nothing else. Accompanied by his suite (and a lagging brother, for Si Bachir already gauged and feared this infidel's ascendancy), the prince made a formal call on Madame Steenackers to ask Aurélie's price. He was prepared to pay anything for such a treasure – absolutely anything.

'But Aurélie is not a slave,' replied the astonished Madame Steenackers. 'She is not for sale.'

The prince is said to have paled visibly, until the *député*'s wife explained that Aurélie could however be *married*.

'So be it,' replied the prince, inclining ceremoniously. If such was the *Roumi* custom, he would marry Mademoiselle Picard. At once. Now. Tonight! It was with difficulty he was edged away to his own apartments. In agitation the Steenackers sent for Aurélie's father. In agitation they awaited his arrival, for Aurélie had announced she would accept the prince's proposal. By now the household was in a ferment. All Bordeaux talked of this extravagant romance.

Spurred on by love and, no doubt, a wish to dispense with the restraining presence of the interpreter, the prince was making rapid progress with his French, though his exotic reputation and the splendid jewels he wore, and now lavished on Aurélie, must have been as powerful an argument as any words to the girl from Arc-en-Barrois. In any case, Aurélie's mind was made up. It was useless for anyone to counsel prudence: she was going to seize this incredible chance. Also, she had begun to recognise a depth of sincerity in the prince's protestations of devotion and recognised, perhaps, how her own feelings for him were growing. Above all, it was through him she would be able to reach that Africa which her father's stories had evoked so tantalisingly.

It was decided that the marriage should take place in Algiers, under French law, as her father stipulated. When the prince and his suite sailed from Marseilles, Aurélie and Monsieur Picard were with them. At that time Algiers was only a huddle of French barracks and military headquarters grouped round the harbour where the new European town was rising beside the cathedral. Behind, like some fantastic backcloth for a pantomime — *Ali Baba and the Forty Thieves* — wound the steep cut-throat alleys of the kasbah, fastness of Arab and Moor, once stronghold of Barbarossa's corsairs, and where, still, strangers seldom ventured. Although there were no more impaled bodies on the city's walls, nor decapitated heads spiked on the great gates, Algiers retained an air of ill-concealed violence. All around lay wild scrub country, mountain gorges and high plateaux, barely begun to be cultivated by the French. Three hundred miles south, on the first expanses of the Sahara, lay Aïn Mahdi, the Tedjani *zaouïa* destined to be Aurélie's home.

In Algiers, preparations for a spectacular marriage were set in train. The entire Picard family, who had now followed Aurélie and her father, and were treated by Si Ahmed as his own people, were installed in a splendid Arab house he had acquired for them. Here Aurélie began to learn some Arabic. Already she loved the graceful, unhurried life in this beautiful old arcaded house with its fountained patios, its shimmering blue and green tilework lining the cool dim rooms shaded from the glare by their fretted *moucharabiyeh*. The few but rich pieces of furniture, low tables and coffers, were of cedarwood inlaid with mother-of-pearl; the hanging lamps were of chased silver, and the divans were deep in cushions and rugs. All round the walls, above the dado of tiles, numbers of elaborate gilt-framed mirrors of varying sizes, of Italian or Spanish origin, were hung at a curious, forward tilt which was a general practice in sophisticated Arabic interiors, where everything is scaled, or arranged for the horizontal, rather than vertical observer. Like the low-silled windows, making it possible for the lollers on the divans to see out easily, so the forward-slanted mirrors reflect downwards, and are thus enjoyed by those below. Musk and sandalwood perfumed the rooms, and countless slaves were always at hand, bringing trays of strange and spiced foods, or filling the coffers with more and more of the sumptuous trappings which were to adorn Aurélie as the prince's bride.

But suddenly this agreeable life was shattered. The French Governor-General refused to sanction a Franco-Arab union. There was no provision for such in French law. He was obdurate and unsympathetic. Did this Arab dare…? All the Picards' pleadings fell on deaf ears. Aurélie wept and the prince raged, threatening to raise a Tedjani insurrection. But officialdom remained adamant. Aurélie, too, remained firm. Marriage or nothing. The deadlock dragged on miserably, until at last she faced a humiliating return to Arc-en-Barrois where the pitying or spiteful looks of the neighbours were an unbearable prospect, especially after a foretaste of life as the prince's wife. She pleaded with her family for more time… Now the Picards turned obstinate. Their daughter could not go round Algiers begging for the right to some native's favours! They would sail on the next ship, and all the jewels must be returned.

Aurélie wept; the prince pleaded. While the arguments and protestations continued, fate stepped in once more: this time, in no less a guise than Cardinal Lavigerie, the Archbishop of Algiers, who was just beginning his great missionary work in North Africa. He was at once visionary and practical; the story of the thwarted lovers interested him. He had noticed the downcast girl who came to pray in his church, and took pity on her situation. In these lovers he saw the embodiment of his ideals for Franco-Arab unity. Cardinal Lavigerie, it will be remembered, founded the Pères Blancs, and his hopes for a pacific penetration of the Sahara were later put into practice by such great figures as Maréchal Lyautey, the Père de Foucauld, and even, in a lesser degree, by Aurélie herself. The cardinal sent for Si Ahmed. Sensing that this ardent young prince could be transformed into either a powerful ally or an implacable enemy, he promised on certain conditions to perform the marriage himself. Sour French officials warned Aurélie she would forfeit her birthright, and that she could no longer look to them if things went wrong. Shrugging, they turned away. But the prince was overcome with gratitude and gave his word to the archbishop. He would marry Aurélie in the Christian manner, as his only wife. From that moment he was always to prove himself loyal to France, always to aid Aurélie in her efforts to further French influences, and to promote peaceful relations.

The simple marriage ceremony was performed by the cardinal in his chapel of Saint Eugene, but the Arab festivities were grandiose, and lasted a week at fever pitch. Night after night fireworks illuminated the sky, hour after hour the musicians made their seducing yet exacerbating music of *derboulka* and *rhaïta* (drum and flute) while the Ouled Naïl dancers postured and swayed in their ritual frenzies, their gold-coined, feathered headdresses glittering in the torchlight, their breasts shuddering and their bellies undulating, their snake-like gestures inviting in the age-old pantomimes of desire. Arab notables had gathered from all over the country, from Morocco and Tunis too, to honour Si Ahmed and his strange *Roumia* bride. But the French colony banged their shutters closed, and predicted disaster.

Then on a morning in late September a great cortège formed outside Si Ahmed's house. The Tedjanis were escorting their shareef and his bride back to Aïn Mahdi. The camels were loaded up with all the baggage of tents and rugs, provisions and cooking utensils and painted coffers topped by Aurélie's European trunks and hat boxes. As the bride, she should have followed her lord and master in a *basour*, one of those close-curtained litters slung across a camel that lurch and heave at every slow step. These are the traditional mode of travel for Arab women. But with that strange instinct which always guided her in her dealings with the Arabs, Aurélie now took her stand. No *basour*, no veils, no traditions for her. She would begin as she meant to go on – of, yet apart from, this Arab world. It was an astute move, for it emphasised her rarity. The enraptured prince could refuse her nothing. Mounted on a white Arab mare saddled in velvet with coral and silver trappings, Aurélie rode out to meet her future, unveiled, *beside*, and not following, her husband.

The journey took nearly a month, for at that time there were no roads and the caravan moved slowly under a devouring sun by day and in an icy grip by night, towards glittering mirages and through blinding storms, such as the dreaded *adjedj*, like some terrible madness or rage of nature, when the sky suddenly blackens and a fierce, suffocating wind lashes round, uprooting tents and terrifying horses and camels while the sands surge like tormented waves. After a matter of hours, or days, a sudden stillness falls, and the *adjedj* is no more. Then a sunrise or sunset of ineffable beauty suffuses everything, and the desert seems reborn.

With each mile, Aurélie fell deeper under the spell of this ardent, yet immobile land. Such characteristics were found again in its inhabitants, lounging, sleeping, going silently about their business, yet, behind the langour, a reserve of force, an animal vitality seldom unleashed – the panther's spring. She noted it all.

At evening, when the tents were pitched and the camels were couched, snarling and grumbling, the loneliness of the wastes that closed round seemed lonelier for the eerie cry of the jackals, answered by the dogs slinking round the campfires. How far, how very far, now, from Arc-en-Barrois; yet, how rapturously happy she was in this new life.

Aurélie's tent was an elaborate affair with all the hangings and cushions of those sultry interiors Delacroix loved to paint. Yet behind the luxury, the voluptuous mood, dangers lurked. Before the tents could be pitched, the ground had first to be prepared by being thrashed vigorously, to scare off lurking snakes or scorpions, as fires were lit to keep off the wild beasts that prowled near. (At that time there were still a few lions as far north as the Djebel Amour range.) But Aurélie was only aware of the beauty and romance of her new existence. On this journey, which might be considered her honeymoon with the prince, she was in fact consummating her love for the desert. And when the huge stars glittered low, and the prince lay beside her, furiously loving, there was a rival: the desert. It already possessed Aurélie – the desert, rather than a man: but any means, or any man, bringing her closer to it must be made to serve her purpose. Thus Aurélie, a woman possessed, possessing.

It was now that she began to realise the full mystical significance of her husband's shareefian title, and the degree of veneration in which he was held. In Bordeaux he had appeared a princely figure of international importance. In Algiers, a *grand seigneur* accorded special prestige among so many other Arab nobles. But now she perceived another side. At each halt along the way, at the wells or by the *douras*, the black tent encampments of the nomads, they swarmed round to kiss the hem of his robes, to prostrate themselves or clutch at his stirrup, imploring the *baraka* or maraboutic blessing which he was divinely endowed to bestow. Si Ahmed was of the noblest shareefian blood which, in Islam, ranks higher than any other, for he traced his ancestry back to Idriss, son of Fatma Zorah, the Prophet's daughter. His was an unassailable position. Aurélie knew she must, at all costs, maintain not only her hold on him but win the loyalty of his followers, the Tedjani, too. Were she to fail, banishment from this land she already loved without reserve would be inevitable.

At last, after passing El Aghouat and threading their way through a landscape of menacing aridity, they came in sight of Aïn Mahdi. Forbidding and splendid, the massive watchtowers and twelve-foot thick walls of the *zaouïa* rose out of the desert. Before the huge iron-studded doors a vast throng had gathered to welcome their shareef, and now rode out, charging forward in clouds of dust, standing in their stirrups, firing their guns, hurling them high in the air, twirling them round their heads and performing all the spectacular feats of the Arab fantasia.

Along the battlements, like some frieze of doom, Aurélie made out a line of veiled women: they were shrilling their *zahrit*, that high, ululating cry which signifies joy, and can be, too, a war cry, inciting the men to battle. It is peculiar to women of the Arab world, from Mahgreb to the Yemen. The women on the battlements were Si Ahmed's wives and concubines. They had been waiting three years for their lord's return, and were now united in their intention to destroy the newcomer, by any means.

Such means were not lacking, for poisons and spells abounded. There were black magics and white, incantations to bring back a strayed lover, to render a rival sterile, to ensure the birth of a son, or the death of a rival's child... frightful potions, such as one quoted to me long ago when in these regions. It was, if I remember rightly, designed to undermine a rival's *ménage*, and one can well believe it might, since it was composed of seven crushed beetles, the droppings of a crow, the pincers of seven scorpions, seven stones from an abandoned tomb, the urine of an aged Jewess, the whiskers of a cat, an ass's bone, mastic and oleander leaves, and a fragment of the shroud in which a corpse had lain overnight in his dwelling (a rarity in Moslem communities, where burial usually takes place within a few hours of death). This fearsome mixture had to be prepared on one specific day, and then thrown across the designated victim's threshold while pronouncing a ritual incantation. After which, I was assured, the *ménage* was invariably destroyed.

It was practices such as these which Aurélie now faced, as well as equally alarming manifestations of nature at its most malign. Enormous bats, scorpions, venomous snakes and deadly black spiders were all part of domestic life in the shareefian *ksar*, as in humbler dwellings. However sumptuous Si Ahmed's possessions had seemed, his costumes and jewels, his weapons, horses and lifestyle, such as Aurélie had known in Algiers, Aïn Mahdi came as a rude awakening.

Besides having the frowning aspect of a fortress, there was that mixture of opulence and decay so typically Arab. It has been said that the desert Arabs possess *'le génie de la destruction'* – an atavistic hatred of permanence, of that which endures, so that the desert always creeps back unchecked to smother what is built, to seep through the cracks, rot woodwork and choke windows and doors. Only the tent survives.

So it was with Aïn Mahdi. Decay to the point of destruction was everywhere. Bats flapped in the falling rafters where the lovely painted ceilings had crumbled; doors hung on rusted hinges; rats had chewed the magnificent rugs and teased the stuffing out of the cushions strewn over the dusty floors; while in the courtyards the mammoth cauldrons used to feed the household, the slaves, and ceaseless flow of pilgrims who passed through the zaouïa were blackened with rancid grease. Even the koubbah, or mausoleum, of Si Ahmed's illustrious father was musty and neglected, and the green standards of the Prophet hung in tatters over his tomb. Only the fountains still lisped softly in the arcaded inner courts of the harem, softening its high-walled austerity. (An Arab wife must see only the sky and the walls of her house, is a local saying.) Here Aurélie was conducted in state, and waited, behind its heavily barred doors and windows, to be greeted by her new family, her mother-in-law, the former Sudanese slave-girl, and her fourteen sisters-in-law, daughters of Si Ahmed's father by another wife.

At once, as if invested with some occult faculties, or guided by some strange prescience, this inexperienced girl took control. At once, she began to set both harem and zaouïa to rights. First, the prince's wives and concubines were banished, pensioned off in honourable discharge, to live at El Aghouat, a discreet two days' journey distant. At once, her new family doted on her, the Sudanese mother-in-law and the fourteen sisters-in-law, like the slaves, marvelling as she opened the barred doors of the harem, coming and going as she pleased — and unveiled. The slaves — Dongolo negresses for the most part — scampered to do her bidding and the dignitaries of the zaouïa respected this Roumia on sight. Only her brother-in-law, Si Bachir, remained hostile, jealously observing her hold not only over Si Ahmed, but the entire complex of Aïn Mahdi. Curiously, when the harem left, Aurélie again showed that intuition or prescience which guided her in her new life. She could not know, at that moment, that she would remain childless, that again and again her hopes for an heir would be dashed. Yet, on her wish, a little boy, Si Ali, the prince's child by one of the concubines, remained at Aïn Mahdi, to be loved and brought up as her own.

Barren women are soon repudiated or slighted by Arab custom. Yet Aurélie's supremacy was never to be challenged by the Tedjanis. It was Allah's will that

Lallah Yamina, as they called her, should come to direct their lives, and it was Allah's will, too, she should be childless. She was a being apart, for both her adoring husband and his people.

At Aïn Mahdi, all Aurélie's French sense of thrift and good management was displayed. Soon, the withered gardens bloomed and household accounts tallied. The mystified slaves were initiated into the uses of a flat iron, and were to be seen laundering Aurélie's complicated underwear, the frilled petticoats, camisoles and drawers that were part of her trousseau, according to Arc-en-Barrois standards. She generally continued to wear European clothes, all buttons, basques and whalebone, for Si Ahmed now showed a marked preference for every manifestation of European living – including champagne, which was in defiance of Koranic vetoes. Though since he was so venerated, the faithful held that on his lips alcohol became milk, and any signs of excess were attributed to mystic exaltation.

Aurélie had brought with her, along with the flat iron, a number of her accustomed comforts, bed linen, knives and forks and such. Si Ahmed no longer ate with his fingers, crouched on rugs, nor slept in the fashion of his people, wherever sleep overtook him, on a divan or the floor, rolled in his burnous or a sheepskin. Bedrooms – rooms set apart for sleeping – were not customary in Arab households. But now he savoured to the full the thrilling novelties his *Roumia* wife introduced. Aurélie had turned one of the tile-dadoed rooms into her bedroom, and installed a double bed of strictly European design. Here, as soon as buttoned into her long-sleeved nightgown, and lying between her smooth linen sheets, she was joined by the enraptured Si Ahmed. Her deliberate emphasis on European ways may have begun by a wish for familiar comforts, but she must soon have realised how much prestige these foreign habits gave her, and so continued them, long after she would have preferred to adapt herself to many local traditions.

Which perhaps explains why, later, she came to make numbers of journeys back to Algiers, there to load up trains of camels with such unlikely objects as grand pianos, crystal chandeliers, billiard tables and whole satin-covered suites of gilt furniture. They breathed splendour and strangeness to the Arab eye. Though, like the garish clothes and enormous feathered hats she took to purchasing during her visits, they were much criticised by the French.

She never stayed long away, hurrying back to the desert as to a lovers' rendezvous. She had come to love the spreading Tedjani lands with that fiercely possessive instinct the French peasant shows towards the soil. All, all must come under her hand. Backed by the bemused Si Ahmed she summoned French engineers and agricultural experts. Tracts of wasteland were irrigated, wells were sunk, new crops sown and new breeds of sheep imported. Forgotten trades were revived, markets established and commerce encouraged. The Tedjanis thrived. Hygiene and medicine saved many lives, while the mystical attributes with which the Arabs invested their shareef were now extended to his wife. Aurélie's touch, too, was believed to bless, heal and even render fruitful the barren. Together Si Ahmed and Aurélie dispensed their blessings from the *zaouïa*, which had been rescued from the tangled state in which a crooked agent had left it upon his dismissal. Once again Aurélie's sense of management, her tact and good sense triumphed. Soon the *zaouïa* prospered, as the land around it flourished. And if, as her detractors were to say, later, she exploited local credulity, accepting, or demanding, valuable presents, tributes of gold and jewels, and even helping herself to the camels, cattle and possessions of the pilgrims in prayer at the *zaouïa*, at least she used these gains for the benefit of Tedjani people and Tedjani territories — *her* lands, *her* people.

Or did she also pile up treasure upon earth for her own use? Did the coffers crammed with gold pieces, precious stones and valuable objects which she flaunted before her astonished French relatives (to whom she was always unaccountably mean) originate in such exploitations? Did she see this accumulation as guarantees against her possible dethronement? Was she ensuring that were she ever to be renounced by Si Ahmed and the Tedjanis, at least she need never be parted from this land of sun, space and solitude which had become her whole life? Giving, giving to it with a lover's largesse was she also taking, taking from it with a lover's greed?

In her life as an integral part of the confraternity, Aurélie came to know much out-of-the-way Arab lore, legends and histories which were stored up by the old women in the harem, or told by the pilgrims or the *harratin* — negro workers on the land. In the early days of their marriage she and the prince had ridden much about the vast territories together, and returning would often choose a track that led by a giant pistachio tree, where a little spring gushed in the desert. This spot was known as Kourdane. Here they would rest, grateful for the great tree's green shade. Dismissing their suite they would watch the sun sink below the desert's rim, while Si Ahmed recounted the legends and histories of his race, telling of heroes and lovers, of El Borak, the Prophet's miraculous winged horse, or the strange ways of the Mozabites, their neighbours across the black stone wastes of the Chebka in the five Holy Cities of the M'zab. There the curious custom of *boumerkoude* – 'the child that sleeps in its mother's womb' – prevailed. *Boumerkoude* was the absent husband's answer if, on returning from a prolonged absence trading (the Mozabites being famous traders), he found his wife had given birth to a child at a most unsuitable date. But it was always acknowledged as his own. He had sown the seed before leaving – two years, three years earlier, it made no difference – the child had simply not chosen to emerge. It had lain sleeping in its mother's womb... The dashing Chaamba tribesmen found this a most convenient doctrine when they rode into one or other of the Holy Cities, and were welcomed by the stay-at-home wives. Nevertheless, to the instinctively jealous Arab man elsewhere, *boumerkoude* was heresy, and they despised the Mozabites accordingly.

These and many more strange tales Si Ahmed tells as he and Aurélie, this oddly matched couple, sit beneath the great pistachio tree of Kourdane. He, the majestic shareef in his flowing robes, the *tespeyh* or string of prayer beads clicking through his fingers as he spins his tales, and Aurélie hanging on his words, her stay-bones creaking in the heat, her china-doll complexion shaded, even under the tree, by a frivolous little parasol straight from Paris. Si Ahmed speaks in Arabic, for his wife has rapidly become proficient in the language of her new life. A fierce sun is declining fast, dipping behind the lilac haze of the western horizon. Now Si Ahmed is telling of the wonderful Tree of Paradise, which is tended by angels and has as many leaves as the sands of the desert, and on each leaf, a man's name is inscribed. In the middle of the month of Shaaban, at sunset, the Tree of Paradise quivers, and the leaves of all who are to die during the year fall to the ground... A shadow falls across their bower, and Aurélie shivers. What if her husband were to die, and she be forced to leave Aïn Mahdi? Now Si Ahmed is recounting the ways of djinns and of their magics, of great consequence in this part of the world. Djinns are believed to be composed of a vapour. They fill the air around us and brush past us, though we are seldom aware of their touch. They must be humoured, for they can be vengeful, though also useful, when invoked to further some nefarious practice. They should always be offered small gifts, *ma'ruf*, a coin, or a dish of salt and ashes, which is their couscous...

I remember a Targui, one of the blue-veiled men from the Hoggar, warning me that djinns are most likely to be about during the hottest part of the day, *el gaïla*, that hour when the noonday mirage shimmers across the desert and the sun seethes in a cruel white haze. Then the djinns and their female counterparts, the djinniyats, are abroad, seeking mischief. It was in Ouargla, at that very hour of *el gaïla*, that my Targui volunteered this information, speaking French in a curiously soft, singsong way. I remember how, abruptly, I was aware of a creeping sense of malevolence overcoming the brilliant day. But then some underlying vein of sinistry is always to be sensed in the desert, however beatific it may appear. Perhaps this is part of its spell.

Aurélie Picard has never been truly assessed, I think, and remains an enigmatic, contradictory legend. She can only be interpreted according to the viewpoint of her interpreter, as I must present her, here. True or false — who now knows? As time passed, it seems that the romantic image of her beginnings, the charming young French girl, bride of the mighty Arab prince, adored by the fanatic Tedjani confraternity and revered as holy by the peoples of the Sahara, gave place to a dominant, matriarchal figure, la Princesse des Sables. That inborn secretiveness and ambition which was hers from the beginning had crystallised, and in the process changed the image. She grew colder, tighter-lipped, more distant with those around her, and took to commanding, the slave-whip in hand, sometimes laying about her vigorously. 'I must be respected,' was her only reply when reproved by her French family. While marvelling at her achievements, they grew critical of her arrogance and avarice. Her mother was left to scrape along on a widow's pension, though no expenditure, no efforts were too great for Aïn Mahdi and the Tedjanis.

She is said to have been beautiful when young, in a sharp-featured French way. The only photograph I have been able to trace is not prepossessing: it shows her in her late thirties, a full-blown woman, tight-lipped and tight-laced, tricked out in Oriental costume, beads, jewels, a fan, and bouffant Turkish trousers from which emerge solid white cotton stockings sagging slightly, encircled by ankle bracelets. But she gazes out complacently, very sure of herself. A forty-inch waist and cotton stockings do not trouble such a woman. Her slightly aquiline nose is haughty, her eyes seem to dart triumph. She is la Princesse des Sables, her powers extending even to the lunar landscape of the Hoggar. In everything she stands beside her husband, the mighty shareef, guiding, controlling, *possessing*; living an inner life of love where no one else can follow.

This state of affairs was made easier for her by Si Ahmed's nature, for he was an indolent voluptuary. Nevertheless he always upheld his religious responsibilities, as he kept to those promises he had made, so long ago, to Cardinal Lavigerie. There was never any question of his taking another wife, or of Aurélie's supremacy being challenged. Both were united in their care of the *zaouïa* and Tedjani affairs, as they were in giving support and hospitality to all those travellers, French administrators, military or civil, who came through Aïn Mahdi, some heading for the dangerous, unpacified regions of the central Sahara. This aid came to be acknowledged and sought repeatedly by the French authorities, and the administrative archives of Algiers at that time, both civil and military, are specific in their accounts of Tedjani cooperation and the prince's support in various projects for the building of schools, and his gift of land to the Pères Blancs for a foundation of their order. Above all, the archives tell of the powers wielded by Aurélie, and in particular, her amicable relations with the intractable Touareg chiefs. These blue-veiled warriors who, in 1881, were to annihilate the Flatters Mission in such terrible circumstances, always showed an especial regard for Aurélie, arriving from their remote fastnesses on their gigantic racing white camels, bringing lavish gifts and promises of goodwill, not always to be relied on, however. The Flatters Massacre, it is believed, might have been avoided if the mission (a military expedition to establish trading concessions) had not set off with such impetuous haste. Although they were accompanied by a Tedjani interpreter, they had neglected to obtain from Aurélie the letters of safe-conduct she was ready to address to a certain Touareg chief upon whose protection they could have relied against the treacheries which awaited them.

Thus the years of love, power and achievement passed for Aurélie; living her Saharan idyll and absorbed by her fierce ambitions, she scarcely noticed the decline of the prince's affections. Concubines came and went, but would things have been so very different had she married a European? Although Si Bachir fostered his brother's infidelities, Aurélie did not appear greatly disturbed. She had become used to Si Bachir's animosity, and shrugged off the menace of other women. She was secure in the knowledge that Si Ahmed's concubines could never come between herself and the land she loved so passionately. Other women might dally in the alcove, but they could never usurp the key position she had won at the *zaouïa*. Nor could they ever weaken the hold she exercised over her husband. He was both contented and proud to leave all in her hands, and grateful for the material benefits of her administration.

Nevertheless it was about this time that she decided to establish herself outside the intrigues of Aïn Mahdi. In 1883, reckoning also on Si Ahmed's weakness for Western comforts and ostentation, she set about building a sumptuous new domain some seven miles distant, at Kourdane, where the great pistachio tree grew beside the little spring. It held so many memories of her early life with Si Ahmed, and was, for her, the heart and symbol of that desert she adored.

Kourdane, begun in 1883, grew rapidly, for Aurélie was impatient to see this pavilion of her heart take shape. She drew up the plans, was architect, mason, engineer and agricultural expert, overseeing every detail of local workmanship. An immense white-walled domed building rose from the sands, Arab in concept, though certain concessions to European living were found in the suites of guest rooms and the kitchens. Balustraded terraces gave on to vistas of garden and orchard, where roses and jasmine scented the air, and fruit trees of a strain imported from France throve in this alien soil. There were great storerooms, outhouses, a flour mill, and stabling for a hundred Arab thoroughbreds, besides quarters for fifty camels and donkeys. The house servants numbered sixty-six, and the grooms, gardeners and farm workers were without number. Kourdane was at once a prince's palace, rural retreat and an agricultural experiment. All the Saharan chiefs came there on visits of ceremony and curiosity. So did the French: generals, Governor-Generals, *députés*, journalists, explorers, all found their way to Kourdane, to be received with princely hospitality, often finding their hostess in the gardens, seated beneath an enormous and elaborate tent, a ceremonial affair of red leather twenty metres in diameter, entirely lined with velvet, which had been presented to her by some of the Touareg nobles.

One visitor describes being welcomed most graciously by Aurélie, who was wearing a *'toilette de réception'* of peacock-blue plush and hung with superb jewellery. She led them upstairs to meet her husband, an obese, panting personage, very amiable to his guests; and dressed, in contrast to his wife, very simply, in a shrimp-pink gandoura, his white muslin headscarves bound by the customary camel-hair cords.

He received them in a vast salon, its floor entirely covered by a gigantic Persian carpet of great value. The tall windows were lavishly draped in silk curtains. A sofa upholstered in black velvet, gold-embroidered with Arabic inscriptions, was the centrepiece. Above, a bronze and crystal chandelier 'such as one finds in churches' hung from the vaulted ceiling, while all around, the walls displayed a marvellous collection of arms, jewelled or damascened, of Arabic and Turkish origin. There was a great deal of pearl-inlaid furniture typical of Damascus, which, with gilt mirrors, are to be found in every Arab interior of consequence. But the proximity of a whole suite of carved French chairs, *style Henri II*, ranged stiffly round the walls, must have looked hideous and, like a large piano draped in embroidered silks, quite incongruous. But then, for all her force and vision, Aurélie was clearly lacking in taste. She had achieved splendour, which had been her goal from the start. The private apartments, which were never seen, were probably more inclined to the Arab style since they had no function to amaze.

The dining room is described as being rather simpler, with tables and chairs, *à l'européen*, to suit European visitors and doubtless to intrigue Arab guests. A large portrait of the then French president was probably hung there for the same purpose. The prodigious banquet which was served started off with a French menu of eight courses, and was followed by an Arab feast of six courses. Not one dish from either could be refused, according to Arab protocol. Besides, the guests were solicitously watched by both host and hostess.

Soon Kourdane became not only a country house for Aurélie and her husband, where they reposed or received guests, but a continuation of the *zaouïa*, for wherever the shareef lives automatically becomes holy, a *lieu* of pilgrimage where every newcomer must be lodged and fed. A family of nomads might plod five hundred kilometres of desert to receive the *baraka*, or blessing, of either Si Ahmed or Aurélie, be lodged at their expense, fed couscous in abundance and bring, as the customary offering, only a donkey-load of desert firewood. Or, in reverse, a group of pilgrims might offer a whole flock of sheep, which Aurélie would brand as hers, and in return she would give them a handful of seeds from her gardens, but which, coming from Kourdane, were deemed to have supernatural virtues.

There was only one shadow over this golden scene. Si Ali, the shareef's heir, had turned out badly. He was irresolute, lazy and drank. Aurélie and her husband feared for the *zaouïa* and all their life's work when he should inherit the shareefian title, though such an eventuality seemed a long way off.

But in 1887 the Tree of Paradise shivered and Si Ahmed's leaf fell. While on a visit to the Tedjani *zaouïas* of Tunis, he died unexpectedly, of blood poisoning. Straightforward poisoning, some said, and Aurélie believed. His death was a profound shock to her, for they had been together through many marvellous years, and he was not yet fifty. Moreover, since he had died away from Aïn Mahdi, his body, by custom, must remain where he died, thus transferring all the shareefian glory and substance of Aïn Mahdi to follow his body. Aurélie battled with the authorities to have this changed, and being a European wife — the only wife, rather than one of a sheep-like harem — her efforts at last prevailed. Si Ahmed's body was brought back to Kourdane where, in the gardens he had loved, she built a simple and beautiful red marble *koubbah* as his monument; the splendours of Kourdane and the well-being of the confraternity were a more fitting one, even though they had been, in fact, the work of his wife.

Now Aurélie had no more part to play in Tedjani affairs, and found, too, that her days at Kourdane were numbered, since Si Bachir, succeeding to his brother's title, was determined on her departure. She had imagined that Kourdane, her own creation, would remain hers. Not so. Aurélie had no more part to play in Tedjani affairs. Si Bachir, the sickly, the malefic, determined on her banishment, not only from Aïn Mahdi but from Kourdane too. Aurélie now faced parting both from her life's work and the pavilion of her heart. As withdrawn in grief as in joy, she retreated to Algiers. Even in this, the most bitter moment of her life, she was dry-eyed. Perhaps she remembered the Arab saying that all is Allah's will — that no tears must be shed at whatever Allah ordains, lest the tears form a river, dividing, forever, the mourner from that which he mourns. In Algiers, in a modest villa and bored by French bourgeois life, she brooded, bitter in the loss of all she held dear. To the French she had become *la veuve Tedjani*, of no more account now she had no more power. But was she of no more consequence?

Yet again, for the third time, we see fate step in to change her fortune overnight. For some while, she had been tormented by hearing, from passing Tedjanis, of the disorder and decay to which Si Bachir's indifference and inef-fectual rule had reduced both Aïn Mahdi and Kourdane the beloved. Gradually the Tedjanis, and even Si Bachir, began to realise that Aurélie's presence was vital to their prosperity. At the same moment, the French administration were becoming uneasy at a growing turbulence and lack of cooperation among the tribes of the southern territories. Such things had not been so marked during *la veuve Tedjani's* days of influence.

They hit on a most ingenious plan and proposed that Aurélie should contract a marriage with Si Bachir, thus returning to Aïn Mahdi to be once more officially associated with the *zaouïa* and all its politics. In spite of their dislike of each other both Aurélie and Si Bachir consented to this arrangement, for it was to their mutual benefit. The marriage took place before the caïd of El Aghouat, Aurélie now taking a particular pleasure in declining the civil marriage which, at last, after many years, the French authorities pressed on her.

Her return to Aïn Mahdi was triumphant, amid scenes of touching devotion from the Tedjanis. Having become, once more, wife of the ruling shareef, she could resume her life's work. She and Si Bachir had agreed to go their separate ways, he to follow the old idling pattern, she to order and restore the Tedjani affairs. Kourdane, she decided, should be her headquarters. With a lover's impatience she set out once more to cross the arid track that lay between her and her adored. The lover's rendezvous once more. But *Ouribet, Khouribet!* says the Arab proverb: *All that is of the desert returns to it.* So it was with Kourdane. Even in so short a while, the beautiful gardens were destroyed and the house become a tarnished mockery of its former glory. However, Aurélie was an undaunted, energetic fifty. With a lover's devotion she set about restoring it, and soon it was as before – but now, all hers, doubly precious for the time of separation she had suffered.

For twelve more years Aurélie lived her Saharan love affair with Kourdane and the marvellous desert from which it had grown. She sought no other company, though she still received in style. Only now she no longer ate with her guests, joining them for coffee, but took her meals in her own rooms where, overlooking the desert's sweep, she was tête-à-tête with her love. She rarely tore herself away from Kourdane, even to order the affairs of

Aïn Mahdi. Time was running out. Every day, every hour, at Kourdane, was precious to her. Every sunset and sunrise there, each flower or fruit it bore, like the rustle of the palms, the cooing of the doves, the song of the slaves, or the starlight silvering the white walls and domes, or spangling through the leaves of the great pistachio tree, were part of this marvellous love affair she still lived to the full.

When Si Bachir died in 1911, Aurélie was sixty-two. Now, at last, she knew that her life of love was ended, for Si Bachir's malice reached out from the grave. He had left her nothing – not even a life interest in Kourdane, which thus became Tedjani property, automatically inherited by the new heir, her stepson, the good-for-nothing Si Ali. He, too, was jealous of her powerful presence, and although generously disposed in material matters, demanded her departure from Kourdane. She was thunderstruck. When he suggested she should take with her anything she chose, her fury was uncontrolled. All was hers by right, she claimed. But all she wanted was Kourdane itself. She refused to leave. At last, implacably, Si Ali had her ejected by law. After her departure for Algiers it was found that she had razed the place. Rugs, silver, linen, furniture, bric-à-brac, the bronze chandeliers, the pearl furniture and the grand piano were all piled into wagons and trundled away. When asked to render the accounts of the *zaouïa* she refused, and for three years remained in obstinate silence, lodged in a small house into which were crammed the glories of Kourdane. Until a few years ago, there were people living in Algiers who remembered the little house and the extraordinary woman, and how, on the rare occasions when someone from the desert arrived, she would spread her superb carpets to overflow the tiny garden, send for dancers and musicians and prepare a feast, a *diffa*, to recall the splendours of Kourdane's hospitality.

Three years of this aimless existence dragged by. Once more, for the fourth and last time, fate stepped in, to bring her once again to that glowing scene which was her destiny. And once again, as in the beginning, chance was heralded by gunfire.

In 1914, France was again in desperate straits, and when the Germans began fostering revolts in North Africa, the French remembered Lallah Yamina, Princesse des Sables. They sent for her and begged her to return to Aïn Mahdi, there to work for French interests among the tribes. Thus for six more years the sun shone on her. A sinking sun, but it warmed her through. Si Ali had become a reformed, if timid shareef and, all the old spites forgotten, welcomed her return to Aïn Mahdi.

Thus, yet again, the Princesse des Sables reigned, to the benefit of the Tedjanis, the furtherance of French interests, and the destruction of German influences. But with the armistice, Aurélie, at seventy-two, felt her Saharan life must finish. Her wartime efforts had exhausted her, the climate began to try her and even Kourdane seemed too demanding. On her own initiative, she retreated — to Arc-en-Barrois: to go home, she said, though her home could never now be in that northern province. She had seized the chance to leave it and had never returned in all the years that had passed. She could not reconcile herself to Europe, either the people, their ways or their petulant skies. Her money and possessions had long vanished. She was very poor, nor was she made to feel welcome among her relatives. She fretted for Kourdane. She was over eighty now, but her love remained as strong as ever, Kourdane, the Sahara… it was all she craved, all that she had lost, had abandoned…

In 1955, in a surge of the old temerity and resolve, she returned to Algeria. Unannounced, she arrived at Aïn Mahdi, having made the journey in a rackety tourist bus, she who had first made it at the head of that extravagant marriage cortège. She was an impoverished spectre, sitting there among the tourists, an old, old woman, but still a woman in love. At Aïn Mahdi she asked to be allowed to return to Kourdane and the Tedjanis agreed. Kourdane was of little account to the confraternity now.

Ouribet, Khouribet! Once more the Sahara had reclaimed its own. Kourdane stood, a lonely ruin, in the fertile wastes that had been her pride. Lizards flicked across the parched fountains, emaciated sheep cropped weeds where once her roses had bloomed; the wells had dried up, the fields lay unploughed, sanded over, dotted by the black tents of the nomads. The desert had crept up, smothering all. *That which is Arab becomes ruin.* Aurélie wept the only tears anyone had ever seen her shed and turned away. The Tedjanis took her to the Soeurs Blanches at El Aghouat. There, in a small room containing an iron bed, an old armchair and a statue of the Virgin Mary, she lay, silently. Sometimes she whispered, in Arabic, seeming to relive those wonderful, audacious days of her Saharan beginnings. The Tedjanis and the shareef's family came often to see her, all solicitude. The French priest visited her constantly, observing that a worn Bible at her bedside was inscribed with her name and a date from her childhood in Arc-en-Barrois. It had been beside her all these years, testimony to her unchanging faith. She was failing fast, now, and received the sacraments, although the sisters did not think the end was near. Next day she asked to be taken back to Kourdane. It was a long and terrible route and the doctor forbade her being moved, but she would not be dissuaded.

'Kourdane – I can only die happy there,' they heard her whisper. The Tedjanis carried her across the desert she had loved to the ruined domain that was still the pavilion of her heart. Twenty-four hours later she was dead. She had wished to be buried there, in a Moslem tomb, beside Si Ahmed, and all the fanaticism of the Tedjanis now rose round her coffin. They claimed she had been, at the end, converted to Islam, though this the French disputed hotly, citing her receiving of the sacraments and her treasured Bible. It was well known she had never adopted her husband's religion, however much she had become one with the confraternity. Therefore, said the French, she must have a Christian burial in the Catholic cemetery at El Aghouat. Such arguments seem trivial in view of her expressed wish to lie at Kourdane. Yet the wrangling continued, faith against faith. Belatedly the French government accorded her the honours they had not bestowed during her lifetime, naming her Chevalier de la Légion d'Honneur and many more high-sounding titles. As 'the first French woman of the Sahara' they gave her, beside their usual *pompe funèbre*, a funeral with full military honours, her coffin draped with the *tricolore* and a salvo of guns to echo across the sands.

But the Arabs designated her a marabout, a Moslem saint, and buried her beside Si Ahmed, under the green vaults of the pistachio tree, surrounded by the desert she had loved more than any man. The Sahara had reclaimed its own.

Bibi Hanum's Medressa

ALL OVER THE EAST, HISTORICAL SAGAS, TALES OF MAGIC OR FOLKLORE have always been an integral part of daily life, like the itinerant storyteller who wandered – and still does – from bazaar to café and street corner, spinning his marvellous tales. Although now on the decline, his livelihood threatened by the rise of literacy, the storyteller continues; especially across the wastes of Central Asia. While few nomads' tents are now without their transistor radio, and in the towns, television sets perform eccentrically, the storyteller can still count on his audience. In remote towns such as Tash Kurghan (much as it was when Marco Polo described it on his way to Cathay) I have watched them in the *chaikhanas*, or teahouses, and marketplaces, surrounded by a circle of rapt listeners, crouching figures, their dark, hawk faces intent, as the age-old tales unfold: tales of mighty caliphs and mythical warriors, Saladin beside Rustem, bawdy harem intrigues interwoven with deathless loves, Nasreddin of Bukhara beside Leila and Majnoun... This is the many-coloured world of the Arabian Nights Entertainment, Eastern world without end, a world not yet wholly given over to oil derricks and housing developments. Here there are still narrow alleyways smelling of spices, musk and dung, where *moucharabiyeh* screen each window, and women go veiled, and some scent of mystery remains. Here everyone is not yet infected with too much schooling. Romantic and supernatural themes still rank as entertainment along with the jugglers, snake charmers, and sometimes, as in the regions between Balkh and Bukhara, those troupes of dancing boys, the *batchas*, whose undulating, sipping steps and provocative postures were esteemed above the charms of women. ('A woman for breeding, a boy for pleasure,' as the local saying goes.)

Here the storytellers still recount tales of magic, and the turbaned lorry drivers climb down from their naively frescoed lorries, which are hung with pious or mystic symbols and talismans, to refresh themselves with tea and (along with radio news bulletins) tales of djinns and peris. But then to people hereabout, both the machinery of the lorry, or the wireless, like the jet plane, are seen as clear proof of magic – the abracadabras of necromancy rather than manmade achievements of engineering. And after all, is a jet plane any less magic than Simurg, the giant bird of Arabian legend, or Borak, Mohammed's winged horse?

Thus the story of Bibi Hanum and her vanishing lover is accepted as truth. Indeed fact and fable are curiously interwoven here, for Bibi Hanum is known to have existed, the favourite wife of Tamerlane, or Timur-i-leng, as he is known in Samarcand, once his capital and seat of all his glories. Moreover, the beautiful *medressa*, or college, which goes by Bibi Hanum's name, still stands there in crumbling majesty, admired by archaeologists and historians alike. And then – fact merging with fable giddily – the Uzbeks and Tadjiks of this region will always point out the soaring minaret above the *medressa* and tell you it was from there that Bibi Hanum's love 'took wing'.

'Took wing': a curious phrase, yet the same words were used when I first heard the story from a rug dealer in Aleppo; and again, years later, when a Turcoman exile in Shiraz recounted it to me. He was originally from Samarcand, where he had traded in karakul skins, like his father and grandfather before him. Everyone knew the story was true, he said. Only strangers like myself ever questioned it, he added, and launched into a dissertation on the power of djinns. But Asiatics, like Hamlet, know there are more things in heaven and earth than are dreamed of, and no explications are ever necessary where lovers or djinns are concerned.

When later I reached Samarcand, it seemed natural to go along with such views, for plainly they were shared by those around me: the Uzbek, Tadjik and Turcoman peoples. Samarcand itself possesses an extraordinary quality of magic, shimmering in the turquoise haze cast by its peacock-bright buildings, its mosques and mausoleums and minarets, all glittering blue, rising from the legendary wastes of Afrosaïb. So I wandered from one marvel to another, from the *medressa* of Uleg Beg or the mausoleum of Tourkan Akha to the lion-fronted façade which dominates the Registan where, beneath each arch or dome, the merchants stack their cannon-ball mounds of green melons, and the citizens sit drinking tea beneath the dappled plane trees. On a breathless summer evening, when I sat in such a *chaikhana* beside Tamerlane's tomb, the Gur i Mir, I watched a storyteller recounting some fabulous legend to a circle of enthralled listeners. They sat cross-legged on wooden bedsteads spread with rugs, drinking green tea out of little china bowls as blue as the dome of the Gur i Mir. I suppose my yearning glances spoke for me, for presently I was invited to join the circle, and by the good offices of a young science student from the University of Tashkent, who offered to interpret for me, I persuaded the storyteller to give me his version of Bibi Hanum's tale. Although the science student seemed disapproving of my romantic choice − shrugging it off as a non-progressive programme − he was indefatigable in relaying the storyteller's words, flowery phrase by flowery phrase.

This is what he told.

Bibi Hanum was a Chinese princess of unparalleled beauty: 'Hers was the loveliness of the full moon; her lips like the ripe pomegranate, her eyes like the darkest jade, her waist slender as a rattan frond...' All the Oriental similes were lavished on this paragon, who was so full of learning and virtue beyond all telling. She was Tamerlane's favourite wife, loved above all the rest of the women in his *anderoun*, or harem.

'There she lived, behind forty silk-hung walls, and the Great Khan sought her company by day and night, taking his joy in her beauty and wisdom,' said the storyteller, at which the circle of turbaned men around him swayed backwards and forwards, clicking their tongues in approval, and shaking their heads in assent, for this is the East, where all is otherwise and a nod stands for no.

Now when the astrologers came to Tamerlane and told him the hour was propitious for his setting out on new conquests, he bade farewell to Bibi Hanum and turned eastwards, towards India. He rode out from Samarcand at the head of a mighty army, accompanied by his generals and scribes, his astrologers, musicians, physicians, his cooks and the master of his horse, his hunting leopards and falcons, two hundred Afghan hounds, horses without number, and a thousand she-camels to provide milk for them on the barren desert crossings. There were, besides, a train of sixty elephants to carry silken carpets from Persia, and ceremonial tents, with their silver poles adorned with yak tails and hangings of gold brocade lined with sable against the cold, for splendour surrounded this mighty khan wherever he went.

When Bibi Hanum parted from her lord and master, 'tears of pearl fell on her alabaster cheeks,' and she withdrew to a painted pavilion on the rooftop of the harem from where she kept watch, 'by sunlight and by starlight,' for that far distant cloud of dust which would tell of Tamerlane's messengers

177

bringing assurances of his love... 'But after thirteen moons and thirteen days had passed,' Bibi Hanum dried her tears and raising her veils, planned to build the most wondrous monument in the world to honour her overlord. It should be a *medressa*, to house a thousand students, each of whom should have his fees paid from Bibi Hanum's own purse, as well as twenty silver *tengas* each month to buy food. The *medressa* must be built without delay, so that it should await the mighty conqueror when he returned in triumph. But there were difficulties in finding an architect worthy of the project, for, as was his custom, Tamerlane had taken the finest with him in his suite, so that they might study the noblest buildings of other kingdoms, and returning do likewise in Samarcand, thus making it Queen of Cities and all man's delight — as it is to this day, added the storyteller, and no one contradicted him.

It is known that Tamerlane's suite did indeed include such experts. The melon domes of Samarcand are said to derive from his admiration for one of the largest mosques in Damascus. When he laid siege to the city he ordered that particular mosque to be spared in the ensuing sack. But the fires ravaged the city and reduced it to ashes, so Tamerlane rounded up all the local builders

A courtyard in Damascus, 1861

178

who knew the secrets of such beauty. Taking them back to Samarcand with him, he set them to work there, to build those ribbed, melon domes which are a derivation of the Damascus original and which became typical of Central Asian architecture. Moreover, Tamerlane's descendants are said to have imposed them in India, where they are found in some of the mosques of Delhi and elsewhere. Further afield, northwards, the same lovely swelling curves and bulbous, onion-domed variations took root in Russia and are also held to derive from a Central Asian inspiration.

But these are architectural digressions. Let us return to the storyteller's tale and Bibi Hanum's dilemma. This was solved by her learning of one remaining architect within the city, young and as yet untried, but of excellent promise. He was commanded to appear before Bibi Hanum. When she descended from her rooftop pavilion to confer with him, he found favour in her eyes, for the plans he submitted expressed all that she had wished for the *medressa*. He was, besides, handsome as a young falcon, said the storyteller. The foundations were laid forthwith and every mason and carpenter and tile worker between Merv and Bukhara was pressed into service. Each day Bibi Hanum came to watch the *medressa* grow, carried there in 'a camel litter hung with silver bells and scarlet tassels and escorted by a guard of archers, and accompanied by twelve virgins of rare loveliness and noble blood,' said the storyteller, now well into his stride, my interpreter panting after him.

'Before the almond flowers had fallen,' he went on, 'Bibi Hanum's beauty and wisdom had inflamed the heart of the young architect so that the twelve high-born virgins of rare loveliness appeared as toads. For twenty more moons the building of the *medressa* continued, growing in all the magnificence that Bibi Hanum had desired.' At last the loftiest minaret was completed, and the tile workers were covering the colossal dome with arabesques of turquoise and sapphire-blue *faience*. Below, in the shadowed vaulting, calligraphers worked on the gilded inscriptions which adorned the walls, while the woodcarvers inlaid panels of cedar wood with ivory and ebony and the metalsmiths plated the entrance doors with sheets of bronze embossed with silver and gold, so that the sound of hammering rang across the city. But now that the *medressa* was almost finished, the young architect knew that his days of happiness were numbered, for soon Bibi Hanum would make no more visits to confer with him and marvel at the beauty he had created... His task would be done and all hope of seeing Bibi Hanum would wither. Therefore he devised a plan by which the finishing touches were delayed: a panel of tiling still wanting from the main *ivar*, or façade; one door still not set aright on its hinges, an inscription unfinished; ever and again some small imperfection remained. At last Bibi Hanum grew uneasy, for rumours had reached Samarcand that Tamerlane had sacked Delhi and was on his homeward journey, a train of princely hostages and captives in his train. Therefore she urged that the work should be hastened. While the *medressa* remained an unfinished masterpiece it would not find favour with Tamerlane, and her proud offering would appear unworthy of him whom she sought to honour. But all her arguments, persuasions or commands failed to move the young architect, who had so marvellously interpreted all her other desires. He inclined before her, promising all she asked, but still there were strange delays, and still Bibi Hanum went to the *medressa* every day, in her scarlet tasselled, bell-hung litter, to urge on the workmen – to confer with her architect which was, of course, precisely what he, her adorer, had planned.

He was clearly a most romantic creature. At this point, I interrupted the story to ask his name and to be given some account of his appearance. All earlier versions of this story had dwelt entirely on Bibi Hanum's charms. He was, the storyteller repeated, handsome as a young falcon and he was, too, strong as a lion and tall as a young cypress: all the Oriental similes again. I imagined him one of those towering Uzbeks, almond-eyed and high-cheekboned, their eyebrows joined in a dark sweep, men who ride like centaurs and tread delicately in their high, soft leather boots, wearing the striped *chapan*, a padded surcoat sashed in rainbow silks from Bukhara and lined with flowered chintzes, a little round embroidered cap crowning that dense dark hair which, among Asiatics, resembles the plumage of some sleek bird. There are many such men in these territories.

'And his name?' I pressed, but for once the storyteller seemed at a loss. While he hesitated, his listeners prompted him, less from knowledge, I fancied, than from a civil wish to satisfy the curiosity of the stranger in their midst. 'Tangrikouli,' said one. 'Moukhouddin,' said another. 'Assadjan Kaloum,' said a third, by which I realised the young architect had passed into legend as Architect, or Lover, and that's that. Let us call him Kaloum, for it is less taxing on the memory than other names from these parts.

For all Bibi Hanum's commands, for all her urgings, summer had passed into autumn, the roses bloomed and fallen and the figs ripened. Still the building was not done, till at last Bibi Hanum grew desperate and threatened to have Kaloum impaled on one of the unfinished gateways. Yet if Kaloum were no more, who could finish the *medressa*? She was about to take counsel with a celebrated necromancer who lived in an ill-famed quarter behind the Registan when a messenger rode up out of the east, telling that Tamerlane was on the march and would reach his capital before the waning of the next moon. On hearing that which once would have rejoiced her heart, Bibi Hanum tore her veils and wept. When Kaloum saw tears falling like dew on the alabaster of her cheeks he swore that would she but pay his price, all should be as she wished, and the *medressa* stand ready for the Great Khan's return.

The price which Kaloum asked of Bibi Hanum was one kiss. When Bibi Hanum heard this, she paled, trembling like a leaf on the peepal tree, for she was the most virtuous of wives. But she was also the most wilful among women – and a wilful woman cannot be denied, said the storyteller, looking round the circle for agreement. All the turbaned heads shook vigorously in assent – shook, for as I remarked earlier, a shaken head for yes, a nodded one for no.

'What then?' I asked, eager for the denouement of this romantic situation.

'Then,' said the storyteller, savouring the whole attention of his public, 'then, Bibi Hanum reflected that one kiss was not so terrible a price to pay, were she to obtain her way. And besides, she had observed that the architect was a comely youth.' So she lifted her veils and Kaloum kissed her.

'Alas! with that one kiss, all this noble lady's virtue and wisdom melted before the fire of Kaloum's desire. Throwing her arms round his neck, like a collar of pearls, she gave him back his kiss a hundred times, and he returned them a thousandfold. Their kisses melted together like honey on their lips...'

Thus it fell that while, by day, the woodcarvers and tile workers and metalsmiths busied themselves completing the *medressa*, by night, when the first stars pricked the darkening sky, Bibi Hanum stole out from the harem, concealed beneath the burqa of a bribed serving girl, and reached a side door in the *medressa* where Kaloum awaited her. There, as the moon swam high, moving to its waning, they lay together in one of the cells where soon some student would begin his studies among the parchments of learning. But now it was a bower of loving, for Kaloum had spread it with carpets from Bukhara and silken cushions, and there the lovers clipped and kissed and sported and Kaloum 'ceased not to play the porter at her door nor the preacher at her prayer niche,' in the words of the Arabian Nights storyteller, and although these were not the exact words used by mine, what he said, according to the science student, amounted to much the same thing.

When Tamerlane's advance guard reached the city, Kaloum knew his hours of delight were done. Bibi Hanum rose up from the cushions and, hiding herself in the servant-maid's burqa, crept back to the palace by byways where none challenged her. There she arrayed herself in her robes of honour. 'Her hair was plaited in many strands and tasselled with jewels. Her girdle was coral and turquoise, her necklace of beaten gold and pearls from Mosul. The veils that fell over her robes of Samut velvet were transparent as the mists of morning and coloured like the sunrise. She painted her cheeks and lips with vermilion and darkened her eyes with kohl, so that they resembled twin lakes beneath the archer's bow of her eyebrows.' Thus her lord and master would not find her beauty less than that of the women of India, those *ranees* and dancing girls whose praises, said the storyteller, returning travellers had always sung.

When Tamerlane entered Samarcand in all his might he saw, rising before him, more splendid and lofty than all the other mosques and palaces of his capital, the *medressa* that Bibi Hanum had raised in his honour. He marvelled at its perfect loveliness. Bibi Hanum was awaiting her lord before the bronze-and-silver-studded doors, surrounded by her women, while his other wives and concubines, finding less favour in his eyes, stood to the rear. As Tamerlane approached, they all knelt, kissing the ground between their outstretched hands. Signifying his pleasure, Tamerlane raised Bibi Hanum, desiring her to name the architect who had conceived so splendid a building. At which Kaloum knelt at the khan's feet, and Tamerlane swore he should be honoured above all other architects in his city. Then, taking Bibi Hanum's hand, he led her within, saying that she and the architect should conduct him about the *medressa* even before he shook off the dust of his desert travels. Standing under the soaring blue dome he marvelled at all the many wonders. 'Here shall wisdom flourish,' he proclaimed. Striking on the door of one of the cells, he commanded it to be unlocked that he might know in what manner future students would be housed.

Now by some fearful mischance, or the sport of some malevolent *afrits*, or spirits, perhaps, it happened that this was the very same cell where Bibi Hanum and Kaloum had spent the noon of every night in lovers' bliss. Moreover, in their haste to be gone and to make ready for Tamerlane's return, Kaloum had turned the key on their paradise not thinking to remove the Persian carpets and the silken cushions, nor the ewer of rose water, the dishes of pomegranates, the drinking cups of jade and the roses, now faded in their golden goblet…

Therefore, when the door was opened, it disclosed, not the parchments and quill pens of learning, but a frame for loving, a nest from which the lovebirds had clearly not long flown. Laughter burst from the astonished multitude, so that Tamerlane was greatly angered. What jokester had dared to trick great Tamerlane and make mock of Bibi Hanum's *medressa*? Tamerlane vowed the culprits should be brought to justice forthwith. While Kaloum stood as if turned to stone, staring disaster in the face, Bibi Hanum fell to the ground swooning and her women laid her down beside the fountain that graced the centre of the inner court. 'When Tamerlane saw her lying there like a broken pillar, he was unmindful of all else, and lifted her veils, that he might know if she still breathed.'

There on the ashy pallor of Bibi Hanum's lovely face a burning mark appeared – the imprint of a kiss, that fatal kiss that had undone all her vaunted wisdom and virtue. Tamerlane let drop the veils. As he rose to his feet, his eyes met those of Kaloum and all was made clear to him. Uttering a terrible cry which reverberated round the great dome and made every man's blood run cold, Tamerlane drew his sword and sprang at Kaloum.

'Shall the dog lie in the lion's lair?' he cried, as his sword flashed above Kaloum's head. But Kaloum leapt aside and made for the narrow, winding stair-way that climbed the minaret, Tamerlane hot in pursuit, while below every eye strained to follow them, knowing that once the topmost gallery was reached, 'the crying place from where muezzin calls the faithful to prayer', Kaloum would be slain like the very dog to which Tamerlane had likened him. There was no way of escape left, nor was he armed.

Here the storyteller paused dramatically, as we hung on his words. As if to prolong the suspense, he called for another bowl of tea, sipping languidly before resuming his tale. Then, it seems, the multitude below saw the two figures emerge on to the gallery, silhouetted dark like puppets in a shadow play, against the blue of the sky. They saw Tamerlane's sword glitter as he raised it – and they saw, or swore they saw, Kaloum leap into the blue and vanish!

'Vanish? You mean he fell to his death?'

The storyteller nodded maddeningly, meaning 'No', in the confusing manner already described. 'Not so,' he said. '*He took wing*. He did not fall to his death, nor did he perish by Timur-i-leng's sword. Nobody saw him fall to earth. His body was never found. No one ever saw him again.'

This was the work of the *afrits*, or the djinns, the good djinns, for there are many such. They took pity on him and letting him take wing among them, he vanished from man's sight, to become one of their own.

'The good djinns have always loved lovers, you must know,' he added, turning his mischievous eyes on me intently. I believed him, then and there, as I do, here and now, writing it all down as he told it.

Next day I returned to the café, but he had gone, nor was he to be found. Find me another storyteller, I begged, but this the Intourist Bureau seemed unable to supply. I told them I wanted to know more about Bibi Hanum; how she had lived. Was there nothing left of Tamerlane's palaces, or possessions or furnishings? Where were the silken hangings that once adorned the forty walls behind which his harem was concealed? Would they open for me one of the cells in the *medressa*? They had almost crumbled away, but perhaps I should come on some shred of a silken cushion, some fragment of a drinking cup, that would speak to me of the lovers. I thought it more prudent not to tell them I was in fact searching for a pavilion of the heart. Even so, the Intourist staff looked blank and suggested the museum (where, surprisingly, there is a Goya) or a visit to the tombs of the Shah Zindeh, or to the huge block of grey-blue marble, the Kok-Tash, said to have been Tamerlane's throne; though neither thrones nor tombs were the sort of furnishings I had in mind. It seemed that all the rest had vanished into thin air – that dry, crystalline air of Central Asia, spirited away, like Kaloum. But then time itself is the djinn of djinns, causing, at last, all things and all men to vanish.

> The samovars of Samarcand
> Stand smoking in the sun
> While melons, tiger-striped and cool
> Are stacked beneath the shattered dome
> Where Bibi Hanum's love took wing,
> And she and Tamerlane and all the Khans
> Lie sleeping in their turquoise tombs.

Laurence Hope: A Shadow in the Sunlight

IN THE BLAZE OF AN INDIAN NOON – THE LAST BRILLIANCE OF IMPERIAL India – a shadow fell across that shimmering scene, merged with the dusk beneath the sinjib trees and was gone, leaving only a legend of some burning love, some perfume of the East, fugitive as a flute song, telling of lovers trysting on the roof tops of an ancient city, of floating enlaced on a lotus-tide; of raptures, revenge by cold steel, tears, sighs, then silence.

This is Laurence Hope's legacy. Three small volumes of impassioned verse, a few scattered memories or letters from those who knew her; the reticence of her son and a host of conjectures which sprang up round the charming, strange, withdrawn, yet forthright woman who, today, is only vaguely recalled as author of some exotic songs hackneyed by misuse.

The Indian Love Lyrics deserved a better fate. They were set to music by Amy Woodforde-Finden and for twenty years the palm courts of grand hotels and bric-à-brac-filled drawing rooms rang with over-expressive renderings of these sensuous poems. 'Pale hands I loved, beside the Shalimar... whom do you lead on raptures roadway far?' so sang the sopranos and tenors, juicily, their accompanist, soft pedal down, swaying in matching fervour. 'I would rather have felt you round my throat, crushing out life, than waving me farewell!'... Loud pedal now, the singer, bosom arched and eyes closed, reaching for the last despairing note... 'Tum tum ti ti tum tum ti' went the accompanist accentuating the evocative Eastern rhythms, drowning the rattle of coffee cups. '...Less than the Dust beneath Thy Chariot Wheels,' the cry of the despairing, adoring Eastern slave-wife was a particular favourite with brisk Anglo-Saxon ladies, until, at last, the beautiful and the violent world of India which Laurence Hope conjured, was forgotten, shouted down by jazz and more clinical expressions of love.

Would she have cared? I do not think so. She wrote organically, for herself, for love of love, of India, in an explosion of emotion, a process of internal combustion, even. It is contended that she could not have expressed such passions without living them, and when first her poems broke on an enthusiastic and titillated London public in 1901 and she was revealed, in spite of the pseudonym, to be a woman, gossip buzzed round her. Every line was construed autobiographically. She was that pretty, rather unconventional little Mrs Nicolson? No, really! well, she simply couldn't have felt that way about her husband they said; he was twenty years older, a stern soldier... Could he have inspired those sort of lines? All those descriptions of – well, of *lovemaking*... of such violent Oriental passions... so *very* frank... No: it must have been some Indian prince, some sepia Romeo. That fitted much better. And then there was her sister, Victoria Cross, who wrote the most daring books, quite often about white women falling in love with Indians. Thus vulgar gossip. The Nicolsons remained an enigmatic pair: they were rarely in London, disliking the chill, petty horizons of civilisation. They returned to India which was their whole life. Three years later both were dead.

To the world Laurence Hope has remained a shade – curious fate for one so vital in both her life and writings. She has always interested me and when I was writing *The Wilder Shores of Love*, I wished to include her among my four biographies, but my research did not give me enough material.

Today I am a little better informed and much indebted to her son's unpublished memoir. But there are still many gaps and no one left alive to fill them. Her son has been approached several times to collaborate on plays or films based on his mother's life: no doubt these would become exuberantly fictionalised, and so, abhorrent to him. 'But of course, the public do not want so much truth as a good story,' he writes.

Yet Laurence Hope's story is a wonderful one – even the little we know, being charged with colour, emotion, adventure and tragedy. Her setting was India – Kipling's India, part of that pattern of empire-building in which England still believed: the India of might and right: of vice-regal splendours imposed on Moghul memories; of inequalities, yet idealisms, too, among the Indian civil servants and military caste with whom she lived, but from whom, in a sense, she was always apart.

I know of no other Englishwoman who penetrated India with the same sensuous understanding as Laurence Hope. Loving it she found, through it, many aspects of fulfilment which her ardent nature craved. It never seems to have occurred to those who analyse her verses, or those who ferret out other people's private lives, that emotions can be transposed to places, houses, things – above all, to countries. Many of Laurence Hope's most impassioned lines can be read in this light. In the blazing nimbus of the East she found the attributes of a beloved – mystery, beauty, cruelty, refinements of *volupté* and ancient wisdoms... Before all else, I think she lived a love affair with a land, striving to possess it, knowing herself possessed.

Her verses, some inspired by legends of the people, by their literature, some from the depths of her own emotion, have left a portrait of this love in many guises. A lover to his mistress, a slave to her unattainable lord and master, an exile to his home; tender legends, terrible ones, the anguished cry of the deserted lover, the call of the prowling jackal at dusk... and always, the scarlet thread of longing – of an atavism stronger than all else, the cry of a being trapped in the aeons of time, scenting, deep in the jungle, some kinship with the first stirrings of this land.

'O! life, I have taken you for my lover!' she wrote. But it was India which was, for her, the incarnation of her passion, the means by which she lived to the full, seeking to be one with the plains and the hills, the animals and the flowers; to know the many races, their beliefs and lives. Often she went among them secretly, living dangerously, beside her husband, in some frontier campaign: riding from battle into the stillness of the jungles, or the latticed world of the *zenanas*, listening to tales of love and jealousy. *The Regret of the Ranee in the Hall of Peacocks, Yasin Khan, The Lament of Yasmini, the Dancing-Girl* or *The Rao of Ilore* are all culled from the people, while she went among them as a woman, as a man (disguised as a Pathan boy), as a European, as an Indian, but always coming closer to the beloved.

'Heart, my heart, thou hast found thy home!' is the opening line of her *Song of the Parao*, something far more likely to be autobiographical than many others held to be so revealing.

These are my people, and this is my land
I hear the pulse of her secret soul...
...Washed in the light of a clear fierce sun,
Heart, my heart, the journey is done.

Over and over she sounds this ecstatic note: in her writings as in her life she
was identified with the East as few Europeans dared or cared to be. Especially
women. In India at that time, Englishwomen held to a code as rigid as any
caste system. The memsahibs of Poonah and Simla or the plains grew fretful
drilling legions of bewildered native servants to recreate the conventions of
Kensington or some country town they had enshrined. For them, India was
exile. They remained uninitiated, playing bridge, planting sweetpeas, or delphin-
iums in preference to the heady blossoms of the tropics, the moghra flowers,
the champa and the lotus which Laurence Hope loved. *Under the Deodar* was
a popular song: at the clubhouse dances they waltzed to it, while sighing for
northern beeches and felt themselves unquestionably more attractive than
the undulating Nautch girls who were said to offer competition, down in the
bazaars.

For women, then, India remained something which, even if it began to charm
them must be kept at arm's length, like some dangerous seducer.

Not for the memsahibs the romantic old *baridari*, or garden houses, set in
mango groves, with marble floors, fretted pillars and mirrored gilded ceilings,
cooled by fountains and water-courses. They preferred gabled bungalows with
chintzy drawing rooms and roast-meat menus. Their lives were lived behind
ramparts of nostalgia. Few, very few of the women, at that time, were truly
interested in India. Flora Annie Steele, and Maud Diver, in their own way; but
it was not Laurence Hope's way.

'If anyone was cabined, cribbed and confined by circumstances, it was she,'
wrote Flora Annie Steele, the novelist and social worker, who lived half her life
in India and knew Laurence Hope briefly, as the bride of an old friend. 'Like
some tropical bird, she was ensnared in the cage of civilisation.' Mrs Steele
described her as 'a small athletic figure in bright-coloured satins... A childlike
face, a pair of wide blue eyes, not by any means unfathomable – they were far
too clear for that – but full to the brim of eager curiosity, keen appreciation
and unswerving directness.'

Another friend described her as 'riveting attention'. She had intensely blue eyes of a peculiarly deep, violet tint, so that her husband always called her Violet. Her build was slight — so narrow (in that wide-hipped age) that she looked like a schoolboy. She did not follow the fashion for piled-up, frizzed-up hair, but wore hers unconventionally, cut loose on her neck, framing her face, in the manner of a Florentine page. The few photographs I have been able to see reveal a strong, rather brooding face, which could no doubt become beautiful in animation, and colour, but which in repose, and black and white, has a quality of wilful determination: the face of a woman who knew what she wanted, sought for it, fought for it, but who knew, too, how to yield: the face of a passionate woman.

What was her background? Adela Florence Cory was born on 9 April 1865, at Stoke House, Stoke Bishop, in Gloucestershire. Her father, Arthur Cory, was a colonel in the Indian Army. Her mother, Fanny Elizabeth Griffen, was singularly lovely, of Irish descent. The family travelled much and Adela Florence and her two sisters spent their time between European cities and a private school in London acquiring the accomplishments then encouraged. Adela Florence was greatly gifted; was musical, composed, played and sang and painted with considerable talent. In the studios and salons of Florence, her artistic development matured precociously, and she is said to have written many verses at this time, though none are included in her collected works. When her parents returned to India, she was marooned in England, to complete her schooling. She seems to have been anguished by the separation: already she was a prey to the force of her emotions.

She was just sixteen when she joined her parents in India, but she was a mature and much-travelled young woman. At Lahore, her father edited the *Civil and Military Gazette* and she began to work beside him. When he fell ill she took over, acquiring journalistic experience, even from so rigid a medium; for it is not to be supposed that this mouthpiece of the British Raj concerned itself with much beyond the perimeter of Government House and the cantonments. (Kipling, however, as a young journalist of eighteen, worked as assistant editor on this same paper.) There is no record of her having written any verses at this time and her life appears to have been chiefly according to pattern, surrounded by the conventions of her kind: dancing, tennis, flirting... but beginning to look about her with those wide and candid eyes and to see another world, infinitely strange and compelling, forever removed from her own.

'And never the twain shall meet,' wrote Kipling whose brilliance was proving most disturbing. While vaunting England's might, he also poured out his spleen on a certain type of Englishwoman in India. But *The Jungle Book*, like some other tales, proved his deep understanding of the country. Beyond the Corys' bungalow lay all that unattainable magic: the musky fragrance of the bazaars, with the opium dealers, grotesque toys and brilliant silks; the clay-daubed fakirs, the painted provocations of the dancing girls, the princely youths, dicing and quail-fighting, their scarlet and orange turbans mounted with jewels; and at dusk, the spangled notes of the sitar floating out across the temples where the carvings of godlike lovers interlocked in eternal ecstasies... But none of this must ever be for the young Misses Cory.

For men, it was different. They could turn inward on native life for their pleasures; tiger hunts and polo with the maharajahs, feasting in their marble palaces; learning something of the mystic-erotic cults of love in the arms of an amber-limbed girl. These men had chances denied to their womenfolk. They worked hard and played hard, learning much about the land they had taken, esteeming its many races and creeds. Still, they generally married some pink-faced miss fresh from home and forgot their flower-crowned nights, while their command of the different dialects rusted. But they had glimpsed that other world and they were never quite the same again. Some echo, or longing, remained.

And what if a woman became aware of the virile beauty of Indian men? These descendants of Akbar and Jehangir? The proud Rajput warriors or a young tribesman glimpsed coming down from the wild hills? 'He trod the ling like a buck in spring and looked like a lance at rest,' wrote Kipling. The Pathans were reputed to be the most vicious and bloodthirsty, but their towering, godlike forms were considered the embodiment of Eastern beauty. These must have been disturbing thoughts for the impressionable, indeed, inflammable Adela Florence and her sister Vivian who, writing later as Victoria Cross, was to enlarge on this theme, as on interracial loves with obsessional force. She is particularly bitter on the subject of English intolerance. Christine is kidnapped by an Arab sheikh and horrifies her friends by submitting; Hamilton pays two thousand rupees for a beautiful dancing girl who is murdered; Stanhope is in love with 'the Pearl of the Desert' who is stabbed; Trevor is desperately involved with Suzee, a Chinese girl... and Frances, a general's daughter, is discovered in her bedroom, in the arms of a Pathan; the general knocks him out, but the lovers escape, to live in a native village. Of course, it all ends badly; intolerance all round. But we are left in no doubts as to the sentiments of the author.

I know nothing of Victoria Cross's personal life: I am not assuming her books to be autobiographical, any more than the poems of her sister Laurence Hope, but both are evidence that each woman, in her own way, was awake to the sensuous spell of the tropics and had few conventional prejudices. One passage in *Anna Lombard* is noteworthy. It was Victoria Cross's most sensational novel, sold 250,000 copies and went into seventy editions and was considered outrageous. In it, she described a martial dance of the Pathans, performed at Government House, before an Anglo-Saxon audience, among them, the heroine who, while sitting beside her long-suffering English fiancé, is secretly married to one of the Pathans and has come to see her husband dance his barbaric dance of triumph there below, 'each dark face between a sword and a sword'. 'It was a sensuously beautiful sight and as such sights are generally rendered by women for the benefit (or otherwise) of men,' she goes on to describe its impact on the white ladies, who sat nervously fanning themselves, shivering with desire. 'A woman whose eyes had once been opened so that she could see that beauty, one whose senses were captured by it would never be free, entirely free, till death released her.'

This was strong meat and although only published in 1901, there is no doubt it derived from the force of the author's youthful impressions, probably shared with her sister. There is no doubt either that the young Misses Cory must have kept their thoughts to themselves. But *their* eyes had been opened and they would always seek for something wild and free, beyond the cage of civilisation.

For Adela Florence the next few years must have dragged. None of the many men she met appear to have interested her. Humdrum marriage with a pukka sahib was not for one who sought the pulse of adventure and for whom India remained tantalisingly at arm's length.

But in 1889 the pattern changed. She met Colonel Malcolm Hassels Nicolson of the Bengal Army. He was a most remarkable man and she must have recognised this at once. He was surrounded by an aura of daring and strangeness.

Here is how one of his officers described him: 'Of splendid build, with a face once seen never forgotten, he at once impressed you as a man absolutely without fear of anything. He had spent his days soldiering among the wild tribesmen beyond Scinde; he knew their language and customs and had imbibed their spirit. But for his colour and Saxon tongue you might easily have mistaken him for a Pathan, when he made up his mind to turn out as one of that fine race. Possessing many peculiar ideas and caring not a jot who did or did not agree with them… he was at once a man you would follow anywhere and a friend who went about seeking whom he might help in trouble.'

This then was the *preux chevalier* who was to prove, for Laurence Hope, the bridge by which she reached India; the man by whom she was, literally, swept off her feet. It was a curious episode. He was leaving for some remote destination, she was at the station seeing him off. The door of his compartment swung open and she was dragged along beside the train. Nicolson managed to pull her up to safety beside him. And so, brought together in the most unlikely manner, they remained together: we imagine them, the stern-faced, adventurous soldier of forty-six and the romantic, adventure-hungry girl of twenty-four, speeding forward into the torrid Indian landscape.

It was a happy marriage. Like had met like: he was the link between her inescapable Western roots and that atavistic urge which was her torment and delight. Their first years together were, for her, of ever-widening horizons. She had found a man who loved India and knew it as she longed to do. In her he found a companionship and daring not encountered in other women.

Malcolm Nicolson was of that special breed of nineteenth-century Englishman at once unconventional and traditional whose legend recurs in the annals of the British Army: particularly in the East. Some were ascetics, military mystics, some were eccentrics; all were men of stern purpose, however exotic their preferences and all knew the East intimately. I am reminded of Colonel Charles James Roberts, who raised the Bengal Lancers, married an Afghan princess, and rallied many intractable tribes to his standard. He lived in style, with Nautch music for the princess and four hundred Rampuri hounds which were massaged daily with sweet-smelling oils. He wore a Kabul turban and his long dark locks falling on his shoulders and administered justice from a fine rug set before his door, carrying a large handkerchief and a club, to weep with the afflicted or castigate the erring, as he saw fit.

Such figures became legendary, 'living the East' dangerously, incorruptibly, in battle, in disguise, but ever loyal to their country; and it must have been intoxicating to one of Laurence Hope's nature to find herself allied to these traditions. Her husband was a brilliant Oriental linguist, speaking Baluchi, Brahmi, Persian, Pushtu and many more. His facility was probably acquired in the classic manner of his kind, among the people, learning love and languages together. Men with this background of adventure could never be dull and it is astonishing that anyone could have ever imagined Laurence Hope found life with her husband such.

Malcolm Nicolson was born in 1843 of Highland Scottish descent, his father before him in the Bengal Army. He saw much active service, in Abyssinia, at the capture of Magdala, in the Afghan wars and was covered in glory and medals. Tales of his daring were many in the frontier regions and Afghanistan, which he reconnoitred, disguised as a Pathan. As a young man it is recorded that he crossed the banks of Magapir leaping barefooted from back to back of the sacred man-eating crocodiles. This exploit, while much admired by his fellow subalterns, has a ring of bravado, but as Gide says: we can never be blasé over crocodiles. Evidently, Nicolson was a man of supreme courage and his wife must have found this as irresistible as the adventures – the campaigns, even, which she now contrived to savour, at his side.

In the autumn of 1890 Nicolson was second-in-command of the Zhob Valley expedition and she followed him, disguised as a Pathan boy, creeping under his tent at night, following the column on the march, spying out the land, crouching beside him in battle and by the campfire. According to her son, to whom I am indebted for much material: 'Probably no woman, outside a novel, has lived so adventurously in peacetime.' But was there ever peace in the north-west frontier regions? Lone, dangerous rides through tribal country, to wild trysting places, in those angry passes; in her own words 'the sky tent-like above us, upheld by jagged peaks.' All the pace and danger of those moments sound in her lines *To the Hills*:

> 'Tis eight miles out and eight miles in,
> Just at the break of morn
> 'Tis ice without and flame within,
> To gain a kiss at dawn...

Or again, in *Yasin Khan*:

> Did we not waken,
> one despairing dawn
> Attacked in front, cut off in rear by snow
> Till, like a tiger leaping on a fawn
> Half of the hill crashed down upon the foe...

and later:

> ...the red tears falling from thy shattered wrist
> A spent Waziri, forceful still in hate
> Covered thy heart ten paces off – and missed.

Jingle, if you like, but how intoxicating to have lived!

Now her blood was up: she could not relinquish such a life. She studied various dialects, travelled about the country widely and luxuriated in her new freedoms. Sometimes the Nicolsons vanished, on long, solitary frontier reconnaissances which were known and valued by the government. Later, for her, there were more and more excursions into native life. Dangerous, hidden excursions into various temple initiations and secret rites – cults which were little known among the Indians themselves, rites which took place in temples carved in the rock, or in caves deep in the jungle. She was believed to be the only European woman – perhaps the only European of either sex – who was an initiate of the Taubuk mysteries. Few dared to approach them, but life in all its aspects, all of that India she loved so profoundly was sought by Laurence Hope. Her curiosity was vigorous, childlike, never prurient. 'Evil slipped from her,' wrote a friend. She wanted to know – to live – all of that stream of life into which she plunged with such eagerness. Mysteries, countries, people.

Not that she welcomed bores. One caller described petulantly how 'she pretended to be asleep when I called. But I noticed she woke up at once when Major Willcocks came in.'

She followed her husband on all his different appointments, preferring the camp life to that of a big station; there she was apt to be regarded as unortho-dox. Mrs Steele, recalling a meeting in Bombay, wrote of her embarrassment, sitting beside this striking figure, 'dressed in a low-necked, short-sleeved pink satin gown, in an open victoria carriage in broad daylight. It seemed a pity, with all those dark eyes looking on, and British prestige looming in the distance.' But she went on to say they were a very happy pair who outweighed thousands in brains and brilliancy.

It was a corseted age and when Laurence Hope received her visitors reclining on a sofa, with bare feet, her hair hanging down her back, she shocked them. Even her sense of humour was mistrusted. Changing clothes with a youthful ADC and driving round the station together was severely condemned by all but the junior officers and her husband, who always understood and indulged her.

Gradually, the life of adventure which the Nicolsons valued became more and more curtailed by his promotions. In 1894, as major general and CB, he was in command of a most important cantonment – Mhow. And now, as once they had ridden dangerously together into the frontier zones, they assumed the responsibilities of this position and the wearing round of official entertaining. Their house had been a small raja's palace; they preferred it to the military headquarters provided and here they received with great elegance – beautiful old silver, fine wines and food and a lavish, almost Oriental massing of tropical blossoms. In spite of a marked reserve which always hedged them, they were very popular: their teamwork was perfect and they were truly interested in every aspect of their post. Sometimes she would lecture the young soldiers and they would listen meekly: she was so disarming, so delightful, so unlike any other woman, they said, and they made her their confidante, trusting her, as did the Indian peoples who sensed her sympathy for them.

Mhow was set in the Great Central Indian plateau, ringed by the Vindhya mountains: a wild and beautiful face of India and a bastion of the British Raj, placed there to subdue any recurring trouble with the turbulent Holkars. The Union Jack fluttered on the ramparts and the guns boomed their salvoes to mark the comings and goings of the commander. Those of his wife were scarcely less remarked, for they were surrounded by an aura of daring. No other woman ever even wanted to go, as she did, alone into the hills and jungles, absenting herself for days at a time, apparently to study strange rites, temples, or some new dialect. To paint too: curiously quiet, meticulous work, faithfully recording the lovely country around her, 'which, as her art matured made very acceptable gifts,' notes her son primly. Even so, her underlying sense of tragedy and drama is apparent. In one, beneath the palms, lies the naked body of a murdered native cradled in a dark stain of blood.

About now, she began to admit, diffidently, that she wrote poems: sometimes she gave them to her friends, or they appeared in local club journals; but always anonymously. It was prudent: some of her subjects would have caused eyebrows to be raised to disappearing point in the curled bangs worn by the other English ladies. Poems such as *The Night of Shiva* would have been considered far too outspoken by polite society then; lines about places, climates, landscapes... they were admirable – to be quoted – 'jagged mountains that gnaw against the hard blue Afghan sky...' But what about the fate of the wanton whose 'body lay with hacked-off breasts, dishonoured in the pass...' Or that *extraordinary* poem called *Afridi Love*...

> When I have slowly drawn my knife across you
> Taking my pleasure as I see you swoon...

or that other:

> Paler and paler grow my lips
> And still thou bid'st them bleed.

Her husband explained away her verses laconically: 'My wife had quite a knack of expressing deep emotion and certain phases of native life,' he remarked to a friend, which gives the lie to those who later insisted he knew nothing of her poems and that on discovering they were engendered by her violent love affair with an Indian prince, he took to his bed and died soon afterwards.

In 1891, on long leave from India, the Nicolsons embarked on a disastrous venture, putting £4,000, a large sum in those days, into a scheme by which, with Sir John Lister Kaye, they would obtain railway, mining and river-navigation concessions in China. After some months of travel in the Far East, fighting to establish themselves in competition with various international syndicates, they were forced to admit defeat. Still, there had been months of travel across China, and meetings with the inhabitants of the Forbidden City. From her poem *Wind o' the Waste On the Wall of Pekin*, we see how, once again the poetess could capture, in a few lines, the *genius loci*, the spirit, or essence of a landscape. It is a strange, cruel poem, matching the scene and the episode recounted. It proves, like her poem *Rutland Gate*, or *Trees of Wharncliffe House*, both inspired by England, how exactly she could convey a climate, or the mood a country aroused in her.

Their return to Mhow in 1899 was joyous: they had come home. Here was the fiery heart of all the fiery kingdoms of India, rich things growing richly, jungles edging down to lakes; nearby the ruined city of Mandu, the red sandstone and marble masterpieces of Pathan architecture choked by vegetation: tombs, domed bathhouses and groves of orange-coloured lantana, where, close by, the tigers burned as bright.

Mhow was not only a military centre: it was also the focal point of official life and made more spectacular by the numbers of Indian princes who gathered there for the polo matches, and the hunting. There were the maharajahs and rajas, and their courtiers; hereditary rulers, such as the Maharajadhiraja Maharana of Jaipur – royal of the royal; his costume 'a living map of emeralds', his heron-tufted turban swagged with colossal diamonds. His white marble palace rose from a vast lake and was ornamented by huge cut crystals, glittering in the sunlight like a thousand more jewels. In their palaces, their lives, their clothes and their proud and beautiful features, these princes were fabled beings, living still in that feudal state which civilisation and the West threatened. As a woman, Laurence Hope must have found them seduction itself. As a thinker, she has left us a poem which speaks of her disgust for much of the West – her own race, holding India in subjection.

> Though many things and mighty
> Are furthered in the West,
> The ancient Peace has vanished
> Before today's unrest...
> For how among the striving,
> Their gold, their lust, their drink,
> Shall men find time for dreaming
> Or any space to think?

For all its former military might, Mhow is remembered for being 'the place where Laurence Hope wrote her hectic verses,' says a traveller visiting the place in 1929. 'The secretary of the Maharajah has reminiscences of her and how her girlish marriage to an elderly man exemplified Hindu ideas on the subject; that marriage is of the spirit and not of the flesh.' Yet whatever, or whoever, fired Laurence Hope's verses from Mhow, they still echo. The captains and the kings depart, the temples crumble and the jungles invade: but the pen is still mightier than the sword.

In the London Library, I found a vellum-covered edition of *The Indian Love Lyrics*, inscribed 'from the Library of HM Queen Mary.' The Queen, as Empress of India, had made a state visit there for the Delhi Durbar of 1911 and cherished memories of that time. I like to think of this great queen, surrounded by her jade and Fabergé *bibelots*, in the sober magnificence of the palace, evoking, through Laurence Hope's ecstasies, those glowing horizons she had barely glimpsed.

Who can tell what sparks a writer – particularly a poet? The stimuli are many. Love, hate, boredom, penury... Confronted by the question of what, or who, inspired Laurence Hope's descriptions of love and longing – which, if we assume they had to be inspired by experience, do not tally with some aspects of her life – it is obviously easier to assume she lived some illicit affair with an Indian lover, for all the implications are there: snatched meetings, secrecy, young love, wild pulses, renunciations, regrets, longings, love, the act of love, even, as in *The Night of Shiva*, or, irrefutable proof to some, the poem *On the City Wall*.

> Upon the City Ramparts, lit by the sunset gleam,
> The Blue eyes that conquer meet the Darker eyes that dream...

Yet we do not know. Were this love between the wife of the British commander and one of the princely Indian rulers to have flamed up, it is certain that the scandal would have been quickly stilled; both races would have seen it as unthinkable – a loss of prestige.

Thus, the mainspring of Laurence Hope's verses still elude us. She was a free soul, true to her own beliefs, who loved her husband deeply. Yet, if she, the younger by twenty years, was swept into some maelstrom of emotion and scandal, involving the clash of East and West, it is her husband of all people to whom she could have turned, who would have understood. It would have been part of that pattern of coming closer to the India they both loved. I do not infer anything so banal as a *mari complaisant*; such a phrase smacks of the facile manners of eighteenth-century France, held to be so authoritative on *l'amour*. Love, as the Nicolsons knew it, was of a very different calibre.

In the dedication of her last posthumous poems addressed to her husband, she writes:

> Small joy was I to thee: before we met
> Sorrow had left thee all too sad to save...

And in a letter, referring to their last year together: 'He said he only wished he had known before how happy life could be...'

What was this gnawing sadness? Why had sorrow marked him, before they met? Perhaps, long ago, he too had lived some tragic folly? In those days, young soldiers of his mettle put their private lives aside. 'Passion blazed in them and was harnessed to work and bodily vigour. A man who wished for marriage before middle age was frowned on: it was an infidelity to the ideal of work,' writes Philip Woodruff in *The Men Who Ruled India*. Perhaps, alone in knowing his story, his wife was sometimes voicing his griefs, too, in her verses?

A biographer's work is always a combination of detection and intuition: if the writer is attuned to the subject there is sometimes a kind of subconscious enlightenment, or communication. This is an experience common to most serious biographers. After the discipline of facts and the triumphs of discovery comes that flash of intuition, of awareness. Studying Laurence Hope with the few facts at my disposal I am of the impression that there was no flesh-and-blood lover – that India, and perhaps some unattained, forbidden passion sparked her already extravagant temperament to produce such fervent verses – and so, send the scandalmongers off on a false trail.

Sometimes, puzzled by the inconsistencies of a character, or by conjecture, convictions, even, which do not seem to tally with facts, I have turned to astrology for clarification. The East has always regarded the casting of horoscopes as an exact science. In the India of tradition, and even today, few marriages are considered suitable unless the horoscope of bride and bridegroom, and the chosen day are all propitious. In the case of Laurence Hope, being unable to obtain the precise hour of birth, only a *speculative* chart could be made. Having insufficient data the astrologer assumed the birth-hour to be after sunset, since this fitted the known facts of the life. Marriage, writing success, elements of secrecy, violent emotions and suicide were all indicated on a chart thus timed. Even with so imperfect a chart the analysis is remarkable. Her character appears to have been violently emotional, loyal, devoted, extravagant, with a very strong sense of justice and also of unconventionality and daring. The urge for unconventionality in many forms is shown by Uranus, placed so that the emphasis is especially connected with the sex life. There are added elements of danger, rashness and drama. But the more benign aspects of Uranus and the Sun indicate that much of this turbulence was harnessed otherwise – in creative work.

'A strong, clear horoscope,' notes the astrologer, Mrs Lind. 'Planetary forces are without ambiguity. Sun in its exaltation (Aries), Venus in its own sign of Taurus, Jupiter in its own sign of Sagittarius, Saturn in its exultation (Libra). Such a subject goes to extremes, with conviction.' I will only add here that in 1895 she appears to reach a climax of extravagant emotions; and in 1896–7 this force continues, stimulating creative forces, adventure, illusion and the secret or sensational; that 1901 was a peak year; that from 1902 on, renunciation and a decline are indicated. In her last year, 1904, where renunciation and sadness gather, Neptune transits Mars, a sinister implication for her, with a natal Mars-Neptune square: this links sex and death, and stimulates her strong potential for emotional suffering, despair, tragedy and self-destruction. Add to this Sun quincunx Saturn, in 1904 – the classic aspect for death. Again, natally, she has the Sun opposite Saturn, which touches off this karma. In this year, all the tragic aspects of her stars, as of her life, combined.

I have been told fantastic stories (as fantastic, some readers will say, as my claim for the verity of a horoscope) concerning Laurence Hope's idyll with a Hindu prince: the whole episode ready-made for Hollywood: how they met at Mhow and lived a brief and burning love, in secrecy and danger, meeting on the lotus lakes, or in the shade of the temples, she disguised as a dancing girl, he as a commoner, their pulses beating to the rhythm of the drums... of how the infatuated prince vowed half his wealth and kingdom to her first-born... how the parchment deed was snatched, at some ceremonial scene, swallowed by a fanatic, or burned by another... how the prince's father tore the lovers apart; how the viceroy himself stepped in to hush up the scandal, how the maharajah was compelled to abdicate. Perhaps this farrago all fits very neatly but I am not convinced. Perhaps she loved – enough to precipitate scandal – but not enough to hurt her husband. Who knows, now? The bombshell quality of Laurence Hope's poems alone was enough to engender the wildest rumours.

In his *Writer's Notebook*, Somerset Maugham makes a reference to the affair as London interpreted it in 1901, the year *The Garden of Kama* first appeared. 'They were talking about VF (Violet Florence) whom they'd all known. She published a volume of passionate love poems obviously not addressed to her husband. It made them laugh to think that she'd carried on a long affair under his nose and they'd have given anything to know what he felt when at last he read them.'

Yes, I expect such people would have enjoyed such a situation. Maugham adds: 'This note gave me the idea for a story which I wrote forty years later. It is called *The Colonel's Lady*.' But when, the other day, I asked him if he could recall anything of Laurence Hope, or the incident, he replied that he was now in his ninetieth year and had forgotten so much. In his same *Notebook*, he writes: 'How often the author makes up his fiction from incidents of his own experience, *trifling*, perhaps, *and made interesting or dramatic only by his power of creation*.' The italics are mine. Laurence Hope's powers of identification, of creative imagination were great. Did she need more?

High passions belong to all ages, all races, but it is the English, for all their seeming reserve, who display in their literature the most ardent emotions, the most lyric tenderness and the most profound understanding of love in all its aspects. Consider the dark face of love as Emily Brontë showed us, in *Wuthering Heights*; the love, at once metaphysical and sensuous, of which John Donne wrote; the heartbreaking desires of Shakespeare's sonnets; or that anonymous fifteenth-century lover whose verse still echoes the cry of every longing lover:

> O Western wind, when wilt thou blow
> That the small rain down can rain.
> Christ, that my love were in my arms
> And I in my bed again!

Here is that same stark note, that same abandonment to love which we find in the Scottish Border Ballads: And which we find in the poems of Laurence Hope.

Not that I am comparing her to the immortals. Still, her voice still vibrates; she still speaks to us of love, and we still listen.

After the whispers of scandal, the fanfares of acclaim. When the general's term of office at Mhow was over, in 1900, their long leave began by a sojourn in Bombay where their only child, Malcolm Josceline, was born in September. Doctors despaired of the mother's life and at this moment we have a clue to the depth of the bond between husband and wife, of some suicide pact even, which later, she was to honour. In a letter to an old friend, the general wrote that he had burned all his papers and meant to follow her, as he had promised. Perhaps her excursions into the mystic cults of India had convinced them of some unity, after death.

But she recovered and back in London, this world pressed in on them. All its conventions stifled them. When in 1901 Heinemann published her *Garden of Kama*, the acclaim was instant. Mr Hope, an unknown young poet – for of course he must be young – showed a fresh and splendid talent. Critics and public wanted more. Then the secret leaked out. It was a woman – Major General Nicolson's wife! Now they found themselves social lions, objects of curiosity and admiration. But financial problems beset them. His leave was indefinite, his next appointment uncertain, although he was still on the active list, a Commander of the Bath, at Court Levées and the Cavalry Club, where appointments are usually sealed.

Forgetting the lesson of their abortive Chinese venture, they now considered tea-planting in Assam, or some lucrative post in Morocco, where they went in 1902. In the great silences of the desert and the sun, the exiles found something of their own climate again. But French-held interests were too powerful for the establishment of any worthwhile venture: once again they were defeated and returned to London. 1903 saw the publication of *Stars of the Desert*; and a disastrous venture, a newspaper, which Laurence Hope wished to run on new, experimental lines. Their whole life was India: away from its fiery shores they were lost. Her poems are not dated, but we can place some precisely. *Trees of Wharncliffe House* is the song of an exile:

> ...your leaves, refreshed by summer showers
> Are naught to me, who feast

My fancy on those other flowers
that burn about the East.

...and again:

I always feel a sense of loss
If, at the close of day
I cannot see the Southern Cross
Break through the gathered grey...

So, in 1904, they returned to India, to await the expected appointment. Leaving their child with the general's sister, they sailed east once more, towards the sunlight. But for them, it was setting, though its rays still warmed them as they wandered from one modest hotel to another (no wild sorties, now, into the frontier passes). A muted note of acceptance sounds in her letters: the rebel has come to terms with life: she loves and is loved, but both of them have known another pulse. She is thirty-nine, he is sixty-two.

Ah! to exchange this wealth of idle days
For one cold reckless night of Khorasan!

are lines which voice their sadness as the years closed round, imprisoning them.

They found life cheap in an Indian backwater. Necessities were few. They no longer entertained officially and so could live modestly. Her songs were sold for sums which, by today's values, seem insulting. Five guineas for one; three for another. Yet she was pleased. How few her demands on life, now.

She wrote home asking for pictures of her baby son and showed, again, how modest her attitude to life. Penny snapshots by a beach photographer, she wrote, were often the best. They could be taken often, every day even, and could catch the subject perfectly. Like many passionate women she was not, I think, predominantly maternal: her husband came first. We imagine the lonely little boy, patting at sandcastles, in the charge of elderly relatives, sent home so early, staying behind when his parents returned to India; loved, but perhaps coming so late into their lives, not having time to become part of it before they died, leaving him forever a stranger.

For some while, the general had not seemed well. Not ill, but not the iron-constitutioned soldier with whom she had shared so much adventure. Suddenly, a chill wind of premonition stirs in the palms. The sun has lost its warmth. In Madras, the general's ill health was diagnosed as trifling; a minor operation would set everything right. It would be better to have it done at once, before the awaited appointment was confirmed. Arm-in-arm they walked round to the nursing home. There was no cause for anxiety and they parted lightly. Next day, 7 August, he was dead. He had been given too much anaesthetic and then suddenly, there was not enough oxygen to revive him. It was a question of time. Frantically, the nurses and doctors tried to keep him breathing. Desperately Laurence Hope rushed from chemist to hospital in a bid for her husband's life. Oxygen cylinders could not be had. When she got back to the nursing home, living a nightmare from which she never again escaped, it was too late. Death had found Malcolm Nicolson, not as he would have wished, in battle, or in the hills, but in the inefficiency of a small nursing home.

For Laurence Hope, there was never any more sunlight: she had entered a twilight zone of grief. Her letters home were heartbreaking: she could not reconcile herself to her loss. She saw her husband everywhere: he was beside her – he was gone; sleeping, waking, she was possessed by sorrow. They had grown even closer, in these past few years of inactivity. Some trivial shopping errand in the town would send her rushing back to him as if she was returning from a long absence. Her grief-stricken letters, at this time, were in truth love-letters, as poignant as any of her verses.

Her friends had not realised how shattering her loss would be. Except in her verses, she never displayed much emotion; now her anguish was terrible to see. She could not rally, and seemed racked by remorse. An old friend, Eardly Norton, the distinguished Madras barrister, lent her his house and here she spent the next month, trying to concern herself about a tombstone and the pension to be paid to her child. For his sake she set about completing another volume of poems for which the publishers were waiting. Sometimes, at night, she was seen wandering about the garden of Dunmore House, a living ghost, 'who cut mysterious initials on the bark of many trees,' wrote Eardly Norton, later. For whom, for what these initials stood no one has ever disclosed. In the opinion of her friends, she was now unhinged by sorrow. Her last poems, *Indian Love*, are dedicated to her husband in moving lines, written prophetically:

Useless my love – as vain as this regret
That pours my hopeless life across thy grave.

By the time the manuscript reached her publishers, she was dead. On the afternoon of 4 October, two months after her husband's death, she killed herself. There were none of the legendary trappings of death in the Orient – of some carved jade poison phial, the thrust of a curved dagger, or the ceremonial of suttee, the widow's immolation on her husband's funeral pyre. For Laurence Hope, a chemist's packet – perchloride of mercury – achieved this end. They are buried together, in St Mary's Cemetery, Madras.

Once, Hindu widows on their last journey to the funeral pyre, flower-hung and adorned as brides, dipped their hand in a jar of red pigment and on leaving their house, imprinted their mark on the lintel of the door. A few old houses still bear traces of this small, lonely hand bidding farewell to life. Laurence Hope, so steeped in Indian tradition, left no such mark. Only her poems:

The years go hence, and wild, and lovely things,
Their own, go with them, never to return.

The Fading Garden and the Forgotten Rose:
A Balkan Queen

THE LITTLE BALKAN KINGDOMS IMMORTALISED AS RURITANIA, OR GRAUSTARK, were once very real, last strongholds of those privileged monarchies that bloomed so exotically all over Europe and grew particularly fanciful as the Danube wound eastwards towards the Black Sea. Now, all over a greying world, former royal residences stand shuttered and dusty, or are put to more practical uses. Pekin's Summer Palace swarms with tourists; the marble halls of the Rajput maharajahs are crumbling under fierce suns. Everywhere, great gilded and mirrored perspectives echo to the shuffle of felt-slippered sightseers. The northern palaces of Tzardom have became museums; their Crimean mansions sanatoriums. The sober magnificence of Marlborough House is given over to Commonwealth conferences. The Emir of Bukhara's Summer Palace and the garden of his harem, where the peacocks still trail their glories, has become a clinic for kidney complaints, starched white hospital aprons replacing the gauzy finery of the odalisques.

Perhaps the most evocative of all lesser royal residences (apart from such monuments of self-indulgence as Linderhof, built by the mad King Ludwig of Bavaria) is the tiny Summer Palace, hardly larger than a pavilion, which Queen Marie of Romania built for herself on the Black Sea coast, at Balcic, and where she was able to express the more untrammelled aspects of her temperament and imagination: where the woman rather than the Queen – even the superb Ruritanian queen she was – could sometimes live entirely in the picturesque manner she favoured. However much she was photographed in peasant costumes, with richly patterned aprons, a weaving shuttle in her hand, her preference was, in fact, for something more exotic. By the time she built Balcic her taste had crystallised and the little villa was, like her style of dresses, a highly personal blend of Byzantine luxury and a note of unmistakably Elinor Glyn romanticism.

This queenly retreat was still much discussed in the People's Balkans, when we arrived there, in 1946. Many of the peasants still clung to the afterglow of royalty, while the party condemned it, but both were intrigued. The royal pavilion assumed a legendary quality, like the stately pleasure dome that Kublai Khan decreed. During the Queen's lifetime it had been scarcely less legendary, being shrouded in mystery and innuendo. Only the most privileged ever penetrated there. But eight years after the Queen's death – after World War II and the establishment of another way of life, the Romanian government used to lend it, on occasions, to those they favoured. Anyone who visited the place always returned with lively descriptions of its octagonal room with the alcove bed. I grew tired of hearing how various high-ranking Allied generals, chiefs of missions and ministers all slept well there – loved the bathing – the boating – the shooting – the Gypsy music...

None of them heard its echoes, or made more than a casual reference to the woman whose turbulence and majesty had stirred even the Balkans, and who had conceived the little palace as her refuge from reality: for even Ruritania had its own brand of such.

This pavilion, or folly, and the larger but less imaginative Chateau of Euxinograd (*faux* French-Renaissance, turreted and pompous) which was built by a neighbouring ruler, the Tzar Ferdinand of Bulgaria, were places we came to know well while *en poste* in Sofia. Both were haunted houses, haunted by phantoms of princes and privilege.

Euxinograd is a pinpoint on the map. There is no village, but the little private bathing beach belonging to the château has one end of its sickle scoop emphasised by a miniature jetty and lighthouse. The little private beach, though that is perhaps too worldly a name for so unpretentious a shore, was still private property when we were there, being then reserved for high-ranking party members, or Bulgarian government officials. In 1946 the Allied Control Commission was still in being in Bulgaria and the military missions and legations had requisitioned villas all along the coast, while some of the Corps Diplomatique – ourselves among them – were able to taste the paradisiacal delights of both Euxinograd and Balcic.

Euxinograd was Arcadia and Ruritania in one. The tiny bay was backed by cliffs tangled in tropic vegetation and sloping, by way of the palmy, still perfectly trimmed royal gardens, to vineyards edging down on to the sands, so that it was possible to reach up out of the water and pick a bunch of enormous, egg-sized grapes which are said to yield a particularly fragrant white wine. Looking inland from the jetty, the fluffily wooded coast, sparsely dotted with villas was rather as the French Riviera must have been in its far away, uncorrupted past. In the middle of the white sand beach stood a ridiculously ornate little wooden pavilion, an orange painted chalet, divided into six or seven cabins, where once the royal bathers used to shuffle in and out of their clothes. A narrow gangplank, with stout handrails, ran down to the sea, but it was rusted and rotting now, half-buried in the loose sand.

I imagined the Tzar Ferdinand and his Ruritanian court, frisking down it to the water's edge; 'Foxy Ferdi' to his detractors, his tiny ferret eyes set too close to his far-too-long nose, smiling his curiously sly smile as he led his guests, in a barrel-striped bathing suit, his plump, white, over-manicured fingers for once bare of the precious stones he loved with such Oriental abandon. I saw the ladies of the party dressed up for their dip, in black stockings and mackintosh mob-caps, bobbing up and down, keeping their pink and white complexions and tong-waved coiffures high and dry, while shrieking and simpering in the shallows.

But these are tougher times. We used to lie on the sand, baking ourselves to crackling, watching a party of lean black-brown Bulgarians; the men in their tiny loincloths, the women with a bandana handkerchief brassiere added, as they swam far out to sea, the flail-like precision of the crawl-stroke churning the dark blue water.

Perched halfway up the cliff there was a little gazebo, a ruined summer house, with trellised arches and a thatched roof. We used to pause there, as we climbed the path on our way home, at sunset. The lilac bushes almost hid it from the path: there were old cobwebs, with dead wasps entangled and sometimes a snake slithered away as we approached. Sitting there, looking through the lattice-work at the fading blue of the sea, and the tiny dots which were fishermen's boats, still out after the few fish which live in this part of the Black Sea, I used to think again of the little Ruritanian court which had vanished.

No doubt the summer house was a favourite rendezvous for those complicated picnic teas beloved of the Edwardians and their contemporaries. I imagined the paraphernalia; the parasols and cushions, the royal ladies and their ladies-in-waiting in tussore dustcoats, buttoned boots and enormous hats with tulle veils which they furled on to the bridge of their rice-powdered nose preparatory to sipping tea. There would be gentlemen – plenty of gentlemen – with whom to flirt, for in that world, few worked except at pleasure. The gentlemen would be wearing white flannels, blazers and straw boaters, or panama hats, for one still dressed formally out of doors. They would be very highly born... the younger Russian grand dukes, a smattering of Hapsburgs, Hungarian nobles and the German princelings, Saxe-Meiningens, Coburgs and Hesses, a stock which peopled the courts of Europe, bringing their blazons and their hereditary taints to each fresh alliance.

While panting footmen staggered along the cliff paths with picnic baskets filled with an elaborate tea, cucumber sandwiches and puffed-up patisseries and spirit lamps and sugar tongs and lace napkins and all the fiddle-de-dee of the drawing room, there would be a lot of tittle-tattle within the perimeter of the *Almanach de Gotha*. Once in a while a lady would glance down over the still blue bay and someone would be sure to say it was just the colour of her eyes. And then, someone else would light a cigarette, a perfumed Balkan cigarette, held in a pale, kid-gloved hand, gloved, even in Arcadia.

O! gazebo, thy name is nostalgia! All over Europe the gazebos and arbours of past dalliance are ruins, now: memorials to an irresponsible, yet charming way of life – charming for those who lived it, that is. Charming for Great Catherine, 'the Semiramis of the North', lying in her favourite's arms, in a Chinese pagoda, at Tzarskoe Selo; for the aristos in the Hameau at the Petit Trianon; for Charles II and his *zenana* of beauties, as he moored a state barge load of them beside the landing stage at Hampton Court.

A mixture of Paul Pryism and tourist zeal made us accept an invitation to visit Balcic. The town, we heard, was nothing special – a few fishing boats, a squalid Gypsy *mahalla,* or settlement, and a few modern villas: but there was Queen's Folly. We left Euxinograd on a lambent August morning and drove east, into the fierce sun, mounting the hairpin bends which connect one great tableland with the next in a series of slab-like plateaux. This is the Dobrudja: chalky wastes, white dust, white oxen, sheep and a blinding blue sky. There are great plains, dotted with dusty scrub and many miles of giant sunflowers with heads like lolling dinner-plates. They are grown for their oil; the seeds, or *semki*, are the Slav equivalent of chewing gum. We stopped to pick some and went on our way chewing, crossing the old Romanian frontier, a sort of Balkan

Maginot Line, sunken fortifications and camouflaged gun-turrets embedded in white rocks.

The Dobrudja has always been a bone of contention between Bulgaria and Romania; it has always been fought over, ceded by one treaty and retracted by another. There is a wild admixture of races here, Turks, Gagaoutz and Tartars. The Gagaoutz are centred in this part of the Dobrudja; they were always very much favoured by the Turks, who considered the whole area, particularly the great forest of Deli Orman, to be a natural frontier defence against the Russians.

In Turkish, Deli Orman means 'The Mad Wood'. Nothing could be better named. The huge tracts of forest – flat forest – sprawl across the plain. The trees writhe in a never-ceasing wind which howls round them by day and night, winter or summer, a restless, maddening wind blowing straight from the steppes, before it rages on, to cross the Black Sea, strike the shores of Turkey and whip the waters of the Bosphorus.

The little town of Balcic is reached by a sudden descent, through limestone crags. It lies basking at the foot of the cliffs, sheltered from tempests and indeed, from life itself. It is quite improbable, having a toy-like quality, as if designed as a backcloth for Mr Pollock's celebrated *Juvenile Drama*, the 'Penny Plain and Two Pence Coloured' sheets which enchanted Victorian children. Act II Scene iii. *A Pirates' Port on the Illyrian Coast*. Ramshackle, doll-sized houses, pink and blue and yellow, cling to the cliffs giddily. The miniature harbour, with its customs, shop and inn are set down between perpendicular white crags and hummocks looking like toy volcanoes. Lemon and fig trees burst from the fissures. One or two over-ornamented, but cardboard-like, buildings, the town hall among them, are pressed against the rocks in tiers, and there are a couple of blue-domed Orthodox churches and a little mosque with coloured-glass lozenges to trim its windows. Everything seemed to come out of a box of children's bricks.

On the cliffs above we found clots of shack dwellings and the ever-irresistible *mahalla* where the Gypsies live; the women in ragged chintz trousers toned down to a faint pastel by the all-pervading white dust. They squatted on their haunches searching their children's heads intently, while the children, a beautiful and dissipated-looking lot, picked ticks off the heaving flanks of the sheep which were tethered by every door. At a haughty distance we saw a line of modern luxury villas, once owned by the rich Romanians who used to follow their queen's lead and flock to Balcic in the summer. But they were standing shuttered and empty now. Turning our steps towards another abandoned dwelling, we left the pretty pasteboard town and followed a road beside the cliff, towards Queen Marie's Summer Palace... the legend we had come to see.

It is no secret that the Queen built this villa as an amorous retreat. Her heart was buried in the Byzantine chapel by the lily garden. In spite of all its highly coloured implications and the exoticism of its architecture and setting (near-Turkish), this royal folly retains a muted, tomb-like quality. But the loneliness, so apparent to us now, was, I believe, always there, echoing, along with self-conscious voluptuousness, some melancholy strain of the Queen's own nature. Although she was generally surrounded by adulation, she remained, in herself, an exile; from that overwhelming love she craved; from her English background and from the pomp and power which was also her birthright, and which she only achieved to a much lesser degree in her adopted country. These undercurrents of sadness, of regret and a quality of defiant bravery are apparent throughout her *Memoirs*. They are a remarkable achievement, quite certainly her own; they bear no traces of the ghostwriter's sickly hand, so abundantly evident in other autobiographies of high-born personages. Her portraits are brilliant; she sees very clearly for one of her rank; it is 'Missy' the unconventional Englishwoman writing, rather than a queen. Even when describing her children, she retains her penetrating judgement; Elizabeth, a silent, cold child with steel-strong little hands, not perhaps a sympathetic character; Mignon, like a full-blown peony, easy-going, loving and giving, 'one of those luminous bridges back to hope, which are given to us occasionally... after great darkness...' Carol, the Crown princeling, at once taken away from her to be brought up by others, brought up wrong; and Ileana, the angel child. 'If Mignon was the child of my flesh, Ileana was certainly the child of my soul.' She is a passionately loving mother, but she is not blinded; she is a queen, her children must share the burdens of monarchy. It is said that during the last stormy days of King Carol II's rule, when a bitter quarrel with his brother Prince Nicolas brought them to the shooting-point, the Queen Mother rushed between her sons, flung her body across that of Carol, the King and so, stopping the bullet believed she had saved the monarchy. But it was lost, one way or another and she herself never fully recovered from the wound.

Two great rulers were her grandparents: Queen Victoria on her father's side; the Tzar Alexander II, 'the Liberator', on her mother's side. As queen of a newly formed, insignificant Balkan country she felt faintly *declassée*. She was irresistibly beautiful, illustriously born… a great catch among the royal princesses. Yet she was married off at sixteen, since her mother, the Duchess of Edinburgh, believed any royal crown, however small, was preferable to a mere ducal one; 'Princesses must be married off young, otherwise they begin to think for themselves,' was one of her beliefs. She herself had not been happy in her marriage; as the only daughter of the mighty Tzar Alexander II, she had felt keenly her loss of prestige at the British court; she had detested what seemed to her its middle-class aspects; she spent much time abroad wearing dull clothes, the magnificent jewels of her dowry unused; her only link with the barbaric splendour of her youth were the glittering ikons which adorned her rooms, and the rich vestments of the priest and two chanters who followed her everywhere to maintain the mystic rituals of her Orthodox faith.

Her three daughters adored her and were in awe of her too. She allowed them a singularly unrestricted childhood… and then all of a sudden it was time to marry. Marie found herself betrothed to Ferdinand, 'Nando', a shy, young Hohenzollern-Sigmaringen prince, heir apparent to the Romanian throne then occupied by his uncle, King Carol I. King George V, then an inconsiderable young naval prince at Malta, under the command of the Duke of Edinburgh's squadron, had fallen a victim to the charms of Missy, the little princess who rode and romped with him, but he was not taken seriously, he was only a second son; the English throne seemed remote. Who could have foreseen then that his elder brother, the Duke of Clarence, would die suddenly and he would find himself heir apparent? At sixteen Missy became the Crown princess of Romania and George, the Duke of York, married Princess Mary of Teck. Together they lived a long life of public glory and private happiness. But for all that it was known that 'May' never quite forgave Missy for having been her husband's special weakness. Such beauty as Missy's always caused pangs all round.

Queen Marie's ambitions grew to match the extravagance of her Ruritanian setting. She came to see herself as a Byzantine empress figure, ruling over the entire Balkans; her dream, that of 'UNIRE'... unity, the wild dream of Romanian patriots, scheming a Balkan empire, Bulgaria, Serbia, Macedonia, Albania... all the territories stretching from Turkey to Austria, and all under her Romanian rule. After the death of King Ferdinand, when King Carol relinquished his kingdom, a council of regency was to be appointed; two elder statesmen, the patriarch and her anointed self. It was her hour of triumph. To become one with her people, she had been converted to the Orthodox faith and now she would grasp that power which had eluded her during her long apprenticeship as Crown princess, and which, during her husband's reign, had not been as absolute as she desired. Her intentions were noble: she had become, over the years, an ardent patriot, a large-minded, courageous woman, a leader who had upheld her country magnificently in the years of battle and stress. But to many she remained the outsider: the Englishwoman, the frivolous beauty, the sorceress, the intriguer... Even her conversion to the Orthodox faith did not win over her detractors.

At the very hour when she was donning her robes of state and all the veils and diadems and cordons by which she dramatised her official appearances, her enemies were denouncing her at the parliament and invoking Salic law. Messengers rushed to the palace to warn her... it was impossible that after such an attack, she could be sworn in. Once again, absolute power had eluded her. Her disappointment was tragic, her fury unbridled. I have heard it said that she flung herself on the ground, rolling backwards and forwards in paroxysms of rage, her jewels scattered, her robes torn. Her Romanov blood seethed and over-boiled; her quieter, more stubborn English reactions, which had sustained her through so many years of strife, were temporarily overcome and both gave place to purely Balkan violence.

This story, like so many others centred round the Queen, may be apocryphal; those who circulated it pursed their lips, as they so often did, discussing her unpredictable actions... Yet, regrettable, violent... whatever they called it, it was in keeping with this figure, so much larger than life, in all her life force, her beauty and daring. She was a queen who had come to identify herself with her adopted country and to assume not only the more theatrical aspects of the Crown, which such a people understood, but also to express her emotions in their uninhibited manner.

Great queens – and in her age and setting I think she was such – have a way of epitomising their country. She herself was aware of this. In her *Memoirs*, writing of the successive coronations of King Edward VII, her uncle and King George V, her cousin, at Westminster Abbey, she emphasises in each case, the sense of sober, unquestioning magnificence.

> The Queens' faces were severe, almost unmoved, the thrones they were mounting were, if I can so express it, seats of peace... Queen Alexandra and Queen Mary: two serene figures... their crowns, although weighted by a hundred gems, did not seem to oppress them... there was an established security about these Queens which made you feel glad for them, not afraid!

In contrast, in prophetic contrast, she saw her cousin the Tzar Nicholas II crowned in the Kremlin; beside him, the doomed Tzarina, 'the young Empress – standing rigidly upright, her golden robes flowing from her shoulders, her face flushed, her eyes tragic, her lips tightly set as though at bay'.

If queens reflect the character of their country, no two better examples of Balkan romanticism, of a sort of stylised monarchy could be found, than Queen Marie and her predecessor, Queen Elizabeth, widely known as the poetess Carmen Sylva. By the time the Crown princess Marie became queen, in 1914, she had evolved her own style – Byzantine – but Carmen Sylva had been Wagnerian. Both were generally swathed in innumerable veils and indeterminate draperies. Both these ladies saw themselves as figureheads – symbols of monarchy. They were, each in their own way, *monstres sacrées*. Both were artistic, wrote poetry, painted, were musicians and fostered the beautiful peasant arts of Romania. But whereas Carmen Sylva was intense and had no gleam of humour, Queen Marie was able to laugh at everything, including herself – except over the matter of her clothes – and here, perhaps she was influenced by her wish to provide the peasant majority with a figurehead in their own terms.

To be royal was to be, in a sense, theatrical: whether she believed, like her ancestors, in the divine right of kings, or whether she moved with the times and sensed the growing artificiality of the *métier*, she dressed the part. Besides, she frankly liked dressing up. With each change of costume she revealed another aspect or mood. The princess in her Carpathian castle, shadowy pillared halls, divans piled with bearskins, walls hung with rare ikons and the Queen, splendid in her trailing robes and jewels, enthroned among her courtiers and admirers. The fairy-tale Romanian princess visiting her remote provinces on a shaggy pony, wearing top-boots and embroidered aprons, who will wave her wand, put on her golden crown and right all the wrongs. The lovely and fecund mother, joy of the dynasty, in a tea-gown, all softness, surrounded by her beautiful brood; the mature woman, the Mother Queen, Mama Regina to her soldiers, in a nurse's uniform, at the front in the hospitals – and here she was playing no part, but was flung into the tragic ordeals of her country, sharing, retreating, upholding with selfless devotion.

In 1916, when everything seemed lost for Romania, there was a question of exile, of forming a Romanian colony in Kharkov, Poltava, or some other Russian province. She was aghast. Her country had become her life. 'This would mean complete exile,' she writes in her journal, 'The thought is so utterly ghastly that one accepts it quietly, without words of complaint or protest, as one accepts the thought of death.'

But she went on fighting furiously. And here she was playing no role, and needed no carefully devised costume. Her loathing of the German enemy was intense. Many of her relatives were Germans; her husband's sympathies and training had been as Germanic as his blood and that of his predecessor, the old King Carol. She was the Romanian, among them all. Perhaps her Russian ancestry helped her to love and understand the Balkans: something wild in her responded to its own wildness. In the mountains, she is remembered as an Amazon – she was unmatched as a horsewoman – galloping across tracks few could follow, riding astride, mounted on a wild Cossack horse, gift of a Russian admirer and wearing a Circassian uniform (sent by another enslaved Slav), a dark blue caftan braided with silver, over a scarlet under-tunic, silver *cartouchières* across the chest and a dagger at her then very slim waist. She describes herself as an over-picturesque apparition. But how pleasing to both player and public. She was undoubtedly narcissistic – delighted with herself – but not self-satisfied. There is a great difference.

That style which might be described as basic Balkan Royal, veils and trailing draperies, which were, in a sense, Queen Marie's trademark, spread from one Balkan kingdom to the next. Her two elder daughters became respectively queens of Greece and Yugoslavia and followed the Romanian tradition, float-ing about their own realms, similarly draped, the apotheosis of queendom.

(It was left to their youngest sister, the Princess Ileana, married to an Austrian archduke and mother of a large family, to face life in exile in America, doing the housework uncomplaining, in tweeds.) But in the last afterglow of royal radiance before World War II, newsreels and press photographs recording great occasions east of the Danube were immediately recognisable, not so much by some distinguishing cathedral or monument, as by the trailing toilettes of the three queens. These bore no relation to fashion, nor, indeed, did those equally stylised but less emotional costumes which Queen Alexandra and Queen Mary of England evolved. But all of them, in their own way, knew that the mystique of royalty must be fostered by every means and that a queen must have every-thing to do with pure style, and nothing to do with mere fashion; still less, must a monarchy appear middle class.

Even in her dying Queen Marie displayed that dramatic sense which lit her life. She had been born to the purple and she asked that for her funeral Bucharest would be hung with purple rather than black. Thus the banal streets through which the cortège passed assumed a drama and beauty, draped in violet, lilac and the Byzantine purple she had always craved.

Queen Marie loved and knew well the peasants; she did not make rounds of scheduled royal visits so much as a series of personal, impulsive, sorties among them; into their villages and houses, accompanied by one lady-in-waiting rather than a suite, or perhaps only one of her daughters, talking to the people in her broken Romanian which always made them smile, but her heart going out to them in a manner they understood. She had, in fact, the common touch, without the patronage which that implies. She would appear unexpectedly in a village, share a peasant's meal with relish, discuss their crops and their hopes, listen to their legends and allow herself to be, literally, taken to their ragged and often noisome bosoms. To such people she was never remote, though among the court she could quell at a glance, as she could charm. Writing of a pair of old crones, 'my two old witches,' she relates being dragged into their arms and their quarrels. To the peasants she was always Mama Regina. 'Your tiny dried up little heart is black as sin,' spat one witch to the other, then pointing to the Queen, 'But Mama Regina's heart is round and red and full of love.'

This was the sort of compliment she valued most, as she preferred the armfuls of wildflowers the ragged children brought her to all the formal bouquets with which her path was strewn. With the years, she and her husband had drifted far apart; Nando had once been, as she says, 'Almost cruelly in love...' but they always remained united in their patriotism and their passion for flowers. Nando was something of a botanist; they both flung themselves into gardening, and both continued to bring each other flowers of all kinds, marvelling at them, together, till the last.

In her early days in Bucharest the princess had been pathetically lonely, cut off, in a strange setting, among strangers, very far from home, surrounded by rigid etiquette, a never-ending round of stern duties, of constraint and criticism; but as she grew to sense her power as a princess, as a beautiful woman, and to sense too, the special flavour of her new country, she sometimes showed an almost outrageous exuberance. Her craving for pleasure, sterner court circles said, was dangerous in one so near the throne. It was a German-held throne, painfully earnest and austere and quite out of touch with the Romanian national temperament. King Carol I, 'Der Onkel' to the young Crown prince and princess, had his hands full striving to raise the European status of his small kingdom, and to inculcate his own strict standards, first to his eccentric wife, Carmen Sylva, and then to his nephew and heir's wife, the Princess Marie. It was grudgingly admitted that she worked tirelessly at her duties, but she *would* dance till dawn... then dash off on one of those wild horses that only she could ride. She *would* know the most unsuitable people... painters, musicians, that fast international set, the Plesses and all those Russian grand dukes... (cousins, but still...) True, she was giving the nation a whole nursery full of splendid little princes and princesses... But she had some *giddy* strain... driving along the Chausée Kissileff at sunset...! (This was Bucharest's Bois de Boulogne, the elegant promenade for *le beau monde* and demi-monde alike.) Not for our Crown princess, said the critics, watching her open carriage bowl past as she smiled and bowed with that almost childish glee, her chic feathered or flowered hat framing those enormous blue eyes that worked such havoc. She wrote fairy stories, painted, built herself a house in the treetops, explored the street markets of Bucharest for antiques...

it was all very unconventional. And then she would summon the Lăutari to her parties. They were the Gypsies whose hot-blooded violins were legendary, but particularly frowned upon by the court. Yet somehow they were always around, their emotional strains undermining royal fanfares.

Her giddiness, like her loneliness, is all recorded with remarkable objectivity in her *Memoirs*. But in the last volume, with the outbreak of World War I, another depth, or dimension, is revealed. She has grown up, at last. Her country's desperate needs, as it was slowly abandoned, overcome and fought back to victory, makes heroic reading. She does not spare us, as she did not spare herself. In Indian heat and Russian cold, which are the extremes of the Romanian climate, she knew no rest. She was all over the country, wherever she could be of use. Beside the troops, retreating, in field hospitals where dead and wounded were piled on the mud-floored huts sanded over with lice; at headquarters, everywhere, she toiled day and night, with ferocity of purpose and tenderness of spirit, lashing at the politicians who dared speak of submission, or defeat; at a base hospital, feeding, for want of anything else, spoonfuls of jam to the gaunt soldiers. In the midst of disease, famine and typhus epidemics she refuses to wear gloves ('They all want to kiss my hand... how can I ask them to kiss India-rubber?') Her journal records this terrible time as she battles on, fighting fatigue, despair and lice too. And still her extraordinary animal vitality asserts itself. She enjoys, sensuously, the sight of a lime tree in flower; or a packet of ginger biscuits, conjuring the far-away securities of an English tea-table on the lawn at Osborne, with Grandmama Queen.

But this is no time for nostalgia. Her tears are kept for memories of Mircea, 'My little Mircea', the baby who died at the beginning of the war and whose grave she has had to leave untended when, with the King and the army, she retreats before the enemy. The thought of the lonely little grave torments her unceasingly. She goes to church: 'I wept, as only a broken-hearted mother can weep, the mother of a dead child, of dead hopes, the mother of a suffering people she has learned to love...' She organises Prince Mircea canteens for the starving children, sends her elder daughters, the Princesses Elizabeth and Marie 'Mignon' off to work wherever they can help. Mignon is a humble worker: she will clean windows, sweep floors or hold a leg steady for amputation with the same self-effacing zeal. The King and the Crown prince Carol are with the armies, her other two children Nicolas and Ileana are too small to do more than accompany her on some of her tours, but they can keep up the people's morale, and she does not shield them from horrors. Except for Ileana, her children are not of her mettle or stamina; Elizabeth collapses at one point, Marie at another; then Nicolas and we sense her impatience... the exasperation of a very strong woman who cannot will others to her own degree of endurance. Perfect health and a good digestion, 'my Russian digestion' as she describes it gratefully, sustained her through ordeals that felled others. But she had her courage; it runs like a thread of challenge throughout her life. And always, at all times, she is fiercely unresigned.

All around her are horrors. 'A long, long day, dark with pain and revolt,' she writes, as they fall back again. Every retreat is also measured by her heart, for its distance from Mircea's lonely grave. One among thousands now. 'We begin to speculate in which way we are to die,' she writes, knowing that for her there can never be any thought of escape. Romania is her life.

She is photographed now in Red Cross uniform, standing defiantly, in contrast to the more soothing poses generally struck by other royal ladies in other afflicted countries. While they are folding bandages, or visiting tidied-up bedsides, she is at clearing stations, where the wounded shriek and die. Unshrinking, she washes open the eyes of a shattered face, one last look of gratitude her reward, and torment. There are no more hospitals, no more guns, no more support from Russia, for the giant is collapsing in chaos and betrayal. Treachery is everywhere, even at home.

Disbanded Russian troops straggle across Romania's ravaged land and are now only so many more mouths to feed. The pro-German clique is strong around the King, himself of German origin. The Queen is uncompromisingly pro-British, pro-French, pro-Allied. As granddaughter of 'the Tzar Liberator' she is half-Russian. The Russian debacle appals her. 'Nicky' abdicates at Mohilev. She knows him weak, a disastrous ruler, overpowered by Alix, whom she cannot like; but the abdication is, to her, betrayal of a sacred trust. No news comes out of Russia, now; as the Revolution takes hold, all is conjecture and rumour. She is anguished for news of her sister 'Duckie', wife of the Grand Duke Cyril Vladimirovich. The Red flag is hoisted over his palace in St Petersburg, for at first he is in sympathy with any movement which will silence the Tzarina, 'the German woman', in her role as dictator and mouthpiece for the monk Rasputin.

In Romania the war drags on. The soldiers have no soles to their boots, now; no more guns; no more hope. Soon Romania is abandoned by her allies and the Germans take possession. In August 1918 comes news that 'Nicky' and 'Alix' and their children have been killed at Ekaterinburg. There had been a moment, before the war, when it was hoped a marriage would be arranged between Prince Carol and the Grand Duchess Olga: the Russians made this flattering suggestion, but the young people showed no enthusiasm for each other and the matter was dropped.

Romania falls under German rule, and the Queen suffers torments of despair and humiliation. All the high offices in the country are held by her enemies, led by the pro-German Marghiloman. In September, she receives another blow. The Crown prince Carol betrays his country and his heritage, in her eyes, by crossing the frontier to Odessa and marrying clandestinely, Mademoiselle Zizi Lambrino, a commoner.

For Mama Regina this is a crushing defeat: but she is as fiercely unresigned as ever, and putting aside her personal tragedy, still opposes every hateful measure of the Marghiloman government, still stands as a rallying point of patriotism.

And still, she fights for beauty. She is a force of nature; sun, air, flowers, laughter, children, love and beauty are still her aura. She is exhausted by her wartime struggles and takes a few weeks off, now, to recuperate in a simple little wooden chalet in the forest, at Cotofanesti. But she cannot rest until she has contrived colour and harmony around her. An old ikon and some Gypsies' brass cooking pots filled with wild flowers help, but still craving a focal point of colour she dyes a bath towel orange and drapes it over the table. Even here, at this moment, she is still setting the stage. Those who criticised her for theatricality should recall that it was, rather, an innate sense of beauty – her own and that of her surroundings; and when there were no luxuries, no Byzantine extrava-ganzas, she still created her own ambience out of nothing – or a packet of dye.

She always loved to express herself through rooms and houses. She had many. She had pined in the dark, heavy Germanic royal palace where she was sequestered in the early days of her marriage. But when at last she burst from the chrysalis, she was able to create Ruritanian splendours at Cotroceni and Peleşor, both turreted castles in the romantic Balkan tradition. Then there was the Foisor, a small forest house at Sinaia and an odd treetop abode, a fairy-tale hut rocking in the pines, where astonished visitors found themselves struggling up ladder-like steps for a picnic tea served in flower cups painted by the princess. Cotroceni's Ruritanian overtones, bearskins, ikons, Romanesque arches and pillared halls were very different to Bicaz, near Jassy, the royal family's headquarters during the war, a thick-walled, low white building in the traditional style of a Romanian country house. And lastly, there was Bran and Balcic, her most loved house. It was an amalgam of all her life; and then, too, it affirmed Romania's repossession of the Dobrudja; it was an emblem of victory, and sovereignty, as well as a romantic retreat. Balcic reflected the country at its most exotic, and it was her own personal interpretation of romance. It was very far from the court and its intrigues, but it breathed secrecy... a house for lovers' meetings; yet I was told by one who had known it as her guest, that it always retained an air of indefinable magnificence: it was a queen's lair.

But to me, seeing it now, abandoned, or worse, inhabited by passing strangers, it was indeed a tomb, a last monument to Ruritanian queens and high adventure. As I sat on the Queen's loggia, watching the evening sky yellowing, the swallows wheeling round the minaret, I resented my own presence there, as the intrusion it was. The gardens were still kept up, much as the Queen had planned them. At every turn there were picturesque vistas; ornamental terraces, Romanesque cloisters and Turkish fountains. Winding paths skirted grottoes and semi-secret nooks, and led to a venerable chestnut tree reefed by chains and hanging out at a right angle over the cliffs. In its green shade stood a white marble Byzantine throne, beside it a low table made from a truncated Roman column. 'Her Majesty's favourite seat for coffee,' said the caretaker, a boldly handsome, dark-eyed man who had followed me to this ghost-ridden terrace.

At a discreet distance from the main house and deep in subtropical vegetation were several cottages, unseen but for their chimneys, peeping from the foliage like rabbits' ears, hidden but alert. These, said the caretaker, had been for the resident masseuse, hairdresser, and dressmaker. I recalled the Empress Elizabeth of Austria, whose sartorial exigencies required two tailors to sew her into her riding habit every morning. No doubt Queen Marie's trailing draperies were less demanding, but even so I fancy a resident dressmaker must have been a necessity rather than a luxury.

Dotted about the gardens were other establishments for the Queen's children, who by the time she built Balcic were all old enough to be fully appreciative of her initiative. Princess Ileana, her favourite child, had a simple little house beside the mill race. Prince Nicolas, a rather streamlined *atelier de luxe* further along the cliffs. But I doubt if King Carol and Madame Lupescu were ever lodged in the Queen Bee's hive. However romantic her view of life, Queen Marie retained an even stronger belief in the monarchy. Nothing, no weakness of body or spirit, must ever be allowed to jeopardise the Crown, and her son's second romantic lapse was a betrayal of her whole life's purpose. That she was equally aware of the mystical, practical, and theatrical aspects of her calling are revealed in many passages of her *Memoirs*. In particular, writing of her accession, describing the scene in parliament, standing beside the new king, her husband, and smothered in mourning veils for the dead monarch...

Suddenly my name rang through space;
'Regina Maria...
'Regina Maria...!'
Then I knew I must bare my face before the whole house, that I must turn towards them with no veil of mourning between them and myself... 'Regina Maria!'... And we faced each other, my people and I. And that was my hour... mine... an hour it is not given to many to live.

'Did the Queen often come here?' I asked the caretaker, who was still hanging around eyeing me speculatively.

'As often as she could. She loved it here,' he replied, 'When she fell ill the doctors said it was no good for her by the sea. They said she must go to the mountains. It broke her heart to leave. She never came back. She wanted to die here... but she told them to bury her heart here, beside the chapel. It's been taken away now, though... Change... change... nothing's the same, except the flowers...'

He snipped the heads off some dead marigolds and stared at me again, his dark eyes bold and questioning.

'You are interested in the Queen? You are English, as she was? You never knew her? But you like this place... the others who come here...' he shrugged, 'They only want to see the bedroom...'

'Her Majesty used to watch the sunsets from the minaret,' he volunteered, 'There's a little staircase leading up beside her bedroom... the moon will be up before the sun is down... you should go up to the minaret,' and offering me a handful of dried sunflower seeds, he lounged off, chanting some sad-sounding song.

The minaret was no doubt a merely secular, or architectural, concession to the locale, having no religious significance, and being more in the nature of a lookout, or a setting for moonlight tête-à-têtes. I went into the house, so disarmingly small and simple in form. There are only three rooms; a big dining or living room, very Ruritanian-Elinor Glyn, and above, an octagonal bedroom with windows on five sides, jutting out towards the Black Sea. Beside it are dressing rooms and a domed white marble Turkish bathhouse. The celebrated bed is on a dais in an alcove. There is a hooded fireplace, flanked by fine candelabra. Firelight, starlight and candlelight... a frame for loving. I climbed the tiny stone stairway to the minaret and reaching the little balcony, surveyed the beautiful and muted domain below where the shadows were gathering. In the limpid evening sky one star joined a crescent moon; it was indeed the frame for love, as the Queen would have wished it.

But is the frame enough? I fancy that when we have achieved the experience, the abandon, necessary to appreciate such a setting, we are too late; we have forgotten that the sort of love we seek does not require a frame. It is come-by-chance, born of the moment. Perhaps today's brisk matings, a kiss beside the collective tractor and no emotional dalliance, is more real. I thought again of the departed Queen, the romantic figure whose ideals and setting time at last betrayed.

> Away with Persian pomps and fineries,
> And wreaths on linden withies nicely wound,
> Search not the fading garden
> For one forgotten rose.*

---

* Edward Marsh; translation of an Horatian Ode.

3

Places

Fragments of a Balkan Journal

THE FOLLOWING NOTES WERE MADE DURING MY TWO YEARS *EN POSTE* IN Bulgaria immediately after the war, from 1946 to 1948. The country was then under the control of an Allied Control Commission – American, Russian and British troops; and a French diplomatic mission to which my husband, Romain Gary, was appointed first secretary.

I saw more of the small details than the whole shifting scene – a range of local colours, rather than Red or White interpretations; a peep show on the panorama as it was at that moment. Much of what I recorded has vanished. Yet, when, twenty-five years later I returned to this country I had come to love and long for, always, I found that some essential quality, perhaps the *genius loci*, the Balkan essence, had remained unchanged.

Love of the Balkans may be an acquired taste, but once you have the taste, it becomes an obsession. No other scene will do. Capital cities, scenery, comforts, cultures... all leave you unmoved, for you are possessed by another love.

This Balkan flavour is hard to define. It is an atmosphere at once subtle and violent, composed of squalor as much as beauty; it does not belong basically to any one country, but is a composite blend of all the Balkan countries: Yugoslavia, Romania, Albania, Bulgaria, Greece and something of Turkey. It is part Slav, part East. It has no relation either to Hungary or Czechoslovakia. For me it begins south of Belgrade, though even so flavourless a city produces faint, unexpected whiffs of it, round the flower market or in the dark, sinister little cafés, behind the station. Every time I made my return to Sofia, after some brief grudged excursion to London or Paris, I was in a ferment, for the journey could take four or five days, then. The war had left many areas still derailed, so that trains assumed the pottering quality of a local branch line. I don't remember when, or indeed if, the Orient Express had resumed its legendary Paris-Istanbul run, but if so it was no longer a symbol of luxury, but just a badly needed piece of rolling stock, all frills forgotten. Even if it had been as before, all traditional glamour and glitter, luxurious sleeper cars, shaded lights, dubious characters and intrigues galore, I should have been indifferent. I was inert for three quarters of the way: sulking through smug Switzerland, impatient to get through Italy and restive at Zagreb. Such a charming place, a real old Austrian town, everyone said, but what did I want with real old Austrian towns? I was heading for the Balkans, with Bulgaria as the archetype and the landscape of my heart. I was in a state of torpor until, as the scene both softened and hardened, becoming at once exotic and fierce, I saw again the first place names written in Cyrillic letters. There again were the blue-domed Orthodox churches, the mosques, the great tracts of rich soil ploughed by water buffalo. The solitary figure beside the well, with its primitive contrivance of dipper and long pole balance; the peasants storming the train with their bundles and children and chickens; someone playing the flute and everyone singing mournful, haunting chants.

Around Nish, where the great gorges were edged by a racing pink river, there were unexplained half-a-day halts; the restaurant car had been unhitched and you were lucky to get some bread and salted fish. In the stillness you heard the ox-carts creaking down the mud track beside the line and the passengers flung themselves into those timeless political discussions which are the core of Balkan life.

With every mile a more Balkan and, to me more seducing, vista was disclosed. This is the scene I love so deeply that I carry it in my mind's eye, always. And each time I returned I was aware of the same trembling excitement, the same beating heart, as if I were going to some romantic rendezvous. It was the Balkans; and I was caught up once more by its binding spell.

I have been here over a week now, a rather tumultuous time. New faces, a new language, new ways. The curious atmosphere of indolence and a sort of hinted violence is intriguing. Last night, we went to dine with an old professor of political economy, Russian by origin and very brilliant, I believe, though the talk was largely in Russian, not the kind I can follow. We walked along quiet streets, scented by feathery acacia trees. A beautiful starry summer night. Outside the professor's door a knot of people was standing silently and made way for us politely. A body lay across the threshold, face down.

'Go on, don't just stand there – step over it,' said Romain. 'This is the Balkans,' he added. Bulgaria is the point on the map where Europe first merges with the East; here the Oriental 'no' prevails. The people nod their heads for 'no', shake them for 'yes'; wildly confusing and amusing to the foreigner. 'They have just come from Europe,' the Bulgarians say of visitors, with respect tinged with disapproval, especially among the more perfervid nationalists.

Roots. Both the Golden Horde and the Osmanli Turks (each stemming from Central Asian roots) have in turn possessed Bulgaria. The original Bulgars themselves were also of Mongol blood. Cumulatively, a strong, a violent strain is here. By comparison with neighbouring Serbs or Greeks, this is easily apparent to people who know the Balkans well, I'm told. Even as a novice observer, I sense this *Asiatic* quality. (Central Asian, with little sips of sugar lingering from an overlay of Sublime Porte dictation.) The people I see around me are generally a swarthy, chunky, low-slung lot, easily part of the Golden Horde. They should be straddling those blunt-nosed little horses of the steppes, not the trotting donkeys or bikes which are everywhere.

Sofia is small but straggling; you can walk across it in half an hour. It is so noisy – clattering on the cobbles, Red Army lorries, political loudspeakers, argumentative citizens and such – that by comparison, Marseille is a sleepy market town. Most of the street names have been changed in a gush of tactful enthusiasm. The Boulevard Tzarina Joanna is now named after a Russian statesman.

I am told one should not judge Bulgaria by its capital. There is a Germanic-suburban air in much of Sofia; shoddy art nouveau buildings, with overloaded old trams rattling past flyblown, empty shops. Greasy cobbles, garbage buckets, overstrained, skeletal horses, mangy cats... such vistas repel. I do not speak of the great heaps of rubble and bomb damage; I do not notice them. After the war years in London they merely add a homely touch. But Sofia has other aspects. Round the Sobranié, or parliament, there are painted sugar-ice façades and curlicue balconies, tree-lined boulevards, very 1900, with the most surprising and delightful golden-yellow paving stones and a backcloth of distant mountains and humpy hills shimmering under a radiant sky, and over all, the great, friendly bulk of Vitosha, the mountain which dominates the plain. It is possible to imagine Vitosha without Sofia, but Sofia without its compensating nearness to Vitosha is unthinkable.

There are few preconceived notions or second-hand opinions about Bulgaria. It was never a 'must' for either the Grand Tour or Cook's. I find it Dionysian and Ruritanian too. The cigar-box-lid landscape of *Arms and the Man* still prevails in spite of the drabness of new standardisations. Beneath it all, the eternal pastoral quality, the unity of man and land. The life of the soil stretching back in an unbroken rhythm, mediaeval, primeval. The roots are pagan. Nothing of the mystical Slav here. Five hundred years of Turkish occupation has left it neither East nor West, but a sort of archetype Balkan middle. Fierce Slav qualities mingle with Oriental languor. The landscape echoes this counterpoint. Harsh mountains and exotic prospects, tobacco, vines, roses and rocks.

Counterpoint is everywhere. The gilded domes of the Byzantine churches, the toothpick minarets of the mosques. The Rose Mosque blooms out of the snow and slush: Gypsies huddle inside verminous sheepskins flung over their bright, baggy Turkish trousers. Even the language, the root base of later Slav tongues, has many Turkish words grafted on. Names are oddly mixed. Hadji Dimitrov; Sultana Petkanov. Music is at once the sombre religious Slav chant and the voluptuous Oriental *mélopée*, 'A song to be sung in blue mornings!' divinely lovely, piercingly sweet, as melting as the frenzied rhythms of the *horo* are wild.

Life here divides sharply; our kind, the Corps Diplomatique and Allied Control Commission kind, has many privileges. The life lived at present by the bourgeoisie varies from precarious to desperate, with few if any amenities. That lived by the peasants still follows an immemorial rhythm. Dressed in sheepskins, eating bread and onion, toiling from dawn till dusk, their only luxuries tobacco and *slivova*, a fiery plum brandy. At twilight, the women stop working in the fields and begin cooking, or spinning their clothes, or household linen. No repose for them by day or night. The men sit in the café, smoking their *narghilyés*, talking politics, politics, politics, the immemorial Balkan topic. There is another small group, the intelligentsia centred round the theatre and opera, both of which are brilliant. There is no aristocracy as interpreted by the *Almanach de Gotha*.

Last traces of Graustark, or Ruritania, are found in the royal guard who have stayed on to adorn the people's junketings. At a government ball given at the palace last week, they lined the swirling marble stairway, splendidly handsome in a rigid Musée Grévin way, noble chests, richly frogged and padded and dazzling top-boots, rakish fur *shakos*, plumed and jewelled.

Everyone dances the *horo*. The soldiers, whiling away an hour on the barrack square; the government officials and their wives at the big political functions; the villagers on Sunday evenings; and the foreigners, more rapturously than skilfully. A great ring-o'-roses, stamping criss-cross steps, wilder and wilder; pursuit and retreat, immemorial coquetry. The *tziganes* have their own especially vicious way of stamping and they roll their bellies in a sort of *danse du ventre*, called here the *Kadunjiebek*. *Horo* music heard from afar produces a curious frisson, a sort of sinister, galvanic attraction to which I am prone.

At the Russian Embassy the little white and gold ballroom was very Petersburg, 1820. I expected to see Tatiana and Onegin come dashing down the parquet in a mazurka. Large wash-basin-sized bowls of caviar were loaded along the buffet. Vodka flowed. Everyone began to dance the *horo*, medals bounced, buttons burst. In the crimson and gold antechamber, the exarch and the high clergy sat remote, a black clot like beetles in jam. The evening broke up late, with me trying to teach a distinguished Red Army general how to dance the polka. Panting, he said it resembled their *gopak*.

Raiina, our cook, is a Macedonian peasant; dark, violent, obstinate, loving and loyal. She can be darting quick and full of primitive cunning. And she can be dull and lethargic, particularly when not in agreement with me, dragging about the kitchen slow as a deep-sea diver. Raiina instantly assumed that we should be able to converse together in a pidgin-blend of Russian and Bulgarian; and though when I arrived I had a little Russian and no Bulgarian, it has worked out well. The desperate necessities of one kitchen crisis after another, combined with the vivid daily dramas of Raiina's home life, is a forcing-house for me. Now we are able to discuss anything from Balkan divorce laws to techniques for dealing with the inevitable bugs.

To her, I am Gospodja – *moia* Gospodja, my madam. Romain is Gospodin, sir, or, more familiarly, *nash* Gospodin – *our* sir – a master figure before whom we females incline.

This country does nothing by halves. Near Sofia there is a lilac forest. A whole forest: another dimension, all colour, into which you can plunge headily. When I spoke of it to Raiina, she began singing some traditional song – The Lilac-bleeding Star – strange and poetic as this country I already loved so much.

'Is that an old Bulgarian song?' I asked her, craving for local colour.

'Bulgarian? No indeed!' she spat. 'It comes from *my* Macedonia... *moi Makedonckaya!*' Raiina has a deep sense of unity with her birthplace and whatever treaties dictate, or ethnographs claim, Macedonia is not Bulgaria. To Raiina, it is something apart – her own.

'And the legend?' I prompt, but Raiina has the cunning of primitive peoples. She has already discovered that I am greedy for the songs and dances and history and customs of Bulgaria; so Raiina is going to dole out her treats, rewarding me with a song, or a story about her uncle, the Bashi-Bazouk (a band of mercenary soldiers, once the terror of the Balkans) when I have been particularly indulgent towards her shortcomings in the kitchen. Fair's fair, she could and often does massacre our meagre supplies, but who else would sing of the Lilac-bleeding Star?

She loves music. Her knowledge of the traditional folk songs and dances are a great bond between us. I am enraptured by their elaborate rhythms. Some of the loveliest originated in Macedonia, her Macedonia. And when their nostalgic, wailing chants, or fierce beats blare from a neighbouring coffeehouse she drops everything and comes running. 'Quick Gospodja! Listen! The *horo*! The *ratchinitza!*' Snatching my handkerchief, she is off in a twirling furiante, while kettles boil over and telephones shrill unanswered, for we are bound by the same spell.

By any standards Raiina is a remarkable character, but her sensitivity, flexibility and her artistic perceptions are extraordinary, considering her uneducated background. She has a painter's eye; her taste is as instinctive and restrained as her judgements on people are shrewd. She loves to pore over the various *éditions d'art* which fill our bookshelves and is particularly fond of Chagall's mysterious paintings. We stand together watching the changing light on the far slopes of Vitosha through the windows. Often, she calls me to the kitchen to see the reflected sunset glow on the distant range of mountains – the Balkans – which ring the plain of Sofia. She is poetic; and sees – seeks – beauty.

A regard for religious observances still flourishes here, in spite of communist discouragement. Our ambassadress has been coaching me – a bewildered atheist – on the appropriate protocol.

'Always courtesy to the Papal Nuncio... He will be here on a visit next week. He takes precedence at all times... When you make your official call on the Igumen at Rila Monastery, be sure to enquire after the health of His Beautitude the Exarch, he heads the whole Bulgarian church, but lives in Istanbul... Always kiss the ikons offered to you in church or at any ceremony... At a funeral, the coffin will be open and the mourners file past to kiss the corpse. You can avoid that, but you must bow to the body, or stand holding a lighted candle and if they give you a little cake – in memory of the departed – you must eat it.'

Atanass is a small *tzigane* who begs outside the Alexander Nevski Cathedral. Sometimes he is alone, sometimes with his mother, who was once a great beauty. Both of them are tattooed with the crescent of Islam on their foreheads, though barely discernible through the layers of dirt. They are old friends of Raiina who knew them when she worked in the tobacco factory at Plovdiv and they were sprawling in the sun-baked *mahalla*, a *tzigane* quarter just outside the town. I wonder if Atanass' mother might be persuaded to come and show the seamstress how to cut *chalvari*, those complicated, gracefully draped Turkish trousers the *tzigane* women wear about the house. R. calls this going native.

Today, Atanass' mother thoughtfully brought along an old pair belonging to her family for me to try on and I had great difficulty in avoiding such a dress rehearsal. However, it all went off well. Mme Violetta, as the local seamstress prefers to be called, cut the *toile*. Atanass' mother crouched on her haunches, directing operations and drinking Cointreau, which Raiina said was all she fancied that morning. I crossed her palm and we parted the best of friends.

Most Bulgarian women are remarkably good-looking. Some are wonderfully beautiful. All of them have an earthy, physical vitality with nothing of the nervous system about it. Repose in them becomes bovinity. Some of the bourgeoisie reminds Romain of *Les Liaisons Dangereuses*: '*Elle est vraiment délicieuse: cela n'a ni caractère ni principes; jugez combien sa société sera douce et facile.*' ('How delicious: she has neither character nor principles; see for yourself how easy and pleasant she is.') I wonder how long it took for him to discover that?

The Alexander Nevski Cathedral boasts many magnificent bass singers. They roll out huge earthy belly notes which resound through the Byzantine domes, rising and falling again, lost in the shimmer of candlelight that glows up from the floor, where candles are ranged in memory of the dead. The Orthodox service is a free, spontaneous affair: it has none of that dank low-church rigidity, nor yet the tawdry theatricality of the Papists. People stroll in and out with bundles and children; soldiers stamp their snowy boots, dump their rifles; there are Russian soldiers too. Since there are no seats, the whole church is a shifting mass of dark figures, silhouetted against the candles. They kiss the ikons, or prostrate themselves before the ikonostas. There are peasants who have tethered their oxen at the door; seedy old men who stand, as if transfixed by time; and always, in the darkest corners, curious little groups of two or three, strange-looking individuals, unshaven, coat collars turned up, who seem to be meeting there on some sinister purpose – their muttering always ceases as you approach. The *tziganes* insinuate themselves here, too, and whine softly as they go from person to person, their slyly seductive faces supplicating; their dirt-caked palms turned up expectantly. And Bortniansky's music is everywhere.

In the tiny church at Boyana, hidden among the plumed foliage of Vitosha's lower slopes, the eleventh-century frescoes are strong proof of that simplicity, of that bucolic matter-of-factness – nothing mystical here – with which the Bulgarians overcame the rigid conventions of Byzantine art. And this at a time when Giotto was yet to be born and the stylised traditions of the ikon were accepted from Constantinople to Novgorod. Yet here, in this remote village, we see the breaking of that tradition and a bold move towards realism. The faces are human, warm, natural faces and very Slav, with their play of emotion.

Naturalistic details abound. The Last Supper is presented in such a manner that it becomes an historic document, a testimony of daily life. We see the table and linen and dishes of that moment. And how unchanging the scene, then and now: everyone is eating onions!

When at the hairdresser's I plough on with my pidgin Bulgarian while someone pours kettles of too hot or too cold water over me. Radka, the pretty proprietor, pins my set, while her old peasant mother crouches by the big stove – as a mark of special esteem I am always given the cubicle with the stove – and Radka's handsome husband Mitko holds the pins and tells me how he used to play Prince Danilo in *The Merry Widow* in Macedonia. And then, while I'm under the dryer, Radka has a rest and sits on Mitko's knee swinging her Russian-booted legs; the children are brought in for me to admire and we discuss Radka's chances of winning a prize, if she can get to Paris for the next International Coiffeur Contest and we drink to it in *slivova*. By the time I get home my set is rather wild.

Rila Monastery is Bulgaria's prime showpiece, an official must for state-conducted tours, which is odd, as it has always been considered one of the most holy places in the land and the present government is distinctly anti-ecclesiastical. Many lesser monasteries and convents are closed, the monks and nuns dispersed. We made our official call on the Igumen yesterday. But holy or no, Rila strikes an oddly secular if not frivolous air.

Perhaps this is due to its architecture which is striped pink and yellow like a layer cake. Picnic parties merge with pilgrims: in their snugly furnished cells the monks entertain their friends. The sumptuously gilded, opera-house encrustations in the church make it seem less religious than the little souvenir shop in the courtyard, full of cheap ikons and holy oleographs.

We arrived around midday, after a four-hour drive from Sofia, by Dupnitza, up and up, always climbing into the high ravine country of the Rila mountains. We drove into the courtyard at full tilt. It was Sunday. There were several char-abancs full of devout pilgrims, a Red Army sightseeing bus and a lorry load of Coldstream Guards, part of the Allied Control Commission personnel. We went first to pay our official visit to the Igumen, or Abbot, who received us most kindly. He spoke beautiful French and had been a distinguished lawyer. We sat on divans covered in fine rugs and were given the traditional *sladko* of welcome, spoonfuls of honey and little blue glasses of a fierce yet mellow liqueur they make at the monastery and I duly enquired after his Béatitude in Istanbul.

Back in the courtyard once more, we were flies, caught in the guide's web. Struggling desperately to free ourselves we were spun from museum to chapel, from cloister to bell-tower. We even walked into his parlour, a pretty little cell with a painted and carved pink and blue ceiling. We visited several of these cells. Anything less monastic, less mortifying, could not be imagined. Some had electric bells, others had yale locks. Brother Timofi showed us his with beaming pride. There was a white stone stove, an iron bedstead decorated with painted panels representing the Bay of Naples at the head and the Château de Chillon at the foot, a number of bright, gros point cushions on the bed and a horribly embroidered and fringed tablecloth. Plants trailed over the deep windowsills and there were quantities of family photographs and football team groups, which on closer inspection proved to be monks arranged in the same pyramid form, arms crossed and button eyes glassily fixed. The captain, or in this case, the Igumen, was in the centre holding an ikon in place of the football usually associated with such groups.

Did I say Rila was frivolous? It is positively operetta. There was a constant coming and going across the cobbles; a white-capped cook bargained with a pedlar; carpenters hammered and sang. A mechanically-minded pilgrim tinkered with his motorbike. With raucous laughter, two American sergeants bought a wooden backscratcher from the souvenir stall. There was all the movement of a market town inn.

The famous frescoes round the church are riotously gay, painted with a child's paintbox. Fork-tailed devils are heartily enjoying the seven deadly sins. Biblical scenes painted with jolly gusto: such blue, blue skies, such pink, pink temples, such smiling, red-faced lions, such Turkish-trousered saints, such rakish haloes... Rila is a holy land in terms of *images d'Épinal*.

After lunch we were overcome and profited by the Igumen's hospitable offer of the one-time royal suite, for a siesta. Returning refreshed to the touristic assault, we encountered some of the Coldstream Guards who, along with their young ladies (mostly luscious local brunettes) had been offered similar hospitality by resident pilgrims. They were describing it as a bit of all right.

At four o'clock exactly, we heard the famous wooden clapper-board call to prayer sounding down the striped arcades. When the Turks forbade church bells, the monks made do with a curious system of sounding-board or *klepalo* still in use. A brisk, booted monk came striding towards us, his black robes flapping, his long board like a narrow, loose paling, which he struck with a wooden mallet; the sound changed according to where he hit it. He flapped his way twice round the courtyard, marked time for some amateur photographers and then led the way into the church, followed by the Red Army, the Coldstream Guards and ourselves. The service seemed a casual affair: tourists and pilgrims went in and out, noisily. There was no singing: the brothers intoned the old Slav chants, their rich, gravy voices echoing impressively. The reek of incense wafted over the garlic-blasting peasants, a counterpoint of odours, sacred and profane.

Against the gilding of the ikonostas, there was a crudely painted coffin, with chintzy roses on a scarlet ground, containing the sarcophagus of St John of Rila. The opening of this coffin is the high spot of the afternoon service. I hung around. Presently the painted lid was raised. Layers of gauze and silk were parted to reveal a peep of mummified flesh, sticky brownish holy of holies. The true believers pressed forward to kiss it in ecstasies of devotion. Both the Coldstream Guards and the Red Army stood firm.

You can book a cell at Rila and stay there as long as you please, surrounded by other pilgrims, cooking in the little anterooms attached to the cells, or in the enormous mediaeval dining hall of the monastery, or at the new restaurant that has been built beside the ravine. Such a sojourn can scarcely be called a retreat in the religious sense, however I think we might enjoy staying here. The rushing torrent cascades beneath the deep-embrasured windows. All around are the peaks of the mountains, sombre and remote. But however pure the cells appear, I'm told bugs are inevitable. The state of most pilgrims makes it a lost battle. As to the sanitation at Rila, there is nothing frivolous about that. A tower hanging over a ravine and a hole in the floor over the steepest drop. Guides – bugs – sanitation. Perhaps these are Rila's special means of mortifying the flesh.

237

Diplomatic wives play a lot of bridge. 'What else is there to do?' they ask plain-tively. Most of them seem to regard life in Sofia as a penance; an exile from more urban or sophisticated cities. But I am laying plans to obtain some sort of permit which will allow me to travel about and see more of the country than official trips reveal. I'm string-pulling right and left – mostly Left, in that sense – and live in hope. It seems that transport is at a standstill. Hardly any trains run, there are no predictable lodgings when you get wherever you are going, and precious little food anywhere: in short, rather like England was during the war.

Atanass' mother has invited me to a *tzigane* wedding. I'm delighted. I find these people perfectly irresistible. There is a large population of them here; musi-cians, tinkers, vagabonds… Like the Jewish and other minorities, they are not persecuted. Most big towns have a *mahalla*, or *tzigane* quarter. At Kyustendil they live in caves in the mountain gorges of the Blue Rocks. At Madara they live in little bright-coloured shacks clinging to the cliff, or so I'm told. No one seems to understand why I am so curious to know more of their ways. They are everywhere about Sofia. Nomadic or static, it seems they live much the same way. Their encampments of painted carts (they don't have caravans) or lean-to huts, are dotted along the roads. They sprawl, splendid and indolent on the piles of sheepskins which, according to Liszt, in his book on Gypsy music, is their only furniture.

Raiina says the wedding will be a very grand affair. I must wear my best clothes. And a hat and gloves. She is stern.

I went out to the airfield to help welcome two plane-loads of underprivileged French orphans who were invited to spend a month's holiday in the mountains as guests of the Bulgarian children. It was searingly hot on the tarmac. A number of Russian machines were lined up being refuelled and some Russian officers and their families came out of the main building to watch the arrival. Every few minutes lorry-loads of spanking fine Bulgarian children arrived, singing, waving branches of evergreen and carrying clumsily, but lovingly, lettered banners which read: WELCOME TO OUR LITTLE FRENCH COMRADES.

It was all rather moving. The woman whose idea it was is a dynamic figure, known as 'La Pasionaria of the Balkans'. Her life has been one of violent drama, in the course of which she has been four times condemned to death, each time by a different political party. She was now quite overcome and melted into tears. So did the Soviet mechanics; and the swarthy ground crews sobbed too, as the planes circled the field. The children were becoming over-excited, beginning their welcome addresses too soon, or having to be rushed off to the lavatory at top speed. The Soviet soldiers hustled them back, all nicely buttoned, well before the planes taxied in.

As the planes came to a standstill, there was a glimpse of pale, sickly faces and sticky paws pasted on the windows. The Bulgarian children surged forward and the reception committee was engulfed in the Lilliputian wave. The French children, looking dreadfully thin and wan (they were picked from very poor families and slum districts which suffered particularly during the Nazi occupation) now came tumbling out banging their heads and barking their shins. The smallest Bulgarian boy, who was entirely extinguished by a mammoth bouquet of gladioli, then piped up with an address of welcome in florid French. It was infinitely touching: an ideal of friendship put into practice. Well might the Bulgarian committee glow with pride, well might there be sobbing and rejoicing.

Yesterday I set off to the *tzigane* nuptials in a taxi; and in all my finery. The *mahalla* is on the straggling outskirts, beyond the Jewish quarter. Suddenly, there were no more houses. The city stopped, as if at some invisible barrier. Here dusty plains, nothingness, begins. Mud-and-dust tracks peter out into rubbish dumps, shacks, refuse, tin cans, dead cats, skeletal donkeys tethered to sparse telegraph posts. The great plain of Sofia lies all around, with its crumpled piecrust edge of mountains.

'Ulitza Tartarli 27,' said the screw of paper that was my invitation. 'The Street of the Tartars', was easy to find, for music and wild thrumming – drum, *gusla* and *kaval* – sounded from afar and the long, unpaved little street was lined with shacks hung with paper flowers and ribbons, like the broken-down fencing. The shacks were more in the nature of low mud huts, with or without doors, mostly slung with a rug or draggled curtain. The entire population appeared to be living or camping outside, cooking on braziers, lolling on rags or broken-down iron bedsteads, shaded by a few stumpy acacia trees. Such places must look terribly squalid in the rain, but the long, golden days of summer gild and soften everything.

They were dancing a *horo* outside No. 27, spinning and shrieking, their bare blackened feet kicking up clouds of dust. They all crowded round, very friendly, almost menacing in their advances. The children lifted my skirt and peeped beneath. The women put their arms round me and fingered my hair. It seems that, as the guest of Atanass' mother, I was warmly welcome. The men, slouching, half-naked, pulled their caps down over their eyes and leered amiably. The babies, who were completely naked except for a string of blue amulet beads, swarmed about chattering and grimacing; they looked scabrous. Little girls of ten or thereabouts were gaudily painted, wore a flower behind one ear and had all the calculated coquetry of the prostitute. These were the degenerate mongrel *tziganes*, corrupted by city life, with none of the pride and tradition of the pure breed, but with the same impelling fascination.

Atanass' mother now appeared, in great confusion at having been absent when I arrived. She launched into a flood of explanation which I did not follow and led me towards one of the houses, pursued by the crowd. *Tzigane* women walk magnificently. They carry their babies on their shoulder like little princes. But it is always startling to see what appears to be a wrinkled, toothless old woman as the mother of a tiny baby. Inside the hut, I was presented to a stoutish middle-aged *tzigane* wearing a well-preserved top hat which he had no doubt inherited from the valet of some visiting diplomat. Atanass' mother said he was the King of the Gypsies, and I daresay he was. Alas! he said, the wedding was postponed till next week. Meanwhile, there was to be another celebration, a big fête. He hoped I would stay. I asked what they were celebrating. A circumcision, he said, with graphic gestures.

Suddenly, everyone began to dance again. *Tziganes* don't dance in couples as we do: men dance with men, women with women. Now the rhythm changed and they formed a chain. They were off, wildly stamping into their own kind of *horo*. Nursing mothers leapt along with tiny babies still clutching their bare breasts. The older ones, just able to sit up, though with lolling heads, were spun round and round like tops. One by one the dancers collapsed on to sagging bedsteads. Some flung themselves down beside the old women who were cooking, or went back to their former occupation of delousing a neighbour's head. I was offered a delicious snack of some sort of pimento and bean stew. The ceremony proper showed no signs of beginning and I remembered guiltily that I was supposed to be at a diplomatic ladies' tea party, quite a different kind of function.

On my way back to the more elegant quarters of the town, I remembered how those same nit-picking rogues had known a moment of greatness. It was a moment near the end of the war, when the fate of Bulgaria's Jewry and other undesirables was to be sealed by the occupying German and pro-German rulers. A first list of deportees was rounded up and a packed trainload stood ready to leave the station when a yelling pack of *tziganes* appeared suddenly and flung themselves down across the lines in front of the train...

Confusion, delays, orders barked out, but not obeyed. A stampede of angry peasants... The train never left the station. Vassili told me this extraordinary story. He had seen it all, standing on the sidelines. (Why was he there I wonder? Romain has warned me never to question anyone too closely.) Anyhow, this story is well authenticated. The Jews crept away and the *tziganes* returned to their *mahalla* to celebrate their triumph, however transitory. It should have been their turn next – they too were undesirables. But the Allied landings in Normandy suddenly changed everything: Nazi regimentation of the Balkans faltered and came to a halt, with the end of the war.

Today, all around, newer persecutions begin to form. Hatreds and denunciations gather strength. Or so I'm told. I don't see much of the political scene and Romain doesn't talk shop at home.

The housing shortage is acute. Our present apartment is hideously furnished and in an inaccessible quarter. But one of the *kavas* at the legation has told us that they are expecting a big purge soon, in which case there will be better accommodation to be had for the asking.

'Do you think he realised what he was saying?'

'Mmm… This is the Balkans.'

It is five weeks since those deprived French children were packed off to their holiday camp at Kyustendil and on the eve of their return flight to France we gave them a big farewell party at the legation. The Bulgarians have done them proud. They filed in, rosy and bulging out of their new clothes. They were splendidly equipped, sailor suits, sun hats, sandals…

'They weigh five kilos more than when they arrived and they all speak Bulgarian,' said their governess. They remained crimson and tongue-tied with us however. We led them to the buffet where a rich array of pastries was displayed. They stood in solid formation, like some massed choir, one behind the other, five deep, stoking rhythmically. One small boy was wearing a very finely embroidered peasant handkerchief tucked into the breast pocket of his sailor suit. I admired it, and in so doing, twitched it out, so that several fag-ends were dislodged and rolled under the table. It was a terrible moment; we avoided each other's eyes and spoke of other things. At last they had eaten enough and the treacly dregs had been drained. We packed them into their charabancs.

'Yes, indeed, it is most gratifying,' said an elderly Bulgarian with a white moustache; he had been closely involved with the whole scheme.

'The boys are fine specimens now and the girls…' he cast a luxuriously lingering glance over the nubile forms bursting so promisingly out of the charabanc windows, 'The little girls have all become young ladies,' he said, and sighed.

The late Tzar Boris died in August 1943 under mysterious circumstances. He was flying home after a visit to the Führer. Heart trouble was the official view. His body lay in state for a considerable while, the bier surrounded day and night by wailing peasants. Long after the burial the peasants were still returning to wail among the wax droppings, the last trace of the great candlesticks that had surrounded the coffin of their king.

The widowed Tzarina Joanna (daughter of Victor Emmanuel III of Italy) and her son, the little Prince Simeon, are still here, sequestered in some unknown remote hideout, heavily guarded and believed to be hoping for permission to leave the country.

Some of the Corps Diplomatique predict that the little prince, as a possible tool in the hands of a royalist opposition, will be assassinated by the Communist Party before he can cross the frontier. This would be quite in the traditions of Balkan violence. (The Serbian King Alexander and his Queen Draga were assassinated during one June night in 1903... they were dragged from hiding, hacked to pieces, disembowelled and thrown from the window...) But Romain thinks such rumours are rubbishy talk, given the present government's need for a public image and credit abroad.

All my life I have heard of Bulgaria's legendary Valley of Roses; I imagined it to be a sort of botanic gardens; carefully tended parterres; a summer afternoon's stroll. But it is a whole region, twenty miles wide and a hundred miles long; a pink province, at once a tradition and a livelihood; a whole world of its own into which people are born, and where they live and work and die, set a little apart from the rest – as it were, becalmed in fragrance.

It seems there are only a few weeks – in June – when the roses reach their apotheosis. Rose culture demands not only the precise moment of the year, but the exact moment of the day – sunrise. The flowers must be gathered while the dew is still on them, before the heat of the sun has drawn out all their perfume. Today is the first of June. Now is 'the time, and the place': but the loved one... Romain is not, at heart, interested in tourism.

He shares the general masculine aversion to picnics. Perhaps his French education is responsible for making him feel anything as serious as eating should be undertaken indoors. As for plants, his life has not brought him into contact with them, except in vases on restaurant tables, or as florists' bouquets – *gages d'amour*.

On the strict understanding that we shall eat at an inn, no roadside pause with sandwiches, Monsieur Mon Mari has consented to undertake the expedition.

We set out in that hushed, half-darkness before dawn, crossing range after range of the beautiful, wild hill country towards Karlova, the rose capital. Vladimir explained that a ton of rose petals is required to yield a pound of attar... (Statistics at such a moment!) We crossed the last pass and suddenly were coasting down into a rosy zone, a limboland of fragrance. Great wafts of sweetness swept over us, enveloping us, sucking us into a heady ambience. The first level shafts of early sunlight were piercing the haze as we reached the rose plantations. As far as the eye could see they stretched ahead in billows of pinkness. At close range, the roses were not such bosomy blooms as I had imagined, but rather austere, single-petalled flowers: yet, the cumulative effect was one of voluptuousness. The pickers were working up and down the lines of dewy, glittering rose bushes, stripping off the petals and stuffing them into sacks with rhythmic precision. They were singing, the lovely *mélopées* which are a Turkish legacy; the women's heads were bound in lilac or lemon or scarlet silk handkerchiefs, always adorned with a rose; the men, too, wore a bloom stuck jauntily into their high fur *kalpaks*. I thought of Baudelaire:

«*Là, tout n'est qu'ordre et beauté*
Luxe, calme et volupté.»

Some of the girls wore stiffly ceremonial dresses of black serge encrusted in gold paillettes which winked in the sunlight. These are traditional garments handed down from one generation to another, and usually worn only on fête days or special occasions. The rose harvest is one such. And more, said Vladimir. The girls go there to catch a beau; the men, to find a wife. As they worked their glances sparked across the foliage – likely lad and comely charmer, pursuit and promise... Love and roses: they are forever linked.

Karlova's distilling factories bring the jam-like sweetness to such a pitch that it is almost nauseating. The little town lies at the end of the Valley of Roses and is sheltered from the north by the great scarps of the Rhodope mountains – purple rock, veined with waterfalls and the setting for much Greek mythology. 'Home of Eurydice,' said the innkeeper briefly, displaying that acquaintance with the classics found, I have noticed, among the simplest Balkan people.

A messenger came from the abbess of a nearby convent, inviting us to sup with her. The painted walls of the refectory were bright with childish saints wreathed in garlands – roses, again. The abbess bowed us to our places with formality. We sat on coarse linen cushions embroidered in stylised scarlet flowers recalling the roses of the world outside. A novice brought us the ceremonial offering, a glass of pure water and little saucers of translucent rose-leaf jam: this is a Balkan version of the aperitif. The jam induces a fierce thirst which, it is inferred, can only be slaked by the host's finest wine. Eat, drink and be merry. The convent saw no reason to be otherwise at supper. During the war, they told me, half the rose crop gave place to baser needs and the Valley of Roses was, in part, the Valley of Potatoes. Even now, we knew conditions were very hard, yet we ate well, among the nuns: great platters of fish from the nearby streams, vegetables simmered in oil and bowls of yoghourt, all presented with simplicity and style: the style of a people who have never known the vulgarity of commercialism. Vladimir told us the abbess had been a great beauty, crossed in love, who found at last consolation in the Church. She had retained all the worldly airs of a hostess. When the bell clanged for prayers and one by one the sisters filed into the dark depths of the chapel, she lingered, telling a peasant's child to lead us to the village square, where the rose-pickers were celebrating their harvest home with torchlight dances.

'My children, you go with my blessing,' she said and picking red roses off the wall, she pinned them on us with a strangely secular grace.

Under the dense walnut trees, I joined the dancers, who formed a huge circle, hand in hand, spinning faster and faster, while the roses scattered from their heads and lay trampled on the grass.

When at last we returned to the inn, they gave us a nightcap of rose-leaf tea. And there were tight-packed little bouquets of roses on our pillows.

Cemeteries seem very revealing of national characteristics. I visit one nearby. At the cemetery gates, some dramatically-minded gardener has contrived two enormous flowerbeds spelling out an awesome message. In geraniums: WE TOO WERE ONCE LIKE YOU. Across the path, in stocks: YOU TOO WILL SOON BE LIKE US.

This is a nice example of the harsh, *masculine* quality of the Bulgarian character, as opposed to the more flowery consolations of cemeteries elsewhere.

Humour is of the broad order here, though it is hard to believe there is no irony in the habit of employing likely and unlikely adjectives for shopkeepers' names. This choice of adjectives is an endless entertainment to us. We collect and swap them daily. Mr Bones the Butcher may be 'Tender' Bones, or he may just as easily be 'Fragrant', 'Merry', or 'Gracious' Bones. The barber's shop is labelled 'Eternal Beauty' Stoyanov. The funeral undertakers are perhaps the best examples: 'Last Care' Petkanov, 'Dust' Zdravkov, or my favourite, Bezoumna Skroub, 'Frenzied Mourning' Ivanov.

A gnome-like man, Baï Tosheff, sometimes calls to trim Romain's unruly hair. His visits are a great treat on account of his conversation, conducted in three or four mixed-up languages. He is quite a wag, but deeply earnest while clipping and combing, and works himself into a lather to obtain what he calls an *Artistiki Effektiski.*

V. took me to a *metoah,* or convent, which was somehow rather sinister and claustrophobic. A group of stone-faced masculine-looking nuns received us and showed us some fine ikons. Dark fir trees brushed at the windows of the refectory like menacing birds. I was glad to leave. On the way back, V. told me that in the past, children – little girls – were sometimes donated to a convent by parents anxious to obtain redemption. The little victims were accepted and took their place, and their vows, beside other nuns. I wondered if any such were among the black-robed figures whose baleful glances I had found so disturbing. Did this terrible practice, this immolation, still go on deep in the still priest-ridden countryside?

Raiina has rapidly assumed the characteristics and standing of a British nanny – she bosses us, loves us, and we love her. But there are scenes. Our relationship is sometimes strained to breaking point over household accounts – arithmetic in Bulgaria brings me, now and again, to striking her, though this seems to be all part of the violent, normal pattern of Balkan life. But then, she knows just how to strike back. Finding I am squeamish about certain things, she bides her time, before returning the blow. The other day, when I was particularly savouring a Bulgarian cigarette she seized the occasion to remind me of the process by which such superlative tobacco is achieved. Or was, years ago, when as a girl she worked in the tobacco factory at Plovdiv.

Intense heat is required during the process of preparation. The rooms where the leaves are sorted were maintained at a sweltering degree. The women – *tziganes* and peasants – who sorted were drenched in sweat; the stench was overpowering. All the windows were sealed for this sweat was a vital part of the process of fermenting the tobacco rapidly and producing that special quality of the celebrated Balkan Sobranié.

As I stubbed out my cigarette I saw Raiina watching me with a marked air of triumph.

Shoes are an anathema to Raiina. She never wore or even saw any, until she left her mountain village for Sofia; and she pads about the house, bare toes clutching the carpet. A nice, roomy pair I bought her hang in the kitchen beside a string of onions. Having observed the startled glances of my guests – Corps Diplomatique and stuffy – as she hands round the canapés, I have vainly tried to insist. Yesterday she produced a pair of baggy white cotton gloves, bought with her own money. 'These shall be worn for visitors,' she announced, 'but on my feet no shoes for no one.'

Raiina's family now play a large part in our lives; they were introduced to me almost before I was unpacked. They are always with us. Tomislav, her drunken dissolute husband, a house-painter by fits and starts, is seldom seen – he lurks in the background, a sinister figure from whom all evil flows. But the children, Minka, Lili, Radja and Borislav – a gargantuam baby whom Raiina is nursing to the detriment of our household routine and the astonishment of neatly gloved Corps Diplomatique callers when she opens the door with the monster brat clinging limpet-like to her bare breast – are a living and very perceptible factor in our lives. And sometimes 'Uncle Bashi-Bazouk' appears, famished and dramatic...

We find it expensive, catering for seven extra people, or *souls* as they are called poetically in Slav phraseology. But there it is. What is theirs is mine too, I know. And what is mine is most certainly theirs, I reflect sometimes with impatience, as they all gather round the kitchen table. This is called giving Raiina a helping hand.

Raiina sometimes adds to the kitchen invasion by introducing a Gypsy friend and his dancing bear. These trained bears are the large brown kind found wandering in the hills; they become pathetic, mangy creatures, rings through torn noses, shuffling wearily from village to village, lumbering round in a sort of tragic dance, to the accompaniment of a zither or tambourine. They are still used as curative agents – that is, they are trained to shuffle up and down the prostrate peasants' spines, providing a sort of furry electric massage said to be highly tonic.

Raiina is a firm believer in the treatment. When no bears are available (they are becoming a scarcity in Sofia) she adopts the substitute of a human being stamping heavily up and down her spinal column. She often fetches in a neighbour to give her a few tonic shuffles, to brace her before cooking dinner. She is fond of recounting the story of an ailing brother, to whom the bear was fetched and, as is the custom, warmed up to its work by a tot of *slivova*. It seems that the creatures are partial to alcohol; it had several tots and waxed too enthusiastic, so that Raiina's brother was in hospital for three months afterwards. Whenever we reach the point of the story where Raiina imitates the bear gulping down its fourth tot of *slivova*, and setting to work on her brother, she laughs so uproariously that the tears run down her face. She has a strong sense of humour.

Raiina's cooking is swayed by her passion, both political and private. We suffer much on account of the Other Woman, a middle-aged Gypsy matron who begs from door to door, and who is unaccountably irresistible to Raiina's husband. Sometimes seething with fury at the Allied peace terms laid down for Bulgaria (politics are bred in her blood and bone, as in all her race) she is unable to produce any sort of meal for several days while political discussions rage in the kitchen and knives are sharpened menacingly.

Her cooking varies with what she considers the social status of the guests. She has her own scale, her own hierarchy, to which she adheres rigidly. For example, Americans, to Raiina, are apart – not altogether human, referred to in capitals THE AMERICANS; something about their exchange rate, the power of the dollar, the nylon stockings of the ladies and the princely way in which the military mission lives in Sofia, dazzles her. The Americans, then, are fabulous, unreal: they must not be given onions, let alone garlic. The British, less fabulous but worthy of respect, must have condiments added. Mustard and pepper are great rarities, but when any of the British military mission dine with us, flavourings are flung about lavishly. Whole avalanches of vanilla ruin the puddings; there are landslides of pepper in the soup. The other legations, she infers, including our own, the French, are not worth a spoonful of paprika. Perhaps she takes the whole Corps Diplomatique with a pinch of salt.

There is no opera house here, but some operas are performed in the theatre, or at a concert hall. Nevertheless, between the splendid choir at the cathedral and fitful opera performances – largely those lesser-known Russian nineteenth-century composers which I love and seldom hear – I am well nourished. Last night, I caught a concert with a symphony by the Bulgarian composer Vladigerov (Tchaikowsky-Bulgar in character) which was lovely.

Lately a young pianist André Boucourechliev, who is foretold a brilliant future, has taken to visiting us, though 'natives' mixing with foreigners is not well thought of by the present regime. I have managed to hire a piano – very 'grand', very shiny. He played some Schumann and I was transported. R. says the piano takes up too much room and the young pianist's visits are too frequent! But then R. is not so much unmusical as amusical. (Boucourechliev later left Bulgaria to become a distinguished figure in Paris as composer and musicologue.)

I'm still not getting anywhere with my permit to move around. So many rulings, so many districts out of bounds. But I'm making endless journeys in my head, poring over old maps, deciding on places I begin to wonder if I shall ever reach.

Bulgarian place names are particularly expressive. They have an almost onomatopoeic felicity. Pamporovo is light, fluffy with snow, like its mountains.

Ichtiman sounds mean, ingrown. Dragalevtzi is a Slav fairy-tale name, direct from the *skazki*, or legends. So is Malevitza, which might be the name of an enchanted princess. Sredna Gora – the name is as sinister as the mountain range which is steeped in the blood of revolt. But Karlovo is all warmth and softness, to match the little white town among the walnut trees in the Valley of Roses. Bachkovo is dark-sounding, noble, as befits the monastery built there by two Georgian princes in the eleventh century and which commands a ravine of the Black Balkans. Madara must be languorous and Oriental, lying on Black Sea shores; and Messemvria hums and shimmers in a heat haze along its Black Sea coastline. Pernik sounds a harsh clangour, like its mines. Loveliest of all, to me, the Rhodope and the Pachmakli – proud names telling of the poetic beauty and wildness of their region.

Two hare-brained Serbian pilots have arrived in scrapped Junker planes commandeered from a deserted German air base, I forget where. They career around as if they were members of some aerial circus. No frontiers seem to bother them, neither weather conditions, nor mountain passes. They flew us to Vienna last week, flying low, swooping too low and skimming between the flanks of terrifying mountain passes. All I saw of Vienna prowling on foot, in bitter cold, were huge heaps of rubble and bomb sites. Everywhere, pathetic messages, asking or giving news of lost persons were scrawled over the crumbling walls. There was almost no street lighting, but at dusk some curtainless windows of the Hofburg blazed out and I could see a crowd of Red Army officers moving about under the glitter of gigantic crystal chandeliers. One of their clubs, I supposed. They seemed an animated lot, but no sound issued from the blackened walls, and I felt I was watching some fantastic puppet show. Outside was almost as unreal. Little or no traffic, only a few army lorries, or a lone ambulance shrieking its way across desolate spaces that had once been that brilliant city. I was thankful to leave.

At last! A nice new apartment has materialised. We moved in, two days ago – days of chaos. Everywhere a move is a trial, but much of the exasperation was lessened here because Nedi, from whom all blessings flow, obtained the services of a celebrated pair of *tziganes*. In Bulgaria the *tziganes* are held to be master-movers. They bring science to their art, balance grand pianos on the nape of their necks in the precise spot calculated to bear the strain. Suddenly galvanised, they swing immense weights about and juggle with packing cases. Round the markets the streets are always full of *tziganes* wearing peaked caps, and hung with stout ropes, lounging around, waiting to pick up some bit of porterage.

Apart from the fact they arrived three hours late, drank most of my remaining French cognac and asked the equivalent of a Bulgarian cabinet minister's salary, the *tziganes* were excellent. I found their antics, their padding bare feet and chatter an exotic diversion. Comparing them to the British removal man, there were certain basic differences. They were quicker – once they began – and there was less of that straining immobility, that, 'To you! To you, Ernie!' or 'Take it your end, Bert!' that accompanies a deadlock on the stairs at home. But they had no sense of time (or fortunately, of overtime). By nightfall they had succeeded in piling all our belongings into the van, which they then placed in a side street. While one settled down among the crates to sleep there and guard it until morning, the other unharnessed the horse and made off towards the *mahalla*. My shrieks did not turn him.

'He has a young and beautiful wife,' said the van-watcher. He flashed his splendid teeth and made an unmistakably ribald gesture. Only after a lot of silver had crossed his palm would he consent to extract our bed and set this up in our bare new lodging. Even so, there were no pillows, and only one blanket.

'Such springs!' said the *tzigane*, prodding with a grimy finger, 'Who would want to sleep?' He made another of those jolly, international gestures called obscene and left us to reflect on the advantages of employing regular removers. I thought longingly of Harrods' white-aproned teams. But Romain, as a child, spent years criss-crossing frontiers willy-nilly, and later lived precariously in small hotels, on air force bases, or some jungly cave after a forced landing, and so does not share my preoccupation with the comforts of the home.

Raiina would like us to bless our new quarters by the presence of two or three small snakes, which she assures us are considered lucky, in the nature of household pets, or mascots. No home was really blessed, if there was not a nest of these writhing terrors beside the warm hearthstone, she said.

When I reminded her that we only had radiators, she admitted that such pets were found less in Sofia than in the open countryside of her childhood.

Peasants who treated snakes badly were always avenged by the Great Snake gods, she said.

That snakes do abound in the forests here makes me particularly vulnerable to Raiina's stories of *smok*, or pythons, which come down to the fields and crush cows and nanny goats to death. 'Nursing mothers, too,' she adds, clutching dramatically at her bosom, 'Why, my own mother's sister had stoned a python that came into the garden and the Great Snake god was angry and punished her. When she went picking tobacco she left her baby son asleep in his cradle under a walnut tree. The Snake god was watching – you do believe me, don't you, Gospodja?' Raiina pleaded and indeed, I was hanging on her words. 'Very well then,' she continued, 'The Snake god sent a little snake into the cradle and told it to slide into the baby's mouth while it was crying for its mother... Ah! Gospodja! believe me, that snake found its way straight to the baby's liver and ate it up in two bites!'

Her voice rose to an anguished Oriental wail as once again, she pressed me to consider the advantage of a few small, good-luck-bringing serpents about the house.

Our nice new apartment is not quite so nice. Last night I went into the kitchen late. The whole floor looked black and heaved and crunched under my feet. Cockroaches: enormous ones. I fled. Now I learn that whatever means are taken to destroy them, they are likely to return. This building is a new, carelessly built block and the central heating, pipes, cellars and all else are a draw to every comfort-loving insect for miles around.

Raiina infers this would never have happened had we listened to her and had a few snakes around, 'Just small good-luck ones, Gospodja,' she pleads, but I remain adamant.

The British legation is in a ferment. His Grace the Bishop of Gibraltar's visit is scheduled for next week. His diocese stretches elastically from Gibraltar to Baku, with Bulgaria *en route*. The English and Americans here have decided on a joint christening for any of their unconsecrated infants. Since there is no suitable church, the ceremony is to be held in the drawing room of the legation. But H.M.'s office of works furnishings (near-Hepplewhite dining room and 'safe'

chintzes in the drawing room) does not include a font. The press attaché has been scouring the countryside for some suitable receptacle, so far, unsuccessfully; and the parents are faced with the alternative of a soup tureen, or a plastic birdbath.

Unbelievably, unexpectedly, my permit has arrived. It was sent from some high-up governmental department and delivered by two heavily armed soldiers who greatly alarmed Raiina. She likes to predict arrests and executions (the climate of the moment and the nature of the race). This precious document is violently stamped in different coloured inks, signed and countersigned. Its Cyrillic confusion has at last revealed that the Gospodja Gary may travel about, much, but not all, of the countryside.

R. has firmly declined to have anything to do with my plans. His work at the legation and the new book he is writing will keep him rooted, he says. Fair enough, I know he dislikes such ethnic outings and would soon fidget and fume. But he is being very understanding about my skipping off and escaping the Corps Diplomatique's social routines.

Now, at last, all I have been reading, or hearing about, will become real. The village where Ivan Vasoff, the great patriot, was killed fighting against Turkish oppression, Koprivchitza, where those elegant old family houses achieve a perfection of local architecture, their wide curved Chinese-style eaves overhang painted frescoes and delicately pillared verandas, secretive mountain villages and monasteries, lonely, in their forests. Oh! how greedy I am for such feasts. *Heiidi*! Let's go! As they say here.

I have just returned from the Shipka Pass. A bleak outing, fearfully windy and for the first time I met some cross-looking black buffalo. They are said to be dangerous, but I never thought them so. Bulgaria abounds in monasteries and convents, the former often going by the latter name; a *convent* full of monks is confusing to the uninitiated. The Shipka monastery is more in the nature of a war memorial and hospice for old soldiers, Russians among them. They are cared for by a few monks. The brilliant-coloured building, scarlet and pink, is brash 1880 Russo-historico in style and has a misleading air, for Shipka is steeped in sombre memories. Its golden fish-scale cupolas start from dark spinach-green firs as you reach the pass.

Here the Russians took their stand beside the Bulgarians, their Slav brothers, struggling to overthrow the accursed Turkish yoke. The pass seems strangely chosen as a battlefield. Dragging the guns up and the wounded down must have been an appalling struggle. For three days and nights six thousand Bulgarians held the pass against forty thousand Turks. When the Cossack reinforcements arrived, there was no more ammunition left, and the Bulgarians were hurling down the corpses of their comrades to stem the advancing Turks. Verestchaguin, the Russian painter who was particularly inspired by the horrors of battlefields in the snow, towers of skulls or scenes of carnage in the Russians' Central Asian campaigns, left several paintings of the Russo-Turkish war. *All is Quiet on the Shipka Pass*, the words of a much-cited dispatch (which was later to be echoed by the book *All Quiet on the Western Front*) depicts a Russian sentry, frozen to death, guarding the pass with its frozen corpses.

A few incapacitated Russian soldiers of the 1914–18 war who, somehow, found themselves marooned in the Balkans, are still here. Bulgarians and Russians lie side by side with nameless Turks in their communal graves. Once again, all is quiet on the Shipka Pass.

The Red Army choir has been here singing to an enraptured public. The Russian troops stationed in Sofia are models of good behaviour and popular with the *chopski*, as Sofiotes are called. They have the bonus of being able to communicate in some sort of Slavic lingo.

The dashing young Major X of the American Army has rocked diplomatic dinner tables by marrying a girl from one of the brothels. He is having no nonsense and stalked into the Allied Officers' Club saying: 'Some of you may have met Mademoiselle Luba at the Maison Rose. Well, she's my wife now.'

They are coming to dinner next week.

At a village near the exotically-named town of Tartar-Pazardjik, Nedi and I chanced on an extraordinary spectacle. A crowd of peasants was gathered round an open grave, a still open coffin beside it. They were wailing and sobbing and offering various foods to the corpse who lay waxily remote from their almost angry solicitations. They are begging him to return and eat his favourite dishes which they have cooked for him, Nedi explained. Being Bulgarian herself, Nedi did not find this as macabre as I did.

My expeditions, alone generally, are becoming an essential part of my life here. Bulgaria contains a great number of strange sects and tribes. The Karakachans are Moslems, like the Pomaks. They live on the high plateaux and are said to be both wild and disagreeable. In some of these communities the women, who are thickly veiled, do all the work, building huts, chopping wood, hunting for game... the men consenting to breed, but no more. When I recounted this at a dinner party, the assembled gentlemen, particularly the Americans, looked sadly envious.

It is now known that the Tzarina Joanna was allowed to leave the country, and the little Crown prince was not assassinated.

The most primitive peasants I have yet encountered on my expeditions were in mountain villages beyond Belovo. The local doctor kindly drove me there in his battered car. I saw the most bizarre make-up worn by the young girls. It was the crude red and white of a painted doll. The doctor said they still use a deadly kind of white pigment (lead?) which blanches the skin for a while, but ends by poisoning them.

These daubed Balkan beauties, so roundly rouged, probably aim at an effect of dazzling freshness, the kind to which Gogol so often refers in *Dead Souls*, 'She was as fresh as blood and milk,' he says with relish; no effete comparison to roses here. This is more in the tradition of the bold scarlet circles painted on the cheeks of high-bred Mongolian beauties. But the Bulgarian make-up is only a passing trick to catch a boy. As soon as she is married, often at four-teen or so, the bride's paint is gone for good. And soon after, her beauty goes too. The peasants age rapidly, becoming wrinkled slaves to their men, who are still treated like pashas, riding ahead on a donkey while the women drag along behind, bent double under their burdens. Bulgaria retains many Oriental customs.

If one can limit one's mind's-eye view of a country to any one colour (without any political implication of course) I suppose red, a glowing pinkish red would be the predominant Bulgarian colour. France has an all-over pearly grey hue which is more of a light, an ambience, than a colour. England is green – where it isn't a sooty drab. In Old Slav, red has always been synonymous with beauty. In Russia, *krassivie*, beautiful, stems from *krassnie*, red – or the other way about. *Krassa* is beauty. In Moscow, the 'Red' Square also means the 'Beautiful'. The *skazki*, or fairy tales, are full of young princes who wear blood-red robes; the peasant boy who wins the princess always wears a red *roubashka*. The walls of the old churches and monasteries are often painted a deep crimson. Rastrelli's original design for the Winter Palace was a burning orange, but this was changed to a dark red; both colours must have glowed out from the snow or rains of St Petersburg. Various religious sects carried a red handkerchief as symbol of their martyrdom.

Here, there are many other examples, such as the Bulgarian custom of exchanging and wearing red and white tokens called *martenitsa*, or *porte bonheur*, on the first of March – spring – which again shows that special superstitious regard Slavs feel for the colour red.

No one seems in the least interested in my travels. Only when I enlarge on the discomforts encountered do they brighten. Having to sleep wrapped in my heavy sheepskin *shuba*, or toast my supper, a kind of local sausage, speared on my penknife and thrust at one of those black-iron stoves called *ziganskis* makes them goggle, while descriptions of a dawdling, lice-infested local train has them shuddering. I'm getting like Dickens' Fat Boy who enjoyed making people's flesh creep.

Prince L. is a rather dissolute-looking old Russian émigré who washed up here after the White Army defeats of 1918. He has a collection of Vertinsky records dating back to pre-revolutionary St Petersburg which survived his escape to Stamboul and a hand-to-mouth existence there. Night watchman in a brothel; pianist in dives at Galata; tutor to some spoiled sultanate brats – he tells it all wearily, but revives when we ask for more Vertinsky songs. Vertinsky! That strange, rasping, cracked voice like nothing else, all nostalgia, all bitterness, white nights, white Russians, *Tosca*, spleen... The prince seems surprised we know about Vertinsky who is a legend to us. Part of our shared Russia, part living memory, part hearsay, Romain's Russia and mine. And The Traveller... I'm reminded of him often, here. Now lore and life merge, or echo round us in this Balkan hinterland.

Some Russian officers are coming for a drink soon. I wonder how it would go if I could borrow the Vertinsky records? That sort of degenerate romanticism is probably banned in the USSR. Yet, essentially, Vertinsky songs are as Russian as 'Black Eyes', or anything sung by the Red Army choir. One of the Red Army officers asked Nedi why I seemed so cold to him when we met at parties. I, cold to a Russian man? Whatever gave him that idea? I must put that right, whatever I do!

The heat is becoming frightful. We are promised leave any day now and will try to drive down to the Black Sea. I would like to make a detour by Tirnovo, the ancient capital, but it is too hot to argue. Once again, I see how Romain blinkers himself away from any local colour, or expeditions, in general.

Euxinograd. We are in paradise here, beside the Black Sea, which really is inky: a dark blackish-blue, though its name derives more from its evil nature. Sudden and terrible storms lash across it from its Turkish or Russian shores and everywhere its treachery is dreaded. It claims a victim each July, say the locals with a certain complacency, I fancy. This profoundly traditional people do not wish any accepted patterns to change. We are very far from governmental Sofia now.

For three halcyon weeks not a tremor has ruffled the limpid waters. We and a few members of the Corps Diplomatique, or the Allied Control Commission, have the run of a stretch of coast once belonging to the Tzar's private domain.

A gingerbread wooden chalet painted bright orange was once Tzar Ferdinand's pleasure dome. Nothing else breaks the sweep of pale silky sand. Where it curves away eastward, gigantic black grapes grow almost to the water's edge. Floating we guzzle: paradise indeed.

However, inland and east, stretching towards the Dobrudja and Romania, there is a demonic area known as Deli Orman, 'The Mad Wood', a vast impenetrable forest. Like the Siberian taïga, it is perilous to man. 'Hunters sometimes go there, but they do not return,' say the locals.

Nearer at hand there is a petrified forest, old beyond time, where twisted, riven roots and branches writhe up out of rank swamps and tangle overhead to form enormous arches casting a perpetual dusk. Nearer still, a forest of stone, ruins of a great temple (date unknown) where pillars, some three metres or more round, and of immense height, circle a mysterious mound. This is the Stone Forest of Dikili Tach. I don't know what that means, but somehow, I feel we shall not budge from the beach and so will never know.

Oxen pull the carts everywhere. Trancy white oxen, or the huge horned meek-looking black water buffaloes, *gamuza*. In spring it seems they are liable to turn ugly and go for anything they see, from a priest to a jeep. These animals were originally imported from Asia. Their ability to survive the Bulgarian climate is remarkable, for when there is heat there is no water and when there is water there is no winter. Meandering along the rice fields, swaying ponderously, often followed by a moon-faced little calf, they transform the Balkan landscape into something Chinese; one's eye searches for coolies. The fur-capped Bulgarian peasant seems alien among his own hills. Legends tell that the buffalo will not be hurried. He will work loyally for his master, hour after hour, day after day, but he will not hurry. He knows he is a heavy, clumsy creature. He does not wish to stampede along, bruising the good earth he loves.

A rattle-trap, springless *droshky* hung with blue beads drove me to Varna today, to sample the hammam there. The old stone building was steaming away traditionally, but almost empty and overhung with a feeling of melancholy. A hideous crone, stark naked herself, pounded me with her withered, claw-like hands and seemed to slap cold water over me with particular venom. No echoes here, of Ingres' *voluptés* – nothing of these luxurious treatments sampled in Istanbul. But the ensuing languor was the same. Even the return journey in that springless *droshky* didn't rouse me.

Nedi & J. have joined us. They drove down overnight, a long haul, but having borrowed a Russian-made car from someone at the Albanian legation, they said it bounced happily over even the most awful roads. However, they're so ecstatically in love, I doubt they'd have even noticed craters.

In the stifling, greenish-lemon twilight that lingers here, we sit on the veranda and Nedi prepares our supper, charring green peppers at a single candle flame; quite a job. From faraway comes the sound of music – the strident wail of the *gaïda* and the softer *kaval*, a rustic flute... Insidious, voluptuous airs. Such music, with its chromatic half-tones, slipping from major to minor and back again, ever shifting, is like the landscape, mountain and farmland; Orthodox domes and Moslem minarets overlapping variations of faith.

Bulgarian folk music – *narodniye piecnyie*, songs of the people – can be meltingly seductive, or with the grave melancholy of early religious chants, then violently harsh, or gently domestic. ('Duna is rocking the cradle but Christo has gone to the Fair.') Abruptly, the mood changes. Womens' voices, singing in that startling, shrill, almost yelping manner which is also found in the Russian villages and called, I believe, *chastouchki*, something quite impossible to describe, but once heard remains unforgettable. Bulgarian folk music has cast its own special spell over me, and I am like one possessed.

Leaving Euxinograd was only made bearable by following a zig-zag, leisurely route which revealed how unspoiled this country remains; so varied, so rich, alternately dramatic or drowsy. Blue-walled villages garlanded with scarlet pimentos drying in the sun. Little Orthodox convents where tiny chapels boast one enormous bell, dangling like a ripe fruit. Plunging streams, great dark gorges, passes linking the mountain chains. Large flat tobacco leaves drying on racks along the walls and roofs; fields of sunflowers with huge lolling heads, spilling their seeds, *semki*, the local chewing gum.

'Tirnovo, ancient capital of the mediaeval Bulgarian Tzars,' I read, and even Romain (not historically minded) agreed to linger, to spend a night in this extraordinary place, this great rock fortress, hanging over the racing Yantra river, far below. Yet with all its grandeur there is something oddly cosy, almost Clovelly-like in the steep, narrow paths overflowing with flowery bowers between small pink-washed houses.

We slept in a broken-down watchtower which commanded the whole magnificent sweep of gorge and forest. Our room contained two iron bedsteads spread with insufficient rugs and a tin bucket, of dubious use. But it didn't matter. Tirnovo was worth every discomfort.

En route once more: a vast expanse of sky and earth. Endless horizons. Sheep moving slowly, their bells sounding across the hills. Shepherds stand like

graven figures, immobile, beneath their long striped cloaks. Sometimes there is
the thin, plaintive note of a flute or reed pipe, reaching back into the pastoral
childhood of the world. Bulgaria is perhaps the last truly pastoral country of
Europe: it is this deep sense of unity with the earth, this Theocritan quality
which remains here.

For how long?

As we neared Sofia, driving through flyblown outskirts, the lovely outline
of Vitosha came into view and I felt welcomed home. This mountain is a
friendly presence: there are no cruel jagged lines, no awe-inspiring peaks, but
instead some warm, companionable, or animal, quality seems to spread over
its humpy bulk. I always find myself looking for it on waking; and I seek its
shadowy outline again, before I sleep.

Winter has clamped down and Romain goes for an early-morning workout
in a nearby gymnasium. It is also the winter quarters of a circus, training for
the spring season. This is very distracting. Buxom charmers in tights ogle him,
hanging upside down by their teeth. Wire-walkers flirt over the top of Japanese
parasols. They are coached by a seedy old man, wildly moustached, wearing
a fur cap and bedroom slippers, Baï Pentcho, the king of Bulgarian circus, and
seventy years in the ring. He pinches the young ladies as they swarm round,
and has offered to coach Romain in a trapeze act. When this offer was declined,
he presented him with his memoirs, flowerily inscribed, from one author to
another. This proved to be a Don Juan travelogue, very racy reading.

Perhaps the most powerful distraction is Fintcho, a fox terrier passionately
anxious to perform on all occasions, forever teetering around on his hind legs,
waltzing, spinning, tumbling, in ecstasies of creative abandon. Winter is dull
for him, his owner says; he frets; he misses his public. He spends much time
curled in the vast lap of Baï Pentcho's fourth wife, now tights-darner for the
show, a sad comedown, for she was once the most sensational snake charmer
of the Near East.

Each morning, from my window I see the guards' *manège* as a woodcut. The
unbroken square of white snow is ringed by the barracks, their eaves festooned
with five-foot icicles. A bugle blows thinly in the knife-cold air: out comes the
cavalry. A ring of horsemen begin to prance round the square, black, very black
against the snow. Round and round they go, rocking-horse cavalry, the horses
snorting and cavorting, Dobbin-like. The breath steams out of their nostrils in

grey puffs. Overhead the rooks circle, cawing. It is a world of woodcut values, black on white. Another bugle sounds. The horsemen trot off towards the stables. The horses sidle and shy at the ice puddles by the fountain. It is breakfast time. Raiina lights the samovar and says the soldiers will be eating bread and paprika and drinking rose-leaf tea. They must be the only troops to start their day on such an exotic brew.

Between us, Romain and I are beginning to know quite a bit about Bulgaria. By that I mean bits not generally discovered by, or of interest to, the Corps Diplomatique. (I don't know about secret agents.) I go for the more exotic, or picturesque aspects of local colour, or a come-by-chance-encounter. Romain's command of Russian opens many doors among the intelligentsia and the politicians, but it is becoming more and more difficult to approach, as to be approached by, them. However much Bulgarians crave contact with the outside world, their frontiers have now become prison bars.

No one talks politics, but we whisper. We whisper darkly, conspiratorially, about the dramas, persecutions and mysterious happenings that are becoming daily life here. It is well known, but never said, that Prince Kyril, the late Tzar Boris's brother, was assassinated a year after his brother's death. And made to dig his grave first. Horrible whisperings, they reach me even in some quiet countryside, when I think I have found an unchanged, pastoral scene. But even that becomes tainted, or grows false, like a scenic backdrop from behind which alien figures emerge – strange figures, imposing alien ways everywhere.

The last few days have been particularly lowering; international tensions at breaking point all round. The minister being in Switzerland on sick leave, Romain is *chargé d'affaires*. His long ikon-face is thunderous. Waiting for a stream of government instructions to be decoded is nerve-racking to all of us. Draga V has been given an exit visa by the Russians, but her relatives don't seem relieved. They've been besieging us all day, sobbing and wailing, asking if she can travel with our courier. They seem to be a morbid lot, convinced Draga's breasts will be sliced off at the Yugoslavian frontier. Romain says it is a classic Balkan gesture.

It has snowed for forty-eight hours. There is little traffic in the streets and all sounds are muffled as the snow deepens. Vitosha is blotted out. Our newspapers are two weeks old. There is no opera this week, even if we could get through the snowdrifts. Romain returns home more ikon-faced than ever. The legation staff are working furiously, burning papers and official documents in the traditional way. Our chimneys block up, regurgitating heavy smoke and undigested scraps of official documents, making it increasingly difficult to breathe. Romain is becoming very tense – too tense, it seems. Suddenly, I remember the relaxing qualities of Beatrix Potter's books. But I have not bought any with me. At the moment of packing they had not seemed essential luggage… Then I remember, there were children in the American mission compound who might have some. I ring through, 'Sue-Ellen, do you by any chance have *Mrs Tiggy-Winkle* around?' I enquire. 'You do? Oh, good, could we borrow her for a bit? She'd be such a comfort to Romain,' and think I hear a faint click on the line, just as my friend agrees to help, 'If things don't get worse,' she adds. There is another distinct click and I imagine the mystified secret police, glued to the line, 'Teegli Vinkoff? Who is? Find!'

I don't know what steps were taken, but the little book duly arrived, and Romain duly relaxed: the crisis gradually subsided, and I was never connected to some unknown spy ring.

The old Russian professor whom Romain loves has a son who has gone into hiding, with a price on his head. He plans a getaway via the Macedonian border. We found him and his most beautiful wife holed up in the mountains. A small dark log-and-stone shelter, a big fire, white bearskins and not much else. We took them some books, newspapers and a huge *kashkaval* cheese. She was wearing peasant costume. He was loading a rifle when we arrived and threw it carelessly against the wall. It was all very dramatic. Or Balkan, perhaps.

Romain came in looking quite shaken. It seems the circus – Baï Pentcho's own where Romain goes for his workout – has been sent to Moscow. Overnight, for a 'Refresher Course'. They have been taxed with 'Formalism' and 'a lack of Constructive Purpose'. 'They are not in line with Socialist Realistic Art,' says the young doorkeeper, busy dismantling the premises. I wonder how this will affect poor, earnest little Fintcho.

Diplomatic life *en poste* is essentially nomadic. There are no roots, no past, no future – precarious present, for as long as the posting lasts; then a *chasse-croisé* to somewhere else. One day, any day now, we shall be moved on – posted else-where, by some inexplicable yet inexorable government ruling. I feel it coming. Everything around me assumes a heart-breaking quality of impermanence. Why have I felt so deeply-rooted here…?

The moment I have dreaded for so long has come. Romain is posted to Paris to work among the *chers collègues* at the Quai d'Orsay. No more of Balkan life. No more parties with the *tziganes*. No more harebrained trips in Junker planes. No more stories about the Great Snake god. No more Raiina. No more sound of *gaïda* or *kaval*, nor any nearness to Vitosha.

All day I have been packing up and crying. Raiina joined me in both occu-pations. Now, at last, she tries to comfort me by telling me the legend she has always kept secret – the mysterious legend of the Lilac-bleeding Star.

In Macedonia, she says, they believe that those born with a wanderlust, those who abandon their true love, or desert their homes because of a longing for faraway lands, are born under the Lilac-bleeding Star. It leads them on, like some lodestar, yet it weeps for them, its tears the lilac-coloured sparks that glitter in a wintry sky…

'Your Star, Gospodja,' says Raiina mournfully, knowing that it is my fate to leave Bulgaria, leave the place I love so much, tearing out some of my heart, because I too was born under the Lilac-bleeding Star.

The Time and the Place

CITIES, LIKE PEOPLE, HAVE THEIR HOUR. THIS IS THEIR MOMENT IN TIME – their supremely personal expression of being, crystallised into an epoch which represents their essence and is the apotheosis of their spirit. Thus we can map time and track the hour and the place through centuries and across the world… 'Last week in Babylon, last night in Rome…' for although all time has existed in all places there is a strange light and shade, or focus, which sharpens our vision of certain places, at certain times, concentrating on that one moment, to make it symbolic of its century and its surroundings. Although this focus must be an individual one, and although it is remarkable how many people's view of the hour and the place correspond; the subject is still highly controversial, the perspectives purely personal.

To me, Munich and Vienna are both Biedermeier cities – only Biedermeier, peopled with a late crop of romantics, wearing stove-pipe hats and bottle-green frock-coats, carrying umbrellas, and playing upon the flute, at once poetic and prudent. For me, there are no Hapsburg glories; no Munich Putsch, only Hermann and his Dorothea, trysting beneath the evening star, repairing to neat domestic interiors, or wandering in the brooding, yet meticulous twilight of Richter or Friedrich.

And Venice: for all its merchants, its Bucintoro splendours, the florid, swirling ease of Tiepolo and Veronese, or Carpaccio's round-rumped young bloods, jostling their gondola craft in the rank canal – for all these, I think Venice only lives imperishably in the eighteenth century. Transfixed, Casanova is forever escaping from the 'Leads'. Behind a Ridotto grille, the *cavalier servente* is always staking his sequins for his mistress, a nun. Longhi and Guardi caught the moment, Galuppi set it to music, and Goldoni staged it at the Fenice. Behind the sinistry of the beaked mask the comedy continues eternally. This is Venice, for all time.

But what of another Venice, you may ask? The city had its greatest being in another earlier age. Yet never was a place so dedicated to one moment – the eighteenth century. Later, the fervours of George Sand and Alfred de Musset seem oddly out of key among such ghostly but quintessential cynicism. So does Garibaldi's heroism, the Brownings' felicity, and the passions of Duse and D'Annunzio. But Cagliostro is at home there.

Yet Florence, surely, can never be *dix-huitième*? It must be the Middle Ages flowering into the Renaissance, with Dante, Giotto and the Medici as part of the noble procession. Here, Alfieri and his Countess d'Albany glide through the Florentine landscape, which is always that of a Benozzo Gozzali fresco, like wraiths, casting no shadow on the abiding Florence.

What makes this sharp focus, this selectivity of vision settle upon one time and place? The Akashic records (by which means some people explain Miss Moberley and Miss Jourdain's famous encounter with Marie Antoinette at Versailles) are supposed to be a never-ending, ever-present series of past events which can be recaptured by those who are attuned. These records do not, I believe, confine themselves to events of an intense, or significant nature alone. All times past are recorded there, to be experienced, and re-experienced by the initiate few.

It is not a city's most noble, or historic moment which is its apotheosis, in this sense. That would be subject to too much variation, according to the beholder. For that way, while the prelate sees Rome as the arena of Christian martyrdom, the classical scholar sees it as the city of the Caesars; though to me being neither, it is the ornate frame for Renaissance and baroque Papal splendours – still a secular rather than ecclesiastical city. That way, too, Leningrad, to the balletomane, is Petroushka's Petersburg, while to readers of the *Daily Worker* it remains an anchorage for the cruiser *Aurora*.

Take Constantinople for example: the climax of Turkish history was most likely reached during the reign of Suleiman the Magnificent in the sixteenth century. And to the painter Liotard, who, two hundred years later was rendering the decaying charms of the Ottoman Empire in his meticulous manner, it was probably that sumptuous epoch – that, or the earlier, dark, ikon-studded Byzantium, which was the city's supreme moment in time. But to me, yet another two hundred years on, Liotard's epoch seems as remote as Suleiman's, or Justinian's, and of all three, I personally find Liotard's the most abiding.

It is the moment when West has conquered East. There is an Arcadian air, a conscious, almost self-conscious *Turquerie*. It is the setting for an endless *fête-galante*, centred around the crumbling Porte Sublime where, in a summer sunset, a veiled houri is wooed with sherbet and sugar plums, and the voluptuous *ghazals* of the poet Nedim, and there is no menace of the Janissaries.

Like all America, New York is still forming. The fabulous city has not had time to distil itself into a past, let alone a perpetual moment, unless it proves to be the Frankie and Johnny era, brash saloons and eager people.

Still mapping the centuries, while Leningrad has, for me, only one abiding moment – St Petersburg, in the grandeur of its early nineteenth-century classicism – its Dekabrist and Pushkinian zenith – Moscow has two periods of perpetuity. It is still the mediaeval Asiatic village, a huddle of cruelty and colour which centres round the onion domes of Vasily Blajeny, and it is still the city of the rich merchants and wan gentry of the 1850s. The serfs are not yet liberated. The aristocrats fawn round the Winter Palace, seven hundred miles west, in St Petersburg. But priest-ridden, greedy, fatalistic Moscow sits round its samovar spooning cherry jam from a saucer, sipping tea noisily, above the clang of a thousand belfries. This, for me, is forever Moscow: the burning of the Kremlin, the genius of Tolstoy and Dostoyevsky – like the Streletzi Revolt or that of the Old Believers – are all manifestations of the Slav spirit, of Moscow's Asiatic vigour; so, too, is that curiously static force which Lenin was later to galvanise into one sweeping, dynamic and constructive whole, and which crystallises in the Red Square. Yet for all its limitless impact, this is not Moscow's most essential aspect. Perhaps this is yet to come, if there is world enough, and time.

London, for all its past grandeurs, its quickened tempo obtained by the war years, and the influx of many races, does not find its moment in time either in its Tudor heyday or in the heroism of the bombardment. I find London was most perfectly itself only in the nineteenth century when, with Regency Corinthians in curricles, tapping the claret and milling the Charlies, the city gathered momentum, and moving heavily but surely on, through vistas of materialism, it reached that unequalled expression of national form found in Cruikshank's London of the 1850s.

This was the London of fogs and muffin men: Hoxton, pantomimes, gin palaces, meek governesses, great statesmen and mean streets. Public hangings. Landseer's lapdog sentimentalities. A tight-laced, strait-laced hour that was, nevertheless, robust, tough and kindly. It was the essence of the city, the century and the nation.

But Paris confounds all theories and eludes all dictums. Paris has the surface charm and flexibility of the true courtesan. Because of this, perhaps, it has contrived for eight centuries to be regarded as the essence of civilisation by each succeeding age. '*Paris? Tu es le coeur du monde,*' cried those most immobile of all Parisians, the Goncourt brothers, seeking no other world. There was a street for every century or mood. It was once for cynics and sentimentalists alike. Paris was the first night of *Hernani* blazing romanticism as a new creed; Voltaire's cynicism, Ravaillac's fanaticism and Dior's taste. The saccharinity of the postcards, and the noble logic of the Code Napoleon. Maxim's and the bistro round the corner. Existentialism and Cora Pearl, 'B.B.' and General de Gaulle stalking up the aisle of a delivered Notre Dame. But lately?

I wonder, does Paris now reflect, or create, claim or repudiate? Is its present Americanisation, *les blue-jeans* and *le drug-store* on the Champs-Élysées something ephemeral, a teenager's dream, or one aspect of this age which Paris has truly absorbed? Perhaps Paris is the exception which proves my rule, that by charting the centuries we can find the setting for each moment in time. Call it the geography of time.

Every Picture Tells a Story

'SEND US A CARD,' IS THE CLASSIC, THE INEVITABLE FAREWELL CRY AS the train pulls out of the station. As classic, as inevitable, the messages which come winging back from all manner of places: 'Having a wonderful time', 'Wish you were here'. For half a century, across a thousand different views the same phrases persist. Across the Sphinx, the Roman catacombs (wish you were here… ?) across the beach at Coney Island, Picasso's *Harlequin*, or the Blue Danube. The range is vast. Jolly, geographic, historic, pornographic or artistic. Waggish, what the butler saw at Brighton; romantic, Rudolph Valentino savaging Vilma Bánky; jokes about plumbing. The matriarchal Queen Victoria, embedded in a living wall of respectful relatives, half the *Almanach de Gotha*; so many of them, it is seen in retrospect, to lose, if not their heads, at any rate their crowns.

These old postcards, so glossy and reassuring, to Mum and Dad, Tiny or *Mon Vieux* are now strewn across the world, impersonal finds for collectors, or just so much paper salvage. Lately, in France, their collection has become a new cult, rapidly assuming the intricacies and enthusiasms of stamp collection. Collectors are forming into clubs and subdivide their cards into sharply defined types. Out-of-the-way places are much sought after. So are exotic scenes, curious types, or outstanding personalities. Some collectors go, too, for the stamp, which seems greedy. When all three combine, as for example, a card of Unter den Linden, bearing Russian Army franking and Mr Churchill's signature, it makes a really royal flush, a true collector's piece.

Some enthusiasts prefer cards of one specific sort, concentrating on one country, or city alone; or railway engines, dogs, cathedrals. Geisha girls. Others go for the writing matter. Many dull cards are redeemed by the subject matter of their message. I have one which shows a group of ample Parsee ladies lounging together, gracefully draped in saris. It is addressed to a gentleman living in Manchester. 'Assassin!' is the unsigned message, brief and to the point. All sorts of speculations arise… Another, perhaps my favourite, shows the Wailing Wall at Jerusalem, wailers in full cry. Across the corner we read, 'Kindest thoughts from Nettie and Papa.' One wonders why kindest thoughts... what were Nettie and Papa doing beside the Wailing Wall that August day in 1907? Delicious vistas open before us as we abandon ourselves to nostalgic fancies... I shuffle my cards; here is the bonbon prettiness of Gaby Deslys ('having a wonderful time' should have been her motto, or device). The Burning Ghats on the Ganges calls for one or other of the classic postcard phrases. What range! A Mexican bullring picked out in sequins. The Alps. Piccadilly Circus on Mafeking night. The Scene of the Massacre Tea Rooms, Glencoe.

The chief fascination of old postcards is their nostalgic quality. They show us a microcosm of some once ordinary way of life, now become extraordinary by its mere distance from our times. Through these cards we glimpse the humours and interests of another age. We see the charmers they chased, the jokes they enjoyed and the events and objects they thought outstanding. I treasure an impressive scene of public vaccination at a town hall during an epidemic of smallpox in 1900.

Postcards are better for being mature. Their vintage years are at the turn of the century; their beginnings around the 1870s. Not much earlier. They are the first flowering of commonplace photography. After the great pioneer days of Daguerre and Octavia Hill came a vulgarised version of the medium that was accessible to all. Postcards record, for all times, aspects of the world which have now assumed legendary qualities. Some cards, as for example the coronation of the last Tzar, have become historic records.

Then, too, old postcards are doubly evocative, for they remind us not only of the places we have visited but, if they are really out of date, they probably conjure up the lost magic of those places which we always imagined romantically, in a way which, alas, the reality so often betrayed. They show us places which we have known and also those we shall now never know. Places that have become inaccessible, or changed beyond recognition. Pekin, the Great Within... Names which haunt our imagination. Queen Tamara's castle in Georgia was such, but if I could go there now, should I find it as Lermontov knew it? Or should I reach it, earn it, perhaps, as a bonus for triple output — only to find it transposed into a shock-workers' rest home? Never mind, my brightly-coloured card of the savage gorges and eagle-nest castle, with some superb Georgian cavaliers in the foreground, is all either I, or Queen Tamara, could wish.

The Sublime Porte, the Street of the Necromancers in Prague, the Kremlin, were other fabulous-sounding places of which I always dreamed. When at last I saw them with my own eyes I felt cheated. I took a bus to the Kremlin; I sighted factories beyond the Sublime Porte... vistas of disillusion. It was not until, much later, looking through my cards (which are invariably found elsewhere, old Turkey in Edinburgh, or the Klondyke in Tunis), that I was able to recapture my original enchantment. This was the world as I had imagined it and only through these cards could I now glimpse Proust's Paris, or Dostoyevsky's Russia.

Like the interests, the popular personalities of other days are incomprehensible to a later generation. The decline in sales of film, or stage-star, postcards can most likely be accounted for by the power of the cinema close-up and the number of magazines which provide suitable pin-up pictures. Thanks to the close-up, fans of today have the illusion of being far nearer to their adored than an earlier generation pining between long-range opera-glass peeps at matinee idols. It is curious to recall that in the late 1890s, postcard personalities included, along with showgirls, a large number of religious leaders. The more handsome prelates are seen in full canonicals thundering from their pulpits. At the time of the Abdication, I cannot help feeling that some enterprising firm must have launched twin portrait cards of Mr Baldwin and the Archbishop of Canterbury as pendant to those of the Duke of Windsor and Mrs Simpson. But I have never seen one.

Politics has a place among picture postcards, but it is a small one. A card which I found, appropriately in Leningrad, of the baby Lenin, in a sort of Slavicised Fauntleroy suit, bubbling over with blonde curls and nestling into a plush armchair, is sometimes regarded as a political manifestation by my more literal visitors. I have seen extracts from Lenin's Order of Battle for the October Revolution made into the same sort of card as Mr Churchill's, 'We shall fight on the beaches'... or the Atlantic Charter, which I saw embossed in Tudor-type lettering. But by and large, politics do not translate happily in postcard terms.

Although we do not, at first glance, associate the postcard with high moral purpose, yet this is sometimes its function. There are cards which list the Seven

Deadly Sins, the Ten Commandments, or a *Tract for the Times*. Temperance societies avail themselves of this paper pulpit, but the only example I have is one publicised by the Ligue Nationale contre l'Alcoolisme, where the very title seems an anachronism in the language of a wine-drinking country.

European watering places nearly always proffer, among the views of the Casino, Jardin Botanique and Plage, a card of forbidding ugliness: this is certain to be described as Le Temple Anglais. All that perpendicular suburban architecture can do to render it repulsive has been done. But there must have been a demand, for the supply is everywhere apparent. I have a splendid example of this kind: it is addressed to a Mrs Gilbert – at a London address. The message reads, 'Wish you were here. Your Gilbert'. More idle speculations: I see Gilbert embroiled in a delicious adventure, dividing his time between some unknown seductress and the gambling tables. I see it all. Emerging from the Casino a crumpled bankrupt wreck, now spurned by the lovely wanton from the Hotel Sumptuoso, he sees the pure dawn breaking and remembers his neglected little wife, his loved ones in London. Will he be forgiven? Not a moment to lose. He must write at once. He rushes to the station bookstall to buy a card. What card? Good God! Not that one – nor that one either. Is there nothing suitable? Ha! Le Temple Anglais! The very thing. Seizing a pencil he writes his message, 'Wish you were here.' The modest little postcard goes on its way, reassuring and homely; it will reunite Gilbert and his loved one as no amount of telegrams could have done.

The different nationalities each have their specialities. English comics for great bawdy gusto, of which Donald Gill was the master, banana peel, lodgers, and smack-bottom fun.

France for frisky stuff. Coy ladies being helped out of their corsets by sleek pink and white *poilus*. Elaborate charts of passion. *Thermomètres des amoureux*, where by an ingenious device a real blob of quicksilver mounts the card, according to the warmth of the hand (the force of passion, it is inferred). Entranced, we watch it soar from one illustrated stage of emotion to the next. From *amour timide*, by way of *amour passioné* to *folie amoureuse*, depicted as an engrossed couple in pastel underwear. There are pseudo-botanic cards, too, the language of flowers, with special emphasis on the message of the fig leaf.

Germany and Romania once excelled at 'feelthy' postcards, where the most frantic antics are displayed with a total lack of aesthetic, or dramatic subtlety, and the singularly unattractive nature of most of the participants is as surprising as the frequent appearances of such extraneous objects as pince-nez and socks.

A rather adolescent form of humour which I much enjoy is to buy with an eye on some specific person, or occasion. Or I may hoard a card for years, until just the right moment arrives. For example, a highly-coloured picture of the Etablissement Thermal, at Vichy, is obviously just the thing for corresponding with someone whose conduct in Occupied France was not altogether impeccable. And that detailed photograph of a head-on engine crash outside Perth, all mangled, splintered scrap iron: that will be perfect to use as a weekend invitation card, listing Friday's best trains.

Many postcards remain teasing puzzles. That smudge beside the fountain, is it an Arabian charger, or an ice cream cart? Is this Europe, or Africa, or South America? Palms and volcanoes are singularly international when presented without a foreground. I peer into the tiny stage for further clues. 'Stands the church clock at ten to three?' and is there honey, or hashish for tea in that lunar landscape? Yes: when all is said and done it is this mysterious quality which is the abiding delight of old postcards. Places we shall never see, people we shall never know. Places, faces, messages. A whole life's drama in a line of faded ink. A vanished epoch on an oblong of pasteboard.

[Editor's note] A postcard sent to the artist Eden Box, from Bulgaria, shows Lesley Blanch, and her husband Romain Gary, standing arm-in arm in a cobbled square. It is inscribed: *Love from Assassins Corner, Sofia. 14 June '46,* and was taken at Stamboliyski's disinterment day ceremonies.*

On the back it reads: *Edie Darling, This pair of Balkan thugs is none other than your own Les and Rom – Chelsea's most gracious living pair. We were swimming across the main square in front of the sacked and looted palace after a vast ceremonial protocol luncheon – 20 a side, white gloved flunkies, on the day of the disinterment of*

---

* Aleksandar Stamboliyski, prime minister of Bulgaria from 1919 until 1923 who was tortured and executed by the Internal Macedonian Revolutionary Organization.

Stamboliysky, a famous Red they've now dug up & are making scenes & incidents in the best Ambler manner. We were both <u>green</u> with heat and high-living. R. had first said, 'I want you back at the Legation by 5 o/c please, as the shooting is going to start about then…' & so that may account for both our expressions. Anyhow, the <u>killing</u> part is – he was right. It did. Such news as I have, sent to Bege this week. Love to everybody. I will write more next week. Scarface sends his fond love & from both of us to dear M, if arrived.

from Stumpoffsky & Thugisttsky.

THE ORIENT EXPRESS

THE ORIENT EXPRESS! ALL THE ABRACADABRAS OF MAGIC, OF FABLED travel lore, lie in those words. To earlier generations (for the great train's first run was in 1883, its last in 1977), the Orient Express held intoxicating promises of romance, danger, luxury and those remote horizons known as the Balkans, where anything was liable to happen and often did. The wild regions through which the train passed like the little Ruritanian cities where it halted were the stuff of adventure, the setting for adventurers. Whether darkling moustachioed figures in fur-lined overcoats with palpably false papers, or ladies of equally dubious origin, but breathtaking beauty and elegance à la Marlene Dietrich, passengers on that train were a breed apart. Commercial travellers, or tourists, were not in evidence, while men of business all appeared to be key figures of international finance. There were regular relays of diplomats and their wives (of which I was one) and of course the embassy couriers shuttling back and forth, now east, now west, carrying the diplomatic 'pouch' or 'bag', chained to their person which lent an air of drama to their movements – even when heading for the lavatory at the end of the corridor. But then mystery pervaded the whole train. It was all part of its magic.

That there is a mystique surrounding all famous trains is undeniable, but even so the Trans-Siberian; the Shanghai Express; the Atchison, Topeka and Santa Fe; the Canadian Pacific; or the Turk-Sib (which linked Lake Baikal with the Uzbek and Turcoman territories of Central Asia, if I remember rightly, for I travelled on it a long while ago) all paled beside that glamour which still surrounds the Orient Express and its legend.

The great monster I knew started from the Gare de Lyon, gathered speed through France, tunnelled in and out of Switzerland and via the Simplon reached Milan and so, sped towards Belgrade. (An alternative route went via Vienna and Bucharest.) Now, at the Yugoslavian frontier, the train began what I always considered its archetypal run, through the Balkans to Sofia, the Bulgarian capital, and Turkey beyond. Mile by mile the same entrancing essentially Balkan landscape unwound itself past the windows — racing rivers, cut-throat gorges, fields of tobacco, valleys full of roses grown for their attars, pastoral scenes, shepherds, black buffalo and minarets rising beside the blue-domed Orthodox churches — for here, Christian and Moslem met. And with each exotic mile east-ward, my heart lightened. I had escaped my bourgeoise roots. What lay ahead?

The Orient Express was the embodiment of luxury, its grooming unsurpassed; its gleaming brass fitments, like its velvety upholstery, soft carpeting and the brilliantly festive restaurant car's haute cuisine and vaunted cellar, all conspired to create a limboland of *grand luxe* lived within its flanks of sleek mahogany panelling. There was a purring content in the subdued rhythm of the wheels which lulled one into a timeless dimension of hedonism... Was it Monday, or Thursday, or yesterday? No matter, it was bliss. As to the uniformed attendants, they too possessed some magic quality, appearing and disappearing djinn-like to gratify one's every whim. After several journeys made together, they seemed to assume another aspect becoming faithful old family retainers, their uniforms now liveries, themselves discreet, indulgent and affectionate. Though they could be critical if they noted a breach of etiquette, or protocol. There were codes of behaviour and a certain accepted style which marked seasoned passengers, very much as on ocean liners. However, the Orient Express spared us the tyranny of gymkhanas or gala dances.

Not that entertainment was lacking; the variety of scenery and the nature of our fellow passengers took care of that. I often thought that these attend-ants, so deftly making up our couchettes for the night, bringing champagne to one compartment, a billet-doux to another, might also have been likened to Cupid's messengers. Three nights aboard had a singularly inflammatory effect on all but the most solid.

Then there were the perpetually renewed delights of the restaurant car. Dinners were formal affairs served with great panache. We were inclined to dress up – to cut a dash worthy of the chef's skills. As I recall that faraway scene, a rosy glow suffuses everything. Pink shaded table lamps, casting a most becoming light over the diners; pink carnations blooming in little silver vases; a roseate sparkle on the impeccable linen, on cutlery and glassware; a shimmer of rose playing over the lobster bisque, or was it the lobster thermidor, the filet mignon or the strawberry mousse? Surely those menus were not entirely of that carmine palette? Yet I still see everything *couleur de rose*, with pink champagne to crown the feast if one was lucky enough to charm one's *vis à vis*. But here I must admit that however romantic and luxurious the fabled train seemed, to me, something of its raptures has always dimmed on the return journey northwards. We were racing towards chill greyness and a too well-known pattern of daily life. Even when, at the end of World War II, the northbound train was sometimes halted by a band of Yugoslavian partisans patrolling the region, one knew it was only a temporary reprieve. These heroic figures used to come aboard to scrutinise our papers. They were handsome, bold creatures in shaggy sheepskin coats and their word was law thereabouts. At that grim moment, all luxury as the train once knew it was severely curtailed. Our meals were largely of a picnic nature, each passenger bringing their own ration. But romance remained and once, one of the partisan leaders took a fancy to me, having augmented my picnic with a bottle of fiery *slivovitz*. He ordered the train to be run into a siding for twenty-four hours while we dallied agreeably, to the fury of the rest of the train and the chaos of any timetable.

But did I not say that romance and adventure were an essential part of that magic spell cast by the Orient Express? It was a spell that never lessened until the wheels slowed to a halt at the terminus, were it East or West, the Gare de Lyon or the Sirkeci Istasyonu, below the soaring minarets of Istanbul. Ah! Match me such magic if you can!

MUCH HOLY DAY IN CHICHICASTENANGO

HIS DIRTY PANAMA HAT WAS STUDDED WITH RUBIES AND EMERALDS, OR what passed for such in the Guatemalan highlands. He clambered up into the driver's seat of the bus. He was about four feet high and his bare toes clamped on to the clutch with agility. 'Good morning sir and lady,' he said courteously, 'My name is Tomàs. My father was a witch.'

'No, really?' we heard ourselves reply, in tinny social tones.

'He died in hellfire,' said Tomàs, 'Much sadness. I take you see his grave. Secret temple.' He eyed us roguishly. 'Many visitors not see but for you...'

As the overcrowded bus ground and shuddered its way up the mountain roads beside Lake Atitlan he maintained a conversational flow, till we became close friends, bound together by ties of mutual interest and suffering. The sun smacked down; dust engulfed us, acrid and choking. Our parched mouths gaped, filling with grit and insects. Baggage flung itself off the rack at every hairpin bend. The cork blew out of a bottle of stomach-mixture, the elixir of life in these parts. Indeed, all journeys through Central America might be described as *voyages aux pays du parégorique*. Although, except in jungle country, one is seldom very far from the pharmaceutical periphery, it is customary to travel with a basic pharmacy. Customary and necessary.

We headed inland: there was a last glimpse of the volcano, San Pedro, reflected, still and majestic in the pellucid depths below Sololá. A signpost said: Huehuetenango via Sacapulas y Quiché... It reads like the purest escapism. The bus plunged berserk into heavily wooded country, live oak, pine and unnamable tangles, where lean pigs thatched with auburn curls rooted angrily. We were heading for Chichicastenango of mysterious legend.

'You been Mexico? Chichicastenango best,' said Tomàs with finality. It was, he continued, market day there; 'And tomorrow, very much Holy Day. Many blessings. You wait see,' and he beamed and squirmed as he negotiated a particularly dizzy bend in the ravine road.

We now began to overtake groups of Indians struggling along, bent double under towering loads of merchandise reefed to their heads by a tumpline. Everything is carried this way: it is a habit begun so young that the typical back-slanting conical skull is said to be the result. Each *cargador*, as these carriers are called, is loaded with upwards of two hundred pounds at a time, and rather than make an easy return trip unencumbered, they usually load up their packs with stones, to keep in training. They trotted fast, with tiny, rapid steps, like little ponies. As they trotted, they chattered in high-pitched Chinese-sounding tones and peeped at us from under their beetling loads with bright slit eyes. The other occupants of our bus now showed unmistakable pleasure. Their granite Mayan faces flickered into life at last. Superiority, pride, achievement… it was all there. They were riding.

As we drove between narrow, windowless, white adobe-walled lanes, Tomàs accelerated furiously and swinging round a blind corner on two wheels, came to a stop by backing into a market stall full of pineapples. Amid shrieks and imprecations, he leant out, took careful aim, and shot forward into a basket-stall kept by an angry man who spat at him. 'My enemy,' said Tomàs; 'Tomorrow I pray for Mercy.' Bowing to us, he moved away from the stall-holder's spittle and fists and was soon lost in the crowd.

We advanced among the mounds of merchandise, buying juicy local fruits, granadillas and cherimoyas, striped tiger masks and papier-mâché jaguar heads, spotted pink and green, irresistible in their comic innocence. These are designed to be worn during the strange dances, rain invocations for the most part, which are still performed regularly hereabouts.

At Chichicastenango the whole elusive Guatemalan scene crystallises. It is the hidden heart of Mayan country, with its own climate of mystical worship, of pagan rites and Papal rituals. The Quiche Indiansé gods are inextricably interwoven. God the Father, God the Son, Great Lord of Retalevleu, the Prince of the Thunderbolts, Holy Mary, St Peter and the Lordly Spirits who attend the Dawn. The Indians are as superstitious as pious. Nothing must be left to chance. After luxuriating in high mass, at the church of San Tomàs, they hurry up into the hills to placate their stone idols with some suitable sacrifice. Some years ago, when all priests were proscribed, the Indians continued to come to church, punctiliously; but soon Rome was blended with pagan incantation. Today, the devout Indian goes to church accompanied by his own special witch doctor; together they make the rounds of the chapels, strewing flowers, different coloured petals, according to their prayers, yellow for crops, white for health, pink for riches, or such. The witch doctor is their mouthpiece, he frames their prayers and directs them where to place their candles. Together, client and priest inch up the great curve of stone steps on their knees, burning copal incense to their several gods.

Most Holy Day or not, Chichicastenango always wears a devotional air. All day, every day, it swims in a mauve haze of incense, curling in perfumed wisps round the brazier, which glows ceaselessly, outside the church door. Here the pilgrims and witch doctors light their censers. Day and night the pious shuffle up the steps, blood seeping through the knees of their rough cotton trousers. But they do not seem to feel pain: their faces are rapt, ecstatic. There is much to pray for: little has been given, here, besides beauty.

At the inn they told us to be up and out early if we wanted to see the processions, and after a night punctuated by explosions, which we later learned were firecrackers let off to propitiate jealous local gods, we were on the main square as the sun topped the far hills and gilded the great bell clanging overhead. Already the village was filling up with streams of Indians and their wives and children gathering from all over the countryside. Each village wore its own distinctive costume. Men from Sololá in pink-and-white-striped, calf-length trousers and tiny Eton jackets embroidered across the back with what looked like a huge, rather sinister butterfly, but which is said to be a version of the double-headed Habsburg eagle of the Spanish monarch Carlos V. Women from across the lake at San Antonio in their tight, scarlet, ankle-length hobble skirts, their goitre-puffed throats hung with as many as thirty gold and silver blown-glass bead necklaces. The Quiché Indians, in virtue of their aristocracy, wore a sixteenth-century costume deriving straight from the Conquistadores, black doublet and hose, their heads bound pirate-wise with a red cotton handkerchief. The proudest families wore extra gold embroideries, blazing suns and moons and were hung with gold chains of office.

They were all forming into processions now. Each group carrying, or rallying round, a life-sized saint's statue which had been removed from its chapel to be paraded through Chichicastenango three times before being restored to its place.

Many of these saints are home-made versions of the original Spanish statue; lovingly recreated Indian versions of the baroque original. They were button-eyed, scarlet-cheeked, jolly figures, hilarious martyrs, at once touching and grotesque. They looked like gigantic toys designed by Steinberg. Some woolly bearded saints carried an infant (but also bearded) Christ-child. They were dressed in brilliant artificial satins, often mixed with fabulous laces, cotton ankle-socks peeping from beneath their fine robes, peacock feathers (symbol of the Cotinga bird, whose turquoise plumage once adorned Montezuma's mantle of kingship), and loops of stiff gold bullion fringe or scraps of cheap ribbon safety-pinned on to them in a haphazard manner. Overhead were arbours of spruce branches hung with little bells and winking pocket shaving mirrors from the five- and ten-cent store.

These extraordinary carnival figures swayed and tottered as they were slowly paraded. Before and after them paced the Quiché nobles, bearing tall staves of office, each topped by a blazing silver-gilt sun. Their grave faces remained unmoved, even when the more uncontrollably devout followers let off fireworks round them, soaring rockets and Catherine wheels, gunpowder play in the manner of an Arab fantasia.

Inside the church, the organ wheezed out a tremolo of Monteverdi from behind the ornate screen. The procession moved towards the high altar, where an old priest waited for them with a smile of welcome. The women, bunched up with shawls and babies, squat, squaw-like figures, followed their men at a respectful distance. Even before God, their place is the lowliest.

At the moment of the Elevation of the Host, the hush was shattered by the roar of rockets, ripping the silence from outside, where some of the witch doctors were acting as a sort of extra-mural congregation: translating the holy ritual into more generally appreciated terms of gunpowder, sulphur and brimstone. Presently, as the church emptied, trotting lines of Indians headed for the hills, making for more ceremonies, while others settled to an afternoon's bargaining, among the stalls full of cotton handkerchiefs, serapes, nameless bits of meat and entrails, coarse household china or tequila booths.

Tomàs, who had followed us into the church and pestered us continually to provide him with a sum suitable to both the offertory and his devout nature, now skipped around us as we moved from stall to stall.

'My father invite you to his home now,' he said, 'Very holy party, much interesting prayer and dance.'

'But I thought you said he was dead?'

'Risen again,' said Tomàs triumphantly, 'My father a Christian witch...'

Eyeing him sternly we said we were busy and shook him off.

As the day wore away and the stalls were packed up, the sound of shooting merged with the rockets; but no one, at first, realised violence was afoot. Presently a terrible wailing sounded. '*Crime passionnel*,' said the chemist's assistant, who had spent a year in Geneva and spoke basic French. A woman rushed out of one house and into another: we saw a heavy, sleepy-looking gendarme waddle across the square, buttoning up his white uniform as he went. There had been trouble between two brothers, we were told. One was dead; the other was dying...

Tomàs made a jack-in-the-box appearance at our side.

'You want see body?' he asked hopefully.

'*Do go away!*' we said.

He went off, looking offended.

The last stalls were dismantled; the tequila booths emptied and the more incapacitated drinkers lay where they fell, giving the empty marketplace the appearance of a battlefield. Tomàs was now among the fallen, his jewel-studded panama hat crushed in the dust. He was snoring gently.

'So much for his very holy day,' Romain said and stepped carefully over him. We did not wish for further solicitations.

The sun dropped suddenly. All at once it was cold: twilight raced over the countryside, and the incense braziers glowed from the church steps. The evening star hung low over the jacaranda trees, as some indignant women began to search among the log-like figures on the ground. As each one found her man, she dragged him up, and went off, scolding and supporting the inert bundle.

That night, nested-down in the enclosed, secret world of comfort and plumbing provided by the Mayan Inn, we watched a marimba band stump on to the patio and settle to their enormous, unwieldy white-wood instruments. They began to play spanking local airs; the macaws shuffled round on their perches, their gaudy plumage lit by the firelight flickering out from the kitchens. They eyed the musicians balefully and began to out shriek them.

In our room a log fire roared up the tiled stove. Far away across the mountains, rockets still soared and sparked; and firecrackers still exploded in night-long rites designed to placate the Gods of Harvest and Rain, and the Lord of the Morning. As if in reproof, the church bell clanged out, suddenly restless. A thin wraith of incense drifted across the darkness outside our window and hung there, like a pale pall. Far away, a dog barked and was answered by another. Chichicastenango slept. It had been, as Tomàs said, a much holy day.

But perhaps, after all, not so very much holy: before midnight the midget reprobate had recovered sufficiently to come scratching on our shutters.

'You want see bad ladies interesting dance?' he whispered.

'Not tonight,' we replied... 'Tomorrow, maybe...'

'Tomorrow no good: not holy day,' he replied, unctuously and giving us no time to change our minds, he disappeared into the night.

CHRISTMAS IN BUKHARA

I HAD GIVEN MYSELF THIS JOURNEY AS A CHRISTMAS PRESENT. FOR YEARS
I had promised myself the Golden Road to Samarcand in my stocking. Now
it was mine. I had spent a most unlikely Christmas Eve in Samarcand, once
Tamerlane's capital, and far from the rustle of gift-wrappings and all the commercial blackmail by which Christmas has come to be represented elsewhere;
I had spent the day lolling on one of those large blue-painted wooden bedstead
affairs that are set under the trees of every *chaikhana*, or teahouse, of Central
Asia. From this vantage point and at the price of endless little bowls of green
tea, I could watch the local population, Arabian Night figures, in their striped
khalats, a sort of padded dressing gown, which, with an embroidered velvet skull-
cap and high Russian boots, is the traditional costume of the Uzbek and Tadjik
men of Turkestan. They were trotting to and from the bazaar on minuscule
donkeys, or seated cross-legged in the white dust before their wares – grapes,
home-made birdcages of netted string, or little mounds of spinach-green
powder, a kind of snuff they place under their tongues and savour voluptuously. Towards twilight, they crowded the *chaikhanas*, lolling beside me and
like myself, contemplating, with a sort of ecstasy, the shimmering blue domes
and minarets of this legendary city. Such an intense blue seems to grey-down
even the cloudless Oriental skies.

Next morning, I flew on eastwards to Bukhara, another legendary and
little-known city, where I had decided to spend Christmas Day itself. I had
not expected the little plane to come down on so short a flight. But it did,
quite suddenly, landing with a thump on the baked, cracked earth of a come-
by-chance airstrip on the edge of the Kizil Kum, or Red Sands, once the
terror of every traveller or pilgrim crossing these deserts. Our pilot emerged
from his cabin carrying a very large plush teddy bear, chocolate coloured
and dressed in mauve check rompers, with a white collar fastened by a pink
tulle bow. The navigator followed, lurching under the weight of a string
bag stretched round several enormous tiger-striped melons. Both men were

wearing a wide gold-toothed grin. 'Here we stopping one-two hours,' the pilot told me in English. He was a Tadjik, my neighbour, a Russian, said, watching him pitch down to earth without waiting for the steps which were now being hurtled towards us by two splendid creatures – again in the traditional *khalat*, now in chintz, printed in the most unlikely bunches of roses or blue and white flowers, but without effeminacy or sloppiness, when worn by such a virile race.

None of the other passengers, Uzbeks, Tadjiks, or a couple of Russian engineers (I was the only tourist) seemed surprised at this halt: but I had only just begun to realise the impromptu nature of local travel; impromptu, but not improvident. Mechanically, the planes and trains were highly efficient.

On the ground, a cold which belied the sun pierced through my sheepskin coat. I hurried towards the shelter of a small wooden hut topped by an aerial, the only sign of life. It was labelled, in Russian characters: KEEP OUT. One side was sheltered from the slicing wind and here I sat down gingerly, thinking about the vipers, monster scorpions, tarantulas and other disagreeable forms of insect life which flourish in these regions and are not discouraged by cold. The navigator stacked the melons beside me and lay down to sleep, his head pillowed on their green gleaming flanks. The pilot, bowing with gallantry, now pressed the teddy bear into my arms.

'You will mind him out?' he asked, nearly colloquial. He seemed in a great hurry to be gone and before I could reply, had flung himself into a decrepit jeep standing behind the hut. The jeep snorted and was off, bucking across the rough ground, dwindling into a dark speck as I watched its progress through spirals of red dust. All around lay limitless wastes, nothingness brought to its apogee in these dreaded deserts, Kizil Kum, the Red Sands, Kara Kum, the Black Sands and Betpak-Dala – the Steppes of Hunger to the Russian armies who took possession of the area a century ago.

Such was the strange country in which I now wandered, or rather, was dumped, on Christmas Day, a large teddy bear on my lap and nothing to eat but a bag of caramels.

The noonday sun beat down strongly now, and the other passengers had joined the navigator in sleep. A young man in Western clothes (and very dull they seemed, after the chintzy *khalats*) emerged from the hut, and settled down beside me, producing a paperback translation of John Braine's *Room at the Top*.

He was, he told me, the wireless operator, and studying industrial relations. I saw it would be useless to hope he might tell me any of the local legends of Nasr-e-din in Bukhara. It was very quiet on the sunny side of the hut, but round the corner the wind whined and buffeted. The teddy bear and I sat staring out across Asia.

During the years I had been collecting material for my book on the Caucasus, I had come across a great deal of extraneous, or, as it were, adjacent material. The Caucasus, the Crimea, the Turkoman Steppes, Uzbek territory, the Pamirs... moving east from the Moslem-held mountains of the Caucasus, all these regions merge, or abut, and the strange characters who peopled them, fought over them, or ventured into them all fascinated me so that I was perpetually sidetracked from my principal theme to follow the exploits of one or another, sharing, in my mind's eye the obsession of this Asiatic hinterland.

Now, at its most stark, it lay before me – the sanded, stony nothingness where countless caravans of merchants and pilgrims had perished. Few travellers and until lately, no tourists had come this way. The khans of Bukhara were celebrated for diabolic refinements of cruelty. 'Bukhara the Noble', so holy that light was said to ascend from it heavenwards, was also 'Bukhara the Terrible'. Beside the most sacred mosques in all Asia, lay the sinister fortress and palace of the Ark, where, between banquets and dalliances, the emirs enjoyed watching the tortures to which their prisoners were put.

Until the end of the nineteenth century, to set out across these steppes was to walk towards death. Around 1830, three English officers had the temerity to try: their mission, to negotiate questions concerning the Afghan situation, border disputes and trade routes affecting the British position in India. Lieutenant Wyburd perished; so did Captain Connolly and Colonel Stoddart. Their slow end, imprisoned in 'the Black Well', their flesh gnawed off their bones by vermin especially reserved for such a purpose, is still a matter of ghoulish interest to the inhabitants of Bukhara. They were at last decapitated in the Registan, or square, before the Ark. The Emir, seated in state on a carpet-hung balcony, had watched the execution with particular relish, for the prisoners had refused his clemency at the price of abjuring Christianity. They were quite alone: no one could or would save them, in this faraway city. Both the Persian and Russian envoys to the Emir's court had tried to temporise. But with their recall, there was no more help. The British government, both in London and in the person of the Viceroy of India, had remained inexplicably inert.

Under a brazen June sky, the two skeletal and verminous figures were led out. Before the executioner's sword they embraced. 'We shall meet again soon, in heaven,' said Connolly. They belonged to that small band of military mystics who were so remarkable a flowering of British arms during the nineteenth century and of which we have particular examples among the officers of the Indian campaigns.

A year or two after the death of Connolly and Stoddart, the English public began to agitate – too late. At which the Reverend Joseph Wolff, a character of such excessive oddity that there is no space to do him justice here, set out for Bukhara, to determine the fate of his friend, Captain Connolly. Beneath the Reverend Joseph Wolff's canonicals (which he wore throughout the three months' journey) there beat a lion's heart. He stormed into the presence of the Emir, thundered his denouncements, quoted the Scriptures, demanded explanations, the bodies, threatened the might of Queen Victoria (who although a woman, was ever an awesome figure to Eastern potentates) and then, having suffered imprisonment and every threat, the parson was miraculously allowed to leave. He withdrew in majesty, his health impaired but his courage unshaken by this dreadful ordeal.

During the rest of the century there are very few records of other venturesome strangers making or surviving a visit to Bukhara the Terrible or crossing the Red Sands, the Black Sands, the Steppes of Hunger.

There were the dreaded wastes of which I had read, so often, in accounts of earlier, less pampered voyagers. Unlike myself, they had not been able to skim the wastes in a plane. They had plodded every parched or frozen mile, on camel or horseback. They knew the anguish of searching for water, of beating off raiding tribesmen or packs of wolves; or of surviving those fearful storms which skip across the desert in great spirals, hurling rocks before them like pebbles.

I remembered a local saying, something a shepherd had told me, in the foothills of the Pamirs: he had spoken arrogantly, as if proud of the harshness of his horizons. 'When creating the World Allah made Baluchistan' – or was it not Bukhara? – 'from the refuse.'

Undoubtedly, nature is hostile here: man is plainly unwelcome. What if the pilot did not return – if the radio transmitter broke down? I glanced round me, furtively. The wireless operator was dozing over *Room at the Top*; a solitary, juicy looking horsefly settled on the melons. The silence was absolute. The sun was inclining rapidly, now, towards the west: a chill crept up from the ground. It would not do to think of nightfall. Clutching the teddy bear closer, I took refuge in history, in that past which was still almost the present, here in Central Asia.

The Russians, expanding their vast empire eastward had taken possession of the Turkoman steppes around 1862. The Caucasus had fallen to them in 1854; the Amur provinces of eastern Siberia, soon afterwards. The next acquisitions were those Uzbek and Tadjik territories stretching between Tashkent, Samarcand and Bukhara. The fighting was violent and soon done. One by one the conquered rulers, the khans and emirs of each province settled back among their women and their dancing boys, the adulated *batchas* of Bukhara, soon exchanging that intertribal warfare which had been their pulse of life, for visits to St Petersburg where they were pampered guests of the Tzar. Their harems languished in perfumed ennui, awaiting their overlords' return, but were consoled by costly presents from the Tzar himself – Fabergé opera glasses, for example. But what were they to watch, in these wastes? Each other? Primitive puppet shows, or the peacocks screeching and strutting along the walls of the harem? There were so few diversions. Presently, echoes of civilisation reached them, even there, at Khiva, Merv and Ferghana, and they began sending for kid gloves and button boots from Paris, while the khans ordered mechanical devices, cigar-cutters, musical boxes and shooting sticks, but all refulgently Oriental in style, dama-scened and studded with precious stones. The khans had now all become loyal vassals of the Great White Tzar. The Emir of Bukhara, with the aid of Russian engineers, constructed a railway line which, from Kokand, served huge tracts of Central Asia and linked Siberia with the Caucasus. The four khans of Merv stopped jockeying for power, imported a Russian physician and exchanged opium for champagne. Not to be outdone, the Khan of Khiva reduced his harem – said to be seven hundred strong – to a mere twenty... Civilisation had triumphed.

Only the people still sat in the bazaars, or under the trees, telling stories of Nasr-e-din, or crowded to pray in the great turquoise-tiled mosques, following the fanatic religious observances of their forefathers. And they whispered, still, of the cruelties and excesses of their rulers, the khans. True, the Russian Governor-General of Bukhara had suppressed the former practice of hurling criminals, trussed like fowls, from the highest minaret. It had been a popular diversion for the public, along with other kinds of public executions, by strangling, or slicing off the head. But still... it smacked of barbarism. Only a handful of malefactors now rotted, chained, in the noxious city jails of Bukhara and were flayed, starved, blinded or maimed, according to their crimes. But this, it was felt, was purely a question of local administration, something outside Tzarist Russia's sphere of influence. Thus the abuses continued until, with the Revolution in 1918, the last of the khans and emirs fled the Bolshevik troops, taking refuge across the neighbouring frontiers of Afghanistan or Iran. Since then, Bukhara the Noble, the Terrible, had declined steadily, till it became a ghost town where only a legend remained, where pure water had been piped in, but where the high walls of the city crumbled, and no travellers came and went through its nine great gates. This was the legend I had come to find, as I sat outside the wireless operator's hut, on the edge of the Kizil Kum.

The stillness of the desert was abruptly broken by the noise of an approaching car. More spirals of red dust; then a rickety bus emerged, to disgorge half a dozen of the handsomest men I have ever seen. They were gigantic creatures, Uzbeks or Tadjiks, I could not distinguish, for all of them had the same traditional *khalats*, the same manner of walking like princes, their velvet-capped or turbaned heads held high, as they advanced on me, displaying the liveliest interest in both myself and the bear. They seemed to be expecting him, for he was seized and passed from hand to hand, approvingly. *'Tchoudessnie!'* Wonderful, they said to me, in Russian. From behind the padded skirts of their *khalats*, I saw a very small girl peering at me fearfully. She was dressed in scarlet silk, with baggy trousers below her skirt. A number of tight, little black braids were hanging from under her gold-embroidered pillbox cap. No doubt the bear was a long-promised toy. I held it out towards her.

'Yours?' I asked, in my basic Russian. But she backed away, shaking her head vehemently. She seemed anxious not to come too near such a fabulous creature. The splendid giants had now settled round me in a circle, sitting back on their heels in that curious upright, yet crouching, attitude seen in the early Persian miniatures. Their brown, beautifully shaped hands were tucked into their long rucked sleeves and their eagle-profiles were dark against the sky. I seemed to be as exotic a spectacle to them, as they were to me and they plied me with questions in their halting Russian.

Why was I here? Where was my husband – home – children? Was it not a big celebration, today, among the Christians? A sort of Ramadan? Well, sort of, I conceded. Then why was I here? Why indeed? What makes a traveller? I felt my Russian was not up to so esoteric a subject, and I turned the conversation to their work – farming, cotton crops, houses – their families (I was careful not to enquire after their wives, knowing that Oriental etiquette forbids such mention), their climate, traditions, music even… So I liked their music? Very much. Evidently my sincerity convinced them, for they began singing in chorus, swaying from side to side, beating their knees and the ground, to accompany the harsh, staccato rhythms. Listening, entranced, I found myself beating time with the bear's stumpy arms. Goodwill overflowed all round. They laughed delightedly, the uncalculated laugh of children.

'Mischka likes our music,' said one singer. (Bears are always called Mischka in Russia.)

Were there such bears in my country? asked the circle. Toy bears? Mischkas? Like this one? All at once I felt the tears come into my eyes. I remembered, so long ago, my own teddy bear, stuffed into my high-chair, sharing my mug of milk… But now I was in Asia, a long, long way from home.

'You love Mischka?' asked one of the crouched giants, plainly puzzled by my tears.

I nodded, feeling foolish, clasping the Tadjik teddy, looking down at his hind legs emerging stiffly from the check rompers. His round, velvet-lined ears and his smiling, trustful expression were the image of my nursery friend. Teddy bears have always seemed to me to be, above all other toys, the symbol of loving kindness. Dolls can look mean. But no plush monkey, rabbit, or even dear Jumbo can ever achieve quite that degree of lovingness expressed by the teddy bear, wherever he is found.

I do not know the origin of the teddy bear, as a toy, but I believe it has some connection with a cub which Theodore 'Teddy' Roosevelt orphaned on a hunting expedition and then adopted as an *amende honorable*. The cub's furry charms were immortalised by an enterprising toy manufacturer, bringing joy to countless nurseries all over the world, forever after.

Russian popular legends are full of stories of real live bears, who come from the forests, to play with the village children. There are many well-established cases of their tossing up crowing babies, catching them and cuffing them affectionately, like their own cubs. Those sad stories of a female bear being shot by hunters, who are afterwards pursued and savaged by the mate seem to me, not so much a proof of the animal's ferocity, as the strength of its love for its murdered mate. Russian and Balkan *tziganes*, whose camps generally included tamed bears, often confided their babies to the bears, who would sit rocking them, held in their huge paws, with almost human devotion. Thus, it is not surprising that the teddy bear has come to symbolise affection – love.

There was a sudden stir among the Uzbeks; they were pointing across the desert to where the jeep was seen racing towards us. The giants sprang to their feet, like uncoiling steel springs; laughing and talking animatedly, they went to meet the jeep. The other passengers began to sit up, yawning. I remained where I was, the bear still on my lap, and the little girl stared at us from afar. The jeep hurtled to a stop and our pilot jumped out, shouting, as he rushed towards me. Seizing the teddy bear and the little girl, he kissed them both extravagantly. With some difficulty I now pieced together what everyone was trying to tell me. The pilot's wife had just given birth to a son, in a nearby village. She had been in labour when we left Samarcand and the pilot had broken the journey to be near her at this crucial hour. He had been counting on a son and bought the teddy bear in anticipation, on his last visit to Moscow.

A son… a son deserved such a fine toy. The pilot, himself a Moslem, like all Tadjiks, shared the Oriental view of male offspring. To the East, daughters scarcely count. 'A girl-child is less use than a stone,' runs a local proverb. 'With stones you can build a house. What use will a girl-child be?' But now the pilot had a son and the little girl, who was his daughter, seemed forgiven for her shortcomings. Now we would proceed on our way and the little girl would take the teddy bear back to her brother. She held it out to me, proudly, to say goodbye. I kissed its plushy snout.

My mind drifted away from the Uzbeks, across the Steppes of Hunger and all Turkestan, to another faraway scene, Sagamore Hill, on Long Island, once the Theodore Roosevelt family home. Now it is a museum, or memorial, left furnished as it was when they lived there. I had been spending one Christmas nearby, at Oyster Bay, and on Christmas Eve we had driven over to join a straggle of tourists peering about the house. We had visited the lugubrious dining room, seen the ample kitchens, climbed the stairs to the simply furnished attics, and followed the arrow to the lamp-lit drawing room with its potted palms, frilly sofas and needlework baskets that Eleanor Roosevelt must have known when visiting there as a young bride. Outside, the raw winter dusk gathered, and the lamplight shone on the bare branches overhanging the house. Christmas carols were being relayed softly and incessantly through the house. It ought to have been corny, but it was curiously moving. Here was the echo of a home: a whole way of life that had been – and was gone… 'God Rest Ye Merry Gentlemen, Let Nothing Ye Dismay,' sang the disembodied choir as I followed the last sightseers to Theodore Roosevelt's library. It was a large, dark, masculine room, full of shiny leather armchairs, heavy desks and sporting trophies.

To give an added air of authenticity to the scene, the curators had arranged a large Christmas tree in the middle of the room. It was gaily decorated and underneath its frost-trimmed branches lay a pile of realistic-looking packages, gift-wrapped, as if awaiting the eager rush of a young family. Among the presents and seated in a child's chair, was a large moth-eaten teddy bear, his arms extended lovingly, his button eyes staring hopefully across the rope which cordoned off the sightseers. As I looked at him, the lights began to dim, the carol-singers were switched off abruptly and a whistle blew announcing closing time. 'This way out please!' We were shepherded to the door, leaving Sagamore Hill and the teddy bear to loneliness. As we went down the hill to where our car was parked I saw the house was already in darkness. God Rest Ye Merry Teddy Bear, Let Nothing Ye Dismay.

And now I have found you again, on an airstrip between Bukhara and Samarcand, and you are still proclaiming your loving kindness, your message of gentleness. And you are no longer alone.

Lesley in the 1960s

Souks, or the Wilder Shores of Shopping

Sūk, souk, bazaar – centre of merchandise, traditional hub of all Eastern and Middle-Eastern life. Today, the tourists' first objective. 'Museums tomorrow, souks today!' their battle cry, streaming across the tarmac, clutching exchange rate cards. What will you find and where? That depends on what you like and what you pay. Something typical, a souvenir, something for the house, or to wear, or give away? Junky toys or pedigree acquisitions?

Souking has been my lifelong passion. Aged seven, I bought a Staffordshire rabbit at London's prime souk, the vanished Caledonian Market and since then, have ranged far afield. Here are some suggestions for worthwhile buys, not to mention the delights of each locale, and be sure to buy recordings of local music, if you want to remember lost flavours…

Istanbul

The Great Bazaar, vast vaulted maze, once Justinian's stables, for rare jewellery, 'turban' rings and 'trembling' brooches, diamond sprays finely wired, that quiver as the wearer breathes: once sultanate harem delights. Antiques include romantic old harem robes, ikons, silver, Turkish and Caucasian rugs (good ones now hard to find). Fluffy woven goat-hair squares, natural colours make good divan covers. Typically Turkish, round brass trays used in cafés suspended from a ring – they defy gravity and loaded with brimming glasses never spill a drop. Handy for serving drinks at home.

Cairo

Khan el-Khalili, still very colourful, a rewarding warren of lanes and courts. The best jasmine essence and attar of roses anywhere. Egyptian cotton, uncorrupted by today's synthetics, is now a luxury; the finest is here, by the yard, or made up overnight into a flowing, graceful *galabiyeh*, costume of the country, lovely

293

for summer. Powdered kohl, the real stuff, in blue, green, grey, black, brown, to protect and line the eyes à la Nefertiti. Egyptian antiquities, real and fake, copies of Pharonic ornaments, ceramics, deliciously frivolous mosque lamps, carved, fretted wood panels, once *moucharabiyehs* – window screens from old Cairene houses; perfect to block out an undesirable view.

Tunis

Souk el Attarine holds the spices of the world, roots, herbs, unguents, perfumes and love-philtres to change everyday living. Fabulously ornate marriage candles, embroidered local fabrics from Nabeul, local costumes, gandouras and the best creamy wool burnous in North Africa. Elaborate Bohemian glass chandeliers and gilded, mirrored beds, once classic harem furnishings, are worth the transport fuss; look for gold trinkets and coins round the striped pillars of the old slave market.

The Trucial Coast

Once the Pirate Coast, now the Petrol Coast, has unsophisticated souks, but both Abu Dhabi and Dubai offer the richly-worked daggers which are everyday wear and beautiful coffee pots (*findjals*) in all shapes and metals; and magnificent pearls – pearl diving being once the only source of revenue.

Morocco

Tetuan's bold local embroideries for cushions, curtains. Fes for metalwork; the plunging alleys of the Medina (old town) overflow with brass trays, table-top sized, pretty chased-brass-framed mirrors and traditional dishes to serve couscous (or anything else) with high, cone-shaped lids. Luxurious in *repoussé maillechort*, a silvery metal; also in basketwork. In Marrakech round the fairground animation of the Jemaa el Fna, more of the same. Acres of souks, shaggy rugs from the High Atlas, Berber-woven wools, embroidered leather, bags, slippers; dramatic caftans (the best are to order, or in sophisticated boutiques of Rabat and Casablanca); everyday ones still charming. Snug hooded woollen *jellabiya*, to defy winter. Irresistible, the gauzy gold lamé caftans village women and servants in conservative households still wear; layer on layer of glitter and colour, orange on rose over lilac… nylon or no, all seduction; cheap and light to pack.

USSR

GUM, the vast government emporium on Red Square for furs, samovars, caviar, vodka. Ikons and Fabergé objects at a price; charming papier-mâché boxes and painted trays, traditional Palekh and Fedoskino work; precious stones from the Urals. Everywhere, superbly produced art books, wide-ranging and multilingual. South, in Samarcand or Bukhara, the chance of Turkestan rugs; in Tiflis, look for Caucasian carpets, samovars, sheepskin toques.

India

In Old Delhi, round the Chandni Chowk, fabulous jewellery, the old coloured enamel-work set with precious stones. Saris vary with the region. In Rajasthan, an enormous choice, both silk and – to me – the more desirable cottons, or tie-dye fabrics. The best antiquities and local crafts in all the government shops; droll toys, alabaster oddments, embroidered cashmere shawls really from Kashmir. Porn, sold slyly, miniatures of frantic antics in traditional style.

Afghanistan

This rugged, lovely country is one vast souk and certainly my favourite. Treasures in every city from Kandahar to Balkh. Lapis lazuli and rare antiquities, Graeco-buddhistic statuary, Nuristan carvings etc. State-controlled, collectors' pieces. In Kabul, splendid carpets, plum-red Bukharans, Turcoman rugs; sometimes rare Samarcands found on junk stalls. Barbaric silver ornaments of the Kuchi tribes, delicious blue glass from Istalif, strange musical instruments, richly decorated weapons, early coins, lengths of turban muslin, velvet, gold-embroidered jackets, semi-precious stones by the bushel. Mazar-i-Sharrif souks sell the best striped *chapans*, the long-sleeved, chintz-lined garments generally worn, a welcome change from the sheepskin *pousteens* favoured by hippies. Tashkurgan's (now Kholm) adorable little souk – still much as Marco Polo knew it – has Central Asian rainbow silks and padded *khalats*, exotic Uzbek wear. The real old Russian dark blue, rose-flowered teapots are now collectors' pride, like the naive painted panels, flowers, fruit, lions, or mosques, with which lorry and bus drivers decorate their vehicles.

Iran

Teheran's venerable brick-vaulted maze of bazaars include whole streets of samovars, bedsteads, and kitchen ware. Copies of traditional Koursi squat metal charcoal grills – on the *hibachi* principle – are practical home fuel savers and decorative too. Local kitchenware is generally worth acquiring, everywhere. More glamorous, turquoises galore, Persian lambskins, old Russian silver, ceramics, Persian miniatures – real and fake – Kurdish embroideries and ornaments, painted Kazvin mirrors with foldover doors 'to shut out the djinns'. Carpets – yes; but fine, old ones are prohibitive (much such merchandise is also found in streets by the British Embassy – souks in themselves). Ispahan's souks, facing the incomparable Masjid-i Shah Mosque, specialise in heavy linen, hand-blocked tablecloths and wall hangings, traditional designs, like the Kalimkari cottons. Shiraz has the Qashqai tribe's exotic silk squares and embroideries; boxes of intricate inlay work, ceramics and all else. Caviar everywhere, even in the supermarkets.

Aleppo

Shakespeare wrote: 'Her husband's to Aleppo gone, master o' the Tiger' – no doubt making for its souks, then, as now, legendary. Dim, exotic paths, old in crusading days; camels and crowds jostling. Pottery, exquisite mother-of-pearl encrusted pieces from Damascus, coffee tables, mirrors and caskets. Vaporous wool *abayas*, cloaks and customary Arab men's wear. Gold-thread-embroidered cloth coats, ditto, lovely for evenings. Intricate trimmings, tassels and braids sold by the pound. Silver-mounted pumice stones and hammam paraphernalia. Bridles and saddles, plain for camels, fancy for horses. Crystallised apricots, fragrant Latakiyeh tobacco, coloured glass *narghilyés* with amber mouthpieces… Ah Aleppo! The Master o' the Tiger knew where to go…

Time and Time Again

'That little ticking sultan who rules your life,' is how a turbaned dignitary of the Ottoman court described the pocket watch that a European ambassador consulted furtively during those prolonged and flowery exchanges habitual to the Orient.

Watch: the word derives from the early English word *wacan* – to awake, guard or keep watch. 'Two o'clock on a fine frosty night and all's well,' called the watchmen who patrolled the streets of London late into the nineteenth century, for a watch was still the prerogative of a well-to-do minority.

From earliest times, watches have stood in a special relationship to man – something which sets them quite apart from clocks. Their close physical contacts with their owner might be said to represent a mysterious link with time itself. Thus the act of consultation, rewinding, or setting becomes an intimate exchange; a ritual of interdependence between man and his time piece.

Pocket watches were first devised during the Renaissance, around 1500, generally in pendant form, as small boxed objects, richly ornamented and suspended from a jewelled chain. Queen Elizabeth possessed several such new-fangled miracles, sumptuous with gold and enamel work to match her fabulous jewellery. These first pocket watches were made in northern Italy and Germany. Their form was round; their cases of rock crystal, or gold, often chased in labyrinthine patterns inspired by the tracery of cathedral windows. About 1550, the oval shape was introduced and became known as the Nuremberg egg, since it derived from that city. As the century progressed, there were hexagonal, octagonal and spherical watches. A massive cruciform design known as 'the abbess' (though quite unsuited to the convent) had, besides the central dial, smaller ones at each side, and above and below. These told the days of the week, the months, the zodiacal signs, and had Latin and Arabic numerals too.

Altogether, pocket watches were becoming a limitless field for fantasy, ingenious mechanism and personal expression. By the eighteenth century we see skull watches, scarab watches, watches in the form of slippers, or guitars; watches that spring out from between butterfly wings, or are hidden in the handle of a lorgnon. Masonic watches in the mystical triangular form bore secret signs and emblems. A bracelet (the forerunner of today's wristwatch) was made for Joséphine Beauharnais by Breguet, the master craftsman of the time. It was one of the innumerable gifts with which the besotted Bonaparte showered his bride on the occasion of their marriage and was, perhaps, a delicate hint that she should cultivate punctuality as wife of the First Consul.

Old watches conjure limitless horizons and romantic reveries. I recall one of Swiss origin, dated 1780, where the names of fifty-three countries and capitals radiated from the central dial like sunflower petals. Many of these names now belong to a historic past: St Petersburg, Constantinople, Siam, Pekin… For what wealthy trader, I wondered, was it designed? I imagine him consulting its inner mechanisms which told the precise hour, or season, wherever his coolies laboured, or his merchantmen put into port to enrich his scattered counting houses. This small, pearl-studded, guillochéed trinket – did it once announce 'the midnight's kind admittance' to some fevered lover? What tragic fatality surrounded the watch that Queen Marie Antoinette is believed to have given Fersen, her *preux chevalier*? The royal family's flight from Revolutionary Paris which Fersen organised so meticulously should have been an affair of split-second timing, the watches – his own and that of the Queen – synchronising like their two hearts. Yet all was lost when, safely clear of the city, with freedom across the frontier ahead, the King dawdled, picking wild flowers, while his massive gold timepiece – the kind known in England as a turnip and in France as an onion – ticked away their last chances of escape.

In the nineteenth century, pocket watches reached the apogee of beauty and craftsmanship. Fob watches were much *en vogue* during the Regency, dangling from the satin waistcoats of the bucks and dandies. Such arbiters of fashion eschewed turnip watches, for their absurdity destroyed the set of a coat. For these gentlemen, who were generally heavily in debt and hounded by creditors and bailiffs, a watch became a real necessity. A curious by-law protected them from arrest between the hours of sunset and sunrise. Thus we see Beau

Brummell and Count d'Orsay eyeing their watches attentively, to gauge the magic moment when they might emerge from hiding and sally forth, arrogant and unmolested. Indeed, the watch has often played a life-saving role. Many a traveller in wild regions has been spared from death by the noble savage's preoccupation with a gold repeater.

There has always been a market for watches which contain secrets: portraits, messages and erotic or pornographic scenes discreetly placed behind the bland watch-face were revealed by a hidden spring. Scenes designed to titillate, or shock were pictured in polychrome, on ivory, or porcelain; Leda's antics with her swan being the mildest of such, while rosy romps and bosoms and less describable anatomic features and situations were rendered with gleeful exactitude.

Some of the least known, most fascinating pocket watches are those wooden ones made in Russia during the nineteenth century, for wood was the mainstay of old Russia. From the endless forests came planks to build houses, logs for fuel, various woods for furniture, household goods, sleighs and carts, while the peasants encased their feet in *laptié* – rough birch-bark wrappings. Thus provincial craftsmen devised these tubby pocket watches, with their large link chains all smoothly fashioned from silvery birch wood, and their works being of splinter-thin bone. I like to think of Tolstoy possessing such a one.

The charming eighteenth-century chatelaine, a feminine delight, was designed to hang from the belt and lingered on well into the twentieth century, for it was both practical and ornamental. The watch took pride of place above all the other dangling objects: scissors, an *étui*, tiny ivory tablets, purses, pencil cases and pillboxes. They were worked in varying metals – gold, silver, or pinchbeck, an alloy once much used – and riotous scenes of classical battles and mythological rapes were rendered, *repoussée,* over every possible surface. I possessed one such, of Dutch origin, and always took it with me on my travels. But when the Trans-Siberian dashed eastward on its six-day stretch, the days changed bewilderingly, breakfast becoming supper and so on. At last my poor little watch could stand no further resetting and ticked its last beyond Chita. But although now only a muted ornament, it remains beside me, snug in one of those embroidered beadwork watch pockets which Victorian sleepers hung on the bed-head to house their watches safely through the night.

Through the Moucharabiyeh

I AM LIKE THE PINE TREE OF HEINE'S FAMOUS POEM, FOREVER DREAMING, on some desolate northern shore, of a distant palm tree in the Eastern lands. Europe remains a base from where I make sorties whenever possible – always southwards – eastwards – to the fabled, still fabulous lands of deserts and palm groves and infinite tawny distances. They stretch from North Africa by way of Egypt and Turkey to Arabia – which is the quintessential golden heartland of the Middle East. Long ago these regions cast a spell over me. Even their names held me in thrall before I knew them. The master of the tiger to Aleppo gone I read, in my childhood, and determined to follow.

Aleppo! Many years later I was to wander in its fabulous souks, among the spices, the pearl-inlaid weapons, the silks and gauzes, heady essences, camel ropes, the dark goat-hair hangings and all the trappings of Arabian living. Baghdad, the Caliph's City, or Damascus, 'the pearl' set among the streams and palms of Ghouta, a vast green oasis known to its inhabitants as the Garden of Eden. Petra, 'the rose red city half as old as time', sumptuous ruin, deep in its crimson-veined rock gullies where the rich Nabataens flourished and the Queen of Sheba and her retinue advanced their way to meet King Solomon and even the little birds have plumage which is tinged with rose... fabled lands, indeed.

These are the regions for which, once you have known them, you are forever hungry. On one of my journeys eastward, I was given a *moucharabiyeh* – one of those carved and fretted wooden screens placed over the window of every Arab dwelling. The delicate interlacings vary according to the country and the status of the dwelling: they can be painted and gilded as in the fine houses of Syria and the Lebanon; of scented cedar wood inlaid with ivory, as in Cairo, all carved cunningly so that the angles of the surfaces of the knobs and fretted pieces deflect the fierce sunlight. Or they can be a rough criss-cross of sticks or woven straw, as sometimes can be seen in the poorer quarters of old Turkish towns; or in elaborate plasterwork such as some of the towering dwellings in the Yemen, but their purpose is always the same, to filter both air and light to the interior and to allow the sequestered inmates of the harem to see, without being seen. Though if we are to believe the *Thousand and One Nights* and other tales of Oriental intrigue, their second function was not always efficacious and they sometimes proved to be, rather, 'magic casements opening wide...' a means of romantic escape.

And so, in another sense, my *moucharabiyeh* has proved to be. At first, when I was living in Paris, I placed it over a window opening on to a particularly grey scene of city rooftops. But I did not see them any more, nor the lowering rain-filled skies of the north. When I looked through its intricacies, their magic conjured the scene and places and faces of those other more glowing regions they once screened – regions which I too came to know, and which through my *moucharabiyeh*, I could now summon at will. I saw again domes and minarets, set against sultry skies: bazaars crowded with turbaned men and veiled women. All the perfumes of Arabia were wafted to me, the heady, heavy scents of jasmine and sandalwood and attar of roses... I heard the curious grinding thump of the Arabian coffee hearth and remembered all its graceful ritual. Then I heard another curious sound, a creaking drone – the *sakieh*, or wooden water wheel turning, forever turning, along the silky stretches of the Nile. And I heard the haunting, compelling cry of the muezzin, calling the faithful to prayer every-where. Over all I heard the wind stirring the palm fronds, a dry, scaly sound evocative of every oasis, from the Sahara to the red sands of Liwa, beside what was once known as the Pirate Coast, on the Persian, or Arabian Gulf, a lovely and little-known area of the Arabian Peninsula.

The *moucharabiyeh* belongs essentially to the desert lands – to the houses and cities and ways of life which have sprung from the desert soil. But however mon-ochrome the general concept of the desert, it is, in fact, never monotonous for it has many variations and its own nuances of colour and form: sudden flashes or oases of colour such as Petra, or Palmyra, with the majestic apricot columns of Zenobia's temple and palaces which, according to the hour, flame orange or glow crimson, or pale, seeming to hang in the moonlight, translucent as the waters of that nearby subterranean bathing pool the Romans knew. Eastwards from this rich desert scene lie the ruined frescoed hunting boxes of the Umayyad caliphs, hidden in the deserts of Transjordan, beyond Amman. Turning northwards, again springing from grim desert wastes, are all the turquoise splendours of Iran, or Persia, as I prefer to call it, having known it by that name when I first read such travellers as Chardin, Morier or Curzon, all of whom evoked it so glowingly.

Eastwards, again across further deserts rise the golden domes of Mashhad and beyond the frontier, all the harsh and wonderful beauty of Afghanistan, with its wild but welcoming peoples. I peer closer through the *moucharabiyeh,* and see very similar ones along the narrow alleyways of the Shor Bazaar, in the old part of Kabul, or in the warrens of Kandahar; and always behind the savage gorges which melt into rich vine-wreathed valleys and orchards I see the vast ranges of the Hindu Kush, a dramatic backcloth to a country which, by its placing and history, it essentially dramatic. Northwards, the Turcoman steppes along the Oxus, with crumbling mosques and bastions of Balkh, 'Mother of Cities'. Now my *moucharabiyeh* pauses in its kaleidoscopic tour to turn puppet show; evoking Alexander the Great feasting, tasting a conqueror's pleasures, taking Roxelane, the greatest beauty of all Asia to wife, but perishing, it is said, by her contriving (a rare pleasure for the conquered) after she goaded him into swimming in an icy river too soon after a banquet.

Across the Oxus, where the Tadjiks and Uzbeks roam with their flocks there are, briefly, no more *moucharabiyeh.* The women here come and go freely about their round felt-covered yurt dwellings weaving the carpets we know as Bukharan. But deeper into Central Asia where all tracks or roads lead to Samarcand and Bukhara, we find again the lattice windows and screened rooftops such as those behind which the Khan of Kokand once maintained nine hundred concubines. It was from hereabouts that my *moucharabiyeh* came, originally, and it shows a tendency to linger over Central Asiatic scenes.

The sequestered lives of women in the East always rouses violent feelings in the West. Today such sequestration is becoming increasingly rare. Yet there is much to be said for protection – something which the ladies of the Women's Liberation movement would not admit any more than the West, in general, would countenance polygamy. But those are subjects too controversial, too vast to approach here. Besides, through my *moucharabiyeh* I never see sociological, economic or political scenes. Nor any of the ugliness, squalor, decay, refuse and flyblown merchandise which is still part of the Eastern scene, however many dazzling new Frigidaires are imported. The particular magic of the *moucharabiyeh* is that through it, all is lovely, glowing, glittering, exotic, strange, at once thrilling and serene and always spellbinding. Perhaps it is the 'sweetmeat Oriental world' of my early longings… but so I always find it on my travels and so it is still conjured for me.

In general, my *moucharabiyeh* seems to share my abhorrence of modern living: perhaps it realises that it is being edged out of existence, itself, by modern contraptions such as air conditioning. Only rarely does it linger on a 'progressive' scene, detesting oil derricks and cement mixers on sight. Yet, occasionally, these objects appeal by the manner in which they are being employed. I am recalling Abu Dhabi, one of the Trucial States, where from desperate poverty, before oil was struck only a few years back, a population of around 15,000 suddenly became heir to an annual income of something like £80 or £100 million. An *Arabian Nights* tale. But the ruler, Sheikh Zaïd, a most enlightened visionary autocrat, by origin a man of the desert, with the finest Bedouin traditions, has conceived and put into place a remarkable welfare state, where irrigation projects, housing developments, welfare centres, free schooling, free hospitalisation and many more beneficent and far-sighted schemes are already in full swing; and in their growth, have not stifled some strangely attractive, open, free, I would almost say innocent quality which I have not encountered elsewhere. Perhaps the setting helps – the wide sweep of dazzling sands, the nearness of the lovely oasis of Al Aïn, backed by the lilac-coloured mountains of Muscat, open country, where the wind blows in from the circling seas, blue green, aquamarine, sapphire, emerald – were there ever such colours as the waters of the Gulf? And then the new buildings which mushroom up overnight: they could be ugly – so out of line with the Arabic tradition. But they are not. Along what will be the littoral, a line of fine palace-like buildings appear; banks for the most part (and with that amount of money gushing from the oil wells, their presence is understandable) but temples of Mammon or no, they are expressed in architectural terms of great beauty, in no way clashing with the impressive contours of the old Portuguese fort which dominates the town, or the basic tradition of Arabic living.

But abruptly as if to infer it has done enough about the contemporary progress, the *moucharabiyeh* shifts eastward again to a setting steeped in legend, one of those many legends that merge all the races and cities into one glorious world of Eastern magic. Let me look closer: this is a scene I know well. Here is Bukhara. 'Bukhara the Noble' from which it was said light *ascended* to heaven above, and Samarcand, where Tamerlane sleeps under a tomb of jade and jasper and in the marketplace, gigantic green-bellied melons are piled beside massive brass samovars, for here, as all over the Middle East, tea is the people's nectar, a delicate brew with many variations of colour and flavour, served in little china bowls. In the *chaikhanas*, or teahouses (*chai* being the common word for tea, from Pekin, via Russia, to Arabia) *chai* is served with the same reverent, ritualistic approach as that found in the Arabian serving of coffee.

It is in the Arabian Peninsula that the *moucharabiyeh* remains most firmly entrenched, for this is Wahabi territory, controlled by the rigid, puritanical tents of that sect, and women are still subject to extremes of sequestration – behind lattices, beneath the veil and behind the mask. This applies particularly among townsfolk. But the women of the nomad tribes and the Bedu generally, live more freely, complying with their own codes, as strictly observed, but less stultifying. The black tents know no *moucharabiyeh* and though the women's quarters are curtained off, removed from one, or the stranger in their midst, the women do not wear those curious beaked butterfly-shaped masks which are so striking and on first sight impart an air of sinistry. Yet how infinitely seductive, how intriguing they prove to be. (I speak here of the shorter kind, which covers the eyebrows, the line of the nose, and upper lip – the longer, leather-covered kind such as those of the Hadramut or the Yemen are altogether too much like mediaeval vizors.) The butterfly curves of the lighter kind seem positively frivolous by comparison and the smiles glimpsed below them, like the glint of the enormous, dark, melting eyes of the Arabian woman, ringed and made more mysterious by a heavy application of kohl, are seduction itself.

But wherever they are worn in Saudi Arabia, or along what was once known as the Pirate Coast – the Trucial States and the Sultanate of Muscat – the wearers contrive to convey an almost overpowering feminine allure, entirely overcoming this barrier. Their garments are calculated to belie the mask of intimidation, being, although enveloped, highly provocative by their very discretion. The ladies are positively smothered in draperies, in veils and cloaks; only a ringed toe or a hennaed finger emerges from dark muslins spangled like a night sky and covering gauzy robes, tunics and shifts and stiff silver-cuffed pantaloons, or *chalvari*, all in brilliant silks, pearl-embroidered velvet and brocades, magenta, emerald, violet or rose, sequinned and shot with gold. Further embellishments are numerous jewelled ornaments, whether from the local souks or Cartier, according to the means of the wearer. But all are brilliant as tropic birds. In the harems of the great sheiks the inmates chitter and chatter, flitting about, their vivid plumage creating an illusion of an aviary, while the beaked masks add to the illusion. They are seldom removed even among themselves, they told me, 'except for sleeping or loving'. Even the poorest women gutting fish along the waterfront appear as if costumed for Verdi's *Ballo in Maschera*, figures of intrigue, emerging from glittering gauzes which even if of shoddy tinsel and nylon, create an illusion of luxury, imparting to them all an air of coquetry, the proper counterpoint to their men – *beau ténébreux* who, hereabouts, are the most masculine imaginable. Mars and Venus, the immemorial mating. (This opposition is something found deep in the Arab character, where sensuous abandon and austere discipline go side by side.)

And when these *beau ténébreux* stalk in from the desert, darkling overlords, commanding figures, still with some air of mediaeval majesty about their traditional robes and headdress *abayas* and *keffiyehs*, some with retainers and hawks, some emerging from Cadillacs it is true, but except in the largest cities, usually dressed traditionally, a dagger, or *khanjar*, thrust through a cartridge-studded belt. It is a reminder that intertribal wars are not entirely a thing of the past here.

These hawk-faced men, who dally with their charmers, dote extravagantly on their little sons (girls being of less account in Arab reckoning) or sit crouched talking quietly at the *majlis*, or sitting place, where men meet at dusk, sipping their interminable brews of cardamom-spiced Yemeni coffee, are first of all, men of desert background, knowing its harshness, rather than city ease. The rituals of the coffee hearth are a refinement they carry with them everywhere; perhaps restricted beside the campfire, but in essence the same. The coffee boy serves with panache, pulling *back* the chased silver coffee pot with a flourish, causing the liquid to spout out in wide arc before it reaches the minuscule cup – marvellous legerdemain, for never a drop is spilled. The skill and general style of the coffee server is taken as gage of his master's standing. They are usually beautifully turned out, their *thobe*, or shirt tunic, immaculate, sashes and turban of the finest stuff, their belts of chased silver; often like the beaked coffee pot inlaid with elaborate tracings of gold. Three cups are ritual offerings to a guest. Shaking the cup delicately from side to side signifies your wish for no more; in short, you are likely to take your leave. The cup will then be removed, again with those gestures of exquisite *politesse* so much part of both the façade and the nature of Arab peoples everywhere.

At the *majlis* the drinkers may appear languid-looking. Foppish figures in their sweeping *abayas* (this costume has not changed for a thousand years or more); their fine-boned hands may appear almost womanly as, with delicate gestures, they perfume them and their long ringleted locks from phials of amber or jasmine essence, or waft little incense burners under their beards, or the folds of their headdresses. They may walk hand in bracleted hand, all softness, but they are also athletes who can undergo the fearful rigours of the desert that surrounds them. They are accustomed to torrid days on camelback, without shade or water, nights of bitter cold without fuel or food (and in the desert fuel is more rare, more precious than food) and while there live forever on the alert for danger, prowling beasts, vipers, or their enemies, for as I remarked earlier, differences degenerate easily into blood feuds here.

Indeed, the merriest festivities are likely to have an undercurrent of violence, such as the sword dances known, I think, as the *Shohu*, perhaps from the tribe where they originated: wild leapings where the men hurl their long naked swords in the air, catching them as they swish down, a warrior's dance, terrifying to the beholder, and not without its terrors for the participants, for when the catch is missed the fingers are likely to be lost too. At which the traditional gesture is to plunge the mutilated hand into the sand to staunch the bleeding – then to resume the dance.

While the *moucharabiyeh* shows me these sort of scenes – from more remote areas such as I have known and loved, they are neither the spectacles nor the people whom the casual tourist might expect to see; least of all those whose business takes them to the ultra-sophisticated centres of the oil trade. There a glittering Western way prevails, and as such, I shall waste no words on it, nor ever wish for my *moucharabiyeh* to recapture it for me. I prefer it to show me simpler scenes, the settings for such figures, costumes and customs as I have described, where all to me is exotic. Camel races in the desert, at Al Aïn, a lateen-sailed *sambuk* entering the creek, or waterfront, at Dubai, where the dhows and curiously-shaped craft seem a direct link with Captain Hook and his crew (for was this not the Pirate Coast?) and a strong flavour of piratic adventure lingers. Dubai is a free port – a *very* free port. Everything goes here. Now I see another port, Jedda on the Red Sea, where the houses are made of coral; 'where are Frankish consuls', and where the merchants still barter for pearls – the real thing, not the cultured Japanese kind, but those for which

Arabia was famous: the kind Cleopatra dissolved in a goblet of wine; the kind so perfect, so translucent, that Pliny believed them to be compounded of dew, itself a rarity in these fevered zones. Another rarity, the bushes growing along the coast which yield a particularly potent incense, besides other oils and essences esteemed for their aphrodisiac qualities.

Jedda is the port for Mecca, the Holy City, core of all Islam, something apart, upon which no amount of oil wealth, or power politics, can impinge. Before all else, His Majesty King Faisal is Keeper of the Holy Places. His temporal powers are of far less count to the faithful. But this is Arabia where piety and fanaticism abound. The various routes for the pilgrims converge on Jedda and now many make the further journey to Mecca, in the interior, in air-conditioned buses, knowing nothing of the ordeal once facing every pilgrim who set out to make the desert crossing on foot, or on camel, under intolerable suns, each man carrying his own shroud, grim reminder that wells were thirty or more miles apart. None but the Moslems may approach the Holy City, nor penetrate beyond the lines of demarcation. No foreign planes may fly near it, no curious eyes spy on it from afar, and so, my *moucharabiyeh* remains blank.

But then this quality of mystery, so much part of Arabia, is found in many other aspects besides the secrecy surrounding the Holy Places. In the darkly-shrouded women, or the screened windows of the houses, or the latticed plasterwork galleries of the rooftops in Hadramut. In the mysteries and terrible spaces of the Rub' al Khali, or Empty Quarter, where few Bedu are known to have crossed. Even the furthest reaches of the Arabian Peninsula, the independent sheikdoms of the Gulf States, or Muscat (a particularly forbidding, forbidden zone to the unwary traveller) posses something of this secret, essentially Arabian quality where all the perfumes of Arabia are better described as the scent of mystery – of the unknown. It is of an overpowering attraction to the beholder. As I peer into the *moucharabiyeh*, seeing again these deserts and oases, these ancient white-walled forts, along the Pirate Coast, those piled-up mounds of shark meat along the harbour, the *barasti*, or palm-frond huts barricaded against the desert sands, which have surged up to engulf them like tidal waves, I am aware of a frisson, a delicious chill… this is still a strange, unknown, wild world. What may it reveal next? What shall I find on my next journey there? What scenes, drama, colours, scents and memories will I gather, then, for my *moucharabiyeh* to store?

IRAN: WHERE ANCIENT AND MODERN COLLIDE

IRAN, THE PERSIA OF THE POETS, WAS NAMED 'THE TURQUOISE KINGDOM' for its *gamme* of blues: marvellous shadings of blue, intense or shadowy; cerulean blue *faience*, lilac blue distances, the brilliant blue of the turquoises mined there; azure skies, sapphire seas... Persia shimmers in a blue haze. Yet there is another *gamme*, a deeper root of sun-bleached stones, deserts and dust-coloured tracks leading to endless horizons, tawny wastes merging with ancient monuments: this *gamme* of stones and sands responds better to the ancient Aryan name – Iran. Each *gamme* sets off the other. Could those Persian blues seem so vibrant, without their tawny Iranian foil? Could the subtle gradations of golden dust seem so infinite and lovely, without those azure skies above?

'*Isfahan nesf-i-jahan*; Isfahan is half the world,' goes the proud Persian saying. 'And all of beauty,' my father would add, quoting it to me as he turned the pages of an old picture book of mosques and palaces, which was an especial treasure in my nursery, where I listened to his tales of Persian djinns and magics. He loved all things Eastern, and exotic, and so do I. Since those early days, I have roamed the Middle East, gone far into Central Asia, and been many times to Isfahan and the other cities of Iran: Mashhad the Holy, Shiraz, Qom, Natanz... Only Teheran, the capital and pivot point for tourism, strikes, at first, an unlovely note.

Isfahan is the Persian city above all others which has always aroused the rhapsodies of Western travellers, seeing it shimmer in its radiance of turquoise *faience*, ringed by its peaked lilac-coloured hills. It possesses a curious quality, as if it were not quite of this world; as if such an amalgam of beauty might, at any moment, dissolve or disappear like some once-glimpsed celestial vision. At least, that is how it first struck me, some twenty or more years ago, seeing it first by starlight, when the stately Royal Mosque glittered darkly, blue and green like some veiled peacock. Immemorial loveliness everywhere: beauty and mystery; the clamorous caverns of the bazaars, the stillness of the cypress gardens. Such pleasure domes, such palaces are gathered here. The Ali Kapu, with its lofty pillared loggia and its inner, secretive little rooms – for loving, drinking, music or nameless deeds? Who now knows? Some of the reception rooms have curious arched and niched ceilings, each niche shaped in the form of a long-necked flask, wine bottle, sherbet or perfume ewer. Curious conceits, unique to this palace. Another, the Chehel Sutun – Palace of the Forty Pillars – is all royal splendour. There are, in fact, only twenty pillars, yet reflected in the *hoze,* or pool, they add up to forty, and forty is ever a number bearing magic connotations to the East. Such treasures as these are now jealously preserved.

But it would take powerful magic to restore Isfahan, as a whole, to its pristine loveliness. Factories begin to impinge, on the Zayandehroud, the river which for centuries flowed under the alcoved arches of the Khajou Bridge, but which now carries a tide of pollution with it. New highways intersect the old city, smog begins to cloud the turquoise domes and the increasing din of traffic overcomes the muezzin's cry, as it floats out from the turquoise minarets – relayed now, it must be admitted, from loud speakers.

Shiraz has always been celebrated for its grapes (and that golden mellow wine from which some say sherry derives) and its roses, which inspired poets with some of their loveliest verses. There are still old rose gardens there, and they are generally open to the public. Their names are as perfumed as their flowers... the Bagh-e Delgosha, garden of the Heart's Delight; the Naranjestan, or Orange Garden; the Bagh-e Eram, named after a legendary Arabian garden, belonging to a desert tribe near Mecca, and cited in the Koran as 'the Iram, adorned with Pillars'; or the Bagh-e Firdows, Garden of Paradise – which is how it still seems to anyone wandering there.

Throughout Moslem lands, water is regarded as holy: in arid lands its scarcity makes it prized, a God-given rarity. In Iran, with its deserts and stony high plateaux, water is life-giving; streams or fountains, and the *hoze,* or pool, which even the most modest garden or court contains, are all cherished. I have often thought that *ame-kari* decoration, those sparkling, many-faceted mirror fragments (also found in the Moghul palaces of India) is particularly admired since its glitter could be likened to a thousand myriad dewdrops, the very apotheosis of water captured or contained.

The ancient name of Iran, it will be remembered, was revived for the West by Reza Shah, on his succession to power in 1925. The 'founder of modern Iran', his was the spadework which laid the foundations upon which his son has built up the present extraordinary edifice of power and progress: his goal, he announces, to make his country, within the next decade, the fifth most puissant industrial world state. But then, the Pahlavi sense of scale is quite apart from all others – larger, better, faster, richer, stronger… a triumphant *force de la nature*, which might now be said to sweep all before it by tidal waves of oil.

I have had occasion to observe the Shahanshah, this grizzled and awesome figure, as he strides through the ranks of bowing courtiers with his eternal air of proud isolation. Then I have seen him, relaxed, in unofficial life, among his family and few close friends, and another man appears, though I think a certain aloofness or detachment persists even then. Sometimes, when he is laughing, setting those around him at ease, and his stern face lightens to an almost boyish grin, as it can do, perhaps at his youngest child's birthday party, or watching the antics of Beno, his indulged dog, it can seem as if the inner man has suddenly emerged from behind the frontiers which surround the monarch. I have heard him criticised for a certain outward air of hauteur, which those who knew him long ago say has grown on him. But small wonder: all those years of unremitting toil, harsh personal disciplines and perils which he has survived, to achieve the metamorphosis of his country, must inevitably have changed something of the man too.

Iran's vicissitudes have been many: great rulers and bad. It is said that this nation, which was puissant and civilised before Greece or Rome, is great when its rulers are great, and sinks when it is ill-ruled. Over the the 2,500 or more years of Iranian history it has known both extremes. Its long chain of rulers is a puissant and picturesque succession of kings, khans, caliphs, atabegs, emperors, sophys or shahs, among them such legendary figures as Darius, Shah Abbas the Great, or Nadir Shah. Not one of their wives, whether styled shahbanou, malikeh, queen or empress, ever shared her lord and master's kingly responsibilities – much less, was crowned. There have been Sassanian princesses, daughters of kings, who ruled briefly – but since the advent of Islam, no woman has worn a queen's crown. This distinction belongs to the Shahbanou Farah Pahlavi – the ancient title of Shahbanou – wife to the Shah – being revived for her. The title has an almost mythical ring. It conjures all beauty, like the land – the Turquoise Kingdom of yesterday – oil well of the world, today.

A walk, a manner of walking, like a hand, or certain gestures, tells much about a person. An imperious stalk, or tread, marks the Shahanshah. The Shahbanou, too, has a very personal way of walking. Hers is a long, loping, almost coltish stride, as if eager to press forward, to get on with the job. This often leaves her shorter-legged entourage scuttling anxiously to keep up with her.

Petrol and power politics are synonymous. In the space of half a century Iran has become the centrifugal force of Middle Eastern policies, the Shahanshah pivot point of this *contredanse* of nations, all, like Oliver Twist, asking for more. More petrol; more aid; more backing; more contracts... Much has been written about Iran's steely ruler. Much less of the woman who stands beside him. Although the Shah had been twice married, neither of his former wives had provided the desired son. A whole generation younger, the Shahbanou Farah has given him the sons he craved for his dynasty, this we know. She is good, beautiful, elegant, cultivated and gives a dynamic lead to countless organisations for the welfare of her country, this we know. Press photographers delight in her presence, and the gaiety and spontaneity of her wide, childish smile. We see her on state occasions, 'a living map of emeralds' as one Moghul emperor was described, or pelting down some vertiginous ski slope, for she is an expert skier on snow or water. We see her in the usual poses of radiant domestic felicity, in flowery gardens, surrounded by tumbling children and their pets. Or in less usual circumstances, seated at a conference table in Pekin, her husband's emissary to Chou En-lai where, accompanied by the Iranian prime minister, they are deep in bilateral treaty discussions. We know that she has earned the title of The Working Empress, and cherishes it. For her, as for the Shah, in the flowery old Persian idiom, there must be no folding of the arms of idleness on the breast of resignation. Now, both romance and queenship are seen in other terms; in the romance of creating a new land, a new image of monarchy, and a new use of that immeasurable wealth which surrounds the Peacock Throne of tradition. A helicopter speeds the Shahbanou about her country, from progressive achievement to dynamic innovation. Schools, clinics, new roads, cultural centres, welfare centres, parks, universities, playing fields, museums... all are her concern.

From 1951 on, land reform was changing the face of Iran and by 1960, was in full swing. Both Crown lands and the estates of the big landowners, many of whom were described by the Shah as 'pleasure-loving absentees, a class of parasites whose days of feudal control were numbered' were bought out, or compensated, their estates redistributed among the small farmers, or cooperative societies. The government fixed their purchase price by reckonings based on the revenue or tax returns made by the owners. Thus, many of these, having fiddled profitably for years, now found themselves hoist with their own petard. Land thus acquired formed the nucleus of a new agricultural pattern. Forests and pasture lands were nationalised. Shares in some government-owned factories became available for purchase by the public. Workers' profit sharing, workers' welfare banks, social security on an ever-increasing scale. Housing projects, industrial reconstruction, the reassessment of labour laws and those of the electorate were only a few expressions of this new concept of Iran, which was forming during the first years of the Empress Farah's reign.

Let us take a skimming flight through time and space, through the centuries and across the mountains, deserts and high plateaux, following the caravan routes, shepherds' tracks or highways known to her ancestors. By way of the halls of Sassanian might, or the pillared majesty of Persepolis, where great rulers held sway, crowned kings of this ancient land, as now her husband, the Shahanshah, their titular descendant is, today. Let us glimpse the ancient Zoroastrian fire temples and know that their flames still flicker, and are worshipped, though while their Towers of Silence still stand, they no longer contain their dead, and the vultures no longer wheel overhead, hungry for their pickings. Skimming on through the centuries, we reach the turquoise shimmer of Isfahan, the golden domes of Mashhad, and the fanciful pigeon towers of the villages – rustic castles, for these birds, since their droppings fertilise the fields, are housed handsomely. Now we see the old walled cities, with their coloured, tiled gates, the elegant pillared houses of the Qajar nobles, ornate with stucco and mirror-work: around them, the warrens of little mud-brick dwellings which form the common roots of this diverse race. All these, and much more, are woven into the tapestried background of the Shahbanou Farah.

Her background has none of the rags-to-riches flavour on which Western journalists, hot for the inexhaustible mine of a Cinderella story, liked to insist at the time of her marriage to the Shah. She is of neither humble nor impoverished origin: indeed, she can claim the loftiest antecedents of Islam, being by descent a Seyyed – that is, one whose ancestry traces back to the Prophet. This descent comes through her father, for no woman may transmit this ancestry. Her family was not of the enclosed court milieu, nor did they possess wealth in extravagant Oriental terms, nor live in exotic indolence, as well-to-do Persians were often pictured by the West. The Dibas were landowners, country nobility and gentry from the province of Azerbaijan, in the north-west, bordering on Turkey and edged by the Caspian. Azerbaijani people are rather different in both character and appearance to more southerly Iranians – Shirazi especially, who are likened to Neapolitans for their love of music, wine and *dolce far niente*. Azerbaijanis are a handsome, fiery race, active rather than languid, who do not, as a rule, possess the long-nosed, heavy-browed, moon-faced and languishing looks immortalised by Persian miniatures.

Although Iranian women have never been so severely subjugated as in some other Moslem lands, they went veiled well into the 1920s, shadowy figures, with no more political rights than lunatics or criminals. Throughout Iran, the *chador*, that black, or darkly speckled, all-enveloping cloak, was customary wear in all walks of life, save among women of the nomad tribes. It took the furious drive of Reza Shah (Reza the Great as he is now known), the present

Shah's father, then bent on modernising his country overnight, to prohibit its wearing. Women were to emerge from both their homes and their *chadors*, to become literate, responsible citizens, along the most progressive lines, or he would know the reason why!

During the first years of her reign and ever since, the scope of the Shahbanou's work has spread in ever-widening circles, reaching out to educational, cultural, medical and judicial areas. She has said that the day Iranian women were legally emancipated from so many crushing injustices was the proudest day of her life. That day, 27 February 1963, when full equality was granted to women, is now celebrated each year as Women's Emancipation Day, though she hopes there will be none of that aggressiveness, that truculence, which marks so many feminist organisations elsewhere.

'There has been such a fuss, internationally, about certain problems concerning women, that our Iranian men are now on the defensive, which doesn't help anything,' said the Shahbanou.

Before the Shah's White Revolution of 1961–2, women's position in Iran was still lamentable. Divorce laws were entirely in men's favour. Women could be divorced by proxy, or even without their knowledge. Moreover in such cases, the woman could only keep her son with her till the age of two, a daughter till seven. Afterwards both children were returned to the husband, and probably, a stepmother. All this has now been changed.

Polygamy, which the Prophet enjoined should be practised with strict impartiality on the husband's part (a ruling as impractical humanly as economically) is no longer legal, unless with the consent of the first wife and a good deal of investigation by the courts: in any case, it is on the decline. Besides, today, four wives might appear to be what the French Inland Revenue would class as *signes extérieurs de la richesse* – outward evidence of wealth – though in terms of flesh, rather than yachts or châteaux, and hardly practicable, with the more stringent economic struggles of this age.

But *sigheh*, a curious old Iranian practice, which lies somewhere between monogamy and concubinage is still in evidence. This is a contract, or form of left-handed union once agreed on before a *mollah*, now before the local authorities, where the duration of the association is agreed on by the partners. This can be for a week, or a term of years or even a day. It is perfectly legal as long as it lasts. Any children born of this union are recognised by the man, take his name, and have full inheritance rights. This practical custom reduces prostitution and promiscuity, protects the children and gives status and some security to the woman, as well as suiting man's inclination to change. There are still numbers of *sigheh* wives, particularly in the provinces, but the institution is no longer fashionable in the big towns.

Persia has an ancient tradition of medicine stemming from the great Persian physician Avicenna, who was known as the Prince of Physicians to the West, and whose canon of medicine was studied there as late as two centuries ago, together with the treatise of Razl, another famous Persian. But in the centuries since they practised, Persia had become apathetic and medical care had dwindled lamentably. With the advent of Reza Shah, however, things changed, and at the time of which I write, there were some excellent hospitals and maternity services established about the country. Nevertheless, the illiterate masses still showed the primitive, age-old distrust of going into hospital; especially the women, who, like their husbands, held to the tradition that birth was a natural function, part of the life cycle of birth and death. Home was the proper place for these events. The villages still relied on wise women and their practices. Hospitals only meddled with nature, they said. Hospitals were cold, frightening places, to be avoided.

It was difficult to reach most women outside the cities by propaganda: few houses had radios then, nor was there television. At that time, said the Shahbanou, the women were often only brought into the hospitals too late, having driven a day and a night, perhaps, across country, in bone-shaking carts.

By one decisive move, the young Empress was to change all that. She decided to remain in the care of Iranian doctors and not look westward – to doctors from Switzerland or America – for the Crown prince's birth (in October 1960). She would go to the South Teheran Maternity Hospital to popularise the first-class maternity services available there. It was downtown, in the poorest section of the city, so it may be imagined how her revolutionary decision was greeted in some quarters, although the Shah shared her faith in Iranian hospitals, and backed her decision.

By deliberately renouncing the luxury and pampering which surrounded her in the palace, she overcame the prejudices which were still so strong. From that moment on, all over the country Iranian women followed her lead and flocked to every available maternity hospital or clinic, and presently, there was a dramatic drop in the maternity and infant mortality rates.

It is one of Teheran's most torrid days. A pall of heat hangs over the panting city, the thermometer is at 112°. The pavements blister; the heat haze, white-hot, shimmers over the distant mountains and reverberates round the high-rise cement blocks of apartment houses and offices. Sometimes a violent, unexpected gust of hot oven air, a dust-laden, sirocco-like tempest, hurls itself across the city, coming from the desert areas of the East, I imagine. At such moments this wind howls round the high-rise apartment blocks so that, blue skies or no, the impression is that of *Wuthering Heights*. Everywhere the trees are whipped this way and that. As suddenly, all is still; the raging tempest has passed. All along the streets of the oldest parts of the city, south of the Bazaar, people are sitting under the trees where the *jubes*, or narrow streams, run beside the pavement. The children are playing in the water and everyone is eating watermelon. I should like to linger there; I love this sawing wood, hammering metal, tinkering with copper cooking pans; outside the hammams, red cotton cloths – towels – are hung to dry... Presently, the garish neon lights will pick out the little mosque, and the muezzin's cry will remind the faithful it is the hour for prayer. Twilight, 'the hour when a black thread cannot be told from a white one'. But I must leave this entrancing quarter and go towards the orderly modern office blocks and governmental buildings, where I have work to do.

In Teheran alone, there are twenty-eight libraries for children and eleven mobile library vans servicing hospitals and outlying quarters. Then there are storytelling sessions for the very young, and specially made films, another brilliant branch of the Institute for the Intellectual Development of Children and Young Adults' work which, like the books it publishes, has won innumerable international awards. There are concerts and recitations of poetry or the visits of personalities likely to intrigue young audiences – perhaps a naturalist, a dancer or an explorer... such visits being accompanied by exhibits, films or music. Mobile libraries are spread about the wide span of Teheran, 118 specially equipped caravan libraries serve 2,400 villages across the country, and go about the summer camps and provincial hospitals or small towns where there are no means of installing a permanent library. For the most inaccessible regions, such as the high pastures of the tribes where they live among their flocks for months at a time, where no wheels can follow, there is the galvanic and practical system of the dashing horseman with his saddlebag of books. Some are school books – primers for the use of a teacher, one of the Literacy Corps, who has accompanied the tribes, and lives among them, holding classes in a special school tent.

'Abandoning their traditional form of architecture, and its manner of family living, in favour of Western-type blocks of apartment houses will turn Iran into a second-hand America, and Iranians into ersatz Americans,' is one architect's warning. All over the country there has been a push towards feckless development. Citizens who pulled down their old houses, thus making room for multistoried blocks, were exempt from taxation for three years. What more persuasion was needed? And always, municipalities could take refuge behind the acute need to house an ever-growing population.

The Golestan Palace, the Sepahsalar Mosque and the Bazaar, are among the few buildings of a truly historic flavour which remain in Teheran. The Bazaar (said to tie with that of Aleppo as largest in the world) hums with activity; its merchandise ranges from carpets to plastic prayer mats, old silver, electro-plated electrified samovars, jasmine oil or Moghul jewellery, all assembled under the intricate brickwork vaulting which roofs its labyrinthine alleyways and courts, little restaurants, and a mosque. But whatever Teheran's shortcomings on the picturesque today, the Golestan Palace and museum is infinitely rewarding. It was here that successive coronations have been held. Here in the open *talar*, or pillared loggia, glittering with mirror work, Fath Ali Shah once held audience and, O! wondrous revelation, his alabaster throne supported by djinns and mythical beasts is still to be glimpsed, from the thronged streets, beyond the palace railings. I have always thought this snatched glimpse of majesty's historic setting is of particular piquancy and far more impressive than close-range visits within the grounds. By this unexpected peep show, seen between dense traffic blocks and the shuffling *hamals*, or porters, carrying their enormous loads to and from the Bazaar, one is suddenly aware of this thread of continuity, of yesterday and today, still present in Teheran, which before all else, aspires to tomorrow's might.

It is such threads that Her Majesty the Shahbanou strives to weave into the texture of contemporary life, where sports stadiums, motorways, museums, concert halls, supermarkets, drive-in cinemas and filling stations are all con-comitant parts of the country's new image. Even the Golestan Palace has to struggle against the encroachment of the high-rise office buildings which now hem it in. Once (and again according to Flandin) there were distant views of the mountains to be seen rising northwards, above the palace roofs. Today, when smog lies heavy over the city, its pall the price of motorised life, the mountains are sometimes blotted out for days on end. Still, they are there, tawny, crum-pled suede in summer, blanketed in snow all winter long. They exist – and I have the impression that even when invisible they remain to Teheran's citizens, however subconsciously, a sort of symbol of strength, and their unchanging roots. Teheranis still speak of their encompassing mountains as if they were living entities, with Damavand as ruler of the Alborz chain. Eastward, great Damavand rises in unchallenged might. This extinct volcano is to Iranians what Fujiyama is to the Japanese: symbol of national pride and home of legends. Damavand dwarfs the mountains of Europe and is only surpassed by the Himalayan giants.

Only those who have never experienced Teheran's traffic and transport problems, would be surprised to learn that a couple of hours – and here, every hour appears to be the rush hour – can be spent inching a few miles across the immense, sprawling conglomerate that makes up the capital's clogged streets. Besides every make of imported lorry and car, there are Iran-manufactured Chevrolets (the German Opel) and Hillmans (Peykan Iran), while the buses are British Leyland, double-deckers, here painted green. All of these vehicles stretch, bumper to bumper, in fuming, honking masses, between the new outlying residential quarters, workers' housing developments, and those factories that mushroom up overnight and spread their pall of death-dealing smog. In the words of the Shahbanou, when addressing America's Aspen Institute of Humanistic Studies: 'The human race is now the victim of its own inventions… Our responsibility is to find a way to tame technology, without depriving humanity of its benefits.'

Today, we see that violence which we associate with Timur the Tartar or the Mongol hordes has become that of our own age, though now manifested in different forms. The idiom of violence is speeded up, mechanised, made scientific: lie detectors instead of poison-tasters, bombs to replace the assassin's dagger, and atomic bombs as the last word all round. Where once Timur, the Achaemenian kings or Nadir Shah rode in triumph between their palaces or plumed tents, with trains of camels and caparisoned elephants, journeying from the plains of Persepolis to the mountains of Ectabana (now Hamadan), imperial planes now skim this vast land. Where once a train of caracoling steeds set out, let us say, for a day's journey from the Castle of the Qajars on the slopes below Niavaran, to reach Rey, or Varamin on the city's southern confines, the imperial helicopters now buzz aloft, forever rising or alighting vertically like so many well-trained insects, securing both speed and security. Today, the imperial couple have come to make most of their journeys aerial ones, between palace and city. Thus, Niavaran has its own landing pad and soft-gliding royal automobiles give pride of place to zooming helicopters.

The Palace of Niavaran lies behind its high, sentry-studded walls and a filigree of leaves and branches; at first sight it surprises, for it has none of the concomitants of a palace, in residential terms of size or splendour. But though it may not possess the legendary grandeur of Windsor, nor the size and studied perfection of Versailles, nor the haunting drama of mad Ludwig's Bavarian splendours, it is, in its own right, interesting. It is an essay in simplified royal living, expressed in contemporary terms, while in no way resembling an informal royal holiday pavilion. The uncompromisingly four-square lofty white cube, strangely windowless on the side approached from the gates, is very modest-looking to house such a monarch as the Shahanshah, and its portico, with soaring tubular pillars, does not impress. While the exterior has no outstanding features, the interior is agreeably personal and inviting. Round the four sides of the cube which forms the entrance hall or foyer, a wide, railed first floor gallery gives on to the private apartments. Below, the state dining room (Gobelins tapestries, places for eighty, candelabras, chandeliers, and cream silk chairs embossed with the sword-brandishing lion, emblem of Iran) bears the imprint of 'safe'or classic French decorators' taste. So do the smaller reception rooms and the main salon: Persian carpets galore, Louis XV *bergères*, a grand piano, vitrines of precious objects, indifferent royal portraits and fine French impressionists; that pure palace style which is to be found behind the façade of most royal palaces, an interchangeable, impersonal décor. Local flavours seldom find a place in palaces.

Here at Niavaran, however, the Shahbanou's taste has overcome the strictures of 'safe', to impose many paintings and objects of Persian origin, some priceless, some simple, pieces: Luristan bronzes, a turquoise-studded *kalioun*, or water pipe, fragments of tiles, florid calligraphy, nineteenth-century naive papier-mâché boxes, and the work of contemporary Iranian painters and sculptors. Such things make even these formal rooms come alive and breathe the spirit of the country. But it is in the Shahbanou's own, lately achieved library (another large cube, added to the east wall of the main building) that her eclectic taste is best expressed – mirror of this woman's many-aspected character and heart of the honeycomb.

Niavaran is, naturally, luxurious: it is a palace. Yet it is very comfortable – comfort not necessarily being the appendage of luxury. You are aware of her presence, her glow, pervading the whole. Then too, that reverential hush, that tiptoed quiet which pervades all palaces can be, here, suddenly broken by the eruption of the younger of her four children, followed by their dogs, tearing through, calling for one or other of their parents.

In Iran's adoption of Shi'a tenets, we may trace this people's fierce spirit of independence. They had, long, long ago, been Zoroastrians; Zoroaster (or Zarathrusthra) being born in Iran about 600 B.C. But the Islamic invasion had swept most of this earlier religion aside. Although the Persians resented the Arab invasion of their country and in due course overthrew them politically, they embraced Islam's faith wholeheartedly, indeed, with such fervour that Persia became one of the major centres of Islamic civilisation.

Shi'ite Islam was based upon a special reverence for the family of the Prophet, and the claim that Ali, his son-in-law, should have succeeded him (instead of the Sunni doctrine, which followed a caliphate succession – elected caliphs being of the Meccan Qureish tribe, which was also that of the Prophet).

This loyalty to the Prophet's own family, to Ali and to his sons, Hassan and Hossein (the second and third imams) remained deeply rooted in Persia, so that, finally, it was this dogma which, during the Safavid era, became Persia's official religion. However, this is a question altogether too involved for these pages – or this pen. Suffice it to say that theological discussions and armed clashes persisted between the two sects for centuries.

Meanwhile, since Safavid Persia's chief enemies were the Ottoman Turks (who were Sunnis), the two countries' political differences were reflected in a religious antagonism too.

But as the political situation changed, so this enmity declined. Today, the Shi'as of Persia live in harmony with the Sunnis of other lands, and also with the large Sunni population within the borders of Iran itself.

The Iranians' age-old culture sounds in the cadence of a song; is found in the typical menu of any popular restaurant, where *chelow kebab*, broiled lamb and ethereal rice, tells of finesse. Or in the delicate little glasses of tea served at any wayside café, or *chaikhana*, perhaps with a rose alongside, certainly with a flowery phrase. Above all, in toleration. Oddly in a country where religious fanaticism persists and the gloomy revels of Muharram are revived yearly, many minorities, Jewish, Orthodox, Christian and Zoroastrian, flourish.

The Shahbanou and I were talking in one of the sun-filled bays of Her Majesty's library. Light played over a huge metal column, or so it seemed to me, though it is in fact a classified and valued piece of modern sculpture. Light glowed through the jar of boiled sweets, which I noticed were beginning to melt – to look far less like cabochon rubies and emeralds; light flashed across the luminous glass stalactite ceiling, reflected down in prisms of colour on the ancient rugs, bringing their soft colours to stained-glass strength... From across the park, through the open windows, very faintly, came the sound of the muezzin... that long *mélopée* that is a call to prayer, a call that punctuates the Moslem's day and night. It floated up to us, from near the little market town of Niavaran, hidden away beyond the trees of the park.

The Shahbanou jumped to her feet, and pushed the French windows open wider.

'Listen!... isn't it beautiful?'

A long silence fell, while we listened to that haunting call, which I can never hear without a feeling of profound emotion. Hearing it, I follow it, as it goes out across the world. I have heard it from Maghreb, across the African deserts, sounding from the minarets of the Balkans to Istanbul, Cairo and Damascus, calling across the strife-torn Middle East, to Mashhad in Iran, to Herat in Afghanistan, to Russian Samarcand and Tashkent, and Moslem India... and on, to that farthest East I do not yet know – China, and the mosques of Indonesia. But always that same haunting call, which morning, noon and evening, calls man to face Mecca and pray, and rouses him from his slumbers at dawn: 'It is better to pray than sleep.'

At last, this noonday call to the faithful died away across the trees, and we turned back from the window.

'Do you consider you are religious – a true follower of the Prophet?' I asked the Shahbanou.

'I try to be: I try to be a good Moslem, though I have not yet made my pilgrimage to Mecca. I go to Mashhad, or Qom, or any shrine when I can. But one can pray anywhere at any time; you do not have to be in a mosque... and all calls to prayer sustain: that voice of the muezzin, just now... or the bells from a Christian church... It's all one and the same, essentially. I am interested in all the religions of the world. Christian, Orthodox, Quaker, Buddhist... We all need religion, we all have a desperate need to have something strong to hang on to – to obtain some inner peace. Isn't religion better than the fashionable psychologist's couch? Not everyone has faith or a philosophy to meet life's challenges.'

In 1970, the Shahbanou acquired overnight, for her country, the superb paintings known as the Amery Collection, then going up for sale in London, at

Sotheby's. These late eighteenth- and nineteenth-century Persian paintings so long neglected had, in the wilful way of taste, suddenly become the rage, their prices soaring, when the Shanbanou rescued them, thus leaving the world of high international art dealers open-mouthed and empty-handed.

Qajar paintings have nothing to do with the more widely known Persian miniatures, being boldly painted, mostly life-sized figures, stiffly posed. Fath Ali Shah is seen crowned and plumed, armoured in jewels, seated rigid on his alabaster throne, among pearl-tasselled bolsters, and surrounded by those ninepin-rows of princeling sons. Acrobatic dancing girls, their breasts looped with pearls, a rose in their navel (as it were, an exotic buttonhole), beckon invitingly or perform frantic antics, balancing on the point of a dagger, tinselled skirts flying... Lovers exchange lascivious glances and offer each other goblets of sherbet, fondle kittens, or each other... All jewelled voluptuous dalliance is here, as luscious as those bowls of tropic fruits, where green parrots peck – the usual pattern of a *nature morte*, in this school.

The Amery Collection had been begun as early as 1905, by Major Harold Amery, then working for the Foreign Office, about the Middle East. The collection was continued by his brother, the Rt Hon. Leopold Amery, a distinguished scholar, fellow of All Souls and Secretary of State for India, during World War II. This collection of sixty-three masterpieces was in the possession of the Rt Hon. Julian Amery, M.P. when put up for sale, and it was these which the Shahbanou Farah was to retrieve for Iran, at the eleventh hour.

She had been returning from the ski slopes at St Moritz, late one afternoon, when she learned quite by chance, that the Amery Collection was coming under the hammer, the next day, at an important sale in London, where the biggest dealers were preparing to do battle. She acted on the instant, instructing a member of her household to go at once – that night – to London, with powers to buy the entire collection, in her name and from her own purse. Her emissary on this occasion has since told me of his dramatic dash, and how the Shahbanou told him: 'You must get them for us at all costs. They must not be dispersed – they must come back to Iran.' And so they did. It was a happy ending.

Or rather, a beginning. For next the Shahbanou devised a special new museum to house them in the heart of Teheran. This is the former small palace of the Queen Mother Tadj ol-Molouk, and is now known as the Negarestan Museum of Eighteenth and Nineteenth Century Iranian Art. To me it is the most perfectly achieved of all the many museums I know. The paintings are superbly displayed on the ground floor. Above, a few rooms show Persian jewels, calligraphy and papier-mâché work, while other rooms house temporary exhibitions. Below ground, there is a lavishly stocked reading room and art library, where all comers may feast. Here are the latest art journals from all over the world, periodicals, *éditions d'art* in many languages, technical treatises, albums and portfolios.

The coronation of Mohammad Reza Pahlavi Shahanshah did not take place until twenty-six years after his accession to the Peacock Throne. The Shah had stated he would never consent to be crowned until he had restored the country to prosperity, and a worthy place among the nations of the world. High words – followed by high achievements.

After twenty-six years of Herculean efforts towards reconstruction and development he judged the time was ripe, and announced that 26 October 1967, his forty-eighth birthday, should be the day of his coronation. He further proclaimed that it would also be that of the Shahbanou – the first queen to be crowned in the 2,500 and more years of Persian monarchy. In an address of that moment, he spoke of his lifelong aims to preserve the independence and sovereignty of his country, and to renew its ancient glories. He also pledged himself to continue the revolutionary progress that had been made in the field of women's emancipation. This was an advancement in which the Shahbanou had played a part only second to himself.

There was, also, another reason for the Shah's decision to crown his consort. In 1966, she had fulfilled all his hopes by giving birth to a second son, the Prince Ali Reza, and thus the dynasty was solidly established. But the Shah knew, too, that his own life was always threatened by a terrorist bullet. He had survived numerous attempted assassinations and coups... but for how long could he rely on that extraordinary chance which, until now, had preserved him? It was essential that the constitution should be amended, so that, in the event of his death before the Crown prince's majority, the Shahbanou could assume Regent's powers.

The coronation of H.I.M. Mohammad Reza Pahlavi was the apotheosis of Pahlavi ascendancy and splendour. All that strict protocol and the Oriental imagination could devise were now brought together. The planning and preparation spread over nearly two years. The ceremony followed that of Reza the Great's coronation by being held at the Golestan Palace, but now there was considerably more pageantry – and a queen – to ride in state beside the Shah.

The country celebrated the coronation for a whole week of junketing: the people of the provinces had poured into the capital to celebrate the birth of the Valiahd, but now they manifested even more enthusiasm. They were feting not only the coronation of their Shah, but Iran's steady rise towards a once unimaginable prosperity. *'Zerideh bad Shahl Zendeh bad Shahbanou!'* they cried, hailing the fount of such prosperity. A steady flow of cars, buses, lorries, trotting donkeys and plodding camels brought them to the city. This was indeed a royal raree-show and they were not going to miss one blaze of fireworks, one salvo of guns. Between the triumphal arches, the streets were festooned with garlands and chains of electric bulbs blazing by day and night. Enormous crowns and unflattering giant metal portraits of the Shah and Shahbanou, outlined in coloured lights, were plastered about the city. The scarlet, white and green tricolour of the national flag fluttered from thousands of flagpoles, and in the Oriental manner, carpets hung out of balconies and windows. Whole sheep were slaughtered, skinned, roasted and eaten at the street corners. Everywhere, the people feasted, danced, sang and slept in the streets. There were the Turcomen, the Baluchis, Lurs, Kurds, Kashgais and more: all the many ethnic groups which are part of the Iranian whole. The nomad tribes came in their best, the women bunched in their bright shawls, their gaudy gold and silver spangled skirts trailing, as they encamped by the kerbside in nomadic freedom. Foreign visitors and the press crammed every hotel. Grandstands were set up round the Golestan where the whole length, from its gates to the shimmering mirror-lined entrance, was carpeted in crimson. The parterres were massed with blooms, and dyed fountains jetted high in the strong autumn sunshine, while on the *talar*, that open, pillared loggia where Fath Ali Shah's marvellous alabaster throne still stands, a large orchestra and choir were assembled to perform coronation anthems commissioned for for the occasion.

For the Shahbanou's coronation, a special crown had to be designed, since there was no precedent for so historic an occasion. Its emerald green velvet cap (green being the colour of Iran) and its preponderance of pear-shaped pearls, the sparkle of its rubies and emeralds, is majesty in a softer, lighter key to the masculine strength, the scarlet and gold and diamond brilliance of the Shah's Pahlavi crown. The Shahbanou had much to say on its design, and worked closely with the Parisian jeweller Pierre Arpels, who was given *carte blanche* to select whatever stones he required from the Crown jewel reserves. Among the 1,469 diamonds, the seventy-two matchless emeralds and rubies, and the 105 enormous, perfect, pear-shaped pearls, the centrepiece of this diadem is a fluted, hexagon emerald about the size of a smallish tangerine. Even so, this crown is delicate rather than massive; it retains a certain charming, light grace, and weighs only 1,600 grammes. When the Shahbanou first tried it on, she was astonished that in spite of its height, and massed stones, it could feel so light. The jeweller, with Gallic *galanterie*, replied, 'May Your Majesty never know a heavier burden.'

Today this crown is to be seen among the rest of the Crown jewels, at the Central Bank in Teheran. Only three persons know the combination of the massive steel doors. Indeed, entering this strong-room-museum is, in fact, entering a gigantic safe. The walls are lined with glass shelves and cases, upon which, backed by crimson velvet and brilliantly fitted, repose what is probably the world's most extraordinary collection of precious stones. Here is the Regalia; the Pahlavi crown and other earlier royal ones. Here one of the golden thrones, studded with jewels. The historic stones like the Noor-ul-Ain – the Light of the Eye. (This fabulous rose-tinged diamond, now centrepiece of a tiara often worn by the Shahbanou, is thought to have been part of the Moghal splendours brought to Persia as spoils of war by Nadir Shah, the Conqueror.) The Daria-i-Noor, or Sea of Light, is the size and the shape of a large decanter stopper and weighs 182 carats. Its only possible rival: the Koh-i-Noor, or Mountain of Light. Here are many pieces of modern jewellery, made for members of the imperial family; and the several diadems and tiaras of former empresses. Here is a snuffbox chunked from a single, flawless emerald; and epaulettes dripping first water diamonds. Here, huge crystal goblets full of what appear to be boiled sweets, but turn out to be cabochon rubies and emeralds. Here are parasols fringed with pearls, the spokes picked out in diamonds, relics of pampered royal favourites... panares of sapphires, tiaras of rubies... and the celebrated Terrestrial Globe which tells of Islam's merging of science and beauty. Standing over a yard high, it is entirely composed of precious stones – 51,000 of them – each country allotted a different coloured stone, with sapphire seas and Persia all in turquoise... an extravagant conceit, very much in the Oriental idiom, originally designed in 1868, some say, to preserve the best of lose stones which lay about in disorder. I prefer to imagine it was created by Nasr-ed-Din Shah to aid the little princes to sharpen up on geography.

In 1960 all the imperial treasures were amassed and catalogued and displayed as we see them today. There are three thousand classified pieces. Most of the Crown jewels can be worn, enjoyed or reset, at will by the imperial family. But they remain, essentially state property, part of the national treasure, for which a permit has to be issued on each occasion of their being removed from the vaults. At the time of Farah Diba's marriage, although the Crown jewels and the whole incredible collection was to be seen, a raree-show, indeed, nothing had been properly catalogued, sorted or displayed as now. But then, as now, they were legendary, something all visitors to Teheran crowded to see; something totally removed from real life, or any calculable value; in short – Aladdin's cave.

Each time I have seen the Shahbanou's coronation crown, glowing out, spotlit, at the centre of this incredible display, I felt it to be *indissolubly* linked with the woman who first wore it and for whom it was designed. This is the Shahbanou Farah's crown – something she has won by her endeavours, a symbol of woman's new place in modern Iran. It was impossible for me to imagine it could ever be worn by a succession of future queens. Was her coronation to be a precedent then, or was it a unique event?

TUNIS

To the Arabs, it is Tunis *la blanche*. To me, it will always be Tunis *la bleue*. The impression which remains is of blueness. A range of blues, subtle or strident, from faded turquoise to Tyrrhean purple. The transparent waters round Cap Carthage, the lilac blue of the far mountains, the livid, magnesium-flare blue of the *café maure* – which they call *bleu diamanté*. This range of blue is everywhere, throughout the country. Blue haze on the alfalfa grass of the high plateau country near the Algerian border. Blue bloom on the Barbary figs of a Saharan oasis. Blue shadows across the Roman temples at Sbeitla. Peacock-bright fishing boats at Monastir. Bedouin women, all blue, elaborate tattoos and traditional blue draperies (more bunchy than graceful and sadly in need of safety pins, as Norman Douglas observed); the blue of *moucharabiyeh* in any Arab street where, behind the lattice, there are shadowy watchers, white veils and kohl-rimmed eyes (the best kohl is made from pulverised bats) and you glimpse all the immemorial mystery of the sequestered Oriental women. Blue amulets hung round the camels' necks; blue everywhere: Tunis shimmers under a blue spell.

There are many civilisations which have each left their mark on the Tunisian scene. Berber, Punic, Roman, Byzantine, Arab, Spanish, Turkish, French: all these different stratas are to be seen and felt, everywhere. Tunisia is like a layer cake of many flavours, forming a rich and a satisfying whole. Of all North Africa it is said to be the least known and least spoiled. It is also said to be less African, more Arabian, or Eastern, in character, than all the rest. Even to the casual observer there is a whiff, of Bukhara and Baghdad. Arabs say that Morocco is the warrior, Algeria the man, and Tunis the woman, and there is a certain effeminate grace, a pliancy about both race and country, at once seductive and baffling.

This mobile quality is especially suited to travellers, who can, within the space of one hundred kilometres or less, change landscape, climate, architecture and people. Impossible to imagine a country which offers so quickly (it is a four-hour flight from Paris) and in so small a space, so many concentrated and variable delights. From the Sicilian fishing villages of Cap Bon to the Sahara is possible in a day's driving. Though no one with any sense of travelling, as opposed to speeding, would rush through such country. There are the mosques of Kairouan, the olive forests round the majestic Coliseum of El Djem. There are the oasis towns, and the extraordinary troglodyte villages of Matmata; and Medenine where the *rhorfas* – fortified stone granaries – must be among the most curious of all human habitations. When I was last there in the fifties, they were as they had always been: but now progress has passed that way, leaving a wake of order and cement. It is at Medenine, too, that the traveller first senses the south: which means not just desert sands and palmy oases, but the Africa which stretches to the Hoggar, the mysterious Touareg territory, to Lake Tchad and far, far beyond. Tunisian signposts read curiously: 'La Manouba 8 km. Timbuktu 3,200 km.'

At Kebili, on the edge of the desert, sand drifts up to the window frames and from the oasis come all the chattering busy sounds of the Arab and African village. Djerba, so pastoral and tranquil, is the Lotus Isle of legend, Lotophages, where in Flaubert's words '*Les oiseaux chantent dans la verdure et ou l'air est si pur qu'on oublie d'y mourir.*' ('The birds are singing in the greenery and the air is so pure, we forget to die.') In Djerba, too, there is the extraordinary spectacle of Hara Srira, the Jewish village which has conserved its traditions for two thousand years, remaining untouched since the Exodus. But Hara Srira is a chapter – a book – in itself.

All these are only some of the general aspects of the chameleon Tunisia. There are so many more specialised interests. A super-abundance of Roman remains; many different races, sects, customs and costumes. All the dazzling merchandise of the souks. The intricate delights of the Arab cuisine.

Every traveller sees the country filtered through his own individual viewpoint: he has his blind spots, his sharp focus. Thus it is impossible for me to judge what is truly outstanding in Tunisia, though most people seem to agree it is, first, the wonderful Roman remains. I was fortunate enough, while in the north, to be staying in an old Arab palace, on the Gulf of Tunis, near Carthage, and the Gardens of Hamilcar. The local train puffs to a halt at Salammbo. Oh, shades of Flaubert! I recall the splendid opening to his tale. '*C'était à Mégara, faubourg de Carthage, dans les jardins d'Hamilcar...*' ('It was in Mégara, a suburb of Carthage, in the gardens of Hamilcar...')

But it is not this beautiful and historic panorama which most typifies Tunis to me. Indeed, I like it less than the wilder, more desert landscape. I remember more clearly all the brouhaha of the Arab towns: the pulse and panorama of street life, everywhere in Tunis; the Place El Halfouine on a Friday (the Moslem Sunday) with tumblers and buffoons in plumed and spangled costumes; jugglers and pedlars, drum and flute musicians and cafés full of immobile groups, smoking the *narghilyé*, or sipping little glasses of mint tea. I remember cafés at Monastir where the tables were covered in birdcages, all brought by their owners to take lessons from a master songbird owned by the café proprietor. Or fortune-tellers squatting in the dust beside the gates of Bab El Khadra, foxy faces, mystical faces, all sorts, twisting paper talismans and tracing hieroglyphics in the sand for their clients. Or the Chara, a religious and civil tribunal, an old Arab court of justice, the sun slanting down through the latticed roof, the crowds surging round the divan; and the porter's lodge, where the litigants were brewing tea, fanning little braziers, while others dictated to the public letter-writer. It was the tension and drama of any law court, but translated into terms of fatalism and green tea. Insha'Allah. *Mektoub*! If God wills. Destiny... those overworked phrases, so eloquent of Oriental philosophy, were to be heard on all sides. I wondered that lawyers are employed, when their clients are plainly resigned to any outcome. Nevertheless, litigation flourishes.

It is, then, these small but vivid details of everyday life which I remember more than any of the outstanding beauties. Arabs carrying little bunches of jasmine and stopping, in the busiest streets, to sniff the perfume voluptuously. A wedding to which I was invited, where the bride sat splendidly enthroned, rigid as an ikon, in her traditional silver-embroidered trousered robes, her black-hennaed hands placed on her stomach, her eyes downcast, in a ritualistic pose, hour after hour. And Arab music: I am haunted by some of the long, slow improvised chants, a kind of *mélopée*, recalling certain Spanish flamencos which, in fact, derive from Arab sources. Other sounds, less musical, but as typical. The harsh voice of the muezzin calling the faithful to prayer from a minaret. But this was Africa – it bore no resemblance to the languorous cadences of the Turkish equivalent: it was a battle-cry.

There is another aspect of everyday, present-day Tunisia and one which is apt to be overlooked by the ecstatic traveller, rushing between black Bedouin tents and Roman colonnades. This is the admirable new French architecture. Schools, administrative buildings and such, are always contrived in local materials and regional forms, so that they blend harmoniously with the surroundings. I remember in particular one at Zriba, a savage Berber mountain-top rock village, not far from Zaghouan, which every motorist should try and reach.

Whatever kind of scene the traveller seeks, there can, I think, be no two minds about crossing the Chott el Djerid. Here is something which is profoundly impressive to everyone. The desolate sand sea is impassable at certain times: it is the northern fringe of the Sahara and links the oasis towns of Tozeur and Nefta with Gabès, the coast, and the Eastern caravan centres such as Foum Tataouine. There is only the shimmering mirage forever renewed out of the waste land. It is Dali-esque, a landscape of despair. This is not a country for a breakdown. The usual procedure is to telephone to your destination before setting out, asking them to come and look for you, if you do not arrive at a given hour, which at first I thought rather fussy: but after I had crossed the Chott, it seemed an elementary precaution, as necessary as filling up the radiator.

The courtesy and hospitality of the Arab peoples is traditional and I had occasion to remark it, again and again: especially in the south where, whether rich or poor, all showed the same exquisite sense of *politesse*. Indeed, there were rather too many kind, but misleading, strangers who always used to tell me trains or buses left at whatever time they imagined I should have liked them to leave, which alas, seldom corresponded with fact. Everywhere I went, there was the same wish to give pleasure. They smothered me in rose water, they offered me eggs or cracked nuts for me: from the Westernised, wealthy, canasta-playing Arab princess who showed me how to cut the enormous Algerian trousers still sometimes worn in the more conservative harems, to the street pastry-cook who showed me how to make exotic Arab sweets.

With that *politesse* goes tact. I remember the unspoken rebuke of an old Arab at Dougga, where we were exclaiming over the wonderful Roman mosaics. The old man looked at them appreciatively. 'Yes, they are beautiful – as beautiful as our carpets from Kairouan,' he said. It was all there, the regret, the pride and the rebuke. I, too, have thought it a pity that so many superlatives are lavished on the glory that was Rome, when all around is the living Arab scene. Surely, it shows a lack of proportion to concentrate on the skeleton of Rome beneath the flesh and blood of Tunisia. Shadow or substance: which is which, you may ask? We come to the impasse of personal preferences. To me, the substance is Tunis, the blue, the beautiful.

Afghanistan Remembered

Although these pages set out to be predominantly on food and local cuisine, it is almost impossible to write of the peaceful country I knew and the Afghan dishes I savoured there when I must recall it today, across barriers of bloodshed and privation. Thus, anything I write here must be taken as a valedictory gesture, hailing the Afghanistan I once knew.

There was still a king in Kabul when first I went there, but his was an austere majesty, with few trappings, and a preoccupation with agricultural development and model farms before palace life. It was among the tribes, such as the Kuchi, that one glimpsed a certain intoxicating glitter composed of coin jewellery, babies ricked out in *kincob*, a sort of gold tissue fabric splashed with bouquets of impossible flowers, their skullcaps gold-embroidered or sewn with pearls and coral beads. As to the cavaliers – they were mud-splashed or dusty, but sumptuous, with velvet saddlecloths, and guns studded with turquoise – a strangely foppish crew, their eyes heavily rimmed with kohl, their turbans rakishly tipped. The women, glimpsed in the tents, were spangled in sequinned veils with a jangling mass of heavy silver ornaments, one and all exotic creatures to find amid the barren wastes. They swarmed down from their rocky fastnesses and enticed us into their encampments to share a stew of goat's meat, or wild partridge, while their huge, angry dogs circled round the cauldrons. Among the Kuchi, I sampled *dugh*, a beverage of watered-down yoghourt perfumed with mint – a change from the usual brew of sweet green tea.

The Afghans, a people who are said to be both genial and cruel, according to their mood, always showed me their genial side. So welcoming were they that every encounter, every meal or casual roadside halt appeared a festive occasion. From the come-by-chance meetings to the hospitality of friends of friends, the garage hands, shepherds, merry marriage parties dancing and singing as they escorted the bride's camel, or the lorry drivers and their beguiling *batcha* boys – all made me welcome with an air of swaggering gallantry.

These *batcha* boys are an essential part of the Asiatic scene: pleasure boys, they were called, in Samarcand, where once they danced for the emirs and became petted favourites. ('A woman for breeding, a boy for pleasure,' runs the Asiatic saying.) The Afghan *batcha* boys I saw had little time for languorous undulations – they accompanied the lorries, rushed to place a big stone under the back wheels when the brakes gave up on a mountain road, and went about the *chaikhanas*, preparing sustenance for their drivers before performing any further unspecified duties required of them.

I came to observe that the more handsome the *batcha* boy, the longer the noonday halt and the more rested and refreshed the driver emerged from the shadowed depths of the *chaikhana*. Thus I took to selecting a lorry with what my nanny used to describe as 'a likely-looking lad' aboard, which ensured I should not be hurried along the way, torn from congenial surroundings such as a *chaikhana* where rug-merchants gathered. In padded caftans they crouched beside their dark crimson rugs, the 'royal' Bukharas (whose traditional octagonal medallion design is said to represent an elephant footprint) and engaged me, language problems or no, in flowery exchanges, pressing me to endless glasses of mint tea. And was it commerce alone that made them so delightfully hospitable? Rather, Afghan geniality.

Recalling such encounters a yearning – almost a homesickness – seizes me for I loved Afghanistan passionately. A kaleidoscope of scenes rises around me as I stand in my Western kitchen trying to prolong Afghan emotions by making *boulani*. This is a kind of wheaten cake stuffed with green-vegetable tops. My driver's two mothers (his father enjoying the Moslem plural) prepared this for me with loving hospitality, one of a dozen or more delights, when I visited the family in their rickety balconied dwelling high above the warrens of Kabul's Shor Bazaar... They made the same *boulani* again, for that sad but hilarious farewell party they offered me at Jalalabad, their winter quarters (for Kabul's winter temperatures are unimaginably severe). It was there I spent my last hours on Afghan soil... Jalalabad... a name now written in crimson for the bloodshed in that frontier region. A saucepan boils over and I am whirled back through time and space to my own kitchen surrounded by stainless steel gadgets, mixers, whisks, a refrigerator and running hot and cold water. How can I hope my *boulani* will taste like theirs? Or that any other of the dishes I ate amid those wild hills could be reproduced here? Yet the spell is potent. I turn away from the electric chop-slice-grind machine and slide back into the dream. I am once more in a large caravanserai, or wayside halt, near Ghazni. Fumes of cooking, a gigantic samovar puffing steam and rows of bright painted teapots (as all over Central Asia, it is customary to offer one to each customer). There is a clatter and roar of gaudily painted lorries drawing up, and the turbaned drivers swagger in to command attention... Now I am airing my few phrases of Pushtu, exchanging a packet of biscuits ('Assorted Hostess'), for some mulberries dried to form a sort of paste. I try to say how sad I am to be leaving next day, at which a *beau ténébreux* who is nibbling a biscuit appreciatively, while looking fierce enough to devour a tiger, flashes his kohl-rimmed eyes (here, the dandies favour a plum-red kohl in place of the usual sooty grey) and presents me with his snuff box. All Afghan men carried such boxes, little gourds, polished and mounted in rough silver, to hold *naswar*, an explosive greenish powder, often their sole luxury. The gourds were topped by a shaving-brush-like tuft of horsehair, by which the snuff-taker brushed away any traces of the powder which might remain. This elegant, curiously sophisticated gesture always reminded me of the manner in which even the most virile Spanish men use their fans, flicking them open or shut, in a sort of personal pronouncement, or signature, of elegance.

I have treasured my gourd-gift through many years, as I treasure every memory of the Afghanistan I knew – once upon a time, a happy, happy time, long ago and far away... now as far away, it seems, as peace, in that tormented land. But, as this is no place for politics, allow me a historical digression.

It has always been customary to imagine Afghanistan as a remote, dour scene, a wild land inhabited by fierce tribes only. The tribesmen – called *moujaheddin* today – are still there, as much part of the land as those cut-throat gorges such as the Khurd Kabul Pass, even more wild than the Khyber of Kiplingesque legend. (It was in the dark defiles of the Khurd Kabul Pass that the British Army of occupation was wiped out in 1842.) Yet behind all the fury and cruelty of such scenes there was, historically, a brilliant setting which requires some effort of imagination. The Afghans understood luxury – in their own manner: many had superb weapons and horses, while fine carpets, priceless cashmere shawls and elephants, jewelled and majestic, were part of that Kabul life which centred round the amirs and khans. One of these, Shah Shuja, possessed the fabled Koh-i-Noor diamond and wore it in his turban, from where it moved first to the sleeve of Ranjit Singh, the Sikh ruler, and finally to the Crown of England.

But then Central Asia *is* extravagant, dramatic and fierce and the violent pride of their Mongol, Turcoman and Affridi forebears became an Afghan characteristic. That is something successive waves of invaders have, over the centuries, learned to their cost.

It is, too, something that can be traced in the Afghan cuisine, extravagant and unpredictable, as varied and coloured as the land itself. From the bleak Turcoman steppes touching Iran to the lush groves round Kandahar, nudging Pakistan, there is great virility in the dishes. Though less sophisticated than Iranian, Turkish or Arabic, Afghan food has its own subtleties. I recall many coloured and spiced rice dishes: *norange*, for example, was rice tinted with orange rind and pimento; while *zamrod*, or emerald, cast a spinachy glow, and dried and powdered grapes were used to impart a violet bloom to grilled meat. *Kebabs*, grilled chunks of meat, attain true perfection here, even at the roughest wayside halt, beneath those giant plane trees that Tamerlane's Golden Horde are said to have first planted. My enthusiasm for Afghan food should not be attributed to any alcoholic haze, for wine is seldom found in Moslem lands, the general Afghani beverage being tea, green or black, flavoured with mint or cardamom, while there is also garlic tea, or a rose-leaf brew, for the more fanciful.

It is by the range of *kebabs* that the Afghan cuisine comes into its own. In the capital – unlovely, yet fascinating, Kabul – even in the most humble restaurants (there were few stylish ones) *kebabs* were an unfailing pleasure. Along the wildest tracks, or by some village coppersmith's booth, the same excellence prevailed. I recall in particular those eaten in the dramatic setting of the bazaar at Tashkurgan, in the north, near the River Oxus, which remains almost unchanged since Marco Polo passed that way. There the low, vaulted saucers plastered into the surface – rare pieces, I fancy, though unrecognised as such for they are casualties of the age-old caravans that followed the Silk Route from Cathay through Tashkurgan towards the West. But back to the *kebabs* we ate from tin plates – adieu the celestial porcelain.

There are many *kebabs*, each originating in a different province. *Pushtu kebab*, from the north-east, has morsels of meat (always lamb) first marinated in yoghourt (or *mast* as it is called there). The meat is then poached lightly, before

336

being grilled fast. Thus tenderised, the succulent morsels almost swoon off the skewer. *Lulu kebab* is little sausagey pieces of minced meat and garlic. Best of all, *khorak* or *kebabi-i-sihri*. Here, small chunks of meat alternate with pieces of fat grilled crisply brown. A preponderance of fatty bits on one's skewer is considered the *bonne bouche*, expressing the cook's regard. Or so I have been told. In any case, as I relished both fat and lean, waves of mutual appreciation wafted between the cook, in his lean-to kitchen and myself, cross-legged and cramped before a rickety mouse-high table on the verandah which served as dining room beside the roads I long to travel once more.

Afghan melons and grapes were always legendary throughout Central Asia. The Emperor Babur, who adored Afghanistan and chose to lay his bones on a verdant hillside outside Kabul, was kept supplied with Afghan melons during his long years of conquest in India. Afghanistan boasts sixty varieties of grape, many of which are dried and stored against the snow-bound Afghan winters. In those long ice-bound months many families across the countryside still lived immured in grim fortress-like *qalas*, high-walled domains built round central courts. Here several generations, with their cattle, domestic animals, stored crops and fuel, were all snowed up until the release of spring. Here they lived, loved, quarrelled, gave birth or died, isolated from any contact with the outside world, for the roads over the mountains that divide the valleys are then impassable by man or beast. In happier times *aft mewa* was prepared in the late autumn months. All kinds of fruits; apricots, peaches, plums, grapes, apples and mulberries were soaked in hot water, until softened, then mixed with chopped almonds and walnuts and left to dry, finally becoming a sort of sticky cake reserved for specially festive occasions. It is the mulberry which provides the most value, nutritionally. The Afghans always took bars of this fruit, dried, to sustain them on the road. Now, probably, it sustains them in battle.

Seshtaranga was to me the most exotic of all Afghan dishes. In fact it is simply composed of eggs laid on a purée of onions, vinegar and sugar added. It would make a splendid emergency luncheon dish with which to puzzle, or dazzle unexpected guests. It was very popular among the Ismaili Moslems, for their sect allows them vinegar which, being a derivation of wine, is theoretically denied the strict Sunni Moslems, and quite out of the question for the even stricter Shi'ite brethren. Sunnis are the majority in Afghanistan, and I have been offered *seshtaranga* at several Sunni tables, and now enjoy it at my own.

And apropos eggs. Those superb horses bred and trained for the national *bouz-kachi* game, a sort of fierce polo originating in the steppes of Central Asia, were fed twenty eggs at a time (in better times no doubt) to keep up their strength. They were as pampered as our Western football heroes. I used to see them, cajoled and cosseted by their turbaned grooms, covered in padded and gaily embroidered blankets, waiting beside their riders, that formidable assembly of almond-eyed, fur-capped centaurs from Maimana and Khunduz, where the game takes the cavalcade thundering across the steppes, seven miles or more, in a single run. Where are those centaurs now? Where their brave horses? Hail and farewell.

MY HOUSE

THE SMALL HOUSE IN WHICH I LIVE AND NOW HAVE MY WHOLE BEING, is small and pink-washed, on a hillside beside the bay of Garavan, still a lush Ligurian rather than Mediterranean shore. My garden is a terraced jungle of bamboo, fig, avocado, jacaranda and jasmine, dominated by a giant cypress tree and a centuries old olive tree. Isn't that enough, you might ask? Enough and plenty I know. Yet at times I still long to be following an unknown road, going towards some faraway, unknown distance. I have the impression my house has forgiven me this disloyalty, for it lets me come and go through its solid doorways and across its four walls into any far horizon I am recapturing in my mind's eye.

When I moved out of Paris and acquired my Garavan house, it was called Villa Paul, which I thought pretentious, too French and bourgeois for its simple self, so I renamed it Kuçuk Tepe (in Arabic, Little Hill) for it was just that, a top-knot on a steep mound reached by thirty-eight steps tunnelled between the giant cypress tree and lush vegetation.

Today it might well be called Phoenix Lodge, since its four walls have risen again from the flames that burnt the original house to ashes, one evil night in April 1994. Now it is strictly utilitarian and minimalistic, named in tune with the times, because the Mairie had the pretentious idea of renaming our little lane, Chemin Vallaya, Avenue Catherine Mansfield, after the distinguished New Zealand writer who

The view from Lesley's terrace
in Garavan, Menton

had once leased a house here for three months. (At first, she was, according to her letters, deliriously happy. Later, having had some searing experiences with the French, I am told that in one of her letters she writes of their greed and wishes she could see their faces, were they compelled to watch a pound of the best butter melting away in the sun.) I have said that my house was originally known as Villa Paul which I changed to Kuçuk Tepe. When the lane where it stood was called Chemin Vallaya, the Arab name seemed quite harmonious. But when the Mairie changed Chemin Vallaya to Avenue Catherine Mansfield, the Arab name sounded absurd, so now I simply call it by its number and bear a grudge against the Mairie for calling such a simple winding lane an avenue.

As Garavan is what might be described as a frontier village, there are always shady characters passing through; sometimes scraping furtively on the gate at midnight having escaped the *douane*, which used to be a particularly efficient one, only a few minutes away.

Our lane was once one of the many sandy, gravelly hideaway roads that led up from the sea into the steep countryside of bare rocky hills, hugging the Bay of Garavan and giving it a special intimacy. Once only a straggle of little dwellings followed its climb. A few fine early nineteenth-century houses adorned with those delightful painted frescoes, garlands, ribbons and doves, which are typical of this area, were also dotted about, but they were gradually being cut up into apartments. There were still a few pink or yellow peasant houses on the steeply terraced land, with small vineyards and eggs for sale before all signs of human habitation petered out among wastes of rock and prickly pear.

The higher one climbed, the more beautiful the distances revealed. Looking northwards – inland – there were the foothills of the Alpes Maritimes where snow lingered late; and westward the enchanting silhouette of old Menton, a hillside clutter of red roofs and ancient churches and chapels and giddy little balconies snugged below the tombs and sanctuaries of the cemetery where the onion domes of a doll-sized Russian chapel bore an historic and princely Russian name. Far below lay the silky blue bay, where the fishermen brought their catch to the market: looking eastwards beyond the towering yellow cliffs of the frontier, were canyons and perilous paths high above my house; often the haunt of those shadowy characters bent on eluding the *douane* far below. Some unintimidating looking barracks and a hut or two announced this frontier, and there a posse of French and Italian gendarmes stood about, uniformed figures set down incongruously in a romantic landscape. Beyond the barriers, the coast road ran away, eastwards, into a lilac coloured distance shadowed by olives: Italy, the Ligurian coast. An upper cliff road, leading to another *douane* post, was once considered too steep for many of the visitors to Menton, and once there were a few little donkeys waiting, saddled, for the climb.

In short, this was a wonderfully remote atmosphere and coming to it from big cities, London, Paris, or New York, I enjoyed it to the full. My neighbours leaned out of their windows to chat, basking in the almost eternal sunshine of this favoured spot. (By official meteorological records, Garavan has more sun, per annum than any other part of France and is also sheltered from the ravages of the Mistral, a wind which is the scourge of the Mediterranean coast.) One friend across the road kept a large strident goose as watchdog: my cats presented me with the snakes they caught and were hurt that I did not appreciate their offerings. The most delightful tree rats, furry grey and not at all repulsive, used to whisk and frisk in the bay tree overhanging my terrace; I never succeeded in taming them, but had to content myself by sometimes catching a beady little eye as it swished itself across my breakfast tray. There were many tropical birds *de passage* in the winter months, making for Africa on the far shore. Ring doves and nightingales are still here, though in diminished numbers. Pesticides and new, repulsive insects from the other side of the world are moving in.

It might be said that the rustic scene I present is over romanticised: what about the railway? True, a small train runs between Nice and Ventimiglia, and indeed runs almost below my window, but it never worried me as it chugged or rattled along; things were much more primitive when I first came here. At night the great Italian express tore past making for the Spanish border at Hendaye, the far side of the French map. It stopped at Lourdes on its way and discharged what were described as the *grands malades* bound for salvation. As it streamed past there were snatches of lighted windows and corridors filled with huge white coiffes of ministering nuns. We possessed our own little station or wayside halt at Garavan. It had been put there for the convenience of Queen Victoria who often spent some winter months nearby in a fanciful gingerbread villa. Her long suffering granddaughters, her doctor and a small court surrounded her daily outings in the bath chair pulled by a favourite white donkey.

How I blessed the old queen for that station! I had no car so the train was my lifeline to the street markets in Ventimiglia, friends along the coast and outings to Nice or occasionally to Monte Carlo, which was never a place I cared for. Our station, like all around, was a rather casual affair, the ticket office was open or shut according to the whims of the station mistress, a wonderful lady, who wielded a flag with authority and was inclined to keep the train standing if some domestic problem kept her in her kitchen. At night the benches were often occupied by those characters who had succeeded in making their way unobserved over the high mountain frontier, or the tramps of whom I write below. At first, I found these sleeping figures rather disconcerting when I got out of the last train around midnight and found myself the only passenger to descend. But I was lucky, I never had any difficulties.

Nowadays as I write this, everything is different. Very smart, electrified trains flash in and out and hideous pylons sprout. An underpass has been made to avoid the unfortunate deaths which occasionally occurred when people used to cross the line on foot, but personally I think the shadowy underpass is an invitation to all sorts of trouble.

Garavan being, technically, a frontier town, there were always numbers of oddball and picturesque tramps who were a permanency hereabouts and usually slept along the benches of the little station at the end of my garden. I came to know some of them quite well; one, a real rag-and-bone figure, was a mysterious massive man, heavily bearded, in bashed almost toeless boots. He pushed a perambulator laden with sacks and bottles, rags and bones. He never spoke and legend had it that he had lost his speech seeing his young wife killed before his eyes. He was said to be Hungarian, but he had no papers and finally no one bothered him: the police were more compassionate then. One cold winter I could stand his rags no longer and begged a Burberry from an English friend. I took this warm check-lined comfort along and cornered the tramp. 'You are not to sell it,' I thundered, 'Put it on this minute.' Unsmiling, he did so, and wore it for the next ten years until its traditional beige became a greasy black. One day he vanished and the pram was found rolling downhill by itself. I was told that his habit, of thrusting a hand through the grills of the restaurant kitchens in Menton, which usually gave him food, had irritated some hysterical chef who had poured boiling soup over him and the shock had killed him, though I preferred another less violent, though equally sad, ending, where I was told the police at last removed him to an hospice for the infirm down-and-outs where he very quickly died.

On the last day of the old year 2000, sleepy-hollow Garavan, on the French-Italian frontier, was shaken to the quick, quite literally, by some very dangerous symptoms of rock fissures suddenly appearing along the steep mountainous bay backing the houses in my quarter, which is called Porte de France. There was instant agitation and every kind of expert measured the cracks which might at any moment result in a fearful landslide carrying away every house in its path. I was just outside the danger slide, but for two days stood glued on my terrace from which I could watch the extraordinary and dangerous manoeuvres that were going on to arrest the disaster. Gigantic naval helicopters hovered, throbbing noisily, dropping enormous rolls of coarse wire netting, the type generally used across harbours to deflect submarines. How the weight of these giant rolls could have been handled as they were by a few acrobatic airmen and experts, balanced on the sheer cliff face, I can't imagine; but the work proceeded smoothly, punctuated by little blasts of dynamite removing inconvenient crags.

Meanwhile, it was not so smooth for two to three hundred occupants of the dwellings on the lower slope of the bay, mostly retired, well-to-do bourgeois couples and some families with small children who were suddenly given notice to leave at once, taking with them only bare necessities, for they were to be rehoused in hotels here, there and everywhere about the town until the danger passed. Considerable confusion reigned and, as always with the French, the sound of their angry complaints, now against nature and the Mairie, resounded shrilly. Next day was New Year's Day 2001, rather cold, with a raw wind blowing. The helicopters and the contortionists hanging on ropes were still working away on the cliffs above us, but at about ten o'clock fearful confusion arose when quite a large procession of Italian cars came streaming towards the frontier, which of course was blocked. The Italians were on their way home after a riotous night celebrating the New Year as far away as Cannes or Monte Carlo and had not reckoned on the drama here. To their surprise and increasing rage they were unable to proceed into Italy by any of the three routes customarily open to them. Both the sea route and the middle route were blocked off. Nor could they go by the Route Nationale, because the frontier tunnel was even more dangerous, and closed. They were, therefore, confronted with the disagreeable fact that they would have to spend a night or two where they were. Naturally no trains were running through and their only other means of reaching home would have been to go back to Nice Airport and wait for a plane to Milan, or charter a boat. The alternative was to stay where they were and – I must stress a fact which I particularly enjoyed – they were all in evening dress, their cars still wreathed in balloons and festive trimmings, while they were clearly still working off what I imagine were terrible hangovers. The situation was very grave here and the army had been called in small measure to assist with the confusion. I understand that the Italians were obliged to spend the next two nights under canvas on the beach as no other accommodation was available. They were not amused and their comments could be heard from a great distance; but we, here, who are becoming crowded out by what is known as *'l'infiltration de la Mafia,'* Italians occupying and possessing houses and acquiring land all around, we enjoyed every moment of it. The final process of dynamiting certain dangerous rocks was still to be got through, before the all-clear sounded about a week later.

The French who had been obliged to leave their houses temporarily had been told to take with them a small suitcase each, and if they needed to return to fetch something essential or feed any cats and canaries left behind, had to ask special permission from the gendarmes and go there accompanied by one, but only for ten minutes, a time limit which was strictly observed by the unsympathetic gendarmes.

It reminded me of a time during World War II in London, when we were used to being turned out of our houses at a moment's notice by the bombing, and had the habit of keeping a small suitcase, ready packed, to hand. These, we called 'snatch cases' and it became quite a game among ourselves to deduce a person's character by the contents of each case. For example, my mother's snatch case contained a large bag of bird seed for her budgerigars, a nice warm shawl (which I knew very well was for the cats rather than for herself) and, of course, a few tins of dog food, as she might have had to be looking after my dog at that moment. My own case was said by my friends to contain an ikon and a very romantic *robe de chambre.*

Watercolour hanging over Lesley's dressing table depicting a Romantic Victorian vision of 'Abroad'

APPENDIX

The Komisarjevsky Method of Acting

THEODORE KOMISARJEVSKY'S ACTORS WERE EXPECTED TO INDUCE AN intensity of feeling and a profound understanding of the characters they played. I found a couple of pages torn out of a book (so the title and author are unknown) tucked inside Lesley's copy of his memoirs, *Myself and the Theatre*, sketching his method.

Komisarjevsky, or Behind the Scenes

The scene is a large room on the third floor of a building in Rupert Street, which runs into Shaftesbury Avenue. It is a particularly ugly room, uncarpeted, uncurtained with walls of salmon-pink and a cracked ceiling from which the paper is peeling mournfully.

In the centre of the room, seated on a wooden form, a woman weeps. She has been weeping, on and off, for nearly three quarters of an hour and one would have thought that by this time her tears would have run dry. But no; they are beginning all over again. For a certain figure, clad in a grey suit, is leaning on the edge of a piano, watching intently, commanding sorrow. And whenever sorrow shows signs of flagging, he commands it again.

The figure in grey is Komisarjevsky; the play is Act III of Chekhov's *Cherry Orchard*; the weeping woman is, of course, Lyubov Andreyevna. Needless to say, there is a good deal of sorrow to be commanded in this act, and, without the aid of scenery, or make-up, or lighting, one might well imagine that it would become monotonous. But no. After endless repetitions one begins to see his idea. He is softening one figure, smoothing her character, as a sculptor smoothes a piece of clay. He is hardening another, making him louder, more aggressive. He is quickening the action of one little group, retarding the movement of another. And when we reached that amazing climax to Act III where the dancing outside the door heightens the gloom-charged atmosphere within, I realised that he was not so much producing as *conducting*. The musical analogy was perfect. And as this idea seemed to express a new and intriguing theory of dramatic aesthetics, I asked him later, over some excellent Borscht (with cream, one shilling extra) if he felt the analogy himself.

'Yes,' he said, 'Look at it in this way. A play is like a symphony. Its acts fall under the heading of, let us say, *allegro, andante, presto* – according to the sequence of emotions which the story unfolds. And just as the conductor of an orchestra must grasp the entire symphony before he begins to rehearse any single movement, so a producer must visualise the whole play before he begins to produce any single act.

'What happens then? Speaking for myself, at any rate, I begin to hear each actor as a series of *notes*. And together, the actors form a fugue, running concurrently or in opposition, in harmony or discord – a fugue which I never allow myself to lose. One might say, for instance, that the main melody was played by the heroine, that the second part was played by her lover and that the minor parts formed the bass. And, to my mind, the producer should *play* those parts, giving their proper significance, as clearly as a conductor stresses a passage for his first violins, or mutes an accompaniment of cellos.'

If you read the above paragraph carefully, taking a deep breath after each comma, it may become a little less obscure than *Sordello*. And if you take the opportunity of seeing the present Chekhov season at Barnes, it should become entirely plain.

Now for the pictorial side of his theories which, after the Borscht, he proceeded to explain. Let us reduce them to their simplest terms. They are, to me at least, extremely stimulating. Imagine an almost empty stage, with half a dozen figures silhouetted against a neutral background, which is relieved by a single tree. Imagine, again, a single act of a play, dividing itself, in the space of forty minutes, into three main emotional divisions, which, for the sake of contrast, we may call joy, love and despair.

During the 'joy' movement, apart altogether from the briskness with which the figures move, the quality and content of their speech, the significance of joy will be expressed by their grouping, not as individuals, but as a whole. It can really best be expressed by the jargon of the Futurists. Certain lines, merely by their abstract form, their relationship to one another, express exhilaration, others express dejection, etc.

Thus, with this particular scene, if you put it in the crudest possible way, you will have a black figure drooping on the sofa, shadows curling darkly and listlessly beneath the tree, and all the movement of all the characters subdued to a series of curves which in themselves are calculated to express sorrow, apart from the lines they may be saying or the way in which they may be saying them.

The English people cannot bear more than two minutes of any theory, so I will not say more. But perhaps, from these few words, some people may begin to realise that the producer is, to say the least of it, more important than they had imagined.

Komisarjevsky told me that in Russia the producer was all-important. You could see fifty productions of the same Chekhov play and they would all be entirely different – as different as a Chopin étude played by Cortot and Orloff.

'It keeps the plays alive,' he cried, 'It would even keep Shakespeare alive, if he were produced properly. Look at *Hamlet*! Nobody here seems to realise that *Hamlet* is a play. They've all forgotten the story because they are so hypnotised by the personality of the actor who is playing Hamlet. But the story is there – a wonderful story. The producer could make that story come to life. Why doesn't somebody try?

'But then,' – and he put his head on one side with that curious little sly gesture which is so characteristic of him – 'the English people don't want to see life. They hate it. It either bores them or shocks them – I don't know which. There isn't a single English character – uniquely English, I mean – being shown on the London stage today.

'Yes,' – he leant forward and pointed through the window to the surging pavements – 'out there are walking the most extraordinary characters which you will find in any part of the world.' And he told me of some of the people whom he had seen during his last Sunday afternoon's promenade – an old woman standing in an alley, gravely letting down her skirt to her knees in order to adjust a recalcitrant corset; an old man at the corner of a deserted street, preaching passionately to thin air... 'What are all your dramatists doing,' he asked with Russian fervour, 'to pass all these people by?'

Sean O'Casey made exactly the same complaint to me in Irish as Komisarjevsky made in Russian. There must be something in what they say.

NOTES

Epigraph

Page ix – 'The eyes of the artist... and that requires time.' Theodore Komisarjevsky, *Myself and the Theatre*, William Heinemann Ltd, London, 1929. p. 33.

Lesley Blanch: Last of a Kind

Page 1 – 'With the death of Lesley Blanch, age 103 [...] the Mitford sisters.' Philip Mansel, Obituary, *Le Figaro Littéraire*, 10 May 2007.

Page 3 – 'She was the greatest influence in my life [...] endearing.' Dana Wynter, email to author, 5 January 2011.

Page 3 – 'a land of memory stretching from Cairo to Constantinople.' Fragment (undated) found among Lesley Blanch's papers. © Georgia de Chamberet, 2017.

Page 3 – 'I turned to gros point as a distraction [...] listening to music.' Ibid.

Pages 3–4 – 'For Nancy Mitford I worked a large pink-pawed mole [...] our shared love of all things Slav.' Ibid.

Page 4 – 'Surround yourself [...] make you happy.' Website www.lesleyblanch.com content created by Lesley Blanch and author and posted in 2006.

Page 6 – 'Perhaps it was due [...] had become my friends.' Ibid.

Page 6 – 'far to go and many to love.' Lesley Blanch, *On the Wilder Shores of Love: A Bohemian Life*, Virago Press, London, 2015. p. 22.

Page 6 – 'I must have been about four years old when Russia took hold of me with giant hands.' Lesley Blanch, *Journey into the Mind's Eye: Fragments of an Autobiography*, Eland Publishing Ltd, London, 2005. p. 3.

Page 7 – 'I asked her once why she had not gone to Russia [...] enigmatic reply.' Ibid. p. 37.

Page 7 – 'At night both streets and houses [...] grilled carrots.' Theodore Komisarjevsky, *Myself and the Theatre*, William Heinemann Limited, London, 1929. pp. 2–3.

Pages 7–8 – 'It may well seem strange that in such circumstances the theatres were still open.' Ibid. p. 5.

349

Page 8 – 'Frequently during performances, the breath of the singers on the stage was visible in such clouds of vapour that they called themselves samovars.' Ibid. p. 10.

Page 8 – 'Where all forms of art [...] took part in the operas.' Theodore Komisarjevsky, *Myself and the Theatre*, William Heinemann Limited, London, 1929. p. 8.

Page 8 – 'His influence [...] debt.' John Gielgud, Obituary, *The Times*, 19 April 1954.

Page 8 – 'Komisarjevsky set up Lahda, a society for the promotion of Russian culture in London, in 1920, with Laurent Novikov and Vladimir Rosing. They organised Opera Intime concerts, ballet performances and 'at home' events at which they performed in the homes of prominent figures in London society.' Philippa Burt, PhD candidate in the Department of Theatre and Performance at Goldsmiths, University of London, email to author, 14 May 2014.

Page 8 – 'When he taught at the Royal Academy of Dramatic Art [...] devotion in his students.' Victor Borovsky, *A Triptych from the Russian Theatre: An Artistic Biography of the Komissarzhevsky Family*, C. Hurst & Co Publishers Ltd, London, 2001. p. 319.

Page 8 – 'He loved young people and knew how to encourage them and bring them out.' John Gielgud, Obituary, *The Times*, 19 April 1954.

Page 8 – 'His education was encyclopaedic [...] European languages fluently.' Victor Borovsky, *A Triptych from the Russian Theatre: An Artistic Biography of the Komissarzhevsky Family*, C. Hurst & Co Publishers Ltd, London, 2001. p. 238.

Pages 8–9 – 'Softly spoken and short, [...] in Lesley.' Ibid. p. 319

Page 9 – 'He possessed [...] in the street.' Lesley Blanch, *Journey into the Mind's Eye: Fragments of an Autobiography*, Eland Publishing Ltd, London, PB 2005. p. 121.

Page 9 – 'Martha's money [...] was running out.' Lesley Blanch's posthumous memoirs, *On the Wilder Shores of Love: A Bohemian Life*, Virago Press, London, 2015. pp. 96 & 149.

Pages 9–10 – 'Diaghilev and Rachmaninov were among The Traveller's circle [...] it did not wither.' Lesley Blanch, *Journey into the Mind's Eye: Fragments of an Autobiography*, Eland Publishing Ltd, London, PB 2005. pp. 54–55.

Pages 9–11 – 'The newly opened art deco Théâtre des Champs-Élysées'; 'Wagner Festival in October-November 1924'; 'An advertisement in one of Théâtre Pigalle's [...] surprises – cabaret'; 'An art deco temple to modernism [...] *Amphitryon 38* played there.' Special thanks to Emmanuelle Toulet and Pauline Girard at the Bibliothèque historique de la Ville de Paris; Matthias Auclair at the Bibliothèque-musée de l'Opéra; the librarians at Arts du spectacle, Bibliothèque nationale de France, Rue Vivienne, Paris, for all their help and granting access to their archives.

Page 10 – 'In a more frivolous vein... exile in Turkey.' Lesley Blanch, *Journey into the Mind's Eye: Fragments of an Autobiography*, Eland Publishing Ltd, London, PB 2005. p. 55.

Page 10 – 'With waves of colourful rugs flowing from floor to divan... Victorian cushions.' Ibid. p. 56.

Page 10 – 'Now I understood the spell they cast... and so many more.' Ibid. p. 71.

Page 10 – 'How I loved him! [...] Trans-Siberian thundering through the house.' Ibid. p. 3.

Page 11 – 'The best play I've seen was *The Three Sisters*... productions of genius.' Marie-Jacqueline Lancaster, *Portrait of a Failure*, Timewell Press, London, 1968. p. 167.

Page 14 – 'the intelligentsia, a shabby brilliant lot who still believed in liberalism, still quoted Herzen.' Lesley Blanch, *Journey into the Mind's Eye: Fragments of an Autobiography*, Eland Publishing Ltd, London, PB 2005. p. 41.

Page 14 – '*Pussinka moiya!*' Ibid. p. 73.

Page 15 – 'A world of their own [...] their progeny.' Ibid. p. 188.

Page 16 – 'All London, Paris, New York focused on Monte Carlo, [...] autumn leaves in Vallombrosa.' Lesley Blanch, 'Brave New Ballet', *Vogue*, May 1938. Lesley Blanch / British *Vogue* © The Condé Nast Publications Ltd.

Page 16 – 'The Traveller's companion [...] never quite clear.' Lesley Blanch, *Journey into the Mind's Eye: Fragments of an Autobiography*, Eland Publishing Ltd, London, PB 2005. p. 174

Page 18 – 'I felt myself abandoned [...] sulked accordingly.' Ibid. p. 82

Page 18 – 'When I am here [...] his meaning was clear: don't pry.' Ibid. pp. 34–35

Page 18 – '*Scandalist!* He was always a *scandalist!*' Ibid. p. 95

Page 18 – 'Peggy Ashcroft took him off me.' Lesley Blanch to author in May 2007.

Page 18 – 'the Russian Don Juan.' Victor Borovsky, *A Triptych from the Russian Theatre: An Artistic Biography of the Komissarzhevsky Family*, C. Hurst & Co Publishers Ltd, London 2001. p. 340.

Page 18 – 'He had nine officially registered marriages.' Ibid. p. 339.

Pages 18–19 – 'A son, Vadim [...] with Komisarjevsky in 1932.' Garry O'Connor, *The Secret Woman: A Life of Peggy Ashcroft*, Weidenfeld & Nicolson, London, 1997. p. 37.

Page 19 – 'Komisarjevsky's younger brother ... in terrible poverty in 1970.' Victor Borovsky, *A Triptych from the Russian Theatre: An Artistic Biography of the Komissarzhevsky Family*, C. Hurst & Co Publishers Ltd, London, 2001. p. 334.

Page 19 – 'because he was a spy.' Lesley Blanch, *Journey into the Mind's Eye: Fragments of an Autobiography*, Eland Publishing Ltd, London, PB 2005. p. 101.

Page 19 – 'He left me, as casually as ever [...] Go with a smile.' Ibid. pp. 139 & 141.

Page 19 – 'I loved him unreservedly [...] at last come home.' Philip Mansel, *Lesley Blanch: My Life on the Wilder Shores*, Cornucopia, issue 37, 2007.

Page 20 – 'As time passed [...] my desire.' Lesley Blanch, *Journey into the Mind's Eye: Fragments of an Autobiography*, Eland Publishing Ltd, London, PB 2005. p. 142.

Pages 20–21 – 'A tattered blue volume carries me to Bakhchysarai... that's travelling.' Handwritten notes for Lesley Blanch's memoirs 2001–2004. © Georgia de Chamberet, 2017.

Page 21 – 'Although he was international in his way of life... impossible to classify.' Lesley Blanch, *Journey into the Mind's Eye: Fragments of an Autobiography*, Eland Publishing Ltd, London, PB 2005, p. 59.

Page 21 – 'Commemorative plaques often mark houses... emotions they once framed.' Lesley Blanch, *Pavilions of the Heart: The Four Walls of Love*, Weidenfeld & Nicolson Ltd, London, 1974. p. 13.

Page 22 – 'It was she who trained [...] wider scopes and greater glories.' Lesley Blanch, 'Ballet Factory', *Vogue*, June 1940. Lesley Blanch / British *Vogue* © The Condé Nast Publications Ltd. Special thanks to Arike Oke, Rambert Archivist, The Rambert Archive, 99 Upper Ground, London, SE1 9PP for all her help, and granting access to Lesley Blanch's letter to 'Darling Mim' dated 20 February 1968, reproduced on pp. 22–24; as well as to the Estate of Diana Gould for granting access to Lesley Blanch's letter to Diana Gould, dated 4 December 1941, reproduced on pp. 28–29.

Page 24 – 'Lesley readily admitted [...] in Richmond.' Lesley Blanch interview with Karen Robinson, *Sunday Times*, August 2006.

Page 24 – 'Had an attractive voice [...] drinking wine.' Handwritten notes for Lesley Blanch's memoirs. © Georgia de Chamberet, 2017.

Page 25 – 'Those people in the set who always discover everything first.' Ibid.

Page 25 – 'Art and drama critic [...] wet leaves.' Philip Mansel email to author, 13 May 2014.

Page 25 – 'The English village and rural life [...] Storrington.' Alexandra Harris, *Romantic Moderns: English Writers, Artists and the Imagination from Virginia Woolf to John Piper*, Thames & Hudson, London, 2010. p. 182.

Page 26 – 'Gate-leg tables, excellent food [...] at 2.30 p.m., in black tie!' Handwritten notes for Lesley Blanch's memoirs. © Georgia de Chamberet, 2017.

Pages 26–27 – 'Chanel demonstrated [...] boredom to bravado, sartorially speaking.' Lesley Blanch, 'Brave New Ballet', *Vogue*, May 1938. Lesley Blanch / British *Vogue* © The Condé Nast Publications Ltd.

Pages 27–28 – 'During the Blitz, [...] free-for-all.' Handwritten notes for Lesley Blanch's memoirs. © Georgia de Chamberet, 2017.

Page 30 – 'London, 1944 [...] a party.' Lesley Blanch's posthumous memoirs, *On the Wilder Shores of Love: A Bohemian Life*, Virago Press, London, 2015. p. 224.

Page 30 – 'found The Traveller again in him.' Philip Mansel, *Lesley Blanch: My Life on the Wilder Shores*, Cornucopia, issue 37, 2007.

Page 30 – 'The arch seducer of his moment, Mosjoukine... studded the walls.' Lesley Blanch, *Journey into the Mind's Eye: Fragments of an Autobiography*, Eland Publishing Ltd, London, PB 2005. p. 55.

Pages 30–31 – 'Jean-Pierre Lasalle [...] Morgiana or Scheherazade.' Anne Scott-James, *In the Mink*, Michael Joseph Ltd, London, 1952. pp. 63–64.

Page 31 – 'From the start she had known what she wanted, [...] She wanted the East.' Lesley Blanch, *The Wilder Shores of Love*, Orion, London, PB 1993. p. 9.

Page 32 – 'In my little, lonely room [...] A big kiss, Pussuna.' An unsent postcard, Summer 1945 addressed to Lesley Blanch's husband at the Ministère des Affaires Etrangères, Quai d'Orsay, Paris. © Georgia de Chamberet, 2017.

Page 33 – 'I like to reach different horizons, to break away from the present and look at the past in far distances.' Lesley Blanch interview with Lorna Sage, *The Observer*, October 1983.

Page 33 – 'Sometimes it seemed as if [...] ultimate goal of fame.' Lesley Blanch's posthumous memoirs, *On the Wilder Shores of Love: A Bohemian Life*, Virago Press, London, 2015. p. 235.

Page 33 – 'Whenever I could not stand the formality of the Corps Diplomatique I would take a train as far away as possible, usually the Sahara, to wander in wild places.' Lesley Blanch interview with Lorna Sage, *The Observer*, October 1983.

Pages 33–34 – 'Darling, it is all [...] Happy Traveller.' Postcard, dated 15 March 1951, Lesley Blanch to Romain Gary at the Ambassade de France, Berne. © Georgia de Chamberet, 2017.

Pages 34–35 – 'At a moment overcast by all kinds of travel restrictions... the sense of my writing.' Handwritten notes for Lesley Blanch's memoirs. © Georgia de Chamberet, 2017.

Pages 35–37 – 'Lesley's artist friend, Evelyn, [...] they called them old hippies.' Mireille Dagostin, interview with author in Roquebrune, 27–28 April 2012, 13 November 2012; and on the telephone 21 March 2013. © Georgia de Chamberet, 2017.

Pages 37–38 – 'Then Romain Gary arrived in New York [...] which cannot have helped.' Gael Elton Mayo, *The Mad Mosaic: A Life Story*, Quartet Books, London, 1983. pp. 182–152. © Georgia de Chamberet, Stephen Gebb, Guislaine Vincent Morland, 2017.

Pages 39–41 – 'Gary wrote his novels, [...] rarely in Roquebrune at the same time.' Mireille Dagostin interview with author in Roquebrune, 27–28 April 2012, 13 November 2012; and on the telephone 21 March 2013. © Georgia de Chamberet, 2017.

Page 40 – 'It tastes so much better from a spoon.' Lesley Blanch, *Journey into the Mind's Eye: Fragments of an Autobiography*, Eland Publishing Ltd, London, PB 2005. p. 4.

Page 41 – 'He was so absorbed [...] very free.' Lesley Blanch interview with Lorna Sage, *The Observer*, October 1983.

Page 41 – 'We had quite a different [...] get up and go.' Ibid.

Page 43 – 'I sought, wherever I was [...] beside The Traveller.' Lesley Blanch, *Journey into the Mind's Eye: Fragments of an Autobiography*, Eland Publishing Ltd, London, PB 2005. p. 145.

Page 43 – 'The Garys' art deco villa in Outpost Drive [...] a terrace and garden.' Dominique Bona, *Romain Gary*, Mercure de France, Paris, 1987. p. 193.

Page 44 – 'One of the most generous and witty hostesses [...] literary figures.' Katia de Peyer email to the author, 7 September 2007.

Page 44 – 'I loved Malraux [...] in their way.' Lesley Blanch interview wish Shusha Guppy, *Looking Back: A Panoramic View of a Literary Age by the Grande Dames of European Letters* Touchstone / Simon & Schuster Ltd, New York, 1991, p. 12.

Page 44 – 'I wore them long before [...] Now nobody thinks anything of it.' Website www.lesleyblanch.com content created by Lesley Blanch and author and posted in 2006. © Georgia de Chamberet, 2017.

Pages 44–45 – 'We both loved it [...] intriguing women there at that time.' Ibid.

Pages 45–46 – 'David Selznick [...] my husband actually.' Dana Wynter, email to the author, 5 January 2011.

Page 46 – 'We had become very great friends [...] very eighteenth century.' Website www.lesleyblanch.com content created by Lesley Blanch and author and posted in 2006. © Georgia de Chamberet, 2017.

Pages 46–47 – 'Like all Americans she can't make love without having to get married.' Dominique Bona, *Romain Gary*, Mercure de France, Paris, 1987. p. 222.

Page 47 – 'He saw a very pretty [...] not talk about books.' Caroline Baum, 'The Wild One', *The Spectator*, May 2007.

Pages 47–48 – 'Gary often visited [...] and felt frail.' Mireille Dagostin, interview with author in Roquebrune, 27–28 April 2012, 13 November 2012; and on the telephone 21 March 2013.

Page 48 – 'He was depressed all of his life; why should he not choose when to go?' Caroline Baum, 'The Wild One', *The Spectator*, May 2007

Page 49 – 'Most writers, [...] Ajar revived his fortunes.' Roger Grenier, interview with author at Éditions Gallimard, 5 Rue Gaston-Gallimard, 75007 Paris, April 2013, translation and revisions approved by email 12 May 2013 and 13 May 2013.

Page 49 – 'Romain Gary left behind him [...] his time.' Olivier Agid, interview with author in Paris, 24 April 2013.

Page 49 – 'A good place to work [...] in my rooftop apartment.' Lesley Blanch interview, British *Vogue*, July 1966.

Page 49 – 'lodestar longing.' Lesley Blanch's posthumous memoirs, *On the Wilder Shores of Love: A Bohemian Life*, Virago Press, London, 2015. p. 315.

Page 50 – 'He spoke beautiful Arabic, [...] an historian manqué.' Website www.lesleyblanch.com created by Lesley Blanch and author and posted in 2006. © Georgia de Chamberet, 2017.

Pages 50–51 – 'In 1965, *Vogue* photographer Henry Clarke [...] He had a hard time accepting she was not available.' Author interview with Susan Train, Paris, 31 July 2010.

Pages 51–52 – 'To know Istanbul truly [...] majestic on the horizon.' Handwritten notes for Lesley Blanch's memoirs 2001–2004. © Georgia de Chamberet, 2017.

Pages 52–53 – 'Once upon a happy time [...] a trace or more essential.' Lesley Blanch, *From Wilder Shores: The Tables of My Travels*, John Murray, London, 1989. p. 105.

Page 54 – 'Japanese Overlord [...] faded paper fan.' Anne Scott-James, *In the Mink*, Michael Joseph Ltd, London, 1952. p. 67.

Page 54 – 'Lesley took to addressing Gary [...] led my steps abroad...' Lesley Blanch's posthumous memoirs, *On the Wilder Shores of Love: A Bohemian Life*, Virago Press, London, 2015. p. 217.

Page 54 – 'Seeing young [...] if they'd managed to get away.' Lesley Blanch interview with Jim Blackburn, *Wanderlust*, June 2004.

Page 54 – 'mother, wife, mistress, muse, or slave.' Article (undated) *Ouled Naïls* found among Lesley Blanch's papers. © Georgia de Chamberet, 2017.

Page 55 – 'The East attracted them […] becomes fact in the living of it.' Lesley Blanch interview with Lorna Sage, *The Observer*, October 1983.

Page 56 – 'For Lesley Blanch, the veil, especially the all-covering burqa of the Afghans […] the mechanics of male domination.' Philip Mansel, *Lesley Blanch: My Life on the Wilder Shores*, Cornucopia, issue 37, 2007. p. 33.

Page 56 – 'Even in her own mind she does not seem decided […] adopts the feminine.' Fragment (undated) found among Lesley Blanch's papers. © Georgia de Chamberet, 2017.

Page 56 – 'In a 1957 diary entry […] admiration for her was total.' Anaïs Nin Diaries 1957, Collection name and number 2066 Anaïs Nin, box 28, folder 5 at the UCLA Library, Dept of Special Collections, A1713 Young Research Library, Box 951575, Los Angeles CA 90095–1575. Handwritten manuscript (7 pp.) read on 26 January 2011. Photocopies received and paid for 15 February 2011 © Estate of Anaïs Nin. Special thanks to Tree Leyburn Wright and Antonia Owen.

Page 56 – '*Journey into the Mind's Eye* is not altogether autobiography... new category.' Obituary, *The Telegraph*, 9 May 2007.

Page 57 – 'Komisarjevsky understood... the Orthodox Church.' Lesley Blanch, *Journey into the Mind's Eye: Fragments of an Autobiography*, Eland Publishing Ltd, London, PB 2005, p. 161.

Page 57 – 'There is only one theatre – *the theatre of life on stage*,' Victor Borovsky, *A Triptych from the Russian Theatre: An Artistic Biography of the Komissarzhevsky Family*, C. Hurst & Co Publishers Ltd, London, 2001. p. 250.

Page 59 – 'Dr Johnson, the Great Lexicographer... which could, often, still be found.' Handwritten notes for Lesley Blanch's memoirs 2001–2004. © Georgia de Chamberet, 2017.

Source Notes

I. PEOPLE

'Anti-beige'

Harper's Bazaar, June 1935. 'No Objections' agreement received via email, 16 April 2015, from Hearst Magazines UK for non-exclusive, one-time use of archive material for which they have no copyright records.

'The Legendary Miss Leigh'

Published on a single-use basis in *The Leader*, 2 June 1945. © Lesley Blanch, 1945.

'A New Personality: Peter Ustinov'

Published on a single-use basis in *The Leader*, 8 December 1945. © Lesley Blanch, 1945.

'An American Director: Billy Wilder'

Published on a single-use basis in *The Leader*, 23 June 1945. © Lesley Blanch, 1945.

'Woman at War: Germaine Kanova returns to Britain bringing with her a picture-record of the violence and suffering'
Published on a single-use basis in *The Leader*, 6 October 1945. © Lesley Blanch, 1945.

2. A TRAVELLER'S TALES

'Perpetuam Mobile: Lise Cristiani'
From *Under a Lilac-bleeding Star*, John Murray, London, 1963; revised by Lesley Blanch in 1995. © Lesley Blanch, 1963 & 1995.
'Loti in Loti-land'
From *Under a Lilac-bleeding Star*, John Murray, London, 1963. © Lesley Blanch, 1963.
'Undulators and Adulators'
From *Under a Lilac-bleeding Star*, John Murray, London, 1963; revised by Lesley Blanch in 1995. © Lesley Blanch, 1963 & 1995.
'Ouled Naïls'
Undated article found among Lesley Blanch's papers. © Georgia de Chamberet, 2017.
'Peace and Plenty: A Plea For Polygamy'
Undated article found among Lesley Blanch's papers. © Georgia de Chamberet, 2017.
'Sultan Murad's Room'
From *Pavilions of the Heart*, Weidenfeld & Nicolson, London, 1974; revised by Lesley Blanch in 2005. © Lesley Blanch, 1974 & 2004.
'Aurélie Picard: A Saharan Idyll'
From *Pavilions of the Heart*, Weidenfeld & Nicolson, London, 1974; revised by Lesley Blanch in 2004. © Lesley Blanch, 1974 & 2004.
'Bibi Hanum's Medressa'
From *Pavilions of the Heart*, Weidenfeld & Nicolson, London, 1974. © Lesley Blanch, 1974 & 2004.
'Laurence Hope: A Shadow in the Sunlight'
From *Under a Lilac-bleeding Star*, John Murray, London, 1963. © Lesley Blanch, 1963.
'The Fading Garden and the Forgotten Rose: A Balkan Queen'
From *Under a Lilac-bleeding Star*, John Murray, London, 1963. © Lesley Blanch, 1963.

3. PLACES

'Fragments of a Balkan Journal'
From *Under a Lilac-bleeding Star*, John Murray, London, 1963; revised by Lesley Blanch in 1995. © Lesley Blanch, 1963 & 1995.
'The Time and the Place'
From *Under a Lilac-bleeding Star*, John Murray, London, 1963. © Lesley Blanch, 1963.
'Every Picture Tells a Story'
From *Under a Lilac-bleeding Star*, John Murray, London, 1963. © Lesley Blanch, 1963.

'The Orient Express'

Handwritten piece for Lesley Blanch's memoirs 2001–2004. © Georgia de Chamberet, 2017.

'Much Holy Day in Chichicastenango'

From *Under a Lilac-bleeding Star*, John Murray, London, 1963. © Lesley Blanch, 1963.

'Christmas in Bukhara'

From *Under a Lilac-bleeding Star*, John Murray, London, 1963. © Lesley Blanch, 1963.

'Souks, or The Wilder Shores of Shopping'

Undated article found among Lesley Blanch's papers. © Georgia de Chamberet, 2017.

'Time and Time Again'

Undated article found among Lesley Blanch's papers. © Georgia de Chamberet, 2017.

'Through the Moucharabiyeh'

Undated article found among Lesley Blanch's papers. © Georgia de Chamberet, 2017.

'Iran: Where Ancient and Modern Collide'

From *Farah, Shahbanou of Iran: Queen of Persia*, Collins, London, 1978. © Lesley Blanch, 1978.

'Tunis'

Handwritten piece for Lesley Blanch's memoirs 2001–2004. © Georgia de Chamberet, 2017.

'Afghanistan Remembered'

From *From Wilder Shores: The Tables of My Travels*, John Murray, London, 1989. © Lesley Blanch, 1989.

'My House'

Handwritten piece for Lesley Blanch's memoirs 2001–2004. © Georgia de Chamberet, 2017.

APPENDIX

'The Komisarjevsky Method of Acting'

Undated article found inside Lesley Blanch's copy of Theodore Komisarjevsky's *Myself and the Theatre*, William Heinemann Ltd, London, 1929.

LIST OF ILLUSTRATIONS

Lesley Blanch: Last of a Kind

Page 4 – The *moucharabiyeh* and *takht* in Lesley Blanch's main room, Garavan, circa 1981. Photo by Georgia de Chamberet. © Georgia de Chamberet, 2017.

Page 5 – Gros point cushion of Russian Minarets by Lesley Blanch for Violet Trefusis. Photo by Gael Elton Mayo. © Georgia de Chamberet, Stephen Gebb, Guislaine Vincent Morland, 2017.

Page 9 – Costume design by Lesley Blanch for Orchidée in *Le Club des Deux Canards Mandarins*, Henry Duvernoy & Pascal Forthuny. Director, Komisarjevsky. November 1923. Le Studio, Champs-Élysées Theatre, Paris. From a Private Collection. © Georgia de Chamberet, 2017.

Page 12 (top left) – Costume design by Lesley Blanch for Agroff in Cimarosa's *Giannina e Bernardone*. Director, Komisarjevsky. Théâtre Pigalle, Paris, May-June 1931. From a Private Collection. © Georgia de Chamberet, 2017.

Page 12 (top right) – Costume design by Lesley Blanch for 'Giannina, femme de Bernardone' in Cimarosa's *Giannina e Bernardone*. © Georgia de Chamberet, 2017.

Page 12 (bottom left) – Costume design by Lesley Blanch for 'Francone, le capitaine de la Police' in Cimarosa's *Giannina e Bernardone*. © Georgia de Chamberet, 2017.

Page 12 (bottom right) – Costume design by Lesley Blanch for Lauretta Karnizka in Cimarosa's *Giannina e Bernardone*. © Georgia de Chamberet, 2017.

Page 13 – Scenic design by Lesley Blanch for Act I, Shakespeare's *The Merchant of Venice*. Director, Komisarjevsky. Stratford-upon-Avon, July 1932. Included in Theatre Art International Exhibition, MoMA, New York 1934. © Georgia de Chamberet, 2017.

Page 13 (bottom left) – Costume design by Lesley Blanch for Portia played by Fabia Drake, Shakespeare's *The Merchant of Venice*. Director, Komisarjevsky. Stratford-upon-Avon, July 1932. © Georgia de Chamberet, 2017.

Page 13 (bottom right) – Costume design by Lesley Blanch for 'Macbeth and household servant', Shakespeare's *Macbeth*. Director, Komisarjevsky. Stratford-upon-Avon, Spring 1933. © Georgia de Chamberet, 2017.

Page 14 – Personal dedication from Theodore Komisarjevsky to Lesley Blanch at the front of Theodore Komisarjevsky's memoirs, *Myself and the Theatre*, William Heinemann Limited, London, 1929.

Page 17 (top left) – Costume design by Lesley Blanch for Chloé, Act 3 'the Winter Scene', from the Balanchine-Ravel ballet, *Daphnis et Chloé*, on which the name 'Lydia Lopokova' appears. Ballets Russes de Monte Carlo. Date and production unknown. © Georgia de Chamberet, 2017.

Page 17 (top right) – Costume design for *Baroque*, possibly a Léonide Massine ballet, on which the name 'Toumanova' appears. Ballets Russes de Monte Carlo. Date and production unknown. © Georgia de Chamberet, 2017.

Page 17 (bottom left) – Costume design by Lesley Blanch for The King in Léonide Massine's *Rouge et Noir*, Ballets Russes de Monte Carlo. Date and production unknown. Included in Theatre Art International Exhibition, MoMA, New York 1934. © Georgia de Chamberet, 2017.

Page 17 (bottom right) – Costume design by Lesley Blanch for The Cardinal in Léonide Massine's *Rouge et Noir*, Ballets Russes de Monte Carlo. Date and production unknown. © Georgia de Chamberet, 2017.

Page 18 – Theodore Komisarjevsky aka The Traveller. All rights reserved.

Page 21 – The cemetery for Russian émigrés above Menton. Photo by Gael Elton Mayo. © Georgia de Chamberet, Stephen Gebb, Guislaine Vincent Morland, 2017.

Page 23 (top left) – Costume design by Lesley Blanch for Jupiter, Ashley Dukes' production of *Jupiter Translated* by W. J. Turner, after Molière's *Amphitryon*. The Mercury Theatre, London, 1933. Included in Theatre Art International Exhibition, MoMA, New York 1934. © Georgia de Chamberet, 2017.

Page 23 (top right) – Costume design by Lesley Blanch for Alcmena, Ashley Dukes' production of *Jupiter Translated* by W. J. Turner, after Molière's *Amphitryon*. © Georgia de Chamberet, 2017.

Page 23 – Homage to Marie Rambert by Lesley Blanch, 1933. Rambert Archive, 99 Upper Ground, London SE1. © Georgia de Chamberet, 2017.

Page 24 – Lesley Blanch caricature-portrait for Dr Philip Gosse, author of *The History of Piracy*. The Beinecke Rare Book & Manuscript Library, Yale University, USA. © Georgia de Chamberet, 2017.

Page 25 – Lesley Blanch caricature-portrait for Clifford Bax. © Georgia de Chamberet, 2017.

Page 27 – Lesley Blanch caricature-portrait *Couturiana*. © Georgia de Chamberet, 2017.

Page 29 – Lesley Blanch at home in Chelsea, 1944. A portrait of *Darling Self* with Mooney by Frieda Harris is on the wall. © Germaine Kanova, 1944.

Page 31 – Romain Gary in 1945. © Germaine Kanova, 1944.

Page 31 – Lesley Blanch and Romain Gary in 1944, St Leonard's Terrace, SW3. © Carol Russell Wood.

Page 32 – Photo of Nedi Trianova, which survived the fire in April 1994. All rights reserved. The Beinecke Rare Book & Manuscript Library, Yale University, USA.

Page 35 – *Le Vieux Village*, Roquebrune-Cap-Martin in the 1950s, photo by Gael Elton Mayo. © Georgia de Chamberet, Stephen Gebb, Guislaine Vincent Morland, 2017.

Page 36 – Lady Frieda Harris, artist and wife of the Chief Whip of the Liberal Party, Percy Harris. All rights reserved.

Page 39 – Christmas card sent to friends by Lesley Blanch in 1951. © Georgia de Chamberet, 2017.

Page 42 (top left) – Christmas card sent to friends by Lesley Blanch. Berne, 1950. © Georgia de Chamberet, 2017.

Page 42 (top right) – Christmas card sent to friends by Lesley Blanch. Paris, 1956. © Georgia de Chamberet, 2017.

Page 42 (middle) – Christmas card sent to friends by Lesley Blanch. Manhattan, 1952. © Georgia de Chamberet, 2017.

Page 42 (bottom) – Christmas card sent to friends by Lesley Blanch. Los Angeles, 1957. © Georgia de Chamberet, 2017.

Page 44 – Le Consulat Général de France à Los Angeles, Outpost Drive, 1959. All rights reserved.

Page 45 – Aldous Huxley, Lesley Blanch, Julian Huxley, Outpost Drive, Los Angeles, Christmas 1961. All rights reserved.

Page 46 – Monsieur & Madame Gary circa 1959. All rights reserved.

Page 55 – Lesley Blanch with Sheikh Zaïd bin Sultan Al Nahyan in the 1970s. © Susan Train.

1   People

Page 61 – Christmas card by Lesley Blanch. 'A Joyeux Noël from Lesley and Romain Gary, New York-London 1955'. © Georgia de Chamberet, 2017.

2   A Traveller's Tales

Page 87 – Christmas card sent to friends by Lesley Blanch in 1958. © Georgia de Chamberet, 2017.

Page 115 – Pierre Loti's house, the Mosque, Rochefort, Charente Maritime, France. All rights reserved.

Page 121 – Ouled Naïl. All rights reserved.

Page 178 – A courtyard in Damascus, 1861. From *Syria and the Holy Land, Illustrated*, engravings by W. H. Bertlett and T. Allom, descriptions by J. Carne, 1861.

3 Places

INDEX